bolivia in the age of gas

bolivia in the age of gas

BRET GUSTAFSON

duke university press   durham and london   2020

Printed in the United States of America on acid-free paper ∞
Designed by Aimee C. Harrison
Typeset in Vectora and Whitman by Westchester Publishing
Services

Library of Congress Cataloging-in-Publication Data

Names: Gustafson, Bret Darin, [date] author.
Title: Bolivia in the age of gas / Bret Gustafson.
Description: Durham : Duke University Press, 2020. | Includes
  bibliographical references and index.
Identifiers: LCCN 2019058963 (print) | LCCN 2019058964 (ebook)
ISBN 9781478009931 (hardcover)
ISBN 9781478010999 (paperback)
ISBN 9781478012528 (ebook)
Subjects: LCSH: Natural gas—Bolivia. | Gas industry—Political
  aspects—Bolivia. | Gas industry—Government ownership—
  Bolivia. | Fossil fuels—Social aspects—Bolivia.
Classification: LCC HD9581.B52 G87 2020 (print) | LCC HD9581.B52
  (ebook) | DDC 338.2/72850984—dc23
LC record available at https://lccn.loc.gov/2019058963
LC ebook record available at https://lccn.loc.gov/2019058964

Cover art by Aimee C. Harrison

When there is oil, capital comes.
—Sergio Almaraz Paz, 1958

It is perhaps the oldest illusion of all to imagine that external contradictions are eradicated simply by seizing control from above.
—René Zavaleta, 1972

The most effective thing against power relations is rebellion, ridicule, disobedience.
—María Galindo, 2019

CONTENTS

ix / Abbreviations

xiii / Note on
Labels & Language

xv / Preface &
Acknowledgments

1 / INTRODUCTION
Gaseous State

**part one
time**

27 / CHAPTER ONE
Heroes of the Chaco

50 / CHAPTER TWO
Imperial Maneuvers

69 / CHAPTER THREE
Las nalgas of YPFB

**part two
space**

97 / CHAPTER FOUR
Gas Lock-In

125 / CHAPTER FIVE
Bulls & Beauty Queens

152 / CHAPTER SIX
Just a Few Lashes

**part three
excess**

179 / CHAPTER SEVEN
Requiem for the Dead

202 / CHAPTER EIGHT
Gas Work

223 / CHAPTER NINE
Quarrel over the Excess

247 / POSTSCRIPT
Bolivia 2020

255 / Notes

271 / References

293 / Index

ABBREVIATIONS

ADN	Acción Democrática Nacionalista (Nationalist Democratic Action)
APG	Asamblea del Pueblo Guaraní (Guarani People's Assembly)
ASOFAMD	Asociación de Familiares de Detenidos, Desaparecidos y Mártires por la Liberación Nacional de Bolivia
BP	British Petroleum
CAF	Corporación Andina de Fomento (Andean Development Bank)
CEDLA	Centro de Estudios para el Desarrollo Laboral y Agrario (Center for Studies of Labor and Agrarian Development)
CEJIS	Centro de Estudios Jurídicos e Investigación Social (Center for Legal Studies and Social Research)
CIDH	Comisión Interamericana de Derechos Humanos (Inter-American Court of Human Rights or IAHCR)
CIPCA	Centro de Investigación y Promoción del Campesinado (Center for Research and Promotion of Farmers)
CNPZ	Comisión Nestor Paz Zamora (Nestor Paz Zamora Commission)
COB	Central Obrera Boliviana (Bolivian Workers' Central)
COBODESE	Consejo Boliviano de Defensa y Seguridad del Estado (Bolivian Council of State Security and Defense)
CODEPANAL	Comité de Defensa del Patrimonio Nacional (Committee for the Defense of National Patrimony)
COICA	Coordinadora de las Organizaciones Indígenas de la Cuenca Amazónica (Coordinator of Indigenous Peoples of the Amazonian Basin)
COMIBOL	Corporación Minera de Bolivia (Mining Corporation of Bolivia)
CONAMAQ	Consejo Nacional de Ayllus y Markas del Qullasuyu (National Council of Ayllus and Markas of Qullasuyu)
COTAS	Cooperativa de Telecomunicaciones Santa Cruz (Santa Cruz Telephone Cooperative)

CRE	Cooperativa Rural de Electrificación (Rural Electric Cooperative)
DS	Decreto Supremo (Supreme Decree)
EGTK	Ejército Guerrillero Túpac Katari (Tupac Katari Guerrilla Army)
ELN	Ejército de Liberación Nacional de Bolivia (National Liberation Army of Bolivia)
ESMAP	Energy Sector Management Assistance Program
EXPOCRUZ	Feria Exposición de Santa Cruz (Santa Cruz International Trade Fair)
FARC	Fuerzas Armadas Revolucionarias de Colombia (Revolutionary Armed Forces of Colombia)
FEGACAM	Federación de Ganaderos de Camiri (Federation of Cattlemen of Camiri)
FEGASACRUZ	Federación de Ganaderos de Santa Cruz (Federation of Cattlemen of Santa Cruz)
FOBOMADE	Foro Boliviano sobre Medio Ambiente y Desarrollo (Bolivian Forum on the Environment and Development)
FSB	Falange Socialista Boliviana (Bolivian Socialist Falange)
GDP	gross domestic product
IID	Interamerican Institute for Democracy
ILO	International Labour Organization
IMF	International Monetary Fund
INRA	Instituto Nacional de Reforma Agraria (National Institute of Agrarian Reform)
IOC	international oil company
LNG	liquid natural gas
LPG	liquid propane gas
MAS	Movimiento al Socialismo (Movement toward Socialism)
MIR	Movimiento de Izquierda Revolucionaria (Movement of the Revolutionary Left)
MNR	Movimiento Nacionalista Revolucionario (National Revolutionary Movement)
MRTA	Movimiento Revolucionario Túpac Amaru (Tupac Amaru Revolutionary Movement)
NFR	Nueva Fuerza Republicana (New Republican Force)
NGO	nongovernmental organization
NOC	national oil companies
OAS	Organization of American States
OPEC	Organization of the Petroleum Exporting Countries
Pemex	Petróleos Mexicanos (Mexican Petroleum Company)
Petrobras	Petróleo Brasileiro (Brazilian Petroleum Company)

PNUD	Proyecto de las Naciones Unidas para el Desarrollo (United Nations Development Project, or UNDP)
PODEMOS	Poder Democrático y Social (Social Democratic Power)
RADEPA	Razón de la Patria (Reason of the Fatherland)
RJC	Resistencia Juvenil Cochala (Cochabamba Youth Resistance)
TCO	*tierra comunitaria de orígen* (originary communitarian land)
TIPNIS	Territorio Indígena y Parque Nacional Isiboro Secure (Isiboro Secure National Park and Indigenous Territory)
TRADEPA	Transformación Democrática Patriótica (Patriotic Democratic Transformation)
UJC	Unión Juvenil Cruceñista (Cruceño Youth Union)
UN	United Nations
UNASUR	Unión de Naciones Suramericanas (Union of South American Nations)
USAID	United States Agency for International Development
USGS	United States Geological Survey
USMILGRP	US Military Group
UTARC	Unidad tactica de Resolución de Crisis (Tactical Unit for Crisis Resolution)
YPF	Yacimientos Petrolíferos Fiscales (Fiscal Oilfields, the Argentine national oil company)
YPFB	Yacimientos Petrolíferos Fiscales de Bolivia (Bolivian State Petroleum Corporation)

I SOMETIMES ADOPT THE TONE AND REGISTER OF THOSE WHOM I AM REP-resenting, for expressive purposes, whether I share their interpretation or choice of wording or not. The reader should be open to shifts in register as well as nuance, subtlety, and irony.

The use of "American" to refer to people of the United States, rather than to all peoples of the Americas, is under question. However, in a book that is in part about US imperialism, avoiding "American" is difficult. At times I use the term for ease of reference. "North American" unduly interpellates Canadians. "People of the United States" is cumbersome. Bolivians refer to the people in question as *americanos* (or *gringos*), so I use "Americans" and "gringos."

The word *indio* (Indian) has colonial and derogatory origins but its usage has widened in Bolivia. I use it as both supporters and detractors of Evo Morales, and Morales himself, have used it, with self-conscious awareness that it can express bold defiance and racist disregard. I follow the Native American Journalist Association guidelines and capitalize "Indigenous." I do not capital-ize indigeneity, which I use to refer to a paradigm. For Bolivians who do not see themselves as Indigenous, "non-Indigenous" is problematic. "Mestizo" is not widely used. I sometimes use *criollo*. When racializing practices are at stake, I use *whitish* to refer to those who claim social distance in racial or rac-ist terms. Bolivian writers sometimes use *blancoide* (white-oid or whitish), a usage that I take to validate my choice. I also use regional identity labels when relevant.

I often include Spanish words and phrases to maintain the feeling of language whose affective or ideological weight is hard to translate. For example, *pueblo*, quite simply, is not just "people." For readers who do not speak Spanish, I appreciate your patience.

Finally, I refer to natural gas as "gas," not to be confused with "gasoline."

THIS IS A BOOK ABOUT THE PAST AND PRESENT OF BOLIVIA'S AGE OF NATURAL gas. Some might date this era to the gas boom that started in the late 1990s, a period that makes up much of this story. However, I start the story of gas in the early twentieth century, with the first oil explorations and their sequiturs. Natural gas politics intensified during the 1960s and 1970s, with the first gas export pipeline. The gas age exploded in the 1990s and the 2000s, taking on intensity with the political upheaval marked by the election of Evo Morales, the first Indigenous president, and a turn toward popular left nationalism. New policies of state spending and redistribution, along with radical shifts in the politics of race, territory, and indigeneity, unfolded during a period of relative economic improvement. These changes did not happen without intense social conflict, events that make up a fair amount of the writing herein. Much has been said about Bolivia and Evo Morales, both celebratory and critical. Rather than focus on Morales and familiar categories like neoliberalism, indigeneity, decoloniality, or plurinationalism, I have tried to write through the lens of natural gas to consider relationships of dependency, power, and excess that transcend particular leaders or political categories. Categories like fossil fuels, fossil capital, and fossil empire and the traps they lay litter this text. Gas preceded Evo Morales, and with the disputed elections and subsequent coup of 2019, gas will be flowing—albeit amid a new kind of politics—now that he is gone.

This book is shaped by my own experience in Bolivia. Some understanding of that may be useful for interpreting the material that follows. During the 1990s, when I lived and worked in Bolivia over several years, I heard many stories about oil. I lived mostly in Camiri, once Bolivia's "oil capital." There the national hydrocarbon company, Yacimientos Petrolíferos Fiscales de Bolivia (YPFB, Bolivian State Petroleum Corporation), by then in decline, underlay virtually everything. From trellises built with old drilling pipe to drill-bit doorstops, oil's history was pervasive. I also worked with Indigenous Guarani organizations in the rural areas. My Guarani hosts remembered gringos who had come through looking for the stinky rock, *itane* (oil). Looking back, I think now that a 1993 encounter I had with a group of Russian "ornithologists" in Entre Ríos, Tarija, might have had something to do with undercover prospecting for gas. One of them had oddly muscular biceps for an ornithologist. My diary notes "that must have been the KGB guy." Or so I fancy. (For the record, by 2018, Russia's Gazprom, during Morales's presidency, was looking to operate in that part of the country.) At any rate, my interests then were in Guarani language and education. Oil seemed to be little more than historical background. The gas boom was yet to come.

In 2001 or so, while finishing a dissertation on Guarani language politics, I was reintroduced to the world of Latin American oil and gas by Ted MacDonald at Harvard University. I took him up on his offer to join a project working with the Coordinadora de las Organizaciones Indígenas de la Cuenca Amazónica (COICA, Coordinator of Indigenous Peoples of the Amazonian Basin). The program brought oil companies, governments, and Indigenous leaders into World Bank–sponsored "dialogues" on the then-expanding industry. The work took us to Venezuela, Ecuador, Bolivia, Peru, and Colombia. It broadened my understanding of (and dread at) the power of the state and multinational oil companies and their backers among the US banks and financiers. (As I understand it, we were later invited to leave the project because the bank and oil participants saw us as too biased toward Indigenous rights.) I thank Ted for starting me down the dirty road of fossil fuel politics.

Though I still work with the Guarani on language and education issues, I started researching gas politics as pipelines created deep divisions within the Guarani movement and conflicts intensified after Morales's election. At this writing, the natural gas industry has largely overrun Guarani country. Although this book is not wholly about the Guarani, this book owes much to them. My Guarani colleagues are intellectual interlocutors as well as participants, victims, and survivors of the processes and events narrated herein. I thank them for their endless generosity. My politics, whether explicitly stated or intimated by the reader, should not be taken to represent Guarani positions, which are heterogeneous and hotly debated. To protect them from repercussions, I leave most of my Guarani friends unnamed. For the record, the Bolivian state also owes much to the Guarani, given that successive regimes, right and left, have for more than a century sacrificed Guarani territory, bodies, and autonomy for the sake of fossil fuel extraction.

Back on campus in the US, my students energized my research (no pun intended) and pushed me to pay critical attention to our own fossil fuel problems, in particular our university's laughable endorsement of the phrase *clean coal* and its ties to fossil fuel industries. I endorse the students' valiant efforts pursuing divestment and I thank the yearly cohorts of anti–fossil fuel activists who are working for a different future. You can borrow my megaphone anytime. And yes, we will win.

Many colleagues facilitated encounters that deepened my academic orientation to fossil fuels. John-Andrew McNeish and Owen Logan are to thank for organizing conferences (and an edited volume) that were instrumental in the early phases of this work. Stephen Reyna and his colleagues also included me in an early volume on the anthropology of oil, from which I learned a lot. Manuel Ferreira Lima Filho facilitated a visit to Brazil to see that side of the gas matrix. For critical insights, support, inspiration, or, in some cases, words of encouragement that stayed with me over the years, I thank William Acree, Alejandro Almaraz, Penelope Anthias, Carlos Arze Vargas, Carwil Bjork-James, John Bowen, Gavin Bridge, Pamela Calla, Andrew Canessa, Mike Cepek, Claudia Chávez, Geoff Childs, Fernando Coronil, Stephen Cote, Talia Dan-Cohen, Michael Dougherty, Nicole Fabricant, Linda Farthing, Fernando Garcés, María Elena García, Lesley Gill, Shane Greene, Natalia Guzmán Solano, Charles Hale, Matthew Himley, Matt Huber, David McDermott Hughes, Ben Kohl, Brooke Larson, Virginie Laurent, Kathryn Ledebur, Rebecca Lester, José Antonio Lucero, Norah Mengoa, Andrea Murray, Shanti Parikh, Tom Perrault, Tristan Platt, Fernando Prada, Raúl Prada, Hernán Prudén, Carlos Revilla, Thea Riofrancos, Tomás Robles, Suzana Sawyer, Chefali Shandra, Julie Skurski, Ximena Soruco Solugoren, Alipio Váldez, Fernanda Wanderley, Michael Watts, and Ana Zalik. A special thanks goes to Guillermo Delgado-Peña, who gave me a copy of his father's memoir and redirected my thinking on the Chaco War. Guillermo also graciously offered commentary on the Chaco War chapter, where his father plays a part. Ubaldo Padilla helped me out with oral histories in Camiri. For research assistance at various stages, I thank wonderful undergraduates at Washington University: Marly Cardona, Marcos Chacón, Nicole Solawetz, Celina Stein della Croce, Hannah Sugarman, and Mónica Unzueta. Burt Fields and the staff at the University of Missouri Ellis Library facilitated my access to Standard Oil's *The Lamp*. Jean Allman and her colleagues at Washington University's Center for the Humanities graciously offered space and time to work on this book. My department chair, T. R. Kidder, gave me time to write. John Garganigo never tired of telling me to get it done. Alex McPheeters conjured up endless adventures on Missouri's rivers and trails that offered an escape from the routine of writing. Sally Falk Moore and Kay Warren shaped my approach to political anthropology and I acknowledge their influence herein.

At Duke University Press, for being an unwavering source of patient support, I thank Gisela Fosado. Gisela's sage advice and encouragement were crucial for finishing a manuscript that took way too long to get into her hands. Despite my enthrallment with the political power of footnotes, Gisela convinced me to send the notes to the end of the book. I urge the reader to visit them often. Thanks also to Alejandra Mejía for guiding the book through and Annie Lubinsky and Sheila McMahon, for valiantly working with me on final edits.

Most of the chapters benefited from feedback from various audiences at myriad campuses and conferences. Too numerous to repeat here, these contributions are acknowledged in the chapter notes. I thank two anonymous readers who helped me sharpen the focus and articulate the chapters more tightly as a historical ethnography of the gaseous state.

Finally, I thank my three children, Bridget, Jack, and Thomas; my mother, Judi; my partner, Patty Heyda (who also helped me with the maps); her mother, Ivana; and my dog, Earl, for holding down the house and putting up with my wanderings as well as musings and rantings about Bolivia; fossil fuels; the ills of capital, war, and empire; and our shared planetary future.

introduction
gaseous state

"THE FACT IS DEFINED, IT APPEARS, BY OUR GEOLOGICAL NATURE. THE PROB-
lem that presents itself is what to do with so much gas." In November 1967,
Sergio Almaraz spoke these words to an audience at the University of San
Simón, in Cochabamba, Bolivia (1967a, 260). Almaraz was one of the
prominent socialist thinkers then demanding the nationalization of Gulf
Oil, the US company that was exporting oil to the United States from its
concessions in eastern Bolivia. Gulf had also found gas and hoped to export it too. Almaraz and other critical intellectuals saw that as theft. The
contract to export was for oil. The gas, he argued, belonged to Bolivia. If
Gulf exported the gas, Gulf would reap most of the surplus profit, just as
it was doing with oil. There would be little left for the people of Bolivia.
Two years later, in 1969, Almaraz and others had turned public sentiment
against Gulf. A military government backed by a coalition of nationalists,
students, workers, and radical intellectuals expropriated the company. In
the words of a retired oil worker I spoke to decades later: "That was the
true nationalization! We sent the gringos packing with nothing but their
ponchos over their shoulders." Though the pendulum of politics shifted
back to the right—again returning more money and power to the foreign
oil companies—by the early twenty-first century, once again, Bolivians
were in the streets demanding the nationalization of the country's gas reserves. Fossil fuels, and the excesses they create, were again at the epicenter of Bolivian politics. And again, the question posed by Almaraz was still
relevant: "What to do with so much gas?"

By retracing historical processes and examining contemporary struggles over time, territory, and excesses of various sorts, this book explores how the struggle over gas radically transformed Bolivia but also reproduced historical structures and power relationships. It is a story riven with contradictions: apparent wealth alongside poverty, social progress alongside corruption and violence, talk of Mother Nature and the embrace of fossil fuels, discourses of decoloniality amid breaches of Indigenous rights and rising violence against women, revolutionary visions of anti-imperialism financed by the circuits of global fossil capital. To try to make sense of political novelty and historical *longue durée* requires revisiting the past and engaging the contemporary moment through the lens of oil and gas. These geological things encapsulate the contradictions since fossil fuels are central both to Bolivia's long history of revolutionary thought and to the global expansion of imperial capitalism. Therein, I suggest, lies the political challenge for the coming generations, as it does for all of us: rethinking radical and progressive change that can move beyond the social and ecological violence inherent in the material things we know as fossil fuels and the excesses they intensify—war, pollution, patriarchy, racial capitalism, and global warming.

In Bolivia, the contemporary age of gas is also shaped by the radical political shift that happened in 2005. After a series of upheavals, recounted in part herein, that year saw the election of Evo Morales, the country's first Indigenous president. It was historic for a country with an apartheid-like history of inequality between the lighter-skinned elites and the country's largely Indigenous majority. Evo Morales led a party called the Movimiento al Socialismo (MAS, Movement toward Socialism). Turning back over a decade of neoliberal privatizations and free-market reforms, in 2006 Morales decreed the "nationalization" of the gas industry once again. Nationalization usually means the government seizes or expropriates the assets of foreign firms. Yet Morales's decree was really just a rewrite of the contracts—a modest rearrangement of the relationship between the landed capital of the state (Bolivia) and the extractive capital of the foreign companies. Simply put, it meant that the foreign companies would receive less of the superprofits that gas activities generate. More rents, taxes, and royalties would stay in Bolivia. It made good economic sense. It was a historic shift away from the past, given that historical colonizers and modern capitalists had been bleeding Bolivia dry for centuries. Morales, and the Bolivians who reelected him three times, invariably referred to the bounty generated by the gas, and its control by Bolivians rather than foreigners, as a revolutionary victory and a gift of the Pachamama, or Mother Earth.

In the 1960s, a revolutionary vision of economic and political democracy motivated the demand for nationalization of gas. Four decades later, a similar vision, along with new words like *decolonization* and *plurinationalism*, congealed in a popular nationalist refrain, "the gas is ours." It was a complex political scenario. US power had waned but US interventionism, long centered on minerals and fossil fuels, continued. The progressive turn in Latin America, known as the Pink Tide, had provoked a reactionary backlash from the right wing and new strategies of intervention and destabilization coming from the United States. Despite the fact that there was very little "socialism" in Morales's actual policies, many in the US circles of power saw Morales's challenge to US hegemony as a threat. In Bolivia, Morales's rise to power also upset the traditional party system, dominated by whitish elites. There was an intensely racist right-wing backlash against his election in Bolivia. Gas was at the center of both tensions, since Morales promised to disrupt the dominance of the US-centric fossil fuel complex and the power of regional economic elites and redistribute wealth more widely.

The complexities are many and are not easily encapsulated in a single narrative. Global warming, absent from political discourse in the 1960s, was increasingly making itself felt in Bolivia. Yet here was a government that spoke frequently of Mother Earth now defending gas drilling. Indigenous rights, nonexistent in the 1960s, were a key part of Morales's platform. But these rights came into direct collision with the MAS prerogative to extract gas (as well as oil and minerals). Despite a long-standing belief that sovereignty might be achieved through state control of gas and its surplus, dependence on gas exports reaffirmed the country's global position as a provider of cheap labor and cheap nature, a relationship of coloniality and dependency (Coronil 1997; Menchaca 2016). And while Morales spoke against the ravages of capitalism, the natural gas industry, whether state-owned or privately controlled, was an infrastructural apparatus financed by and for global capital, or, more precisely, after Andreas Malm (2016), "fossil capital." Evo Morales became an embodied icon of these contradictions through some fourteen years of volatile and conflictive politics, contradictions only partly resolved by the widely shared belief that "the gas is ours" (figure I.1).

Though both criticism and praise are heaped on Morales, gas dependence and the fossil capital behind it generated its own political forces and effects. These will continue into the foreseeable future. Gas and mineral extraction shape politics in particular ways—generally distorting political incentives, intensifying inequality, and weakening democratic processes. Changing this

FIGURE I.1 Evo Morales campaign poster, 2005. Combining the multicolored wiphala of plurinationalism, the tricolor of the Bolivian state, and drilling rigs on the horizon, the poster states, "The People, the Constitutive Power. Evo, President." Photo by the author.

requires more than electing an Indigenous president. As René Zavaleta intimates in one of this book's epigraphs, political transformation requires thinking beyond merely capturing the state. In this book I try to do so by offering an account of Bolivia's age of gas across historical time and space, at different scales. My aim is to document the heroic efforts of social movements seeking progressive change and to offer a critique of fossil fueled capital(ism) and the troubled relationship, past and present, between the left and fossil fuel nationalism. Much of what is happening in Bolivia exceeds the terms that are often used to describe it—neoliberalism, populism, socialism, indigeneity. Instead of reducing Bolivia to any singular category, I borrow a phrase sometimes heard in Bolivia and offer in this book a historical ethnography of Bolivia as a gaseous state (*el estado gasífero*).

To suggest that Bolivia became, for a time, a gaseous state or, like many Bolivians say, it was gasified (*gasificado*) or gaseous (*gasífero*) is metaphorical, in ways I explore herein. Yet the concept also acknowledges the somewhat deterministic force of fossil fuel economies. The imperatives of gas extraction as a material process generated direct and indirect impacts tied to the production of surplus (in the form of rents, violence, and other kinds of excess) and the reshaping of legal regimes, geopolitical calculations, and political potentiality (Mitchell 2001). I examine what this means through three lenses—time, space, and excess. Temporally, the gas economy demanded (particularly of Evo, but also of social movements) the subsumption of longer histories of struggle and visions of political futures into the contractual temporalities and enticements of fossil capital. Gas came to dominate talk about the present ("look at the wealth gas brings") and the future ("we need to find and extract more gas"). Spatially, the decolonizing struggles of Indigenous peoples and rethinkings of a new political order were also gasified, such that fossil capital exerted a kind of transterritorial sovereignty that privileged certain territorial projects (like that of the regionalists and a particular expression of nationalism) while subsuming other more radical political utopias (like that of Indigenous autonomy). In terms of excess, with a more utopian politics sidelined, Bolivian politics was again reduced to a quarrel over the percentages, the trickle-down of rents that bring some material benefits in spatially and socially uneven ways, even as these generate new forms of violence, also experienced differentially, against people and nature. I return to these three themes, around which I structure the book, later in this introduction.

IN ATTRIBUTING BOLIVIA'S POLITICAL FATE TO GEOLOGY, ALMARAZ WAS ONLY partly right. Hundreds of millions of years ago, the land mass now called South America was sutured to that now called Africa. Three hundred million or so years ago, the continents split and water rushed in to form a massive sea. Over a few more million years, organic matter settled to the sea floor and was covered and compressed by sediment. Over a few million more, the organic material slowly cooked into oil and then cooked some more into gas. Along the way, the waters receded. The oil and gas accumulated far underground, beneath what are now the edges of the Atlantic Ocean, offshore Brazil and offshore west Africa, and farther inland. Fast forward a few million years and continental collisions folded and thrusted geological layers upward, forming the Andes and bringing these fossil fuels closer to the surface. In Bolivia this Andean fold-and-thrust belt made the aboveground and the underground something like a blanket bunched up at the foot of a bed, wrinkles in geological time that brought the past within reach of the present. In Bolivia the oil- and gasmen speak with glee of the Huamanpampa and the Devonian, labels for these deep geological strata where oil and gas might be found. This geological history set the stage for the political and ecological quandaries of the day.

Geology set the stage, but as Almaraz also noted, it was not until the rise of fossil capital in the early twentieth century that Bolivia became entangled in the dilemma of having too much gas and too much of the noxious, violent politics it brought with it. Most of the gas is in the rugged area of Bolivia between the Andes and the Chaco (map I.1). And much of that disheveled geological blanket makes up the ancestral lands of the Indigenous Guarani people, now living alongside Bolivian neighbors of various origins. Gas there was, and a lot of it. Germans, British, Chilean, Bolivian, and US prospectors first sought oil in the region in the early twentieth century, some of whose history I trace herein. Fast forward many decades, and it was gas, not oil, that was most abundant. In 2000 the United States Geological Survey (USGS) World Petroleum Assessment labeled the area the Santa Cruz–Tarija Basin and ranked the area seventy-fifth on the list of the world's seventy-six priority hydrocarbon regions. Notably, the geologist's-eye view sees neither Indigenous nor national territories and, conspiratorially or not, only highlighted the two political centers that would become the main opposition to Morales: Santa Cruz and Tarija (Klett et al. 1997; Lindquist 1998; Ahlbrandt 2000).

Most of Bolivia's gas comes from a few megafields clustered in the central part of the region: San Alberto, San Antonio, Margarita, and Incahuasi (map I.2). All of them are in Guarani territory. This is a region seen as a remote backwater by those who do not live there. Along with the rest of eastern and southeastern Bolivia, it was long treated as a frontier periphery by an Andes-centric state heavily reliant on mining. For many Bolivians, saying the word *Chaco* brings to mind the Chaco War, and oil. The Chaco is thus central to the national imaginary, even if stories are rarely told from the perspective of those who live there. It is often imagined as a space somewhat disconnected from the true Bolivian nation (Delgado-Peña 1996). In other senses, as a space of war marked by decaying monuments of earlier booms and busts, the Chaco is also often spoken of as a space of relics and ruin, similar to its representations on the Argentine side (Gordillo 2014). Yet of late, as in an earlier age

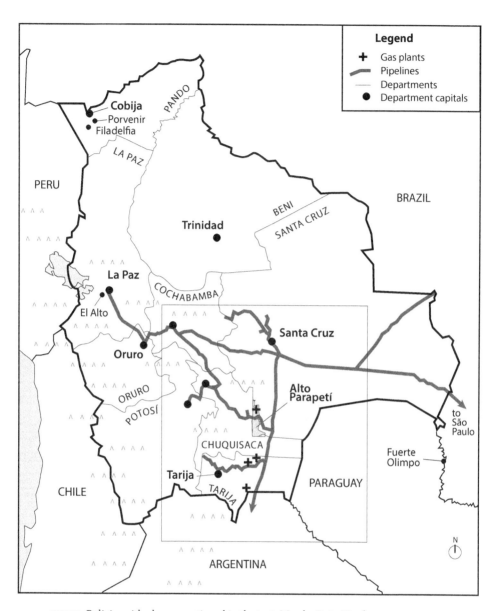

MAP I.1 Bolivia, with places mentioned in the text. Map by Patty Heyda.

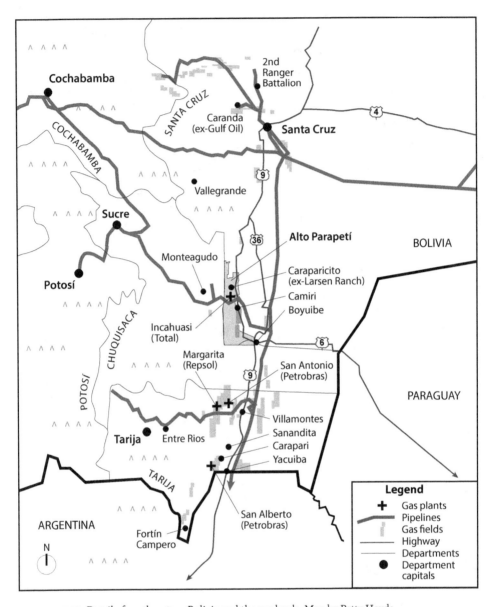

MAP I.2 Detail of southeastern Bolivia and the gas lands. Map by Patty Heyda.

of oil, the gas lands of the Chaco and eastern Bolivia have taken on renewed political importance on the national and global stage, with "Chaco" and "gas" now anchors for imagining once again an elusive national unity. Because I have spent most of my time in Bolivia working in the Chaco and its environs, much of this book is centered there as well.

When Evo Morales decreed the nationalization of gas in 2006, it made good economic sense for a poor country like Bolivia. But it was not as radical as many on the nationalist left wanted. The country did revitalize its government-operated oil and gas company, Yacimientos Petrolíferos Fiscales Bolivianos (YPFB). But the foreign firms were still the dominant players. These included Brazil's Petrobras (a semiprivate firm part-owned by the Brazilian state) and Spain's Repsol. France's Total was not far behind. Others—including British Gas, Shell, Exxon, and, of late, Russia's Gazprom—also came to the table. These companies all invest in shared-risk partnerships, such that any one gas operation may have linkages to various sources of global capital. A range of service companies, from China's Sinopec to Houston's Halliburton and Schlumberger, also work in Bolivia. Despite the rhetoric of indigeneity, decolonization, socialism, and anti-imperialism, Bolivia in the gas age was still pretty much a system of fossil fuel capitalism, albeit capitalism with a much larger government role in redistributing the excess wealth generated.

As gas operations ramped up, the volumes of gas exported out of the Chaco backlands increased. During the course of each day, millions of cubic meters of gas are piped out of the earth, processed to separate liquids, and pumped into thirty-inch underground pipelines. Like arteries, one set of pipelines runs north and east, for over two thousand kilometers, to Brazil.[1] The main line across Brazil takes between 40 and 50 percent of Bolivian production.[2] Bolivian gas generates electricity across Mato Grosso do Sul and in the capitalist industrial heartland at São Paulo and also fuels the Brazilian agro-industrial complex via a fertilizer plant at Tres Lagoas, in the heart of Brazil's soy and sugar cane region (Correa Vera, Serrano, and Añez Rea 2003, 67–68). Petrobras, the Brazilian company extracting gas in Bolivia, can thus be said to control a cheap energy production apparatus for Brazil. Though Brazil's offshore oil and gas—and its growing turn to renewables—now threatens to diminish its demand for Bolivian gas, at the moment Bolivia is an energy colony. Or as a Brazilian law student in a bus crossing Mato Grosso do Sul told me, "Bolivia is like a little thing stuck to our body, an appendix."

Another pipeline feeds Argentina's energy demand with 20 to 30 percent of Bolivia's production. These operations are mostly controlled by Repsol and/

or Yacimientos Petrolíferos Fiscales (YPF, Fiscal Oilfields), the remnants of Argentina's national energy company, purchased by Spain's Repsol before its partial renationalization. With the help of Chevron and despite valiant opposition, Argentina hopes to frack its way to gas independence in coming years, along with all the toxicity that will bring. This may also reduce Argentine demand for Bolivian gas. Yet during the age of gas, and for many decades prior, Argentina had long jousted with Brazil, and in turn with the US, for access to Bolivian gas. So, to a lesser extent, Bolivia has also been an energy colony of Argentina.

On a smaller scale, Bolivia's own domestic gas pipeline infrastructure and internal consumption have expanded in recent years, fluctuating between 15 and 25 percent of overall production. Expanding public access to gas was crucial for maintaining support for gas extraction. To that end, YPFB installed new gas lines in thousands upon thousands of kitchens in humble urban households. One of the more frequent political rituals in recent years has been the president or vice president opening the gas valve in a kitchen, as the beneficiary (invariably a woman representing the grateful housewife) looks on. Evo Morales, or his vice president, Álvaro García Linera, would celebrate the moment as one of domestic progress, modernity, and the outcome of a long revolutionary struggle against imperialism (e.g., ABI 2013).

All of that gas flowing out of the country brings in millions of dollars per day in royalties, rents, and taxes. Between 2007 and 2017, what is called the "government take" has been around $22 billion (YPFB 2017). Unlike any time in recent history, Bolivia has consistently led Latin America in measures of economic growth, fiscal stability, and foreign reserves. Plenty flows into the coffers of the gas companies as well. In Bolivia, through a complex set of funds, legal stipulations, metrics, and political calculations, percentages of this new government wealth were redistributed in multiple forms. Some of the money goes directly to department and municipal governments. Other percentages go to the military, the universities, and the national oil and gas company, YPFB. Other percentages serve a rural development fund. Still others are used by the national treasury for expenditure on public works. Others help fund various cash transfer programs, to children, the elderly, and expectant mothers. Regions where the gas is found—Santa Cruz, Tarija, and of late Chuquisaca—receive more money than others. (Though most of the gas wealth comes from underneath Guarani land, the Guarani bear most of the direct impacts and benefit much less than one might expect, having only been offered project-based compensations and some new public institutions and the jobs they offer.) In some cases, such as that of Tarija, departmental governments have received so much money that they could hardly spend, let alone steal, all of it.

Energy and Empire

Any account of Bolivia and its natural resources must grapple with a longer history of US intervention, a relationship to "empire" and "imperialism" that occupies a central place in Bolivian political discourse. Culturally speaking, I seek to capture the rich Bolivian language of anti-imperialism, with its vocabulary of useful words like *lackey* (*lacayo*) and *country sell-out* (*vendepatria*). An anthropologist would be remiss in not taking these meanings seriously while acknowledging that this can reflect combative militancy but is often merely discursive flourish. In addition, written from the perspective of a North American, and considering that many who read this are also reading from the US, a subtext of this book is a critique of US foreign policy shaped by a long history of fossil-fueled expansionism, intervention, and militarism (Mitchell 2001; Huber 2013). To this end, I use the term *empire* as many Bolivians do, to refer to the United States and its long history of efforts to control the path of Bolivian politics and economics. Empire refers to a specific territorial configuration in which the US seeks to exert influence over the course of state policy. As Greg Grandin argues (2006, 2), Latin America has been a proving ground for American empire, a kind of testing ground for "extraterritorial administration," economic policy experiments, techniques of "soft power" like conditioned development aid, as well as a long history of unilateral use of military force. Without reducing local complexities to external forces, and recognizing that many Bolivians are willing to serve the interests of the United States, I follow Fernando Coronil (1997) to "oscillat[e] between a critical localism and a critical globalism." The point is to consider how the concept of empire is useful to "capture the way that US power is enacted in the Western Hemisphere" (Gill 2004, 233). This is not to suggest that US imperialism is an all-powerful force. Indeed US interventions, carried out frequently with willing Bolivian collaborators, have failed as often as they have succeeded (Lehman 2006). The rise of Evo Morales is a testament to this power of resistance. And his fall in the coup of November 2019 was not (only) the result of US imperialism. Yet when viewed through the lens of the US private fossil fuel industries and their intellectual, military, and political backers, Latin America remains squarely in the sights of the most base elements of the US imperial urge and its local backers: to assure access and, by extension, some control over the course of oil and gas development in the region.

Even so, in much of the academic and the policy world, dominated as it is by material interests and forms of knowledge production that serve the imperial urge, the reality of empire is denied and its invocation often mocked. This is clearest among the hawkish hard-liners of the US Republican Party, but neither have the Democrats fallen behind. Indeed, in January 2010, when Barack Obama was US president and Hillary Clinton secretary of state, Clinton sent an envoy, María Otero, to the inauguration of Morales's second term. Otero, a Bolivian American with ties to Beltway insiders and Bolivia's wealthy elite, echoed what must have been generalized condescension toward Morales in Washington, DC. Upon her return to Washington, she emailed Clinton to complain of "countless hours of speeches and indigenous rituals," "barbs" aimed at the United States that were "blasts from the past," and the vice president's embrace of a "socialist" future for Bolivia. Otero had made the trip with then secretary of labor Hilda Solis. "I have to say," Otero (2010) wrote, "sending two Latinas to represent the 'empire' was disarming [to the Bolivians]."[3] The putatively humorous juxtaposition of one category deemed marginal but noteworthy for its representation in the heights of power (*Latina*) with another deemed hegemonic but ridiculous (*empire*) projected innocence on the United States while reducing Bolivian defiance to caricature worthy of mockery.

Nonetheless, the effort to situate Morales's position as "past," and the notion of socialism as inviable, betrayed the ongoing urge for control that is central to the imperialist project, whether represented by two Latinas or the US Southern Command. The US quest for hemispheric access to fossil fuel resources, couched in the language of "energy integration" and "open markets," is a core component of energy and empire today. The efforts to bring down the governments of Hugo Chávez and Nicolás Maduro in Venezuela have everything to do with oil (Tinker-Salas 2009; Schiller 2018). US foreign policy toward Mexico, including promoting privatization of Petróleos Mexicanos (Pemex, Mexican Petroleum), was equally centered on US fossil capital interests (Breglia 2013; Menchaca 2016). US support for violent dictatorships in Bolivia during the 1970s had everything to do with oil and gas. US efforts to defeat Evo Morales, both electorally and through political subterfuge, are also connected to—if not wholly determined by—the politics of gas. As an intention, if not always an achieved reality, the imperial urge is palpable and real, and deeply tied to fossil fuels.

In combining an ethnography of the Bolivian state with a critique of US imperial history, part of my purpose is to help North American readers understand the problem of "fossil capital" (Malm 2016) and fossil fuel dependence in the United States as well as Bolivia. This is not only because of concerns about climate change but because of the ways that fossil fuel political economies are central to the reproduction of patriarchal and racial capitalism and the militarization of social life. Fossil fuel economies generate multiform toxicities that are arrayed against our own bodies as well as ecological systems. What is clear is that the material thingness of fossil fuels, if not singularly determinant, plays a decisive role in entrapping us in a socially, politically, and ecologically toxic world. In infrastructural, political, and economic terms, we are all in the grip of a fossil empire that shapes, in its own ways, the making of modern politics and modern political subjects. By the same token, although with different measures of responsibility for the damage done, Bolivian gas consumers and car drivers in the US—and everywhere—are subjects of this fossil empire. This sets up a disposition by rulers to open their borders, change their laws, and repress their citizens, whether in the Bolivian gas lands or the Oceti Sakowin territory of North Dakota. Alternatively, rulers can try to convince us that fossil fuel dependence is good and right by telling us that we are in the midst of a revolutionary process (Bolivia) or we are enjoying the freedom that molecules of gas bring (US). At the end we are asked to acquiesce so that capital can grow through the monetization of fossil fuels.[4] Fossil empire relies on the reproduction of fossil colonies, and colonized imaginaries. We are all, in a sense, in that trap. Whether renewable energy might lead us out of it is open for debate, but our current situation of fossil fuel entrapment is clearly dire.

Anthropologies and Energy

The anthropology of energy has also experienced a boom. In earlier generations, scholars pursued general theories of the relationship between energy and social and cultural evolution (e.g., White 1943) or social power (e.g., Adams 1975). Yet most anthropologists tended to take energy for granted, at best, or pursued other theoretical turns. Laura Nader's 1981 essay was an early exception that sought to combine theory, ethnography, and political critique, in a piece showing how engineers charged with thinking about energy transitions were ill-equipped to do so because of their narrow forms of reasoning tied to technical specialties and existing infrastructures. The argument holds today. Yet anthropology failed to take up Nader's call. Save some exceptions, the poststructural turn and the rise of neoliberalism kept anthropologists engrossed in other things. Only in recent years, amid rising awareness of global warming and the intensification of the latest round of endless oil wars in the Middle East, has new work of various forms taken off.

In broad strokes, anthropologists are again interested in the relationship between social, cultural, and political-economic processes and energy, understood broadly. On a general level, Dominic Boyer offers the phrase "energopower" to refer to a way of thinking about "political power through the twin analytics of electricity and fuel" (2014, 325). Scholars have traced linkages between nation and state formation and oil (Coronil 1997; Apter 2005) and the effects of violence, terror, and resistance on the ground (Reyna 2007; Behrends, Reyna, and Schlee 2011).[5] Others have argued for a cultural or humanistic approach, one that seeks to understand how people's lives, imaginaries, and senses of self, place, and time are shaped by energy and material things like oil (Rogers 2015b; Boyer and Szeman 2016; Pinkus 2016; Wilson, Carlson, and Szeman 2017). The infrastructural turn has prompted work on "things" like pipelines, power plants, grids, and electrical flows (e.g., Gupta 2015; Bakke 2016). Studies of science, technology, and society have also returned our attention to the role of experts imagining new energy futures (e.g., Günel 2019). These approaches are crucial for making visible how human ways of producing and using energy, long taken for granted and now urgently demanding change, are imbricated in both intimate details of our lives and seemingly intractable structures of power.

Thinking about political power, the sociotechnical effects of energy infrastructures, and cultural meaning all resonate with the story I tell here. Yet beyond pursuing an anthropology of energy narrowly focused on gas or its infrastructures, I offer a historical ethnography of the Bolivian state, as shaped through the politics of gas and, to a lesser extent, oil. I take inspiration from political anthropologists interested in how states are made real through their effects (and affects), an approach renewed of late in Latin America (Krupa and Nugent 2015). Coronil's (1997) pathbreaking work on Venezuela's oil industry recenters the politics of value and nature into a Marxian critique of oil and state, drawing our attention to the ways that oil capital exploits nature (as well as labor) and oil—transformed into monetary rents—was deployed to reproduce imaginaries of the nation and state (see also Schiller 2018). Other work has examined conflicts between corporations and peoples, and resistance to fossil fuels. Susana Sawyer's work (2004) on oil and Indigenous rights in Ecuador draws attention to the ways that neoliberal (capitalist) ideologies were congruent with the interests of the oil industry. Elana Shever (2012) traces contours of oil and neoliberalism in her study of oil labor and reform in Argentina. A parallel approach focuses on the daily life of those living in oil zones—something oscillating between resistance and resignation, such as Michael Cepek's (2018) intimate portrait of Cofán struggles in Ecuador or Lisa Breglia's (2013) exploration of oil and local politics in Mexico. Lesley Gill (2016) offers a historical study of an oil town in Colombia, illustrating how oil, labor, and revolutionary politics created a cauldron that the state and paramilitary forces addressed through years of systematic violence. Martha Menchaca's (2016) examination of oil, labor, and asymmetric dependency between the US and Mexico shares much with my historical approach to Bolivia and the United States as seen through the politics of gas. And David McDermott Hughes (2017) offers a critique of the immorality of gas in Trinidad.

My approach also takes inspiration from critical scholars outside anthropology whose work has examined the intersections between state power, fossil fuel infrastructures, and the dynamics of capital, territoriality, violence, and hegemony (among others, Mitchell 2001; Huber 2013; Malm 2016; Valdivia 2008; Watts 2001, 2004a, 2004b; Zalik 2004). As with political anthropology, albeit with more emphasis on spatiality, this work is concerned with the ways that fossil fuels intersect statecraft, power, culture, and rule, and how people in distinct social positions seek to transform, resist, or promote the imperatives of fossil capital as these intersect with ongoing political and historical processes. If my efforts might be condensed, I pursue a critical historical and ethnographic account with a spatially attuned sociotechnical and materialist approach to gas. This requires an ethnographic sensibility to meaning and its material effects as well as an empirical acknowledgment of the harder geopolitical and economic materialities that fossil capital and its infrastructures entail.

A spate of recent studies of Bolivia composes another set of interlocutors. Bolivia was held up as a quintessential example of the broader turn to the left in Latin America, the so-called Pink Tide. Roughly from 2003 to 2008, as the MAS fended off right-wing and US-backed destabilization efforts, a number of writers, myself included, wrote optimistically of the progressive transformation underway. As did many Bolivians, foreign academics expressed solidarity with the "process of change" while offering critical assessments (among others, Fabricant and Gustafson 2011; Canessa 2012; Farthing and Kohl 2006). As state-led development collided with Indigenous rights, corruption multiplied, violence against women intensified, and judicial institutions came under political pressure, disaffection with Morales and the MAS grew. The 2011 police attack on Indigenous marchers during the Territorio Indígena y Parque Nacional Isiboro Secure's (TIPNIS, Isiboro Secure National Park and Indigenous Territory) struggle over a new highway through the lowland forests was a breaking point for some (McNeish 2013). The realities of natural gas dependence and the imperative to consolidate and centralize power began to reveal their contradictions with decolonial and socialist ideals. At various times, even from the beginning, committed revolutionaries began decamping from the MAS. Andrés Solíz Rada, one of the last of the nationalist leaders of the generation of Sergio Almaraz, was ousted for demanding that Morales stand up to Brazil. Another old anti-imperialist, Enrique Mariaca Bilbao, whom I introduce in chapter 4, left after the government frustrated his efforts to audit gas contracts with foreign companies. Raúl Prada, an early theorist of plurinationalism, left after the watering down of the constitution. Alejandro Almaraz, the son of Sergio Almaraz who plays a major role in chapter 6, was an early MAS militant forced out for being too committed to Indigenous rights. That all of these prominent leftist figures are men is part of the problem, as various radical feminists, to whom I return at various points, were less inclined to board the androcentric train of fossil fuel power in the first place. Many are the most vociferous critics of the MAS government today.

Similarly, observers have shifted to a more critical stance. What may have begun as a "plebeian" uprising (Dunkerley 2007) has arguably become a "passive revolution," a reformist apparatus largely sustained by petty capitalists in alliance with the big capitalists of agro-industry and fossil fuels (Webber 2017).[6] Brent Kaup (2012) argues that a new form of neoliberal capitalism has emerged. Nancy Postero (2017), focusing on the discourse of decolonization, suggests that much of what passes as decolonization is mere performance (see also Anthias 2018). While some have described the new progressive extractivism, with all its warts, as "commodity dependent left populism" (Riofrancos 2018), others have described Bolivia as "redistributive reformism," with the MAS unwilling or unable to radically transform capitalist and imperialist relations (Petras and Lora 2013, 90).[7]

Though these analytical reductions may resonate with some Bolivians, they also risk obscuring other readings of Bolivia, past and present. As an attempt to remedy this, by writing both from within and without, I have drawn inspiration from Bolivian intellectuals and activists whose work has a bearing on past and present interpretations of the politics of gas. This includes the nationalists of the left who produced political and historical critique of Bolivian subordination to foreign economic and political interests. Analyses of the role of these figures, their oeuvre, and the ideological complexity of "resource nationalism" have been done more ably by others (e.g., Tapia 2002; Cote 2016; Young 2016). I engage these figures in a different way, rereading them as historical voices that shed light on heroic resistance to fascism, racism, and authoritarianism, and on the dilemmas and limitations of oil- and gas-centric socialist thought. I found inspiration in their fearless use of biting prose against oligarchs and dictators, clearly surpassing my own capabilities but contributing to much of what I write herein. Facing off against military dictators (Marcelo Quiroga Santa Cruz, among many, many others, would eventually pay with his life), these writers instilled fear in the powerful because of their commitment to the written truth.

My mimicry includes what Mauricio Souza Crespo describes as René Zavaleta's affinity for paradox, juxtaposition, and digression (Souza Crespo 2013a, 18–19). By drawing connections between past and present, making linkages across time and space, juxtaposing historical events, and borrowing categories and redeploying them in new ways, Zavaleta sought to generate insight—or theory—through an accumulation of events, or in Souza Crespo's terms, an "accumulation of senses." Part of this strategy involved historical digressions, something that happens throughout this book. This includes my foray into the Chaco War and American guns, oilmen, and bankers. This also involves a series of parallel histories of struggle, from Che Guevara to the oft-forgotten urban revolutionaries of the Comisión Nestor Paz Zamora (CNPZ, Nestor Paz Zamora Commission) and notes on various heroes and villains who played historical roles. Some of these digressions are in the text; others are relegated to the notes. I encourage the reader to digress with me, and to read the notes alongside the main text. Through this piling up of interconnections, I encourage the reader to feel and see the intersections that add to the accumulation of political senses that I hope some might find useful for confronting the fossil empire of today.

The patriarchal terms of the conversation are clear in the fact that much talk of popular and socialist nationalism (not to mention the patriarchy of the conservative right) was and is dominated by men. I recognize that deploying nationalist male writers to critique an androcentric gaseous state has its limits. This is part of the analytical point. A key challenge is articulating critical thinking about lines of violence and inequality tied to race and sexuality with their political and economic anchors in systems like the gaseous state. As a remedy, however incomplete, I also offer forays into the underside of extractivism (Gómez-Barris 2017), to expose the gendered and raced toxicities and violences of the gas industry. Rereading the historical "defenders of the gas" critically—and taking up the more raucous and indignant critics of the present—allows for thinking more clearly about alternative politics not wedded to the toxicities of fossil capital. There has always been a heterogeneous constellation of other forms of resistance that finds echoes in the anarchism, the spirit of *desacato* (disobedience), and the anticolonial *janiwa* (No!) of the Indigenous movements. These are finding resonance in the age of gas with anarchist, queer, antiracist, feminist, and ecological currents waging a slow insurgency. Writer-activists like Silvia Rivera Cusicanqui, Raúl Prada, and the anarcho-feminist María Galindo, though not always talking about gas, have established a language of critique from the underside, critique that uses parody, satire, and acerbic humor, some of which I try to *recuperar* (recover) herein. Between the heroes of the old left and new figures of desacato, Bolivia offers inspiration in a world where capitalism, guns, and oil have led to rightward neofascist political shifts and intensification of war and human and ecological crises globally. The world has much to learn from Bolivia.

To see how this story unfolds, one needs to take on the state both from its center, and the iconic figures of its leaders, but also from its peripheries (Krupa and Nugent 2015). A fair amount of this book explores state policies and actors, including Evo Morales and others. A fair amount is also written from the perspective of the southeastern Bolivian region of the Chaco, home to the Guarani and the location of most of the country's gas reserves. Just as the Chaco is seen as a periphery in Bolivia, Bolivia is frequently seen as a periphery on the edge of global capital. Yet both are central to understanding how global circuits of fossil capital and empire operate. Following June Nash (1979), who saw, during Bolivia's age of tin, peripheries like Bolivia as a crystallization of a global condition, there are questions here that link all of us. For example, how might we escape the tentacles of fossil fuel capitalism amid deep relationships of dependency, inequality, and ecological crisis? After Ananya Roy, this calls for analyses that are not merely attempts at viewing regional particularities of the Global South and from there extrapolating how these "underdeveloped" areas relate to the developed Global North. This implies, instead, rethinking theory and knowledge production from what Roy called these distinct "places on the map," such as the rugged Chaco of south-eastern Bolivia (2009, 822). I hope to offer a reading that interprets how the politics of gas were experienced on the ground, or on many grounds, from the fascists of Santa Cruz to the anarcho-feminists of La Paz and to my Guarani friends in the Chaco, all mobilized to shape the direction of change.

The Structure of the Book

The book is structured chronologically around three interwoven dimensions of the gaseous state—time, space, and excess. Part 1 offers three historical sketches that provide the frameworks for thinking about the contemporary battles over the past that shape Bolivia's present relationships with gas. Re-sources have a temporality, which is to say that when transformed through the deployment of capital and the work of human labor, things like gas take on social and cultural meanings that are imbued with multiple and often con-tradictory senses of time. As Mandana Limbert (2010, 11) argues for Oman, entanglement and dependence on the fossil fuel industry generate multiple and overlapping temporal and political sensibilities, from the contractual time linking industry and state to the time of historical memory, that ani-mate political struggles and aspirations. These are not standardized, despite the shared form of oil and gas extraction worldwide, but collide with local and national histories and cultural forms of imagining the political. The purpose of part 1 is to set up a basis for thinking critically about the historical and con-temporary linkages between finance capital, militarism, war, and fossil fuels; the particular role of the US in aiding the expansion of military infrastruc-tures in direct relation to oil and gas infrastructures; and the masculine excess produced by fossil fuel economies, all of which coexist with the dispossession of native peoples and the exercise of multiple forms of violence against femi-nized bodies and nature.

In chapter 1, through the lens of the Chaco War, I set up a historical framework that involves thinking in the longue durée of the long oil and gas century (1920s to the present) to consider how Bolivia's political quandaries can be understood as shaped in part by efforts to build the infrastructures and establish the political conditions to extract fossil fuels. In chapter 2, I revisit the post–World War II era of authoritarian development to consider how the urge to expand oil and gas infrastructures was central to the US-backed mili-tarization of Bolivia's east. In chapter 3, I return to offer a critical look at the underside of the oil boom of the 1970s, a time of exuberance, debauchery, and distorted politics that foreshadows the decadence that characterized the late 2010s. The effort is to show how contemporary political struggles are animated by discourses on oil and gas that bring the past into the present in selective ways while collapsing past political struggles and present political imaginaries into a form of consent to ongoing gas activity. Against the backdrop of these multiple temporalities, I focus on the ways that the temporality of political struggle, primarily that of the social movements, as expressed in the recent cycle of resistance (2000–2005), was absorbed by the temporality of gas as a commodity in circuits of global fossil capital. Historians have argued that Bolivians, especially in the Andes, have deep reserves of revolutionary memory and constantly replenished revolutionary horizons that, in certain moments, are central to mass mobilization (Hylton and Thompson 2007; Gutiérrez 2014; Dangl 2019). The point is that gas, as mediated through the crucial figure and voice of Evo Morales, freezes these imaginaries in the present with the idea that the revolution (of sorts) had triumphed. The collapse of historical time and memory into the temporality of gas extraction and sale had a numbing effect on Bolivian politics, contributing to feverish struggles over rents and the gas assemblage, and dislocating and distorting other political projects and visions.

The second section of the book considers the theme of space and territory (Watts 2004a, 2004b; Labban 2008; Zalik 2011). When states open their borders to foreign extractive capital, the state cedes some sovereignty and access in exchange for the ability to monetize nature (gas) and generate some return as rents to landed capital, that is, the state as a landlord. The sovereignty that is left over, which is constrained by the urge to monetize gas, is fought over in territorial terms, as the priorities of the gas industry are to produce "governable spaces" (Watts 2004b). This has not spiraled into widespread or systemic "petrolic violence," as Michael Watts describes for the Nigerian case, yet we see an ongoing cartographic reconfiguration as national, regional, and Indigenous territorialities are subjected to new pressures to conform to the infrastructural and discursive needs of the gas industry. At the same time, conflicts between and within these scales and spaces intensify as spatial integration with global fossil capital generates spatial fragmentation internally (Labban 2008). There is thus a constant tension between the intensification of nationalist sentiment, and its aspirations for an imagined unity and shared history, and the intensely regionalized ways that struggles over gas rents and its sequiturs create other intense claims on a share of the excess. The chapters in part

2 consider three scales of spatial dispute: the national, the regional, and that of Indigenous territorialities. Chapter 4 considers the conflictive moment of the Gas War of 2003, and its sequiturs, arguing that despite the popular uprising, the configuration of fossil capital and local power imbalances set up a legal and infrastructural carbon lock-in for the export of gas. Chapter 5 takes on the reemergence of regionalism in Santa Cruz, offering a critical account of the ways that anti-Andean racism, cultural appropriation, and the objectification of women articulated with a political claim for regional autonomy. This would manifest itself again in the coup of November 2019. Chapter 6 examines conflict tied to Guarani demands for territory during a crucial moment in the early years of the MAS government. In each case territorial orders are contested through a combination of legal and extralegal maneuvers, often shaped by violent clashes.

Part 3 explores the gaseous state as a series of interlocking struggles over different forms of excess—excess violence, excess work, and excess money. Drawing on the vision of Bolivian historian and political thinker René Zavaleta, whose Gramscian notions of hegemony and state formation revolved around consideration of politics as a "quarrel over the excess," I trace the politics of gaseous excess. The gaseous state produced phenomena that exceed our capacity to reduce them to familiar analytical terms but invade, disrupt, and inflect the political and economic dynamics of territory and capital discussed in the first two parts of the book. In chapter 7 I argue that excess violence, the making of dead bodies (and the political work that they do), was and is central to the struggle over hegemony. The final two chapters examine the circulation of gaseous excess through struggles over compensation and labor (chapter 8) and battles over what Morales allegedly did with all the excess money (chapter 9). In all cases—violence, labor, money—there is a deep political and moral ambiguity about these excesses, part of the distortionary impact on politics that suggested to some the success of the MAS government, and to others the decadence of what was once a process of revolutionary potential. In sum, the age of gas was a time of hope and paradox, marked by progressive change but deformed by an increasingly grotesque form of politics, the latter intensified by right-wing tactics that would coalesce in the coup of November 2019, discussed in the postscript. In hindsight, Bolivia evidences the "crisis of futurity," described by Coronil, through which putatively leftist states ended up "doing the work of capital," as the commitment to the monetization of nature through gas extraction yielded a pragmatic politics that erased (or extended into the distant future) more radical and utopian political projects (Coronil 2019, 142). With the right-wing resurgence, the struggle will continue.

A Note on Method

This book is the outcome of hybrid methodological strategies and writing efforts that emerged out of particular historical moments. I have worked largely through "diagnostic events" (Moore 1987, 730). These are moments of political conflict or gasified social encounter. I reconstruct these through interviews, ethnographic observation, and documentation from digital and print media sources. These events provide the anchors for considering broader political and historical processes, as well as conflictive interpretations of the moment, in light of local experience. I seek to document and reflect on these events to ask what they teach us about the underlying dynamics of fossil fuel capitalism and the particularities of the gaseous state. It is important to note that I have not attempted to write an ethnography of the gas industry itself, whether of the corporations, the workers, the infrastructure, the gas molecules, or the inner (and largely inaccessible) political negotiations that shape the workings of the industry at the national level. For that, the reader will have to look elsewhere.

On Global Warming and Critique

In this book I try to offer critical understandings of Bolivia as a gaseous state. I might have followed the path of Hughes (2017), who delivered a scathing critique of the Trinidadian gas industry and Trinidadians' immoral complicity with global warming. Hughes, rightly I think, demands that we acknowledge the existential dilemma we all face and recognize that burning fossil fuels is basically immoral. We are trapped and dependent, which is why we must resist. As I write, my lights and computer are powered by a coal-burning utility here in St. Louis, one that exercises corrupt and outsize influence over an obedient legislature. We resist in ways that might seem laughable in Bolivia— they block highways and topple governments; we tweet and sign petitions. Certainly, there is concern about global warming in Bolivia, but it is coupled with a recognition, rightly so, that most carbon dioxide emissions and global warming have been caused by the US and the overconsuming Global North. And gas, beyond being a source of carbon dioxide with toxic effects on nature and people, means many things in Bolivia. Structural, historical, and political-economic forces make of Bolivia's current gas dependence something that goes far beyond individual or even collective moral decisions. As you sit in your parked car idling and spewing exhaust, remember where the real problem lies. So, it is not my purpose to criticize Bolivians for embracing natural gas. This is not to absolve Bolivian political leaders or fossil fuels, which are the targets of much critical reflection herein. Rather, it is an attempt to let Bolivians tell the story. My hope is also to point out that moral critique must be accompanied with radical structural change, which entails mass collective action. As Maristella Svampa (2017) writes, the left of the future, if there is to be one, will have to be an ecological left—united in its critique of racism, patriarchy, capitalism, and militarism—all of which are closely linked to the fossil fuel industry as we know it. I hope this book contributes to that conversation.

time
part one

1 heroes of the chaco

ACROSS THE CHACO REGION OF SOUTHEASTERN BOLIVIA AND WESTERN Paraguay, Indigenous peoples carved out relations of conflict and exchange long before the arrival of Europeans. In what is now Bolivia, the lands were the ancestral territories of the Guarani, with parts of the southern edges home to the Weenhayek and Toba. By the late 1800s, the Guarani had been subjugated by a combination of violence, forced labor, and missionization. The Toba were decimated and pushed into Argentina. The Weenhayek still live along the Pilcomayo, below Villamontes (Gustafson 2009c; Langer 2009). With no territorial recognition for the Indigenous peoples who survived settler colonialism, the Bolivian state asserted its authority by the early twentieth century, although its borders with Paraguay remained in dispute. On the ground, power was contested between landlords, soldiers, and the Church, all of whom competed for control of Guarani bodies, land, and labor. Though it is a truism to say that all land was Indigenous land, it is important to recognize the centrality of Indigenous dispossession, historical and ongoing, in Bolivia's history of oil and gas. As I explore in the following chapters, the Guarani in particular have been and remain central actors in the gas lands, even though most nationalist and popular histories of oil and gas rendered them invisible.

Running north to south, the rugged hills of the Incahuasi range rise up to the foothills of the Andes to the west. Further south, the range known as Aguaragüe drops into the Chaco flatlands. The Guarani grew corn in fertile valleys and hunted in the rugged hills, and had long known about oil and gas seeps along streambeds. The Guarani called oil itane (stinky rock) and used it for lamps and salves. Gas seeps in creek beds were marked with toponyms like *ivo*, literally bubbly water. This knowledge was later taken up by Spanish and Bolivian occupiers. In the early colonial period, Spaniards pursued oil as an alternative source of fuel to burn for Andean mineral processing, given the scarcity of wood, llama dung, and yareta, a mosslike plant. Yet the effort yielded little, given the challenge of transport. By the late nineteenth century, the quest for kerosene, then produced in Argentina, re-intensified interest in oil. Local knowledge about oil was going global. Preparing for an exposition in Italy in 1900, the Franciscan priest and catechizer of the Guarani, Doroteo Giannecchini, wrote in the catalog that Aguaragüe was "pure rock, silicate, which for its hot and boiling springs, sulfuric, salty, and oily, must enclose in its breast volcanoes of fire. In many of its creeks there are springs of gas and oil" ([1898] 1996, 278). The advent of automobiles and the demand for gasoline would follow soon after. As Sergio Almaraz wrote, where there is oil, or gas, capital will not be far behind.

With much intrigue, German, Chilean, British, Bolivian, and American capitalists started sending exploratory expeditions to the rugged region. Through subterfuge and buying out opponents, Rockefeller's Standard Oil, then a growing transnational behemoth, eventually acquired most of the concessions across the Guarani heartland in southeastern Bolivia. In both exploration and production, many Guarani were put to work doing manual labor (figure 1.1). An infrastructure of roads, outposts, work camps, and trading posts arose, changing the landscape and overlaying settler colonialism with a new apparatus of domination, the oil industry (Cote 2016). By 1926 Standard Oil was extracting oil from its operations in Fortín Campero, near the Argentine border (see map I.2). The company even built a clandestine pipeline across the Bermejo River to illegally export oil to Argentina, a point to which I return later in this chapter.[1]

Standard also began drilling in the area around what is now Camiri. The company eventually built a refinery there on a piece of Guarani land sold to it by the Vanuccis, an Italian settler family. In coming decades Bolivians from all over the country flocked to Camiri to work for the oil industry or to provide goods and services for those who did. Camiri, sitting atop much of the oil, came to be known as the Oil Capital of Bolivia. Along with the expansion of cattle ranching and corn production, oil development pushed the Guarani further to the margins. Camiri became a crossroads of Bolivia, between Santa Cruz to the north, Sucre and points beyond to the west, and the vast, arid Chaco and on to Paraguay and Argentina in the south. Far from the Andean

FIGURE 1.1 Standard Oil men paying Guarani laborers, 1924. From "Remote Bolivia," *The Lamp* (Standard Oil), February 1924.

mining centers and the state power structure centered in La Paz, Camiri and the Chaco were at once peripheral and central to Bolivian politics and the Bolivian political imaginary, especially when it came to fossil fuels.

WHEN I AND A COLLEAGUE, UBALDO PADILLA, STARTED COMPILING ORAL histories from retired oil workers in Camiri, it quickly became apparent that talk about oil, gas, and labor, past and present, had little to say about the Guarani. Rather, the history was invariably framed through the lens of the Chaco War that Bolivia fought with Paraguay between 1932 and 1935. For virtually all Bolivians, it was a war over oil that remains central in the national imaginary. Like historical wrinkles in time, stories about the war and the struggle with Standard Oil in the 1930s were folded into stories about the struggle against Gulf Oil in the 1960s. These in turn were folded into stories about Evo Morales and gas nationalization in the early twenty-first century. A unifying trope was pervasive: the affective urge to defend (*defender*) or to recover (*recuperar*) Bolivia's natural resources from foreign control. Though the history of the Chaco War is well-trodden terrain, understanding the age of gas and ways of speaking and thinking about the meaning of time, memory, and fossil fuels requires revisiting the war here again.

Here I explore the ways that Bolivians came to narrate the war through the lens of oil, imperialism, and nationalism. I emphasize Bolivia's early entanglement with what I call the fossil fuel-military-capital assemblage in the United States, by which I refer to the interconnections between militarism and war-making, the private oil industry, and finance capital, all expanding from the United States in the early 1920s. Thinking historically, spatially, and relationally allows for understanding how these fossil fuel assemblages (Watts 2004a) cross borders and exert forms of transterritorial sovereignty. As such, the story requires making visible the connections between the Chaco and the US government, Standard Oil, and banks, capitalists, and arms dealers from the US, Britain, and elsewhere. In ways that are more complex than saying the Chaco War was "fought over oil," it was, like virtually all wars fought in this long oil century, fought because of oil's inseparability from militarism and capitalism and vice versa.[2] Understanding fossil fuel dependence and attempting to think beyond it, whether in Bolivia, the US, or elsewhere, requires reflecting critically on the interdependence between normatively "good" cultural symbols, affects, and desires and the fossil-military-capital nexus as an apparatus of war and death.

IN CAMIRI, IN 2007 THE RETIRED OIL WORKER CRISÓLOGO MIRANDA, THEN seventy-five, started telling his life story this way: "My mother's name was Amalia Barahona Saavedra. My father was a lawyer. His name was Miguel Miranda Ramos. He died in the war of the Chaco, in the last retreat at Picuiba. In the midst of combat my father died in defense of the oil."[3] With that phrase, *died in defense of the oil*, Miranda encapsulated a cluster of meanings that sutured fossil fuels to Bolivian soil, nation, and sacrifice, now part of nationalist mantra. Germán Molina, another old oilman, recounted: "My dad came from Yacuiba and my mom from Tarija. They were merchants, they came here to make their lives around commerce. And *mi papá* went to war very young." Another retiree, Eusebio Vargas, recounted the story about his father going to war and dying young, telling my colleague Ubaldo, "That's right, you know that we men in this passage through life have to be useful to our *patria*, our fatherland, and my father was one of them." Like many families of those killed in war, coping with the death of their loved ones involves believing, rightly or not, that they were on the side of moral righteousness, or at least that the death had some meaning. In dying for oil, or for the nation (patria), the deaths made of the defense of oil a sacrosanct idiom of the Bolivian nation. Those who fought and died there have since been sacralized as the "Heroes of the Chaco." Although the Chaco War was a bloody folly of tin-pot generals and their capitalist backers, this mythos of heroism and sacrifice in defense of the oil is a difficult one to question in Bolivia today.

IN 1884, AFTER A FIVE-YEAR WAR WAGED OVER NITRATE, CHILE WON AND seized Bolivia's Pacific coastal territories, making a country dependent on the export of minerals a landlocked nation. As intense as oil and the Chaco, the issue of Chile and the sea still roils Bolivians today and would also come to shape gas pipeline politics over a century later. In 1903 Bolivia also ceded territory after losing a war with Brazil, over rubber.[4] By the 1920s, reeling from territorial loss, the mining-dependent economy was struggling with economic crisis and rising social discontent. Bolivian president Daniel Salamanca thought that territorial conquest in the Chaco would lead to economic diversification, particularly with oil. Standard Oil was operating in the Bolivian Chaco but had no way to export oil. Standard was also drilling in Argentina's northern Salta region. Yet Argentina, then more aligned with British capital and interests in Paraguay, and hoping to defend its own embryonic national oil company, refused to allow Standard to export Bolivian oil through its ports. The Bolivian generals hoped to assert control over the disputed territory of the Chaco and seize Fuerte Olimpo, a port on the Paraguay River (see Map I.1). With a pipeline to this port, Bolivia hoped to find a way to get its oil out to the Atlantic (Cote 2016). Though Argentina and Paraguay played a hand in stirring up long-standing border tensions, in 1932 Bolivian generals made the first moves that precipitated the war.[5]

Though cast in the language of nation-building, rightful claims, and heroic sacrifice, the Chaco War, like most wars, was also a tool that the rich used to wage class war against the working poor. World War I had increased demand for Bolivian tin, but the Great Depression had collapsed it. Bolivia expatriated most of the tin wealth and was wracked with debt, mostly to US and British banks. Unemployment was high. Along with ongoing Indigenous resistance, the period saw new forms of struggle as militant workers, students, and intellectuals inspired by Marxism and anarchist thought began to challenge the mining-backed oligarchs (Lora 1977; Lehm and Rivera Cusicanqui 1988). The army had recently responded to miners' strikes with mass killings, events that met with public repudiation. Against rising discontent, the generals hoped that a war with Paraguay might stir up nationalist

my first book

sentiment and breathe life into an authoritarian regime composed of tin barons, military officers, and their foreign backers. As one anarchist leader recounted of the era, "In 1928, 1929, 1930 there was no work. . . . It was a terrible crisis. We workers were suffering, eating the 'poor man's pot' in the churches, we had nothing to eat. The people were in a social convulsion, and the struggle was intense. That's why we [Bolivia] entered the war; because [the regime] detested the workers, they declared war" (Lehm and Rivera Cusicanqui 1988, 124). Marxists and anarchists were stalwart opponents of the war, which they saw rightly as merely promoting the interests of foreign capital and the bourgeoisie. In response, the military regime repressed, jailed, and exiled many young labor leaders, greatly weakening the organized union movement.[6]

Paraguay was better supplied, better motivated, and better led. After three years of mutual slaughter, the Bolivians suffered a series of key defeats and withdrew to the line of settlements between Camiri and Villamontes. By late 1934, Paraguayan troops were threatening to take both cities and the oil fields. It was then that the old oil worker, Crisólogo Miranda, just a toddler at the time, lost his father, Miguel. Yet as any Bolivian will tell you, in that dire moment their troops mounted a heroic defense of Villamontes. One can revisit it through photos, mounted machine guns, and dioramas in the little Chaco War museum in Villamontes. When Paraguayans tried to cut the line between Villamontes and Camiri, they were again stopped by Bolivian troops positioned atop a big escarpment called the *muela del diablo* (devil's molar). It juts up south of Camiri. As any Bolivian driver can tell you as you pass by, "that's the devil's tooth, that's where we stopped the *pilas*," using the slang for *pata pila*, the barefoot ones, the Paraguayans.

As the stories unfold, the defense of the oil—alongside the mythos of the heroes of the Chaco—exists today almost as if the war were yesterday. The heroes of the Chaco are all those Bolivians, then and now, who stand to "defend the oil" from foreign usurpers. The sentiments are intensely felt. I once suggested to a colleague, an urbane intellectual with leftist and ecological sensibilities, that the Chaco War was an aggressive war seeking a port, not a defensive one. Taken aback, he reminded me a bit forcefully, "Yes! Maybe. But in Picuiba and Villamontes, that's where we were defending the oil!" Somewhere therein lie collapsed many other historical facts and fictions, many disputed, among them the role of the US and the fossil fuel assemblage: US capitalists, arms dealers, and Standard Oil.

Rockefeller's Oil Company

Through years of studying Latin America and living in Bolivia, and long before embarking on this project, I had internalized the story that Standard Oil (on the Bolivian side) and Royal Dutch Shell (on the Paraguayan side) were to blame for the Chaco War. The simple version was that it was a proxy war between two rival imperial powers (the US and Britain). Standard, backed by the US dollar capitalists, was pushing Bolivia to capture territory from Royal Dutch Shell in Paraguay, backed by British pound sterling capitalists. The two countries, companies, and currencies were then jousting for control over oil regions globally, a struggle that was in fact being waged across the oil lands of the world through competition (and sometimes collusion) between US and British oil interests (Mitchell 2001; Arrighi 2010). Cultural residues of this history live on in the Chaco. Given the once dominant role of British capital in the rubber industry to the north, the tin industry of the Andes, and the lumber and cattle regions of Argentina, Bolivians in the Chaco still tell folk tales about discovering hidden treasure chests holding *libras esterlinas* (sterling pounds). In contrast, stories told about contemporary oil and gas wealth and corruption usually speak of tables covered with *dólares* (dollars).

Given the reality of proxy wars over oil elsewhere, and Standard's corrupt and criminal practices in the US, Standard's culpability in the Chaco War is eminently plausible. In 1940 the Chilean poet Pablo Neruda wrote the poem "Standard Oil," which reads in part:

> Standard Oil arrived beforehand
> [With its lawyers and its boots]
> With its checks and its rifles
> Their obese emperors
> from New York are suave
> smiling assassins
> who buy silk, nylon, cigars,
> petty tyrants and dictators.
> They buy countries, people, seas,
> police, county councils,
> distant regions where
> the poor hoard their corn
> like misers their gold:
> Standard Oil awakens them,

clothes them in uniforms, designates
which brother is the enemy.
The Paraguayan fights its war,
and the Bolivian wastes away
in the jungle, with his machine gun.

Antes llegó Standard Oil
con sus letrados y sus botas
con sus cheques y sus fusiles
con sus gobiernos y sus presos
Sus obesos emperadores
viven en New York, son suaves
y sonrientes asesinos,
que compran seda, nylon, puros,
tiranuelos y dictadores.
Compran países, pueblos, mares,
policías, diputaciones,
lejanas comarcas en donde
los pobres guardan su maíz
como los avaros el oro:
la Standard Oil los despierta,
los uniforma, les designa
cuál es el hermano enemigo,
y el paraguayo hace su Guerra
y el boliviano se deshace
con su ametralladora en la selva.[7]

IN HIS MONUMENTAL *OPEN VEINS OF LATIN AMERICA*, EDUARDO GALEANO argued that Standard Oil's crimes elsewhere were encapsulated in the Chaco
War (1973, 163). Galeano pointed to the fact that postwar negotiations were
even overseen by Spruille Braden, American diplomat and capitalist investor,
who himself had oil concessions in Bolivia in the 1920s and later sold them
to Standard Oil.[8] The inseparability between government, capitalists, and oilmen suggested a general conspiracy behind all of Standard's actions. Indeed,
it was in these early years of oil and empire that the US government and its
growing military apparatus became increasingly indistinguishable from the
interests of private oil companies, as in many ways, they continue to be today.[9]

That Standard Oil and Rockefeller interests were behind a number of
imperialist pursuits in Latin America is unquestionable (Colby 1995). None-

theless, the story of Standard Oil's responsibility for the Chaco War has been questioned by US historians. Herbert Klein (1964) argues that while Standard was operating in a corrupt way, and its contract breaches were a reasonable justification for nationalization, Standard was not to blame for the war. More recently, Stephen Cote (2016) points out that territory was pursued by both sides, with at least some notion that oil was one of various resources at stake. Bolivia did seek an outlet to the Atlantic, and did so in part because it hoped to export oil. Yet for Cote, Standard was not the protagonist. Standard was doing what oil companies did everywhere, sitting on its concessions to hold them until a global oil oversupply evened out. Cote argues that Bolivian elites had their own territorial ambitions and did not simply respond to the machinations of Standard Oil. The fact that during the peace negotiations the Bolivians continued to demand a navigable port on the Paraguay River seems to confirm this reading (see also Rout 1970, 69). Formally at least, Standard Oil and the US government declared themselves neutral. In point of fact, Standard did little to help Bolivia's war effort, and even sold oil to Paraguay from its Argentine operations. Had it been a proxy war, the logic suggests, Standard would have at least done more to help Bolivia win it. Leslie Rout Jr. (1970) suggests that the "blame Standard" narrative was just a later story told to create unity among fractious political classes and between Latin American nations, and to absolve the Bolivian military of blame in the aftermath of a disastrous war.

With little explicit evidence to show that Standard had a direct hand in instigating the war, one might conclude that Standard, the US, and Wall Street were innocent. The "blame Standard" story could be written off as nationalist or left-wing propaganda. This is, at least, the story that Standard's official history tells (Larson et al. 1971). Yet if we know anything about the oil industry, it is its penchant for untruth. As with contemporary attempts to suggest that the endless wars in the Middle East are not about oil, the effort to absolve Standard from the war is politically and intellectually naïve. To absolve oil is to ignore the realities of fossil fuel capitalism and the militarist nationalism it engenders, in both the US and Bolivia, and to obfuscate the ways that war and oil entice us to embrace a politics of death while calling it sacrifice. The Bolivian oligarchs, Standard Oil, and the US financiers were entangled by oil, guns, and debt, and were virtually inseparable. On Miranda's cue, or at least in the name of his father and tens of thousands of others who died in the war, I thus pause to reconsider the "blame Standard" narrative with a bit more nuance to conjoin two dimensions of the war—the racist contours of the Bolivian state and the question of debt, money, and guns. I draw here on historical work and my own digging into the links between the banks and Standard Oil.

MUCH HAS BEEN WRITTEN ABOUT HUMAN SUFFERING IN THE WAR. SOL-DIERS risked death from battle, as well as from tropical disease and lack of water (Zulawski 2006). The suffering was intensified by the war's colonial and racist character. On the Bolivian side, a whitish oligarchic caste was sending mostly darker-skinned soldiers to kill and die. Officers enjoyed better living conditions, food, and access to medical care. Foot soldiers were treated on the front lines much like they were on the haciendas and in the mines, as less than citizens, something disposable. As the anarchist leader cited above said, they were workers, detested by the elites. The Bolivian revolutionary thinker René Zavaleta (1984) excoriated this oligarchic antinational state, the incompetence of the military, and the racist disregard that the elite had for workers and Indians alike. For Zavaleta, the racism of the ruling caste was expressed in the hubris with which soldiers were sent to die in the Chaco.[10] He wrote that "decimating men [of color,] without reason, evidenced a secret desire to suppress them, part of the logic of social Darwinism" (Zavaleta 1984, 353). Recalling Hans Kundt, a German general in command of Bolivian troops who sent two thousand to their deaths in an ill-thought assault at Nanawa, Zavaleta wrote that the elites did not care for the loss of human lives "because in the end it was the loss of Indians [indios], that is, something that one could afford to lose" (355–56). In another essay, Zavaleta (1977, 48) suggests that the racist hubris of the oligarchs and Kundt was such that it was hard to know if they had as much disdain for the Paraguayans "who they thought they could defeat in a few weeks, or toward the Bolivians, who were sent to be killed with the tranquility of one who is contemplating the extermination of locusts" (figure 1.2).

Here the sublimation of sacrifice for oil as a call to national unity confronts its first disruption: the deep racism of colonialist and capitalist disregard for the indio and the unruly worker. For the oligarchs, these were neither heroes nor sacrificial victims; they were cannon fodder. There was of course, intense critique of the war even in its midst. This counterimpulse is often obfuscated in contemporary nationalist rememberings of the Chaco War as the heroic defense of the oil. This impulse was to resist the war altogether, through the Bolivian anarchist spirit of desacato (disobedience) and dissent. A recently published memoir of the war written by Trifonio Delgado Gonzales (2015) offers an illustrative taste, starting with its title, Carne de cañon: ¡Ahora arde, kollitas![11]

FIGURE 1.2 The German General Kundt with Bolivian soldiers during the Chaco War, 1933. Bettman via Getty Images.

At the outset of the war, in 1932, Delgado Gonzales went to the trenches. He was in his twenties. By train, truck, and forced march, he and thousands of others were transported from the high Andean mining and agricultural centers to the unforgiving battlefields of the Chaco. Already steeped in the experience of labor struggle in the mines, and no stranger to the linkages between tin, oil, and empire, Delgado Gonzales was both foot soldier and radical intellectual. Though many anarchists and radical thinkers had gone into exile to avoid going to war, Delgado Gonzales, for circumstances beyond his control, found himself on the front lines. He concluded, while trying to stay alive, that the war was premeditated, funded, and promoted by Wall Street and the oligarchs: Simón Patiño, the absentee baron of Bolivian tin;

and Standard Oil, the rapacious oil company of the North. Here, he was right, as we shall see. Yet Delgado Gonzales was no naïve purveyor of cheap patriotism (*patriotismo*), a derogatory word for nationalist sentiment. In fact, his diary is a blistering critique of the blustering "patriots" and the generals who swept them into war. In contrast to Germán Molina, who seemed resigned to the idea that one's destiny was to sacrifice himself for the patria, Delgado Gonzales lamented the sense that "we somehow had to fulfill our duty, that we had been called [to war] by the random chance of life, by the nation-state, by the oil, and by *Standard Oil*" (2015, 48). He recalled soldiers calling for "revolution," not for a war for oil (67). Much a Bolivian version of Joseph Heller's Yossarian, writing his own *Catch-22*, Delgado Gonzales wrote: "We were always reflecting on the absurdity of this war, as absurd as the physical space in which we acted, we killed, we died, anonymously, surely serving as a support for the political ambitions of neurotic and paranoid mestizos for which, in the voice of the people, we were defending the oil of *The Standard Oil Company of Bolivia*" (132; italicized portion in English in the original).

Read in this way, the issue was not so much whether Standard instigated the war; instead, the problem was that all those Bolivians died not defending the oil from Paraguay but defending Standard's oil in the service of corrupt military rulers and their Wall Street backers. For Delgado Gonzales, the blame was shared between fossil capital (Wall Street), its primary investment (Standard Oil), and Bolivia's ruling classes. The Chaco War was a senseless counterrevolutionary blood-letting that articulated racial capitalism, the power of the oil and arms industries, and the pathologies of military men and financiers. Against the remembrance of war heroes defending the oil, and thus justifying the sacrifice, again, Delgado Gonzales saw the death as senseless.

> We continued advancing, with difficulty, taking hand by hand a few miserable stretches of this sterile and treacherous land; and as we advanced we left in our path, made brothers by death, *pilas* [Paraguayans] and *bolis* [Bolivians] laid out with their face to the sun, amid puddles of blood and in the most grotesque poses: some clenching their rifle, others face down, some huddled around their possessions as if they were trying to dodge death. All of these cadavers appeared to protest silently and sinisterly against the remote instigators of this cruel massacre. (2015, 159)

After the defense of Villamontes, growing international pressure and the financial and military exhaustion of both sides led to a truce. By the end of the war, in mid-June 1935, some fifty thousand Bolivians and thirty thousand Paraguayans were dead. Bolivia lost much of the Chaco but kept the oil fields. Paraguayans moved the border definitively westward.

Money, Oil, and Guns

The story of Bolivia's war dead—whether worthy sacrifice in defense of the oil or meaningless cannon fodder of a racist state—must be considered within a broader context of capitalism, debt, and imperialism that set the stage for the Chaco War. After World War I, the United States, flush with capital, briefly became a creditor nation; much of this wealth came from oil exports for the war itself. The US had been spared the devastation of war. American finance capital was a rising power. Banks—most virtually indistinguishable from the oil industry itself—and the US government hoped to lend money to expand consumption of US goods and extend US political influence through debt. This dollar diplomacy, both before and after World War I, was aimed at countering the influence of the British pound sterling in favor of the dollar while also gaining access to natural resources needed by the oil-military-capital assemblage. Bolivia, which had tin, oil, and other minerals, was one of several countries targeted.

This involved the sale of Bolivian bonds by American banks to buyers in the United States. The banks, after taking a cut, would give the money to Bolivia for future repayment. Invariably, the agreements required that Bolivia use some of the money to contract goods and services from US firms. In 1917 a bond issue was to be used to hire an American firm to build the Yungas railway. In 1920 the money was to hire Ulen Corporation to build a sewer system in Cochabamba and La Paz. In 1921 and 1922 bonds were issued both to pay back prior debts and expand railway infrastructure, also of US construction. In 1924 and 1927 bonds were issued to pay back the now-mounting debts and finance new infrastructure projects. Much of this lending involved speculation that oil discoveries would finance repayment. But default was also built in as a political tool. Across Latin America, the mechanism was similar.[12] US banks, through bribes and other forms of kickbacks to receiving governments, sold bonds to North American investors, large and small. The banks skimmed off lucrative fees. If the bonds defaulted, as virtually all of them did, the intermediary banks and the government were off the hook. Most of the risk was taken on by the buyers of the bonds, and the Bolivian people, from whose labor repayment would be extracted. This was the context of finance capitalism and debt that set the stage for the Chaco War.

The connections between the bonds, the US government, and Standard Oil were most evident in the 1922 loan. The negotiation of Standard's entry into Bolivia was preceded by the floating of a large bond issue remembered as "El empréstito Nicolaus" (the Nicolaus Loan) of 1922. The St. Louis investment firm Stifel Nicolaus (today simply Stifel) participated in the bond offering of $24 million along with other banking groups. Yet at the center of the loan was the Equitable Trust Co., a Rockefeller bank built out of capital accumulated through the activities of Standard Oil and its affiliates.[13] Walter Teagle, president of Standard Oil, was a trustee of Equitable Trust. Thomas Armstrong, who headed Standard Oil's operations in Bolivia and who negotiated the Standard contract with the Bolivian government, was a treasurer of Equitable Trust (State of New York 1920, 416). The banks were the oil companies, and vice versa, with guns thrown in for good measure (figure 1.3).[14]

The relationship between Rockefeller's bank and Rockefeller's oil company is noted by many Bolivian historians but rarely discussed by American historians who question the "blame Standard" narrative. Three points are significant. First, the distinction between capital and oil was blurry, if it existed at all. After Malm (2016), this bank-oil fusion was fossil capital incarnate; both oil and debt were mechanisms of capital accumulation, as was war. War was a primary means of expenditure which consumed both capital and oil and necessitated more debt and more consumption. It was in fossil capital's interests that Bolivia (as with the US) waste its oil and money on war. Second, against Standard Oil's claims that it did not instigate the war, the blurred lines between the bank and the oil industry show that it did indeed finance the Bolivian military build-up, even if instigating the war was left to the Bolivian generals. Third, the bribes, the payments, and the loan itself were used to encourage Bolivian oligarchs to take on debt and reward Standard with a generous concession, giving the oil-capital assemblage significant power over Bolivia.

The bond issue contract, with terms onerous for Bolivia, was signed in May 1922. In a clear quid pro quo, the contract with Standard Oil, with terms equally onerous for Bolivia, was signed in July 1922 (Zapata Zegada [1964] 2015). The oil contract granted Standard concession rights for fifty-five years, a very low royalty to the state (11 percent), and no surface rental fees until production began (Cote 2016).[15] In signing the contract, the Bolivian gov-

FIGURE 1.3 Thomas Armstrong, of Standard Oil, New York, ca. 1930. Armstrong, son of a Texas rancher, sat on the board of Rockefeller's oil-funded bank (Equitable Trust) and spearheaded the negotiation of Standard Oil's first contract in Bolivia. King Ranch Collection, The South Texas Archives & Special Collections, James C. Jernigan Library, Texas A&M University–Kingsville.

ernment ignored its own 1921 Petroleum Law, which placed a moratorium on new concessions. The imbrication of the banks, the oil company, and the Bolivian government was clear. In Klein's terms (2003, 166), there was "little question . . . that Bolivian negotiators had been corrupted." Of many mechanisms of corruption there included payments to Supreme Court justices, payments to newspaper outlets, direct bribes, and government concessions to Bolivians who could in turn enrich themselves by selling these concessions to Standard Oil (Almaraz 1958). The Bolivian state was largely, if not entirely, brought under the thumb of US fossil capital through the legal mechanism of debt finance.

In the case of the bonds, the contract stipulated that the debt would be secured by mortgages on existing and yet-to-be-constructed railroads and customs and tax revenue on most exports. In an early version of the deal, even taxes on future petroleum exports were to be subject to collection by the American bankers. Had this clause held, it would have meant that any revenues generated by Standard Oil activities (above and beyond their profits and share of rents) would also be returned to the Rockefeller-controlled banks themselves as payment on the bonds. Fierce public outcry led to the removal of this clause in the final version. Yet the agreement still handed over sovereignty. To ensure collection of all available money to service the bond repayment, the bond issue established a permanent fiscal commission to oversee tax and customs revenue collection. Two of the three members of this commission would be named by the North American bankers.

Consider how this worked through one example. In 1926 Pompilio Guerrero, a humble customs agent monitoring Standard Oil's activities in the remote border post of Fortín Campero, reported to his boss in La Paz that he had discovered a clandestine Standard pipeline exporting oil illegally to Argentina. This was a breach of contract, since Standard repeatedly claimed that it had not yet discovered oil and any exports would be subject to tax and royalty payments. Guerrero's boss told him that was impossible, since Standard Oil was a reputable foreign company. The boss fired him. It turned out that his boss, the national director of the Bolivian Customs Agency, was one William Magowan, a US citizen and former employee of Standard Oil. Magowan had been given the job as one of the conditions imposed by the loan, a mechanism through which the oil banks could extract repayment on the debt and Standard could evade the law. Guerrero was later vindicated, but Standard had so much power in the government that this breach of contract was not addressed until after the Chaco War. In nationalist lore today, Pompilio Guerrero is yet another hero (Zapata Zegada [1964] 2015).

In short, Bolivia's elites mortgaged public works, revenue, and sovereignty in order to access (fossil) capital. The state also turned over control of oil exploration. As it was in the 1990s, when deeply indebted and interpenetrated by World Bank and IMF functionaries defining policy, the Bolivian state in the 1920s was a hybrid entity. The loan propped up the Bautista Saavedra government, which had no political or economic base outside the small oligarchic elite and its dependence on mineral export taxes. More precisely, Standard, through its bankers and agents, American and Bolivian, literally seized control of much of Bolivia's political and financial infrastructure as well as its potential oil-producing territories.

The Standard concession was achieved through the enticement of a bond issue that all parties knew Bolivia could not repay.[16] In 1908 Bolivia had no foreign debt. By 1927 it owed $40 million. In 1928 the principal items on the Bolivian budget were debt payment (25 million bolivianos, about 50 percent of total government income) and the department of war (11 million bolivianos, about 21 percent). By 1929, on the eve of the Great Depression, Bolivia was spending 37 percent of its revenue on servicing debt and 20 percent on its military (Marsh 1928, 90).[17] In addition to earlier support from British investors, US capital—derived from oil sales combined with US investors large and small—was thus largely used to build the Bolivian military apparatus. Margaret Alexander Marsh, a radical intellectual who studied the US banks in Bolivia in the 1920s, called it a "subtler kind of imperialism." For Marsh, the relationship was pursued by the Bolivians and it was being carried out not by the US government but by private members of an (oil) banking syndicate, one whose power would increasingly rival that of the US government (1928, 134). But the underlying assumption was that in case of default or the nationalization of Standard assets, the US government would step in to defend Standard Oil and US capital.

Yet just as oil capital worked transnationally, so did the radical ideas that sought to resist it. A digression is worthwhile. Marsh is another long-forgotten hero. She studied the US loans to Bolivia based on several months of fieldwork in La Paz between 1925 and 1927. Marsh's work was financed by the American Fund for Public Service, a foundation created by the eccentric son of a Wall Street banker, who, in a crisis of conscience, offered his inheritance for radical research. Marsh's book was included in a series edited by Harry Elmer Barnes, part of a circle of socialist and libertarian intellectuals who were critics of war, the banks, and the arms industry. Marsh went on to teach sociology and anthropology at Smith College (Curti 1959). In Bolivia, Sergio Almaraz and other nationalists writing in the 1950s and 1960s drew on Marsh's *The Bankers of Bolivia* (1928), which had been published in Spain and circulated in Bolivia as *Nuestros banqueros en Bolivia*.

This bond-based oil imperialism hit many countries in Latin America and elsewhere in the world. In virtually all cases the countries were in no condition to repay. Princeton economist Edwin Kemmerer led an advising mission to Bolivia in 1927. His report led to the redesign of the Bolivian banking system to make it more amenable to US capital interests. Although Kemmerer concluded that Bolivia was overborrowed, his mission was followed with a new bond deal arranged by the Dillon Read investment firm. No subtlety here: Kemmerer's mission was financed by Dillon Read itself (Drake 1989, 175–211). A significant portion of the Dillon Read loans of 1927 and 1928 went toward the payment of debt to Vickers, the British maker of machine guns later used in the Chaco War. Kemmerer was right. The Dillon Read bonds were in default by 1931. But that was the goal. Default triggered mechanisms that further deepened the control of the US banks and dependence on future dollar debt. The US banking and capitalist apparatuses of railroad, oil, and construction interests were complicit in what California senator Hiram Johnson, who led the charge against the banks in the 1930s, called a "big orgy of flotation of foreign loans." (For another digression, consider Lawrence Dennis, another traveler in Bolivia in those days who offered brilliant testimony to Congress on these loans to the Andean countries.[18])

As Bolivia slid recklessly toward war with Paraguay and confronted its own antiwar movements, the United States also saw the eruption of antiwar movements on both left and right. These included Americans who conjoined their criticisms of Wall Street and the arms industry, blamed for pushing the US into the carnage of World War I. Exposés of the arms industry, such as *Merchants of Death*, written by libertarian scholars, were interconnected with critiques like that of Marsh (Engelbrecht and Hanighen 1934).[19] In those years, these critics also began to see the US oil industry, with Standard as its dominant representative, as wielding too much independent power. Franklin D. Roosevelt even floated the possibility that the US government take control over oil reserves and pipelines in Saudi Arabia then held by Standard. Imperialist, to be sure, Roosevelt's idea was deemed necessary to arrest the unfettered power of the private oil industry. By the same token, the arms industry was outspoken in its opposition to pacifism and neutrality. No surprise there; its business relied on war. This led to the Senate convocation of the Nye Committee, named for Senator Gerald Nye, the North Dakota progressive who chaired it. The committee was charged with investigating the arms industry and considering whether it should be placed under government control. Behind the creation of the committee was the work of the antiwar Women's Peace Party, part of the Women's International League for Peace and Freedom, then led in the United States by the tireless activist Dorothy Detzer, another oft-forgotten hero of the time.[20] Pacifists and isolationists, as they were known, joined together in the push against the arms and oil industries and their power in the US government.

By nationalizing both, it was thought, profit could be taken out of their motivation for skullduggery (Seidman 1934; Mitchell 2001). Roosevelt and the Nye Committee, though often at odds, faced an uphill struggle against the conjoined power of big oil, factions of the US military, and the private arms industry.

In order to grow, capitalist arms industries need expenditure of armament through war, an expenditure also needing oil and thus useful to an oil industry that needed to constantly boost demand to keep prices high despite oversupply. In this post–World War II moment, the Chaco War was one of only two major armed conflagrations globally and was thus a mechanism for wealth production elsewhere. Bolivia played a central role in the Nye Committee hearings on the arms industry in the US Congress. Flush with capital from the US oil banks, Bolivia purchased weapons from the British, the Germans, and the Americans. Paraguay, financed by Argentine and British capital, would do the same. (According to Trifonio Delgado Gonzales, who handled some of these weapons on the front lines, much of the British matériel they had was recycled weaponry from World War I.)[21] As with the oil industry, the Nye Committee hearings revealed that bribery was common in the weapons industry, as arms dealers sought to convince governments to sign contracts, doing their best to sell to both sides (Seidman 1934; Gillette 1970). The hearings brought to light the ways that peripheral places and bodies, like those of the Chaco and Bolivian soldiers, were also treated with racist disregard by white businessmen leading US companies like Colt, Remington, Winchester, and DuPont. A Remington executive complained that new rifle designs were necessary when it came to the Chaco War, given that their Enfield rifle, at more than eleven pounds, was too heavy for the "pygmy Indian soldiers of the South."[22] Another saw no contradiction with selling to both sides, arguing that it would make little sense for someone in the gun business to be bothered by a conscience. In the final report, the Nye Committee held up the Chaco War as a key example of the complicity between debt financiers, arms makers, and militaries.

> When a limited amount of matériel, such as machine guns, was available, Bolivia could be forced into ordering them on the threat that unless she acted quickly, Paraguay would get them. Killing the back-country Indians of South America with airplanes, bombs, and machine guns boiled down to an order to get busy because "these opéra bouffe revolutions are usually short-lived, and we must make the most of the opportunity." . . .

The committee finds, from official documents which it has not entered into the record, that the sales of munitions to certain South American nations in excess of their normal capacity to pay, was one of the causes for the defaults on certain South American bonds, and that the sales of the munitions was, in effect, financed by the American bond purchasers, and the loss on the bonds was borne by the same people. (United States Congress 1936)

Thanks to the efforts of US pacifists like Detzer, in May 1934 Roosevelt's government passed a unilateral embargo on the export of US-manufactured arms to the Chaco combatants.[23] But plenty of weapons were already sold and those already contracted were given exceptions. Gillette points out that arms were relabeled as machinery and exported anyway (1970, 296; see also M. Hudson 1936). More would be smuggled through Peru and Chile. Europeans from Norway to Belgium to Germany to Britain were also shipping arms to both parties through Chile and Argentina. The war dragged on. In January 1935 Paraguay took the upper hand, seizing the area around Boyuibe, in the heart of Guarani territory and the Bolivian oil fields. Now on undisputed Bolivian soil, Paraguay was labeled the aggressor and the League of Nations moved to relax the embargo on Bolivia so as to force Paraguay to the negotiating table (Streit 1935). Debates on regulation of the arms industry in the US continued, with one reporter arguing that "the War in the Chaco had been a trump card so far as munition salesmanship." In other words, testimony showed that war-mongering paid off. Paraguay, it was feared, would nonetheless "have the oil fields" by February (Speers 1935). Peace talks were imminent but both armies fought for advantage at the negotiating table, meaning more dead in the waning days of the war. It was then that Miguel Miranda died "in defense of the oil." The hostilities finally ended in June 1935. That same month, on June 3, with the bodies in the trenches, the *New York Times* reported that the "tin hermit," Simón Patiño—one of the world's richest men, Bolivia's minister to France, and a financier also partly responsible for bankrolling the Chaco War—celebrated his seventieth birthday in a luxurious Paris apartment (Associated Press 1935).

Peripheral as it now seems, the Chaco, converted into a vast killing field, was central to the birth of Bolivian popular oil nationalism and to debates over isolationism, oil, arms, and intervention in the United States. The contours of oil, guns, and war remain relevant today. The US oil companies, recognizing that their survival relied on government-backed private control over oil reserves both at home and in other countries, resisted pacifism, isolationist neutrality, and government regulation. Powerful factions of the US military sided with the private arms companies and the oil industry to oppose government takeover of either one. War assured continued private oil industry domination. In order to secure oil supplies during World War II, the US government ended its antitrust activities against the oil industry, including Standard Oil, in the United States. Meanwhile, the antiwar pacifists and isolationists, like the brave anarchists in Bolivia, faced accusations of treason as World War II approached. War and oil was as counterrevolutionary in the United States as it was in Bolivia. This came despite the fact that it was not the pacifists but Standard Oil and other US firms that had been collaborating with Nazi Germany. Standard would go on to gouge the US public while profiting from US government loans to Europe after the war's end.[24] Isolationists like Nye and some in Roosevelt's government as well had tried to unwind some of the militarist and fossil capital power that had captured the state. It was a fertile political moment but one in which the convergent interests of the oil companies, a militarist foreign policy, and private banking apparatus prevailed.[25] This was the same largely private apparatus, rooted in fossil capital, that enabled the Chaco War.

IT IS WORTH NOTING THAT MOST BOLIVIAN WRITERS NEVER ESPOUSED THE simplistic version of the "blame Standard" or "proxy war" arguments that have motivated such historical questioning. René Zavaleta wrote that blaming US imperialism entirely would mistakenly absolve Argentina, the "demented" leaders of both sides, and Bolivia's "rancid" oligarchic class, who lived in a closed society absolutely foreign to that of the true nation, that of the Bolivian masses (1977, 43–45). Sergio Almaraz (1958) also argued, as I have tried to show in this chapter, that the war had multiple villains, chief among these the US banks, the oil money backing them, and the complicit Bolivian oligarchy.[26] Standard Oil, which was part of this governing assemblage, was guilty as well. It had facilitated the war by financing Bolivia's generals, whose expenditures sank the country further into debt and assured further control by the US banks. The war was about capital, capital was in large part about oil, and war was about both—a form of bloody expenditure of excess labor, bullets, fuel, and matériel, all of which meant more production (of arms), more returns to fossil capital, and more debt.[27] Or, in terms of the historical fiction of Rafael Ulises Peláez, author of the oil novel *Los betunes del Padre Barba*, the war was about trucks and drivers, basically moving water, gasoline, and soldiers' bodies, dead and alive, back and forth to the front: "Thousands of trucks, only

trucks. If the vehicles got stuck they had to be liberated by other trucks. . . .
War was a machine of motors and it was oil that was in charge of moving this
machine. . . . Without oil, who knows, there would not have been a war, or
maybe, because of oil, they turned to war!" (1958, 215–16).

As oil prices dropped and Standard's interests in Venezuela became more
significant, Bolivia's oil lost importance. Standard had hoped to hold its concessions to keep them out of the hands of others (Cote 2016). As discussed by
Timothy Mitchell (2001), keeping oil in the ground and controlling potential
transport corridors were strategies key to the interests of capitalists whose
investments relied on controlling oil price and supply. Almaraz, preceding
Mitchell by forty years or so, sketched out the same argument. Almaraz noted
that Standard could afford to be indifferent as to the outcome of the war. If
Bolivia won, Standard's interests were maintained. If Bolivia lost, Standard
could renegotiate with Paraguay.

IN ANY CASE, THE OLIGARCHS, GENERALS, AND BANKERS UNDERESTIMATED
the Bolivian masses. The public outrage against Standard Oil coalesced with
outrage against the political and military classes. At the core were labor movements and Chaco War veterans, among others, who backed the rise of a generation of military officers who called themselves socialists. Led by Colonel David
Toro, the country followed the Argentine model by creating a national oil company, YPFB. In March 1937, officials of YPFB, accompanied by Bolivian military
officers, walked into Standard Oil's office in La Paz, kicked the employees out,
and took everything. Standard Oil's chroniclers lamented that "not a chair or
pencil was left for the Company's staff" (Standard Oil Company of Bolivia
1939, 7). Though Argentina had sided with Paraguay during the war, the postwar negotiations with Standard brought Bolivia and Argentina, and their militaries, somewhat closer. From 1935 to 1940, as Standard Oil enjoined the State
Department to intervene on its behalf, Argentina, pushing a nationalist and
military-backed effort to expand its own YPF, pressured Bolivia to open its oil
reserves for Argentina. Hoping for a favorable settlement with Paraguay, Bolivia
played Argentina against the US, in effect siding with what had been its indirect
adversary in the Chaco War. The subsequent construction of the Santa Cruz–
Yacuiba railroad, oil exports from Bolivia to Argentina, and exchanges between
YPFB (Bolivia) and YPF (Argentina) were the result.[28] Backed by the newborn
YPFB, the military saved itself by conceding to the popular movements.

Writing in the 1960s, Zavaleta called the Chaco War a war between "mul-
titudes" of "naked soldiers," a "phenomenon after which began the conscious-

ness [raising] and the rebellion of the national classes." For Zavaleta the war was a "cartographic" failure of liberalism's alliance with imperialism (1967a, 138–40). What he meant was that in attempting to consolidate national borders alongside the interests of Wall Street, the tin-pot generals and Bolivian capitalists had made a grave geopolitical miscalculation. Not only was territory lost, but the foot soldiers who were its main protagonists would return to the towns and cities to make a deep claim on citizenship after the war unsettled the caste-like society of the country.

OVER THE DECADES THAT FOLLOWED, THE WAR BECAME A TROPE ITSELF, constantly invoking for Bolivians the value of oil, and later gas, given the killing and dying that took place. Taught as quasi religion in Bolivian schools, everyone repeats that Bolivians fought and died in defense of the oil. The remembrances have become more energetic in the age of gas. In 2006, Morales and the MAS named the decree that nationalized the gas industry after the "heroes of the Chaco." Around that time, the military refurbished a Chaco War–era water truck and parked it on Camiri's main square, as if to refresh people's memories. A decade later, as I worked on this book, Evo Morales, in one of his many commemorative tweets, reminded the nation that Standard Oil had betrayed Bolivia during the Chaco War, even "selling oil to the enemy army at the height of the war." On that day, March 13, 2018, Morales was remembering the nationalization of Standard Oil on that date in 1937. Yet as with the age of gas in the twenty-first century, the "defense of oil" and the sublimation of a certain expression of nationalist militarism also lured the popular movements into a trap: anti-imperialist critique voiced through the idea of blood sacrifice in defense of oil actually facilitated deeper subjugation to the power of global fossil capital.

With this detour into the Chaco War, I have traced some of the symbols, affective impulses, and reconstituted memories that pervade the discourse on gas today. I have also outlined a latent counterdiscourse, that of the anarchist veteran Trifonio Delgado Gonzales, and others who sought to disrupt this absolution of war, capital, and oil. I have attempted to set up a critical posture that recognizes the interlinkages between oil, racialized fossil capitalism, and militarism, and the ways that these linkages brought the United States and Bolivia into a closer relationship characterized by imperialism and resistance to it. On the ground, the Chaco War and its aftermath also situated Bolivia in the epicenter of a new geopolitics of fossil fuels, involving the United States, Argentina, Brazil, and Chile. These are all processes, patterns, and relationships that would reappear during the age of gas.

2 imperial maneuvers

THE CHACO WAR WAS A MOMENT OF HISTORICAL RUPTURE IN THE COUNTRY, the dawn of a new era of national consciousness and the organization of the working classes. Yet because of the association with the "defense of the oil," the expansion of the army, and the clamor for the nationalization of Standard Oil, popular forms of Indigenous and worker resistance were undermined by their interdependence with the oil-capital-military nexus, a kind of Achilles heel for the left that would shape the country's politics, more and less, to the present day. Words like *nationalism, Marxism, socialism, popular,* and *revolutionary* characterized various political parties, factions, and even some segments of the military. Yet not only had the Chaco War engendered new popular consciousness; it had also created new expressions of a militarized politics in which oil nationalism crossed ideological lines. For example, Razón de Patria (RADEPA, Reason of the Fatherland), a secret society (*logia*), appeared within the military. This society and other overtly fascist elements of the military hoped to forestall public critique of the army in the wake of the Chaco defeat and purge the government of incompetent rulers (Lora 1977). They were also, selectively, nationalist. Underlying complex ideological and factional disputes was a political-economic structure that depended on mineral (tin) exports. The generals hoped to diversify into oil. Whether from tin or oil, the surplus (taxes, foreign exchange) flowed to a small, concentrated elite, its dependent bourgeoisie, and to the army, which was the elite's instrument of labor control. On the other hand, the military "socialists" who seized power after the war, created the YPFB in

1936, and nationalized Standard Oil in 1937, challenged these arrangements somewhat. But they were soldiers, first and foremost. They were structurally dependent on the rents from exports of raw materials. They were not workers, despite their adoption of various pro-worker policies. Once the military consolidated political control, its alliance with the workers, some of whom were espousing actual socialism, was dismantled. Under pressure from the mining oligarchs and the United States, the more conservative military sectors tied to the mining oligarchy toppled the "socialists" and returned to power in 1939. Despite the bloodshed of the war and the victory of oil nationalization, more entrenched powers—dependent on foreign capital in a codependent relationship with a pro-capital, not a pro-worker, military—maintained control (Lora 1977).

In the wake of the expropriation, Standard Oil hoped to make an example of Bolivia and pressured the US government to refuse loans or aid to Bolivia unless Standard was compensated. Bolivians voiced staunch opposition to any compensation for Standard Oil. But after the "socialists" were ousted, in January 1942 President Enrique Peñaranda bypassed Congress and authorized payment of $1.7 million to Standard Oil. The next day the US signed a $25 million loan package. Much of that money was tied to implementation of the Plan Bohan, named after the US economist Mervin Bohan, whose mission to Bolivia that year prescribed the building of roads, the settlement of the east, and the reopening of oil reserves to private foreign investment. A portion of the debt was conditioned on it being used for oil development to be carried out by US oil companies. Bolivia even requested assistance in reorganizing the administrative structure of YPFB, along American lines, an effort ironically backed by Nelson Rockefeller, then active in Latin American affairs (Randall 1985, 96). Wary of supposed Nazi sympathizers making inroads in Bolivia on the eve of World War II, the US also sent its first military mission to Bolivia that year (Wood 1961). For Sergio Almaraz (1958), writing years later, the compensation of Standard Oil and the reprivatization of Bolivia's oil resources were crimes. For Almaraz, the realignment of Bolivia with the US government and oil industry was a sign of the return of the oligarchic *vende-patria* "sell-out" elite.[1] This pattern of apparently radical political rhetoric, followed by tactical alliances with and subsequent sidelining of social movements, giving way to the restoration of the fossil-capital-military nexus, would continue in subsequent decades.

In this chapter I consider this pattern by revisiting the period between the nationalization of Standard Oil (1937) and the nationalization of Gulf

Oil (1967). With the ebb and flow of international oil prices, internal politics, and economic dependency, it was a period that shifted from nationalist to more capital-friendly policies and back again.[2] The period ends with the subsequent reopening of Bolivia's gas and oil reserves under the dictatorship of Hugo Bánzer Suárez in 1971. Revisiting this era is useful for creating more grounded understanding of the age of gas during the early twenty-first century, given the limitation of much of our vocabulary—plurinationalism, decolonization, indigeneity, socialism, neoliberalism—for grappling with what the state actually is, was, and does in relation to fossil fuels. I trace four interwoven elements. First, I examine the role and expansion of a conservative expression of the military shaped by the Cold War, a process which also had a geographic particularity given its rootedness in the eastern Bolivian oil and gas lands. Second, I follow the contours of nationalist and socialist resistance, as radical intellectuals sought to convince factions of the military—often through the masculinist language of the national hero—that their openness to the US companies made them (feminized) sell-outs. The military, as it were, was a fickle ally. Third, the era saw the effective retreat of oil as the primary commodity at stake and the rise of natural gas as the key resource that would shape fossil fuel politics for the next fifty years. The slow build-out of first oil and then gas infrastructure would lock the country into a trajectory that it is still on today (Kaup 2012). Fourth, I highlight the role of the United States, which promoted the deepening militarization of the country and greatly influenced the direction of Bolivia's hydrocarbon economy. This is not to take agency away from Bolivians, many of whom were willing partners of the United States, even as others were vocal opponents. The purpose is to reflect on the wider transnational fossil fuel complex and an imperialist urge charged with racism and white supremacy, the expansion of US counterinsurgency logics (imported from Vietnam), and the deepening of the capital-oil/gas-infrastructure complex that would saddle Bolivia with debt well into the twenty-first century. While breaking these chains of dependency has always been the goal of the most authentic socialists, the pursuit of sovereignty by way of oil and gas development has generally tended to be a trap. This is due to the fickle politics of the military, the persistent power of oligarchic elites, and the structure of indebted subordination to foreign capital. It remains so today.

From Tin to Oil and Gas

From the perspective of Bolivia's oligarchs and generals and their international financial backers, the pursuit of oil development was an attempt to address the economy's overdependence on tin. The Chaco War was motivated by dreams that oil would diversify the economy and provide a buffer against tin dependency. But there was simply not enough oil and still no good way to export it. Tin dependency continued to shape Bolivian politics through the coming decades (Dunkerley 1984). Bolivian tin barons and their British investors tried to keep prices up through a cartel with Malaya, Nigeria, and the East Indies. But Bolivian tin was expensive and a global tin surplus exerted downward pressure on prices. US demand for cheap Bolivian tin increased as World War II loomed on the horizon. So the US moved to displace British capital and undercut the cartel by buying and stockpiling Bolivian tin. In 1940, to outflank the United Kingdom, where most Bolivian tin was smelted, and fearing the Germans might bomb British tin smelting out of commission, the US built the Longhorn Tin Smelter at Texas City, Texas (Dorn 2011, 18–19). Bolivian tin moved outward by rail to the Pacific, and then north through the Panama Canal to the Texas coast. It was a supply chain meant to support the US war machine. Or, in the memorable words of one US ambassador, the goal was to allow "bachelors and newlyweds in the United States [to] enjoy life with . . . Bolivian tin-lined canned spaghetti with meatballs, Campbell's tomato soup and Portuguese sardines" (figure 2.1).[3] Enjoying life and fighting wars meant extracting cheap nature and labor from elsewhere. As Almaraz wrote, Bolivia subsidized the US during World War II with cheap tin, sold at the so-called democracy price of forty-two cents per pound. The market price was then close to five dollars (1967b, 432). The Korean War increased tin demand and global prices once again. Yet under the leadership of a young senator from Texas named Lyndon Johnson, the US maneuvered to impose the "lowest price of tin" possible (Dorn 2011, 138). In Bolivia, twenty or thirty cents one way or another was enough to generate or navigate an economic crisis, such that commodity prices and imperial interventionism were emblazoned in the national consciousness. Dependency on tin, and the United States' control of markets in the service of its military-industrial machine, ultimately led to the fiscal implosion that helped pave the way for the 1952 Revolution.

After a decade of political upheaval, the Movimiento Nacionalista Revolucionario (MNR, National Revolutionary Movement) led the 1952 Revolution that finally displaced the old mining elite. The MNR government was led by

FIGURE 2.1 American workers processing Bolivian tin, Texas City, Texas, 1942. The original caption read: "Production. Tin smelting. Emptying bags of raw tin ore from South America on a conveyor which feeds the crusher of a Southern smelter. The crusher reduces the larger particles to uniform size and discharges ore ready for the first stages of the smelting operation. Additional processing units now being added assure a much heavier output in the near future. The plant is already producing large quantities of tin for the countless war needs of the United Nations." Photograph by Howard R. Hollem, July 1942. Courtesy of Library of Congress, Farm Security Administration and the Office of War Information collection.

left and centrist middle classes, with miners and peasants as its more radical foundation (Klein 1982; Dunkerley 1984). Yet in a state that had long exported its wealth in return for rents either sent abroad or controlled by private elites, the MNR needed external economic support. To that end, the government nationalized the tin mines, yet these were in permanent decline. Although YPFB was producing some oil, since it was not for export it did not generate dollar income. With high debt and a weak political base, the MNR again reopened the country to US investment.

The Korean War was raging and the US was in full Cold War mode, fearing that communists were everywhere. The MNR, looking to stay in power, both exaggerated the internal communist threat and marginalized the left wing of its own party to gain favor with the United States. It also rather quickly rolled back the nationalist approach to oil. Just a few months after seizing power, the MNR offered its first private concession to an American oilman, the flamboyant Glenn McCarthy of Houston, Texas. With echoes of the arrangements with Standard Oil in the 1920s, the terms of the concession included a clause that would force Bolivia to purchase oil from McCarthy, if he found it, in US dollars at the Gulf of Mexico price. In other words, Bolivia would have to buy its own oil from McCarthy as if it had been exported to the US and then resold to Bolivia, even though the oil would have never left the country. Almaraz lamented that the MNR was further "denationalizing" Bolivian oil and forcing Bolivia to "buy national oil as if we were foreigners [in our own land]" (1958, 211). The Texas wildcatter-turned-millionaire flew out of Houston and landed in La Paz in 1954 (New York Times 1954).

McCarthy is a useful character for thinking about the political and cultural configurations that shaped oil and the imperial urge of the US at the time. With oil came the rise of Texas and its nouveau riche political and economic elites. McCarthy was one of them. Seen by many as iconic of the oil-fueled American dream, McCarthy played the role of the risk-taking, rule-breaking, whiskey-drinking, bar-fighting rough-and-tumble white man who made America great. In the 1950s, with oil prices high and demand rising, independent producers like McCarthy, trying to compete with big companies like Standard, responded to the increasing scarcity of domestic oil by pursuing new finds in foreign countries. Justifying access to the oil of other countries had long been done by stating a doctrine of white supremacy that sustained US foreign intervention and the ethos of the oil industry. In simple terms, the oil industry—and the US government—maintained both publicly and privately that backward places and races needed white people to develop their resources (see Mitchell 2001, 87). McCarthy unabashedly embodied this and much else central to the US oil industry (and Texas): intense opposition to government regulation (despite demands for government subsidies and military support), a glorification of guns and masculinity (recall the photo of Thomas Armstrong in the previous chapter), and unapologetic racism.[4] In an early version of 60 Minutes, Mike Wallace puffed on a cigarette while grilling McCarthy about the morality of his oil wealth and his racial politics. McCarthy, having recently returned from Bolivia, blamed Latin America's economic troubles on racial mixing, which he said explained why Latin America was "a hundred years behind" (Wallace 1957). The views were convergent with Bolivia's internal racism and colonialism, since the criollo upper and middle classes saw the rural Indigenous population through a similar lens. American-style racism also found its echoes in eastern Bolivia, especially in the area of Santa Cruz, where most of the American oilmen ended up. Almaraz, with deep insights on US oil politics, described McCarthy as a "brutish North American who arose out of the oil jungles of Texas," with a fortune derived from the famous 27.5 percent depletion deduction and the "political machinations between Texan oilmen and fascist groups" (1958, 216). Almaraz was referring to the proximity between Texas oil interests and the fascist character of anticommunist and anti-Mexican hysteria. He also recognized the depletion deduction, still in existence today, for what it is: a government subsidy that facilitates private oil-based wealth accumulation. McCarthy's concession was in Guarani territory, an exploration block called Los Monos, south of Camiri. In a sign of what was to come, he found gas but not oil. At the end of the day, with no means for transport and no market to sell it, he sold off his lease rights to a consortium of American multinationals including Monsanto and Tennessee Gas (Carmical 1956; *New York Times* 1957). In the end, independent wild-catters like McCarthy were small fry compared to the power of big oil. He abandoned Bolivia and returned to Houston, where his decline continued in an accelerated way.[5]

During the 1940s and 1950s, Bolivia's national oil company, YPFB, had produced a modest amount of oil in the Camiri region. But rather than encourage the growth of YPFB, the US, in collusion with conservative factions of the MNR, sought to defend the interests of the US oil industry. This meant keeping access open for private US business investments. The MNR hoped to counter the possibility that YPFB would become too independently powerful. For the US, the goal was to avoid popular social mobilization and stave off the anti-imperialist nationalism that boiled in Bolivian consciousness, both of which were threats to US capital accumulation and access to Bolivian resources (Young 2016, 152–53). In 1956, at the behest of the United States, the MNR passed a new oil law called the Davenport Code, named for Schuster and Davenport, the New York law firm that wrote it. In return, the MNR government got a new tranche of aid, which is to say, more debt, and paved the way for foreign companies to take a dominant position in Bolivia's oil fields (Philip 1982, 79). Shortly thereafter a deal was made with Gulf Oil, offering the company key reserves held by YPFB in exchange for the construction of a pipeline to export oil through Chile, leaving YPFB with mostly declining fields while the US firms took more productive areas. By 1957 Gulf, with ten million hectares of concessions to explore, became the dominant force in Bolivian oil. By the 1960s, Gulf, Shell, Occidental Oil, and Chaco Petroleum, formed from the Tennessee Gas–Monsanto buyout of McCarthy, were all operating in the Bolivian east (*New York Times* 1956, 1958). Many of them still are.

Meanwhile, the giant next door, Brazil, had also nationalized its oil industry and created Petrobras in 1953. Brazil was pushing to trade investments in Bolivian infrastructure for access to Bolivian oil and, eventually, natural gas. Argentina, with its own national oil company, YPF, also had its eyes on Bolivian gas. Shrewdly, the US-written Davenport Code prohibited any foreign government investment in Bolivian oil. This permitted access for private US capital (as much a proxy for the US government as any) and excluded Petrobras of Brazil and YPF of Argentina. Gulf dabbled with the idea of an oil pipeline to Brazil yet nationalist opposition in Brazil scuttled the plan. So Gulf looked toward the Pacific and helped finance an export pipeline from Santa Cruz, across the Andes to the port of Arica, Chile. New Gulf Oil wells, like Madrejones, the first well drilled with US capital in the postrevolutionary era, were touted in the US press (*New York Times* 1958, 1959). In 1961 Gulf was exporting twenty-five thousand barrels per day from Bolivia to refineries on the California coast. After Gulf discovered that its oil wells also had natural gas, it began crafting a plan through which the World Bank would finance a gas pipeline to Argentina (Klein and Peres Cajías 2014, 149–50). It was increasingly apparent that natural gas, rather than oil, was the coming boom in Bolivia. For its part, YPFB was relegated to its declining wells and reserves slated for domestic consumption.

Money flowed northward to Wall Street in many ways, first as exported oil (bought cheap, sold dear), second as returns on capital for US-built infrastructure, and third as interest paid on debt. In the United States, gas pipeline companies were expanding as natural gas, once flared (burned off) for lack of markets, was increasingly being used for industrial electricity and slowly replacing heating oil and coal in homes (Raley 2008). Yet there was only so much need for pipelines, and staying in business meant building gas infrastructure elsewhere, thus deepening the reach of fossil capital. As infrastructure, pipelines are forms of solidified capital that set up durable relations of dependence. If hegemony over the spaces the pipeline connects is sustained, along with the markets, these massive infrastructures assure returns to capital over a long period. Oklahoma's Williams Brothers, which built Gulf's pipeline to Chile, and

Tennessee Gas, which bought out McCarthy, were looking south for contracts. Bolivia and Argentina would borrow American dollars to hire American firms and buy Caterpillar tractors and the like (*New York Times* 1958). Bolivia was being reoriented, and more deeply connected, in infrastructural, economic, and political terms, with the US-dominated fossil fuel assemblage.

Santa Cruz and the Militarization of the Bolivian East

A few points are crucial to the story told in the chapters that follow. The first is the rise of the city of Santa Cruz as a kind of oil-fueled political and cultural satellite of the United States. As with Texas, which used oil to challenge the dominance of the political elite of the US northeast, with oil in Bolivia a shift had begun away from the traditional center of economic power in mining and the Andes, rooted in La Paz, toward the agricultural and oil frontier of Santa Cruz. The arrival of oil companies from Texas and Oklahoma further influenced the society and economy of Santa Cruz, including, for instance, the emergence of the wealthy neighborhood known as Equipetrol. As Miguel Tinker-Salas (2009) writes of Venezuela's experience with US oilmen and companies, the most pervasive effect of long interactions was the assiduous cultivation of American notions of white middle-class life, with all the racial prejudices, consumer aspirations, and political preferences that went along with it.

After the 1952 Revolution, the government of the MNR faced new pressure from Santa Cruz. The Santa Cruz Civic Committee was born out of a demand for oil rents, giving rise to the demand for 11 percent of oil royalties (or rents) to be assigned directly to the oil- or gas-producing departments. With street battles that nearly brought down the MNR, the victory of the 11 percent became a rent-seeking battle cry that still shapes Santa Cruz's regionalism today (Whitehead 1973; Prudén 2003). By 1963 the *New York Times*, in a laudatory piece, wrote what many would repeat decades later: Santa Cruz was becoming a new geographic center of the country, in large part thanks to US foreign investment in highways and to Gulf Oil, which had made recent discoveries (*New York Times* 1963). It was no coincidence that like those in Texas, Santa Cruz's whitish elites worshipped their cattle and despised the darker-skinned classes who worked the land they coveted, such that a particularly Bolivian version of the oil-cattle-racism-fascism nexus was not far behind, a reality I explore further in chapter 5.

Another point to consider is the Bolivian military. On one side there was a more nationalist, at least rhetorically, socially conscious and anti-imperialist

FIGURE 2.2 US President Lyndon B. Johnson (*second from right*) and his family welcome Bolivian president René Barrientos (*fourth from right*) to the LBJ Ranch in Texas, July 1968. Bettman via Getty Images.

sector that saw the military as a necessary tool for addressing poverty and underdevelopment. On the other was the more familiar right-wing sector, many of whom were from Santa Cruz, who saw the country's poor population as a threat to internal stability. For this latter sector, defending the interests of private, mostly foreign capital and its patrons, the United States, was the priority. To influence these factions, the US increased its military aid as the Bolivian army was rebuilding in the wake of the 1952 revolution. The transformation of Santa Cruz into an oil society went hand in hand with the US-backed Cold War–era militarization of the Bolivian east. The aim was to shift the meaning and practice of soldiering away from the heroic popular nationalism invoked by the Chaco War (in "defense of the oil") and toward the anticommunist paranoia of Cold War national security (for "national security"). The imagined enemies were Bolivians themselves, indios, miners, leftists, peasants, and other would-be revolutionaries: in other words, the working poor. Organized people of any sort, especially the laboring classes in countries of great inequality where US businesses had interests, were anathema to the United States (Field 2014).

The vision was shared by conservative Bolivian elites. In 1962, with the US embroiled in containing civil rights struggles at home and in the Vietnam War, the US transplanted counterinsurgency infrastructures to Santa Cruz. An agreement with the Bolivian government allowed for the arrival of a detachment of US Green Berets as trainers, justified because of supposed internal security threats: "Recognizing a possible threat to the internal security of the Republic of Bolivia in the Oriente, specifically the 3rd, 4th, 5th, and 8th Division Areas of responsibility, it is agreed that a rapid reaction force of batallion size capable of executing counterinsurgency operations in jungle and difficult terrain . . . will be created in the vicinity of Santa Cruz" (USMILGRP 1962). The gringos named the unit the "Second Ranger Battalion," in English. Virtually under the direct command of a foreign army (that of the United States), the unit was a replica of the American Second Ranger Battalion of Special Forces based in Panama. It was not a coincidence that the Ranger base, just north of Santa Cruz at Montero, was built just twenty miles from Gulf Oil's operation at Caranda. The Americans offered that "this in no way precludes the Bolivian Army from designating this unit by any historical or traditional name that it might desire." The Bolivian Army, to this day, has stuck with "Rangers" (in English). They still wear green berets. The cultivation of closer social and ideological ties between the two militaries proceeded much as it had elsewhere in Latin America. By 1963 Bolivia had sent more officers than any other country to be trained at the notorious School of the Americas at Fort Benning, Georgia (Corbett 1972, 406; Gill 2004). As historian Thomas Field (2014) summarizes it, the American philosophy of development went hand in hand with authoritarian militarization. The key point is that this had a particularly regional anchor in the Bolivian east, where American oilmen and American soldiers, both with an antileftist and racist view of the world, would insinuate themselves into the social and ideological world of Santa Cruz.

Despite having shifted to the right, the MNR was unable to manage popular demands for deeper social transformation. In response to the instability, pro-US factions of the military under René Barrientos seized power through a coup in 1964. Barrientos, a School of the Americas graduate, moved Bolivia more deeply into the tutelary relationship with the United States. With US financial support offered to both Barrientos and the conservative faction of the MNR, left-leaning activists and labor leaders were marginalized, persecuted, and exiled. The CIA ramped up its covert funding to split social movements and unions and root out any perceived influence of communists, nationalists, or progressives, including the left wing of the MNR. With US funding for his campaign, the dictator Barrientos became President Barrientos after a sham election in 1966.[6] In June 1967, Barrientos ordered the army to open fire on striking tin miners at the Siglo xx mine, killing at least twenty, among them children. In October 1967, the CIA and US soldiers helped their protégés, the Bolivian Ranger Battalion, hunt down and kill Che Guevara, then operating in the Camiri area. In 1968, by then president, Lyndon B. Johnson hosted Barrientos at his ranch in Texas (figure 2.2). There he raised a glass to him, calling for stability, integration through free trade, highway and river basin development, and the construction of the (Gulf Oil Co.) pipeline to export natural gas to Argentina. Johnson said he looked forward to "full exploitation for Bolivia's development of its oil and gas resources" (Johnson 1968). It was not communist insurgency that was a serious threat in Bolivia. It was the possibility that an organized population might undermine the extractive interests of American capitalists, the American oil industry, and their Bolivian caretakers.

Nationalization and Right-Wing Reaction, Again

These were the times that Camiri's old oilmen remember as full of "el Gulf" and "los Misters," referring to Gulf Oil and the gringo Americans who worked there. These were also the days when charismatic socialist intellectuals rose up to challenge the empire and shame the sell-outs of the Bolivian military. Figures like Sergio Almaraz and Marcelo Quiroga Santa Cruz, following on earlier writers like Carlos Montenegro and Augusto Céspedes, led the way. The socialists were ideologically committed but the military nationalists were fickle. Part of the socialist strategy was to encourage dissension within the military ranks by appealing to a masculine defense of the nation, and of the oil and gas, from foreign usurpers. Marcelo Quiroga Santa Cruz, then a congressman, penned both analysis and critique, and led the denunciations against the Barrientos government for dismantling national sovereignty. In 1966, with Barrientos in office, Quiroga Santa Cruz bravely spearheaded a debate in the Bolivian Chamber of Deputies, where he laid out the antinational orientation of the oil policies of the government. These writers highlighted the draining of Bolivia's surplus wealth, the *excedente*, pointing out that ten years of Gulf Oil activities had contributed little to the national treasury or national development. The Davenport Code, in particular, Quiroga Santa Cruz said, was unconstitutional. It had been written as it if it were American oil law, even giving companies like Gulf the 27 percent depletion deduction. The law enriched the region of Santa Cruz, like Texas, rather than the nation. The royalty scheme only forced Gulf to pay immediate royalties, the 11 percent, to Santa Cruz. On the other hand, the national government would receive only 7 percent, and only then after the depletion deduction and the repayment of Gulf's capital investment. This meant that it would take thirty years for the national government to receive significant royalties, and even then they would be minuscule (Quiroga Santa Cruz 1967). By pitting region against nation, this is how spatial fragmentation was built into Bolivia's integration into the circuits of fossil capital, via American-backed oil legislation (Labban 2008). Furthermore, Gulf paid royalties calculated on a lower price per barrel than what YPFB paid. It was highway robbery sustained by the antinational factions of the Bolivian military. That, Marcelo Quiroga Santa Cruz said, was the "madre del borrego" (mother of the lamb), in other words, the origin of the relationship of exploitation between Gulf and Bolivia (1967, 29).

Of principal concern was natural gas. Gulf had made a large discovery of gas at Caranda, near Santa Cruz, and YPFB had found gas in the Monteagudo region. In fact, the famous Texan well-fire killer Red Adair had to go to Bolivia in 1967 when YPFB's gas wells at Monteagudo blew out, spewing millions of cubic feet of burning gas into the air (de Onis 1967). While YPFB's gas was to be oriented to local demand, Gulf wanted the higher prices from export and now needed a gas pipeline. Gulf was sending its oil east to the Pacific and California, but gas was only profitable in regional markets (and liquefied natural gas [LNG] was not yet a possibility). So Gulf looked toward Argentina. The World Bank stepped in to finance a pipeline plan with investors that included the New York State Pension Fund. The Williams Brothers, the Oklahomans who had built the oil line to Chile, would come back to do the job. German steel would be used to make the pipe in Argentina. Gas and money was to flow by 1969.

Critics saw this as theft. Marcelo Quiroga Santa Cruz (1967) argued that the word *hydrocarbons* in Gulf's contract referred only to oil, not to gas. Whether it came up in Gulf's well or not, the gas belonged to Bolivia, not to Gulf. Gulf used the time-proven strategy of fomenting regionalist support against national interests by offering to give some of the gas to Santa Cruz for free. The growing city hoped to use it for electricity generation. The Americans were also deepening their involvement in the electricity infrastructure of the region. In those years US companies had advised Santa Cruz on the expansion of its electricity system, through the establishment of the Cooperativa Rural de Electrificación (CRE, Rural Electric Cooperative), on the model of rural electric cooperatives in the United States. The CRE was quickly captured by the Santa Cruz elite as an anchor of economic and political power distinctly opposed to central government control. What the nationalists saw as theft was part of a regionalist strategy aimed at US- and Gulf-backed empowerment of Santa Cruz's economic and political elites.

Even so, the wider public in the Andean cities, led by the radical socialists and the unions, was calling for the nationalization of Gulf Oil. After Barrientos died in a helicopter crash in 1969, his vice president, Luis Adolfo Siles Salinas, took over. Siles Salinas sought to stave off nationalist discontent by telling Gulf Oil it could stay but had to give the gas to the whole country for free. It was too little, too late. Next door in Peru, General Juan Velasco had seized Standard Oil's facilities in 1968. The US, uncharacteristically, did nothing. In 1969 Bolivian military officers of the nationalist factions decided to do the same with Gulf. General Alfredo Ovando, who at one time had shared power with Barrientos, maneuvered to seize power under the mantle of nationalist defense. The key issue was whether Bolivia was being robbed by the foreign companies. As Ovando wrote in a public letter:

> In order that the country be ours, the basic industries must belong to the state. The highest priority must go to metallurgy, without which we can never break the barriers of backwardness and integrate ourselves economically into the reality of a continent undergoing change. There cannot be a strong army without the complement of a strong heavy industry. Natural resources, and the terms of their exploitation, also constitute an inseparable part of national sovereignty. The country must move toward the control of their full exploitation through its own resources and entities. With reference to petroleum, the Davenport Code must be annulled as soon as possible, and a tax established that reaches 50 percent of the gross production; special regulations for gas must be established; and control for the state obtained over its refining transport, marketing and industrialization through YPFB. The best committee for the defense of the natural resources, and the most legitimate, is that constituted by the people and their armed expression, the national army. (Corbett 1972, 413)

As Bolivian analyst René Zavaleta argued, the nationalist factions of the military, most from Cochabamba or La Paz as compared to the more reactionary officers who hailed from Santa Cruz, created a pact with the intellectuals and sought to bring the power of the masses over to their side by embracing the nationalist project (Zavaleta 1972). Ovando annulled the Davenport Code as his first act in office and named the fiery socialist Marcelo Quiroga Santa Cruz to be minister of mines. Twenty-one days later, with Quiroga Santa Cruz overseeing the process, Ovando ordered the seizure of Gulf Oil facilities.

In Camiri, decades later, in 2009, the old oil worker Eusebio Vargas recalled that moment with great pride, as a "true" nationalization compared to the later one carried out by Evo Morales: "That time was nationalization with honors for Bolivia. Because it was a true and legitimate nationalization, where the *gringos de la Gulf* had to leave with their ponchos on their shoulders, without taking a single screw. That was the nationalization carried out by the paladin of democracy, the socialist, Marcelo Quiroga Santa Cruz, whose works until this day continue to serve as the true example of the true Bolivian who recovered Bolivian oil from the claws of the transnationals! At that time, we were filled with joy."

"With your poncho slung over your shoulder, and not taking even a screw!" It was an apt image of defiant Bolivians booting out carpet-bagging gringos. Yet it was not quite so glorious. Ovando was no socialist. He went on to crush the ill-fated Teoponte guerrilla movement, composed of young university students who had taken to the jungle to push the regime leftward. The bloody slaughter provoked Marcelo Quiroga Santa Cruz's resignation. Ovando then went on to set up compensation for Gulf Oil with $78 million. Once that happened, the World Bank, which threatened to hold up its loan for the gas pipeline to Argentina, had no qualms about lending money to yet another military regime.

As the pipeline plans went forward, the political situation intensified. Confronting pressure from the left and the anticommunist right, Ovando's power eroded by late 1970. Despite his willingness to kill young students seeking progressive change, Ovando was deemed insufficiently anticommunist by the conservative "professionalist" officers (Corbett 1972, 418). By nationalizing Gulf and doing away with the Davenport Code, he had dared to question the US military and its oil industry. As the right maneuvered to seize control through a military junta, the more ideologically committed and left-leaning general Juan José Torres mobilized workers and seized the presidency instead. Unlike Ovando, seen by some as an opportunist, Torres is remembered as one of the more critical left-leaning representatives of the army. In office, he attacked the US development agenda as being overly militaristic, blinded by rabid anticommunism. Speaking to the Inter-American Defense Board, an entity set up by the US military to promote its interests in the region, Torres said in November 1969:

The armed forces do not have to be . . . typecast as organizations exclusively dedicated to checking the political phenomenon of international communism, but fundamentally as co-participants and efficient agents of the battle [against] economic underdevelopment from which follow the elements that later go to make up the political setting that has set off the subversive struggle in the continent. . . . The arch conservatives see in the armed forces an exceedingly efficient instrument to return to the night of the past while they remain allied with the foreign monopolies. For their part, the popular classes look at the armed forces as the truest instrument of redemption since they [the armed forces] will no longer accept the role of [being] simple wardens in an unjust order. (Corbett 1972, 419)

Torres kicked out the Peace Corps (accused of sterilizing Indigenous women) and nationalized the zinc industry. He also allowed the organization of mass movements into an embryonic experiment called the Asamblea Popular (Popular Assembly). Like the US government, the *New York Times* worried incessantly about this "new nationalism" and fretted in its reporting that some Bolivian newspapers were offering "anti-CIA" bracelets to readers in La Paz. All this was sacrilege to the empire and too much for the right-wing military entrenched in the Bolivian east. The US, under Richard Nixon and led by Henry Kissinger, started plotting against Torres, as did the right wing of the Bolivian military. Torres lasted only eight months in office.[7]

The US-financed gas pipeline to Argentina remained in discussion and the battle over control of the state intensified. In January 1971, Hugo Bánzer Suárez, a rightist army general from Santa Cruz, the land of cattle, sugar, cocaine, and Gulf Oil, launched his first coup attempt. Bánzer was a petite but vicious man who had trained at the US Army's School of the Americas in the 1950s (Gill 2004). Foiled in his first try, Bánzer rallied the support of Brazil, then also led by a military dictatorship. The US was clearly aware of Bánzer's goals and was actively planning a way to topple Torres, though it might have preferred an MNR government. President Nixon, at Kissinger's urging, ordered the CIA to plan an intervention. The US offered military aid and ordered cash to be delivered to key contacts in the media and opposition parties, chief among them the MNR and military officers opposed to Torres. At the same time, in June 1971, the World Bank underwrote the coup and raised the stakes of state seizure when it rewrote the terms of the gas pipeline loan. Robert McNamara—former president of Ford Motors and, as secretary of defense, Vietnam War architect—by then head of the World Bank, signed the loan agreement that month (the New York State Pension Board lost its stomach and withdrew its planned investment) (World Bank 1971).[8]

While the CIA handed out cash to army officers and laid some groundwork, there may also have been direct involvement by US military personnel on the ground. The US may also have worked through Brazil. By August, Brazilian troops massed in support of Bánzer on the border. Brazilian army planes dropped off arms and supplies in Santa Cruz. Bánzer also relied on the US-created Rangers battalion to back him up. Ultimately, after bloody street battles in Santa Cruz, troops loyal to Bánzer rose up in La Paz, where university students had organized to resist the coup. In response, Bánzer's forces bombed, strafed, and occupied the main building of San Andrés University. The students and workers and their small armed militias, as well as the handful of troops loyal to Torres, were no match for the armed putsch. Hugo Bánzer Suárez seized the reins of government in August 1971.

In "Extremism Spits in the Face of the Nation," a pamphlet published soon after the coup, Bánzer's Ministry of Information claimed to represent the true "popular nationalist" alliance, against those "infantile leftists" who idolized Cuba's Fidel Castro and Chile's Salvador Allende. With support from the fascist Falange Socialista Boliviana (FSB, Bolivian Socialist Falange) party of Santa Cruz (which also used the word *socialist*), and with backing from the right wing of the MNR (with the word *revolutionary*), the new military regime appropriated the language of the left, claiming that the "Nationalist Revolution led by Colonel Bánzer is a movement of the unity of the people, from the peasants, workers, and middle classes" (Ministerio de Información y Deportes 1971). That the coup was largely about control of the gas boom to come is clear.

RENÉ ZAVALETA OFFERED A SUCCINCT ANALYSIS OF THE MOMENT IN *New Left Review* in 1972. On the one hand, he wrote, it was clear that the left had not come to terms with the need for its own base of armed support, given that the army was fickle and unreliable. On the other hand, the US fear of democracy, that is, mobilized people, was a determining factor. As he wrote, "The Americans did not regard the loss of the zinc mines as of fundamental importance; nor were they too concerned about the expulsion of the Peace Corps, who Bolivians saw as just a bunch of scruffy Protestants. What was dangerous was that behind Torres the masses were moving, and with certain positive results, given that the workers were no longer isolated" in the mines and factories, but had evolved to make key alliances with students and vanguardist revolutionary sectors (Zavaleta 1972, 78–79). Yet what the left had not done, he suggested, was move beyond arguing about its program to thinking about its survival. The army, he argued, with patriotic elements or not, could not carry out a popular revolution. Fatefully, he wrote, the left "ignored the question of military organization. The left neglected war, but reaction won by war. Nothing should ever happen in vain" (82). These dynamics and shifting tensions between the social movements and the military would reappear during the upheavals of 2003 and 2019.

Bánzer moved to reverse the anti-imperialist content of Bolivian oil and gas law and passed a new hydrocarbons law in March 1972. Bánzer also participated, with US backing, in Plan Condor, the coordinated effort between the military intelligence agencies of Chile, Brazil, Uruguay, Paraguay, and Argentina to hunt down, torture, disappear, or kill progressive activists, students, and movement leaders. Lesley Gill (2004, 96–97) describes how, during these years, Bolivian soldiers who trained at the Colegio Militar (Military Academy) in La Paz studied the "internal enemy"—plotting forms of attack on the headquarters of the labor union, Central Obrera Boliviana (COB, Bolivian Workers' Central); peasant communities; and mine workers' communities. Even former allies of Bánzer met their ends. The military man Andrés Selich, who helped Bánzer gain power, was choked to death in his house. An ambassador deemed a threat was murdered in Paris. In 1974 General Juan José Torres, the nationalist hero who had been toppled by Bánzer, was living in exile in Argentina. In June of that year he was snatched off the street, blindfolded, and executed. The death squad threw his body under a bridge outside Buenos Aires. Unsurprisingly, Bánzer denied any involvement (Dinges 2005). The socialist "paladin of democracy," Marcelo Quiroga Santa Cruz, by then under threat for his own life, bravely continued to speak from exile. He denounced Bánzer's negotiations with Brazil, through which Brazil's support for the coup would be rewarded with access to Bolivian gas and iron ore resources, and territory to build a petrochemical complex on the eastern border ([1975] 1997). In addition to this "capitulation" to Brazil, as a new imperial force, Quiroga Santa Cruz referred to Bánzer's hydrocarbons law, reopening access to private foreign investment, as an "authorization for the legal exercise of theft" (1973, 21).

Through everything, the oil, and now gas, flowed. Gas started to flow to Argentina in 1972, and debt payments to the World Bank and compensation to Gulf flowed back to the United States. Prices were high during the so-called oil crisis of the 1970s. The military government and its base of power in Santa

Cruz reaped most of the rewards from this boom. As with military regimes in Argentina and Brazil, oil and gas flows were fiscal machines, the key to financing military governments that had little popular (or legal) legitimacy. Santa Cruz expanded with privileged access to royalties, helped in no small part by the cocaine trafficking and land-grabbing boom that also flourished under Bánzer. Hugo Bánzer Suárez lasted in power until 1978. He left a country in debt and crisis that would be snapped up once again by the moneylenders backing the neoliberal project in the 1980s and 1990s. Even so, the decade of the 1970s, flush with cocaine dollars, land grabs, and new oil wealth in Santa Cruz, was a time seen as the *auge* (boom) of oil—which takes us back to Camiri, and the heroes of the Chaco.

3 *las nalgas* of YPFB

DURING THE 1970S, WITH THE GAS FLOWING TO ARGENTINA IN THE NEW pipeline, Hugo Bánzer Suárez oversaw brutal repression of dissent while he channeled money and land to his cronies.[1] The state was flush with rents from high oil prices and gas exports—and cocaine. The military had control over YPFB and virtually every other state entity. Meanwhile Bánzer borrowed heavily, leaving the country saddled with higher debt. By the 1980s, with oil prices down and oil reserves declining, the World Bank and the International Monetary Fund (IMF) pushed Bolivia toward austerity and privatization, upon which future aid and loans were contingent. This would also involve pushing to export gas through deals with big multinational firms like Enron and Shell (Hindery 2013). In the 1990s, President Gonzalo "Goni" Sánchez de Lozada (1993–97) initiated the privatization process and moved gas negotiations forward. When Bánzer, the ex-dictator, managed to get reelected as president in 1997, he continued the privatization process, and would oversee completion of the gas pipeline to Brazil (about which more in chapter 4). Yet given the distortions of politics that gas would later wreak during the early twenty-first century, it is worth revisiting the oil boom and its sequiturs. A rethinking of political futures requires questioning both the capitalist addiction to fossil-fueled growth and the nationalist aspiration for revolutionary oil, since both share the same dirty underside.

By the 1990s, after Gulf had pretty much exported much of the oil and the government started dismantling YPFB for privatization, Camiri was not much of an oil capital any more. There were monuments to oil along with ruins of the past, like the old refinery stacks. A huge arch is at the terminus of Camiri's

FIGURE 3.1 YPFB facilities in Camiri, 2018. The sign reads: "In the service of the father-land." Photo by the author.

main avenue, called La Avenida Petrolera (Oiler Avenue). The arch marked the entrance to the old facilities of YPFB, whose initials hung on a sign dangling from the top (figure 3.1). But YPFB was pretty much gone. Free market reforms were exacerbating poverty in the 1990s and the Chaco region, one of Bolivia's poorest, was attracting significant development aid. The city had become an epicenter for nongovernmental organizations (NGOs). In those days, since there was not much in the way of oil, we joked that the letters Y-P-F-B meant Ya Pronto Fallecerá Bánzer: Bánzer will soon die.

The dismantling of YPFB left only residual administrative structures in Camiri. It also left nostalgia, at least for some, most of them men, for the oil days of the past. Fossil-fueled nostalgia for the past works as a reserve to generate feverish excitement and anticipation of fossil-fueled well-being in the future. These feelings—nostalgia and desire—are deeply charged with remembrances of the Chaco War and, for some, a sense of unfinished struggle for liberation from foreign domination. These impulses are expressed in stories that are as much about forgetting as they are about remembering. The struggle over Standard Oil and the Chaco War that I sketched in chapter 1 can certainly be read through the lens of heroic anti-imperialism and the rise of a new political consciousness. As I pointed out, the nationalization of oil and gas, for the Bolivian socialists, as with the left throughout Latin America, was at the heart of a revolutionary agenda (Gledhill 2011). Yet the yearning for fossil-fueled prosperity also locks political economies into a system that fuels, and is fueled by, other structural contradictions, desires, and violences. These are decidedly unrevolutionary. Much of Bolivia's recent history unfolded, as has the age of gas, within this space of political contradiction.

As I tried to craft my own historical understanding, I set out to learn a bit more about what the oil boom years were really like in Camiri. That led me first, as I described in chapter 1, to the heroes of the Chaco. Then it took me to the US-backed militarization that went hand in hand with oil politics, as I explored in chapter 2. It ended up, as I retell in the following pages, in kissing *las nalgas de* YPFB (the butt cheeks of YPFB). Or at least that is where the stories of the old retirees, the *jubilados*, took me, so that is where we will go in this chapter.

NEXT TO THE ARCH WAS THE OLD YPFB COMPANY STORE, A STUCCO AND cement *pulpería*, now boarded up. Down the street was the entrance to the "Campamento"—now called the Ex-Campamento. Campamentos were where oil companies built temporary and sometimes permanent residences for laborers. Standard built a work camp there in the 1920s, and it stuck. Under YPFB and later Gulf, Camiri's Ex-Campamento became a suburban-style neighborhood, with largish houses and yards with fences, where YPFB and Gulf engineers and managers lived with their families. The Oil Hospital, called the *caja petrolera*, was still functioning there. This was one of the residuals where retired oil workers or the families living off their pensions got medical access and treatment. With YPFB gone, the Ex-Campamento had filled with gringo missionaries, cattle ranchers, merchants, NGO employees, and others, like local politicians, who had more money than most.

Outside the gates of the YPFB complex stood the retirees' union hall. Out front, in the avenue, rises a looming monument to the *petrolero boliviano* (Bolivian oilman) (figure 3.2). His muscular back ripples as he bends over a manual casing tong. Bulging biceps, forearms, and veiny hands grapple with the iconic tool that drillers used to grab, hold, and screw drilling pipe together.

FIGURE 3.2 Monument to the Bolivian *petrolero*, Camiri, 2005. The oilman holds a ca. 1955 Web Wilson tong. Photo by the author.

In both life and statue, it is as if bodies were fused to steel to drill into the earth. The tong's curves extend the physical orientation of the rig worker bent over the drilling pipe. With chains and pulleys for creating torque, the worker connected or disconnected pipe, with the bit far underground. "Throwing chain" is still a part of drilling rig labor. Judging by YouTube, throwing chain right, with élan and efficiency, is a point of masculine pride for rig workers worldwide, and long has been. This moment of drilling, the perforation (*la perforación*), was the iconic event of oil labor, the moment that would make or break the venture. Somebody took care to give the statue a fresh coat of paint each year. Web Wilson—the name of an American oil tool inventor—is stamped on the tong.[2]

Inside the union hall, murals represented similar scenes, linking the heroic driller and oil to the progress of the nation (figure 3.3). But there was no more drilling going on, and the only thing left at the union hall were the

FIGURE 3.3 Mural to the oil workers, retirees' union hall, Camiri, 2009. Shown are the heroic driller, the Mary-like mother, and oil flowing, supporting the family and nation from birth to old age. Photo by the author.

jubilados. These former YPFB employees had stayed in Camiri and now lived off their pensions. Like the old-timers, the union hall was a bit run-down.

Two doors down stood the Hostal Marietta, another historic landmark. The owner was a venerable old Italian widow named Doña Ana de Fosfori. Her husband, Federico, had been the honorary Italian consul. Doña Ana built up a pharmacy, the hostel, and a restaurant that thrived through the days of the oil bonanza. There, in late 1966, Doña Ana and Federico had even hosted—unknowingly, she assured me—the Cubans, Argentines, and Bolivians who were heading into the hills to join the revolutionary struggle with Che Guevara. After the Bolivian army captured Ciro Bustos, one of Guevara's Argentine compañeros, and Regis Debray, a French journalist, they were put on trial in the oil workers' union hall. This brought the global press to Doña Ana's little restaurant (Falacci 1970). On one occasion when I was staying there, Doña Ana brought out a box of magazine and newspaper clippings about the trial. She told me how she cooked food that Elisabeth Burgos, who eventually became Debray's partner, took to him in jail. As Ana cooked up Italian fare for the oilmen, the military, and the journalists, she and Federico built up quite a business. The streets were still dirt then, she recalled: "It was dusty all the time, but they all came here." By now, though, these were all just stories of the past. Doña Ana took some satisfaction in the fact that all of that revolutionary dust had settled. Sorting through her clippings, she pointed to a letter from Burgos, who wrote after she and Debray had returned to France. After all that, Doña Ana snorted, "she wrote me to say that the idea of the armed struggle was over."[3]

Over at the union hall the YPFB jubilados were still alive and kicking. They hung out there during the day, and some spent evenings around the corner drinking and playing cards at a local billiard hall. The old oilmen were still mobilized as a union (sindicato). No state pension in Bolivia should be taken for granted, so its defense was a motive for staying organized. These were obligations that the state had to those oilmen who had sacrificed their labor for oil and the fatherland. These pensions were also all that was left of YPFB, and they were crucial for the city's economic livelihood. After the NGO boom receded, Camiri basically lived off these pensions for oil workers, teachers, and soldiers. It was a city dependent on state rents (la renta) and on its rentistas, as retirees are known. At the end of each month, when pensioners cashed their checks, there was an influx of money in the market. People talked about this as the movement or circulation of la renta, in ways that ran parallel to the rents that regional and city governments now receive from gas development. There was no shame in this dependence, only anxiety about its possible disappearance and contests over access to it. Now and then a black ribbon appeared on the front gate of the union hall, announcing that a wake was being held for one of the old-timers. A coffin would be set in front of the stage in the main hall. If there was no widow to claim the retiree's rent, this meant one less pension obligation for the state. With YPFB's arch in decay and the oilmen slowly leaving the stage, it seemed that the history of oil was also becoming a thing of the past. Seeking to juxtapose this oil history with the gas boom under Evo Morales, I wandered into the retirees' union hall one day to find someone to talk history with, which led me to the stories I recount here.[4]

DISTINCT FROM THE MANAGERS, ACCOUNTANTS, OR TEACHERS IN THE YPFB schools, these men—most of them former rig workers—tended to emphasize the same thing: the hard physicality of manual labor in difficult rural conditions. In southeastern Bolivia, the oil, like the gas today, lies under rugged terrain traversed by ill-maintained dirt roads often rendered impassable by deep sand or mud. The brush was spiny, thick, and unforgiving, with mosquitos, bugs, snakes, and creatures of all sorts, not to mention the blistering heat. Oil workers in the field might spend weeks at a time traversing the bush or encamped at an exploration site. They may have been on exploration crews, taking geological notes, or on seismic crews, laying lines with explosives to detonate to generate sonograms of the underground. Once drilling sites were identified, the drilling crews went in. Most of the men told stories of the drilling crews, those whose actions finally led to the flow of oil. In these stories, these were the real men, the real heroes.

Eduardo Cabrera, then fifty-one years old, recalled one such hero of those days, a famous tool pusher, the boss of the rig, named Gerardo Sasamoto.

> Don Gerardo Sasamoto came to a well site at San Roque, where a tool had gotten trapped. We were trying to wet [the drilling hole] with liquids so it would soften up, *pero nada*, we couldn't do anything. He gets there and asks how many rotations were on the pulley [controlling the drill pipe] and told the mechanic to engage the three motors. He got out his helmet, his coca, and then says, "Everybody get down, I'm going to pull." From afar we watched the tower bend under the force and he was all alone there. He didn't want to risk anyone else's life, only his own. That's where one realizes the valor of the man, one who hides behind nobody and takes up his responsibility. He was a man with *cojones* who inspired admiration and respect. It was this type of man who made this business grand, those men, many of whom I've seen lose fingers, be mutilated, or die in an accident. I even saw, I don't know if for bad luck or pure *desgracia*, another man who was pulling on a tensioner pulley, and [it came loose]. Unable to dodge it, it hit him like a club and smashed his head in. It was like seeing a chicken when you wring its neck. What can you do? Nothing.

Sasamoto was a Bolivian John Henry of sorts, deified for his physical strength and knowledge of the task. Those who died were seen as heroes, martyrs for oil, and martyrs for the nation. These working-class men, like the Bolivian miners June Nash (1979) described so memorably, had deep knowledge about their jobs, and, like many who labor face to face with the earth, often dismissed the engineers who came to tell them how to do their jobs.

In this atmosphere of intensified masculinity, the man on the rig—like the statue in the street—was held up as the pinnacle. At the top was the tool pusher, the guy who gave orders on the rig. The tool pusher is configured, almost globally, as a hero of the oil patch. Given the role of the US in standardizing oil cultures, in Bolivia, the English words *tool pusher* were even used, rendered as *turpurshe*. They were legendary figures.

> If you realize it, these were the great jefes, the bosses, of the well, the great tool pusher or the company man as they call them now; those people were the ones here who had gotten to third or fourth grade. Don Alfonso Sánchez, for example, a great tool pusher [*un señor turpurshe*], the boss of all the tool pushers, was in charge of all the equipment. Don Jorge Cruz Castro, nicknamed Guasaco, Don Gerardo Sasamoto, Don Raul Domínguez, Don Loro Rodríguez. These are people who never set foot in a university but became grand bosses [*señores jefes*], grand YPF-Bers [*señores yacimientistas*] that loved their company. I was lucky enough to work with them. Don Lucas Ferrufino, for example, didn't know how to write, so I had to write out his daily report for him. But they knew it in practice. I worked with Don Celestino Salazar and Don Olegario Galvez, since they didn't know how to write. I helped them, I earned their trust. It was a spectacle to see these men work; sometimes they worked in the darkness with their hands—they knew the tools, their dimensions, the types of [drilling] thread. I learned good things from these great men.

And so many stories went: Of the manliest of men, who through deep knowledge and hard physical work modeled principled sacrifice and loyalty to their nation and to YPFB. Of the time spent in the camps, in the countryside; the hot days on the rig; the accidents. Of the men at one site who washed away in a flash flood. Of the truck that wrecked, with eleven men killed on the eleventh day of the eleventh month. (You can visit their eleven fenced-off graves in Camiri's cemetery, where a special monument stands today.) The stories were full of emotive words like *fatherland*, *sacrifice*, and the company itself, *yacimientos*. As with schoolteachers, soldiers, and revolutionaries of the popular era of struggle in Bolivia, oil workers referred to their relation to the job as having a *mística* (mystique).

To here, one cannot help but think that against the power of the United States, Standard Oil, and the sell-out factions of the military and oligarchic elite, Bolivia's intellectuals, social movements, and workers had indeed been heroes who managed to wrest control of the industry—at least for a time—to pursue a sovereign path of development. Indeed, the retirees often invoked the brief moment in the 1960s when Bolivia, under YPFB, achieved gasoline sovereignty, producing enough gasoline for its own consumption. However fleeting, at least in these stories that kind of sovereignty was truly heroic.

Yet as I pursued stories of labor in an attempt to think more deeply about the longer political history of fossil fuels in Bolivia, I did not find revolutionary struggle of a radical, alternative, or transformative sort, much less anything deeply Indigenous. Distinct from the tin miners described by Nash who were radicalized by Trotskyism and Andean ontologies, the old men shrugged off my questions about whether revolutionary aspirations or rituals to Mother Earth played a role in their labor. They were manifestly not indios. Indeed, most were migrants to the region from Sucre and did not identify with indigeneity, neither in the Andes nor here in the Chaco. Other than the consciousness about the nature of their manual labor—and their resistance to alienation— they were not radical political actors. This was different from other cases like Colombia, where oil workers were often in the vanguard of radical struggle (Gill 2016). Here in the Bolivian southeast the oil workers were a labor aristocracy. And the more we talked, the less we heard about labor and the more we heard stories about good times, money, and abundance.

Often, the conversations turned nostalgic for the golden days of oil. One of my confidants, Doña Teresa, whose ex-husband had worked for YPFB, often told me about the old days when the oil workers "had everything." There were luxuries. Mexican movies were shown in the town's cinema, which now stands (empty) in the plaza, right beside the Bolivian Central Bank. In his memoir, Ciro Bustos, the Argentine revolutionary, also remembered watching through his jail window as people went into the movie theater, right across the street from the military officers' club. Movies were a huge affair in the remote southeast, rare in Bolivia in the days before widespread television. Yet here in the periphery all could view the latest film. Reportedly, the Mexican movies were the best. Decades later I often sat and listened to Doña Teresa as she smoked and knitted and watched movies of the Mexican comic Cantinflas on her cable TV. Cantinflas always sparked memories of the *cine* of YPFB. This was all thanks to the oil.

There were other material benefits, and YPFB families had many of them. A retired worker listed them: "We got a production bonus, we got groceries, we got the gasoline bonus and the kerosene bonus, the butcher shop bonus, work clothing, materials for school for [our children], pens, books—they had a bus for the children that picked them up from kindergarten through high school, there was a bus called 'The Heroes of the Chaco,' contracted exclusively for [YPFB] students and the professors." There was also a lot of talk about the pulpería, the company store. There, unlike most others in this poor rural backwater region, the oil workers had access to the best food, sugar, meat, and flour, including fine products from Argentina. With access to consumer goods as well as state services, the oil workers and their families lived above the means of most people in the poor, hardscrabble Chaco. I was told the oil workers' hospital was the best-equipped hospital in the entire Bolivian southeast. And the men remembered the social clubs and the sports, particularly soccer. As one recalled:

> YPFB brought players from Argentina and Paraguay. I'm telling you Yacimientos was the father of all of the great teams of Camiri, Sport Boys, Petrolero Camiri, Litoral, Bolivar, and others. Some of the department heads at YPFB loved soccer and were named presidents of the clubs, and they could make affiliates of workers for the teams, and then some of their salary would go to support the team. Since they earned a lot of money, these deductions did not hurt, they [earned] good money [*buenos billetes*], and so they paid players to just play. [This was the origin of] Oriente Petrolero, the only team still in Bolivia's professional league. . . . We even had the third lighted stadium in the country, even before Santa Cruz [had one].

One worker, invoking the extractive imaginary that pervades Bolivia, a mining country, equated Yacimientos with a *veta* (mine). It was a place where if you got a job, you could strike it rich: "Yacimientos was the biggest *veta*; everyone dreamed of being a petrolero."

Rural towns like Camiri formed after the dispossession of native Guarani lands. Wealth was extracted from the land via corn, cattle, and exploited labor, that of the Guarani. The only other economic activities—soldiering, teaching, or drilling for oil—depended on the state. Commerce grew around both sources of wealth, but again, Camiri was a town of rentistas, those who lived off their right to a monthly portion of the labor they did for the state. Teachers, less well paid and a bit more radical than the oil workers, were always striking for higher wages. Soldiers, especially the officers, were kept happy. But the oil workers were kings. As another recalled, "Undoubtedly that situation made it such that the petrolera families had a privileged level of life in Camiri. In other words, we were, we could say, the highest class in Camiri; on top of us were maybe a few merchants and cattlemen but nobody else. It was the petrolero that moved the economy here in Camiri."

All the heroic talk about masculinity had another side: women. "Even the soldiers were jealous of us sometimes," recalled one. "One of our men was killed by an officer in Villamontes, over a woman. Whenever [we] oilmen came to town, all of the women went to look for us." The economic structure, as in the mining regions, made men the privileged wage earners by a wide margin. Women, as Nash wrote of the mines in those decades, were doubly or triply dependent, and exploited—first by the global economic system, then by the mine, and, finally, by their husbands. And by this we refer to urban women. Rural peasant and Guarani women were further subjected to a violent, racialized regime of debt labor in which sexual violence perpetrated by the landlords—and by some oilmen—was common. For urban women in Camiri, marrying a petrolero was one avenue of survival. These economics of rent distribution were mediated in large part by kinship, which was in turn mediated by sex, perhaps motivated by love but, more often than not, by other desires and dependencies.

As my interlocutors shifted from heroic nostalgia to humorous head-shaking, a good part of the stories turned to tales of lovers, mistresses, adultery, cuckolds, and sex, which in Camiri was a sweaty and often illicit affair. The brutal oven of *chaqueño* heat, with dry season temperatures routinely passing 105 degrees Fahrenheit, made tangled bodies in unconditioned spaces a mess of what locals called *entrepiernados* (tangled up in legs), *empapados* (frothy), and a mess of sweaty *sopa* (soup). Illicit liaisons, in cars, along the river, in the once vibrant brothels, or in the town's "motels"—the place of the red light bulb and hourly room rentals—were frequent, or so the stories go. Stories were told of being caught in flagrante, or not. Rumors floated about one or another lover. Vocabularies of suspicion and infidelity were rich. Doubtless the same in many places, these stories struck me as culturally intensified by the oil boom, as hidden and not so hidden sex, sex work, and sexual violence are key features of masculine-centric oil economies. Stories were reminiscent of *La novia oscura*, Laura Restrepo's 1999 novel about a Colombian oil town and its main protagonists, the local prostitutes.

Asking questions of women about the golden days of oil generally revealed not nostalgia but ambiguity and bitterness, through refrains about the infidelities and violences of the petroleros. The petrolero was indeed flush with money. But part of the culture of masculine labor solidarity, the key means of accessing and keeping a job, meant spending some of this money hanging out with your coworkers drinking during your time off. This led to the pursuit of sex. As such, and at the risk of offending Bolivian readers, we might read the Oil Capital of Bolivia, Camiri—remembered as the bastion of defenders of the Chaco, the epicenter of the national treasury, the bulwark of gasoline sovereignty, and so on—as a masculinist hell for many, an epicenter of rumor, sexual innuendo, familial strife, and *chiverío* (cuckoldry).[5]

Women countered the heroic masculinity stories with their own stories of petrolero drunkenness, domestic violence, and abuse. Oil workers usually spent a week or two in the field and then came home for a week or a weekend. When they arrived in the city, flush with pay, as an older divorcée of an oil worker complained, the man cashed his check, dropped his bag at home, and, if she was lucky, turned over the voucher, or chit, for food at the company store to his wife. He then headed for the bar or the brothel. This was followed by drunken returns home, and accusations that it was the wife who was being disloyal, followed by beatings.

When asked, the men also remembered the brothels. Older men remembered with laughter and fondness one of the most famous, La Bonanza, appropriately named for boom times in an oil town. The Bonanza was staffed, it was said, by women who, like the best soccer players, were also "imported" from Argentina. In Bolivia's racist imaginary, these lighter-skinned women were superior to the locals. The Bonanza lured in oil workers, destroying some families and creating others. Children born to the women who worked at the Bonanza were called *hijos del pueblo* (children of the people) because nobody knew who the father was. I spent one afternoon being driven around old oil camp sites by a friendly older fellow whose nickname was indeed El Hijo del Pueblo. His mother had been a sex worker at the Bonanza, and his father? Who knows? I did not linger on his nickname, which his drinking friends had bestowed on him. But this particular son of the people assured me that many of the women at the Bonanza were indeed loved. In fact, some even ended up marrying oil workers and engineers. A number of those *putas*, he said, using the word for whore without malice, became "grand ladies of the local Rotary Club." A cruder version emerged around the question of the identity of all *camireños*. In Bolivia, regional identity is privileged, such that being *paceño* (of La Paz) or *cruceño* (of Santa Cruz) or a *cochabambino* (of Cochabamba) is a big deal for attributions of qualities, loyalties, and political affinities. Camiri was in the department of Santa Cruz but was geographically more like the Chaco. Was it cruceño, with more affinities to Santa Cruz? Or was it chaqueño, with closer connections to the Chaco? One group of men, all sons of oil, resolved the anthropological question in their own joking way, as did El Hijo del Pueblo, who resolved his own identity by telling me a common joke, "What are camireños?" they ask us. "We are all children of whores [*hijos de puta*]."

This patriarchal and generally misogynistic ideological field had everything to do with the structure of the extractive oil economy. The wives who stayed in town raising children while the oilmen were in the field would, if they were lucky, receive a chit for the company store. Wives would queue up there after pay day. Imagine the husbands in the bar or the brothel and the wives lining up beside the YPFB arch to get food for the family. And the pulpería was big business, which leads into other stories. Those charged with managing the pulpería could make lucrative money from kickbacks, buying Argentine maté tea, say, at an overprice, and fudging the daily numbers reported to La Paz to keep the difference. The chits the women received, just as good as money, were also the source of conflict. A wife would sometimes show up to claim her groceries by identifying her husband's name on the roster. More often than not, families were riven apart as mistresses would show up first, having been told by the oilman that she could get goods in his name. As another oil wife recounted, "My mother worked at the pulpería, and she had problems with many women, because they went with their pulpería card and my mother had to tell them, 'But they've just taken the goods in the name of that worker.' And the women got furious. Sometimes the workers promised their chits to several different women."

Dramatic battles, or so the stories go, tell of women—some wives, some lovers—fighting as they lined up for meat, milk, or dry goods at the YPFB pulpería. One long-circulating story that a local car-racing fanatic told me had two women battling over a dead oilman's pulpería card at his wake. "Right there in front of the coffin," he said, "they went at it." Often these battles played out over accusations of paternity, since a child born of an oil worker became a means of making a legal claim on wages or health care. Divorce was common—families with children from one, two, or three marriages equally so. The stakes were high. It was not just the chit for the company store but the right to the pension and the health care. As in oil towns elsewhere, it was a fragmenting social history. Despite the illusions of wealth, grandeur, and heroic nation building, I was told often, "It was *un chiverío total*"; for lack of a better way to translate generalized cuckoldry, it was a goat fest.

The oilmen blamed much of it on the women. Stories of infidelity invoked the vocabulary of the *chivo* (goat), that is, the man who is cheated on by "his" woman. From this masculinist angle, the petrolero was a victim. Sent to labor in harsh conditions in the rural area, the laborer was serving his patria (never mind that much of this rural labor also involved seduction or rape of rural and Guarani women). But the petrolero always worked with the anxiety that another man was back in town trying to seduce his wife. The other man that made one anxious was the *pata de lana* (wool-footed one), or the back-door man. These lovers snuck in and out of houses quietly without being heard, hence the wool feet, making clandestine love and dodging the all-seeing eyes of the neighbors in the dark of night. One was always risking discovery in a small town of prying eyes and wagging tongues. Innuendo about infidelity was rife. There were the *alcahuetes*, those who gossiped about illicit love affairs or tried to instigate them for others, always seeking some benefit, invariably generating conflict. This generalized condition of chiverío was sometimes called *alcahuetería*. That was Camiri. As another divorcée—and victim of domestic violence—remembered:

> It was the eternal routine. He arrived on Friday and he disappeared until Sunday. That's the way most of the oil workers were. He'd come back home Sunday night and sleep off his drunkenness until Monday. And sometimes even Monday he was "sick" and would claim medical leave to justify not going to work. Those things are stamped on me. It's not that I'm just speaking badly of the petroleros, because I'm not the only one; I know lots of women and the history is the same. It was a very easy life, that of the petroleros. They gave them all sorts of privileges: when they wanted a pay advance, they could get it; they had special clubs—oh, you could see drunkenness there, street fights, petroleros sleeping in the streets. It was a disaster, because they never showed up at their houses to sleep and the company gave them everything they wanted. It's true, I am a witness. I was humiliated to go out in the streets; I would be ashamed to encounter my husband with his lover. One day I came out of the market and there he was kissing her in front of the market, right in front of me. That was the life of the petrolero.

One older petrolero acknowledged that the women in Camiri were "admirable" because they put up with this. He said, "The one who understood and learned how to manage money was the wife [*mujer*], and even the lover [*amante*], because a good part [of the pay] went to the lover of the oil worker that everybody knew he had." Yet this sexually mediated distribution of oil rents in the form of surplus benefits to workers was insufficient to maintain two or three families. The divorcée quoted earlier lamented her need to make bread, take in laundry, and do seamstress work to keep her kids well fed, well

FIGURE 3.4 YPFB, oil workers' guard station, 2009. On display are conflicting images of the gaseous state: the YPFB flag with the slogan "There is a new country with its own energy"; and a MAS calendar for 2008–9, with Morales in a hard hat and the headlines "Democratic and Cultural Revolution" and "For equality and social justice for Bolivians." Photo by the author.

clothed, and in school. Indeed, much of her husband's pay was going to the brothel or the lover. All this extra labor on the part of the woman came in addition to putting up with her husband's violent outbursts and beatings.

In the oil camps, a major threat to oil labor unity and discipline were the rumors, gossip, and incessant macho joking tied to these two figures, the chivo and the pata de lana. Or maybe you were both? Start talking about chivos among a group of men in this sexually charged discursive field and you are liable to start a fight. The issue was so significant that there was an explicit counterdiscourse against gossip in the union. On my tour with El Hijo del Pueblo, we peeked into an old worker's trailer. Newish calendars graced with Evo Morales and calls for equality and social justice hung beside older pin-ups and hand-drawn cartoons of the Chilean cartoon figure Condorito, beseeching workers to stop all the gossiping (figures 3.4 and 3.5).

This chiverío stemmed in large part from the privileged place of the oilman in the structure, economics, and spatiotemporality of gendered in-

FIGURE 3.5 Cartoon in an oil workers' trailer near Camiri, 2009. The popular Chilean character Condorcito exclaims, "Please, enough with the gossip and *alcahueterías* between us." The counterinscription reads, aspirationally: "principles, honor, and glory." Photo by the author.

equality and oil work. Compared to the tin mines, where miners worked in closer proximity to their families, here the physical movement of labor in relation to the domestic space further distorted gender relations and labor militance. As Nash recounts, the miners, despite their revolutionary ideology, held on to patriarchal gender norms that stymied their capacity to maintain strong revolutionary commitments, especially when that would require more female protagonism. The sociospatial arrangements of oil labor were distinct, not that oil workers were anywhere as militant as miners, a point to which I return. But the separation between rural labor and city domestic life was part of oil life and a part of chiverío's intensification. Oil workers left the city in buses, trucks, or planes, to go to remote areas to work. When they came flying back from the field, the stories go, the planes buzzed the city first. Always joking, but then again, maybe it was true, camireños said the pilot would do everyone a favor and fly over the city once before circling back to land. The "chivero is coming," people said, referring to the YPFB plane as a goat transporter. The fly-by was a warning to all of the lovers, the wool-footed ones, to grab their clothes and get out, because the petrolero was coming home. Or so the stories go.

One of the heroic moments that sticks out in these tales was that of a quietly gay man of the town, a hairdresser who ran a salon on the main square. He was still cutting hair there when I first went to Camiri in 1993, when I first heard the stories told about him. Heroic indeed, he was routinely referred to as the *maricón* (queer), in a region where machismo is law and homophobia rampant. He had a bouffant hair-do and a garish salon with posters, as many have in Bolivia, of lighter-skinned men and women with different hairstyles. As one story went, the gay hairdresser was mercilessly mocked by the oilmen. As the oil workers' trucks drove by his salon, the petroleros would shout "*maricón, maraco, marica,*" and more epithets, all derogatory references to homosexuality. Having endured constant harassment from these most masculine of local men, one day he is said to have waited for them in front of his salon in silent protest. As the trucks filed by heading for the rural oilfield camps, he stood quietly on the sidewalk and held up the severed head of a goat. The oilmen, at least that day, or so the story went, passed in silence. Fact or fiction, the image I conjure in my head sticks with me today: the bouffant hair and the goat head, a rebellious queer critique of the system. Now that was a true hero of the Chaco.

HAVING COME TO THESE HISTORIES OF OIL AND GAS BY WAY OF MANY YEARS of work with the Guarani, what stood out to me was the virtual absence of any references to the Guarani. As in the nationalist histories, indigeneity and Indigenous peoples as distinct social and political realities were invisibilized, given that their presence challenged the nationalist paradigm. Even stories of the Chaco War were "whitened" or "mestizoized," largely making invisible the devastation the war wrought on Indigenous lands and lives (Richard 2008). Chronotopic narratives like the defense of the oil and the heroism of the Chaco War came to define the region as functional to fossil fuel extraction and nation building, which also entailed invisibilizing indigeneity. Prior to the war, oil entered the narrative of Bolivian nation making by way of the settler-explorer, those deemed by contemporary writers as the "pioneers" of the "miraculous discovery" (Royuela Comboni 1996, 36). In these accounts, the Guarani guides and laborers are labeled cambas, a term used much like indio, a generic, laboring subject marked as racially inferior (recall figure 1.1). As such, oil labor and the circuits of rent that flowed through it were largely "whitened." Even so, all the oil sites, wells, and camps were positioned in (that is, on top of) Guarani places and communities. And as settler armies did with native names (Apache helicopters, Tomahawk missiles), as far back to the days of Standard Oil, the oilmen frequently named geological strata and wells after local Guarani places: Tatarenda, Igmiri, Kaami. The oil places became Guaranized, even if the real Guarani were silenced. Places like Mandiyuti (the place of cotton, *mandiyu*), where whitish settlers putatively "discovered oil," were not treated as a sociohistorical site of Guarani existence but as a geological waypoint, a token of Bolivia's entry into the vortex of global fossil capital. The oil camp became an enclave within Guarani lands, and it enacted both violence and erasure.

What is significant is that the age of oil—as would the later age of gas—exacerbated gendered forms of exclusion and violence and also largely excluded, while deeply affecting, Guarani lives and spaces in the rural oilfields. The only times that Guarani came up in oil stories I heard was in reference to the sexual conquest by oil workers of a Guarani woman, the *kuña*. Part of the regional vocabulary of race, sex, and violent subjugation, conquests of the Guarani kuña were another component of the oil workers' philandering ways.[6] As early as the days of Standard Oil, Stephen Cote (2016) recounted violence against Guarani women by members of work crews. If the oil workers in the city were said to have made Sons of the People, here in the Guarani communities around oil camps people talked about the "children of Yacimientos" (*hijos de yacimientos*). Similar phrasings refer to other lighter-skinned children as either *hijos de cura* (children of priests) or *hijos del patrón* (children of the landlord). When asked by one of my Guarani colleagues about relations between criollo Bolivian YPFB oil workers and local Indigenous women, an elderly Guarani woman in the Charagua area recalled: "Did they leave children here? Sure they did, several! So-and-so's son, the one they call 'blondie,' he is a child of *yacimientos* . . . and the others, I don't remember, all those [women] who worked in the camp, as laundry women, cooks, they all brought children home from there." "From there" means from inside the oil camp, or what are called man-camps today, a space of potential wage acquisition but also masculine trickery and violence. She went on to recount that the oil workers would be drilling up in the hills and they would come down to the towns and communities "to drink and trick women" and leave them pregnant: "We worked hard [but] lots of women were tricked. The oil workers said they were single [men], but they were deceiving women [into sexual relations] in exchange for diesel fuel, for trinkets. It was no good." Among the masculine heroes and machismo petrolero, Indigenous lands and livelihoods, as something worthy in their own right, were made irrelevant and invisible. They were absorbed into a place of subservient functionality to the fossil fuel apparatus which abstracted geological space and extracted nature. It is from within and against this history of erasure and selective, often violent appropriation of sex, territory, and labor that Guarani continue to struggle in the age of gas, a question I return to in the following chapters.

YPFB: The End of an Era

Camiri was full of stories about oil workers and illicit rendezvous, but besides the stories of Che Guevara, I never heard much about class struggle and labor resistance. I prodded the old retirees for such stories, but not much emerged. The oil workers did strike—or threaten to—at various points during the Cold War years. In 1958, for example, the oil workers' union spoke out against the MNR's Davenport Code and went on strike to defend the YPFB (Young 2016, 155–56). Yet true to the form of a small privileged sector, subordinated to the dominant parties and the military, the strikes or actions in later decades were generally tied to support for one or another administrator of YPFB. There was little direct articulation with any kind of revolutionary or class politics, despite the fact that the oil workers were affiliates of the national Central Obrera Boliviana (COB).

This is not to say that some union leaders did not speak the language of class struggle. The most famous oil workers' leader, Enrique Martinez, was an outspoken critic of privatization during the neoliberal years. But one older worker, reflecting on privatization, said without prompting that compared to the combative mining centers in the Andes, oil workers were "submissive, passive." Most remembered the time there was a bit of labor unrest in the camps when YPFB workers were again confronted with foreign companies. The gringo employees ate and labored in better conditions. The Bolivians demanded not their expulsion but *portacamps* (trailers to sleep in) and better food. The time is remembered as a small victory, the time of "American food" (*comida americana*). With the towns of the oil region dotted by military bases, there was more proximity between oil workers and soldiers, with the latter frequently arrayed against peasants and miners. In fact, it was a YPFB worker who handed over León, one of Che Guevara's revolutionary soldiers, to the military. Being a radical labor activist was no way to keep a job in the Bolivian oil industry.

The military, in fact, was in direct control of YPFB for most of its existence. From the first nationalization of the 1930s, to the dictatorships of 1965–71 (whether the right-wing Barrientos or the populist interludes of Ovando and Torres), through the Bánzer era (1971–78) and the narco-dictatorships of the early 1980s (1979–82), YPFB was administered by army officers. This served as a control on labor militancy. It also created a patronage system that brought the military and the parties into competition over distribution of jobs and rents. Depending on who was in power, the army or a political party, one had to know someone to get a YPFB job. One older man recalled how he *almost* got a good job. He tried to use his connections to a local merchant and political figure but came to a dead end. Finally, he took a job that had him loading sacks of baritine, a chemical used in drilling fluids. One day a manager came and asked who knew how to use a typewriter. He spoke up and ended up with the relatively cushy job of sending telegrams with production figures to La Paz. But when he tried to move up the chain, the particularities of military rule complicated his efforts.

> In that moment [Luís] García Meza [dictator, 1978–81] was in as president of the Republic and General Otto López was the president of Yacimientos. The commandant of the Fourth Division [in Camiri] was General P. R. and Colonel R. C. was the head of the presidential guard, and he was the right-hand man of García Meza. The daughter of this Col. C. had been a classmate of my wife in the local school; he knew us well and we had *muñeca* [wrist, i.e., connections, the ability to take advantage of a relationship] with him. But just when I was about to send my papers along with the commander of the Fourth Division, there was another coup d'état. My "wrist" (i.e. my influence) was done [*Se acabó mi muñeca*].

As the retiree reeled off names and surnames of army officers, bringing up a thirty-year-old memory, he highlighted the significance of social connections between Camiri's petroleros and the military structures of power. Social affinities between YPFB workers and the military officers show their relatively conservative positioning vis-à-vis miners, urban workers, and Indigenous peoples.

So, despite its nationalist origins, YPFB was, most of the time, not part of a popular revolutionary project. It was like a mine (*mina* or *veta*) or a war booty (*botín de guerra*) disputed between the military and political elite, both dominated by the political right. After the return of electoral democracy in 1985, even as policies aimed at dismantling YPFB, the industry became the battleground of the political parties. Another worker recounted his experience.

[The workers affiliated to the parties] carried out barbarities [*barbaridades*]. One day I went out to the camp with another worker who was an MNRista [a militant of the ruling party, MNR]. He had processed the per diem for both of us for a week, and we went to get our money when we got back. I got 240 Bs and he got 500 Bs. He was no engineer to be on another per diem scale. I saw that and asked why he was getting more.

"No," he tells me, "it's just that they're paying me the professional scale."

"But you're not a professional," I tell him.

"But I'm an MNRista," he answered.

That was the little huge difference [*la pequeña gran diferencia*] and of course there was nowhere to go complain because if I complained I was fired, because our boss was also an MNRista.

By the 1980s, it became clear to workers that the government was bleeding out the company. By the 1990s, the IMF, alongside willing Bolivian political leaders, pried open the oil industry by privatizing retail gasoline sales. The plan was to break up and sell off different pieces of YPFB to foreign multinational firms. After other gradual shifts, in 1996, President Sánchez de Lozada passed the new law of hydrocarbons that sold off more chunks of YPFB and further opened up Bolivia's gas industry to foreign investors, with generous conditions for foreign capital. Havard Haarstad (2009a) describes the broader political goal of free market reforms: to weaken organized labor and transform the entire political space for making social demands on the state. This hit the Andean miners the hardest, many of whom migrated east or to the Chapare to seek new livelihoods in farming or coca growing. In the case of the oil workers, things were distinct. The government in the late 1980s and 1990s was still largely dependent on YPFB for revenue even though neoliberal policies were designed to gut it. In 1989 almost 47 percent of taxation revenue still came from the company. Transfers to the state from YPFB were *increasing* through the neoliberal era from 1985 to 1991 (Haarstad 2009a, 242). What this meant was that while the government pushed the ideology of the "free market," it was emptying YPFB's coffers even as its privatization plan would ultimately undermine the patronage system that parties relied on for survival.

In a speech given in 1985, when Víctor Paz Estenssoro was president and Sánchez de Lozada was minister of planning, Sánchez de Lozada described the situation as one of chaos, where YPFB and the unions had too much power (Sánchez de Lozada [1985] 2018). His vision of privatization was already gestating and Sánchez de Lozada suggested the need to "decentralize" YPFB, a euphemism for privatization. The strategy was really aimed at bolstering the MNR apparatus. In fact, in reference to the strikes by mine workers and the COB against the 1985 neoliberal decree, Sánchez de Lozada acknowledged that the goal of the state of siege and the seizure of parts of YPFB was not to destroy the unions like Augusto Pinochet but to "dominate the unions . . . in the sense that they should belong to the governing party" (512). Though referred to as decentralization and couched in the language of good economic sense, for workers it was clear that the MNR government and its successors were looting the company.

The fact that some workers say they adopted a similar attitude is not surprising. By the end, said Rosstel Alvarado, "there was no more mystique [*mística*]," referring to that commitment of noble sacrifice to the nation and to YPFB. Another old timer said, "We all robbed, absolutely everyone. It was a sacking of the company [*saqueo de la empresa*]." A worker recalled how one scheme operated, as political parties sought to capture rents in multiple ways, many under the table.

> Politics was the cancer that rotted everything. You know what they did? They [the political parties] put their people in strategic places: for example, the head of acquisitions, because that's where the deals [*negociados*] were done. A pen in the market that cost 1 boliviano came in to Yacimientos at 10 bolivianos. And why did it come in at 10 Bs? Because the guy who requested [the pens] had to take his part, the one that authorized his request had to take his part, the one who received the shipment had to take his part, and the guy who wrote the check had to take his part. In other words, it was a chain of corruption that made everything expensive, and I'm not just talking about little things. Pens are just an example.

In the end, as in the Argentine case described by Hernán Palermo and Cynthia Rivero (2011) and Elana Shever (2012), the neoliberal government was astute in its means of pushing through privatization. The sale of YPFB assets was partially used to create pension funds that would own shares of the newly privatized companies. The plan also funded a small retirement benefit for the elderly (the Bonosol), paid by dividends from shares of the newly formed private companies. This gave the government, in the figure of Sánchez de Lozada, a way to say that the benefits of YPFB's privatization, called "capitalization," would remain in the hands of the Bolivian people. The government also offered to sell shares in these newly formed private companies to YPFB workers to encourage their compliance. When I asked whether there was resistance to the privatization of YPFB, one of my more critical interlocutors recalled:

> There should have been a social and political scandal! The workers and their wives and kids should have marched from here [Camiri] to La Paz, one thousand workers with their wives. It would have had to be a huge movement to get attention but would not have been able to change anything because they had stuck us with the scheme [the privatization plan] from all four sides so there was no way [to resist]. They put the worker to sleep; they took away his capacity to react with everything. For example, they started offering to sell shares of Transredes [the new company formed with YPFB's pipeline infrastructure], of Chaco [the exploration company formed out of YPFB]; they messed with their consciousness, their subconsciousness, and their unconsciousness to accept privatization. They said take your severance and buy two hundred or three hundred shares of Transredes so you will become a businessman shareholder [*empresario accionista*] of the companies. So a lot of [the YPFB workers] burned up their little coins there. The business of neoliberalism went well for those who designed it, but the rest of us were left riding in the back of the truck, on top of the tarp.

His metaphor, *nos quedamos en la lona* (on top of the tarp), was revealing: the less fortunate on Bolivia's highways hitch rides sitting on the top of loaded trucks, on top of the tarp that covers the cargo. The more privileged ride inside, or drive. The government encouraged YPFB engineers and managers to create their own businesses, or small cooperatives, so that they could become service firms when the big multinational firms came in. As Shever (2012) described for Argentina, which implemented a similar strategy, the shift was as ideological as it was tactical. The oil worker was no longer that heroic laborer, the tool pusher or the martyr for the nation, but was to become an entrepreneur. Many YPFB employees embraced this possibility. Structurally though, only a handful could be successful. Alvarado recalled how this started before Sánchez de Lozada and continued during the Bánzer presidency. "Bánzer told us, 'Form your cooperatives,' so, you see my colleagues did that and created the oil services business called 'Gran Sararenda.'" Another group of YPFB teachers and administrators bought one of the old elementary schools run by YPFB and turned it into a private school. Others were encouraged to retire early. The government split the older workers in factions by lowering the retirement age for some workers and offering relatively generous packages for them to go out on their own. Those who were not yet old enough would be left out of the deal. With classic Bolivian ingenuity, an industry of birth-date transformation arose.

> Ohh . . . Yacimientos and neoliberalism came up with a bunch of tricks to convince workers to go along with their [privatization] plan . . . and then the offers to change your birth dates began to rain down, in order to get into the retirement system. So for 800 dollars, [or] 600 dollars, lawyers who were still in the residual offices [of a downsized YPFB] began to change birth dates for workers. In other words, the doors were opened to corruption so that everyone tried to save themselves however they could, paying whatever they could to assure their older years [*para asegurar su vejez*]. I don't think it's been written down yet, everything that neoliberalism fabricated [*todo lo que maquineó*], everything neoliberalism articulated, to hand over Yacimientos to the multinational [firms].

There was a brief window of mobilization when the plan to "capitalize" the oil company was announced in 1993. The old union leader Enrique Martínez tried to rally opposition at a national workers' assembly at Cochabamba. The police promptly jailed him. Eusebio Vargas recounted to my colleague Ubaldo Padilla how he tried to mobilize resistance in 1996, when privatization became law: "[We hoped to act] before 1,500 jobs in the Southern District [of Camiri] were erased with the stroke of a pen." By then already retired, Vargas tried to create a "Strike Committee," the first thing one needs. Yet against the backdrop of the corruption, the theft, the muñeca, the strategic placements, the kickbacks, and so forth, the struggle was futile. Vargas implied that leaders were bought off: "It hurt us, we were being wounded and lacerated, not so much because of the interests of the multinational firms but because of Sánchez de Lozada's 'country selling' [*vende patria*] Bolivian government. That was a national humiliation. But we carried out the strike. We were on hunger strike for several days but unfortunately, as you know, when money talks, the truth is silenced [*cuando manda la plata, la verdad se calla*]."

With its own form of theft, the privatization regime privileged profit maximization over social redistribution. Haarstad suggests that the discourse of efficiency was meant to do away with the idea that the state, by way of the efforts of organized labor or state-owned economic production, should have a key role in economic redistribution. As is evidenced in the memories detailed in this chapter, it was a question of not only reducing the labor force but transforming what Haarstad calls the "political space for labor organizing," that is, the very meaning and possibility that workers, however ambiguous in their political consciousness, should have an organized role in pushing for economic democratization through a redistributive state project (2009a, 244).

Similarly, the history of oil nationalization in Bolivia is politically ambiguous. Though born of a popular nationalist demand for prosperity and sovereignty, the military, the parties, and eventually the international finance agencies all whittled away at it. One account described YPFB as increasingly and intentionally *carcomido*, worm-eaten like an apple or bore-holed like wood attacked by termites. Despite the stories of corruption, debauchery, and disenchantment, an optimistic reading would be that there were still elements of political potential that resided in the oil workers' organization, until it was also dismantled by the neoliberal project.

Even so, and despite the heroic narratives of the Chaco War, the reality of imperialism, and the admirable resistance to it, YPFB and fossil fuel development were problematic as progressive instruments. Given its structural realities—a small, privileged sector of largely male labor, spatially distant from the more militant unions of the Andean political center and spatially closer to military infrastructures, and with few political or economic articulations beyond the region—its transformative and democratizing potential was limited. In addition, in social terms, with the family break-ups, the violence, the bordellos, the destruction of Guarani landscapes and livelihoods, and the abuse of women, it is not surprising that another oilman's divorcée said that the golden age of YPFB was a *desastre* (disaster). Even within the men's more limited self-critique, the programmed rotting out of YPFB was also internalized as a disaster: "It's impossible to return to the old YPFB that I knew. Nope, I don't think so. In those days we [YPFB workers] used to say, 'Where might we find the butt cheeks [*nalgas*] of YPFB so that we can go give them a kiss?' Because in Yacimientos everyone did what they wanted—not just the workers but the cliques of bosses; they're the ones that led it to disaster. It would be hard for it to be like it was before." Another of the retirees, José Ponce, summed up the feeling at the time: "It was a structural crisis that Camiri lived through. It was a crisis that affected even the dogs, the parrots, and the cats. It was a structural crisis so profound that nothing remained like it was before: not the market, not the bars, not even the brothels."

And then came the age of gas.

space
part two

4 gas lock-in

IN 1991 SIXTY PLANES FULL OF BRAZILIAN BUSINESSMEN AND FUNCTIONARIES reportedly arrived at the El Alto airport outside La Paz. They were shopping for Bolivian gas and pursuing other investments, much of it in agro-industry. The Brazilians wanted a gas pipeline running from the Chaco across eastern Bolivia to the Atlantic, to provide energy for the country's industrial center at São Paulo. Agro-industrialists had parallel interests in Bolivia: land, fertilizers (made from gas), and eventually biofuels. Engineers already knew there were large gas reserves under Guarani lands in the far southeast, and the Brazil pipeline idea had been gestating for some time. As early as the 1920s, the idea was floated, and it was debated again in the 1960s. In 1974 two right-wing dictators, Hugo Bánzer Suárez (of Bolivia) and Ernesto Geisel (of Brazil), signed memorandums to move the plan forward (Quiroga Santa Cruz ([1975] 1997). Yet political and economic conditions did not coalesce until the late 1980s, with neoliberal ideas ascendant and investors keen on taking advantage of high gas prices. Finally, in 1993, even before the pipeline was built and the privatization law passed, President Jaime Paz Zamora signed a contract to sell gas to Brazil (Hindery 2013, 42–44). Bolivia was locked in to several decades of gas exports.

Meanwhile, the networks linking US foreign policy hawks, industry-funded university centers, think tanks, and the private fossil fuel industry in the US were looking at Bolivia as a potential continental center for gas supply and transport in South America.[1] If Bolivian gas was seen as a cheap source of energy for Brazilian industry, it was also seen as a way to alleviate then scarce supplies for the US consumer and prop up US fossil fuel companies with access to foreign reserves. In September 1994, oil- and gasmen gathered at the Dallas Petroleum Club in Texas. It is a swanky club lined with polished hardwood, one of the social hubs of fossil fuel capitalists. A Bolivian government representative was in Dallas at the club that day where those present christened Bolivia as the future "Gas Hub of the Southern Cone" (Miranda Pacheco and Aliaga Lordemann 2009, 35). The idea was to build out liquefied natural gas (LNG) infrastructures, pipelines, and liquefication plants on the Chilean coast, to export Bolivian gas northward. As opposed to oil, which can be moved in a barrel or in massive supertankers, gas in its gaseous form has a high volume to value ratio and is dependent on pipelines for transport, with the spatial limitations on profitable marketization that that supposes. Yet with higher prices and new technologies, natural gas can now be piped to a coastline, superchilled to liquid form, and then shipped in ocean tankers like the mobile commodity that oil is. This has finance capitalists rubbing their hands with glee, since massive infrastructures require capital investment, a more mobile commodity allows more flexible pricing, and traders can speculate on liquefied gas futures, as they now do with oil (Zalik 2008). A vision emerged of a giant ring of pipelines: an *anillo energético* (energetic ring) that would encircle Bolivia, connecting both coasts and encouraging unfettered flows of gas and capital. Against the nationalist vision of a strong government-controlled fossil fuel company that would produce wealth for social redistribution, the dominant catch phrases in the US were energy security, energy integration, and energy cooperation. These were all euphemisms for market-friendly energy policies that would allow foreign private industries access to Latin American reserves and markets, privileging the interests of fossil capital, and the US, over social and redistributive demands on the ground (much less the climate and the environment).[2] Bolivia's elites, then closely identified with the neoliberal free market ideology of the North American capitalists, embraced this vision of integration into the circuits of fossil capital.

This chapter examines the conflict over the gaseous state at a national level, tracing the ways that the gas assemblage secured a hegemonic position in Bolivia, one that would persist through and despite the nationalist turn from 2005 to 2019. At stake was a battle over the relationship between landed capital (the state, Bolivia) and extractive capital (the foreign fossil capitalists), and the financial conditions through which the former would, if at all, cede spatial access to the latter in order to monetize underground reserves (Labban 2008). Despite the later turn away from neoliberalism in the 2000s, the hegemonic power of a foreign-dominated gas assemblage was in many ways prefigured by processes already underway in the 1990s. This unfolded through forms of carbon lock-in and a struggle over hegemony. By "lock-in," scholars refer to legal and technical infrastructures, the debt obligations to capital that underlie them, and the social relationships of power that these establish within the state form, all of which set constraints on the capacity of organized citizens to dismantle or radically change the system. The question was never whether the gas should be exported; it was by whom and on whose terms.[3] In terms of hegemony, against the threat of refusal of access by national governments, foreign extractive capital seeks free movement for capital, profits, and the material commodity itself. Often in alliance with the landed capital of the state (as it was during the neoliberal era), the gas assemblage relies on a combination of coercion (violence) and consent (through discursive, redistributive, or legal strategies) (Zalik 2011). In this chapter I trace these conjoined processes—the build-out of a form of carbon lock-in through legal and infrastructural devices—and the conflict over hegemony in the form of discursive disputes over the meaning of gas and space and intense violence of the Gas War and its sequiturs. While this spatial integration with the circuits of capital conjured up a shared national space of contestation, it also produced deep spatial fragmentation, the legacies of which persist today (Labban 2008).

AS THE GAS PIPELINE IDEAS GERMINATED IN THE EARLY 1990S, CARLOS Miranda Pacheco, a Bolivian expert who tended to side with foreign capital, was involved in promoting the idea of Bolivia as the "gas hub of South America." As a Bolivian who tended to favor the position of foreign extractive capital, he offers a useful contrast to the nationalist figures like Sergio Almaraz and Marcelo Quiroga Santa Cruz, whose fiery critiques I shared in previous chapters. As such, Miranda Pacheco offers a contrastive window onto the social relationships that shape the political world of fossil fuels in Bolivia. Miranda Pacheco helped negotiate compensation for Gulf after the 1969 nationalization and was later the national director of hydrocarbons during the Bánzer dictatorship in 1974. Though Bánzer called himself a nationalist, the dictatorship's interests lie in monetizing gas for expanding political power in the east, not for social redistribution. During that time, Miranda Pacheco also helped Bánzer pursue the (unrealized) sale of gas to Brazil, a plan that was deeply unpopular in both countries, given the opposition of unions and nationalists on both sides.[4] He returned again to oversee the privatization of YPFB during the first government of Gonzalo Sánchez de Lozada. As an ideologue for fossil capital—and distinct from the nationalist position—he wrote that the vision of Bolivia as a gas hub for energy integration within the free market framework of the Washington Consensus was the "most advanced" idea that Bolivian elites had ever come up with, an "intelligent and important geopolitical action" (Miranda Pacheco and Aliaga Lordemann 2009, 39). Never mind that it was first presented at the Dallas Petroleum Club. Like Oklahoma, the environmentally and economically degraded oil and gas hub in the United States, it seemed as apt to describe Bolivia as a future energy colony. Promotion of the plan depended on the privatization of Bolivia's production, transport, and commercialization infrastructures, what the Sánchez de Lozada government later called "capitalization." This set the stage for the ideological and affective battle over consent, since this also had to dismantle the nationalist idea that gas was the property of the state whose riches belonged to the people.

Privatizing YPFB

Behind the scenes, President Sánchez de Lozada worked with World Bank experts led by an Algerian, Chakib Khelil, to write a new hydrocarbons law.[5] The task was to offer favorable conditions (i.e., low taxes and high profits) to multinational private oil and gas companies. This enticement was deemed necessary to attract investment but encouraged the repatriation of gas superprofits—the extraordinary returns to capital from fossil fuel extraction that go beyond normal returns on investments—to investors and creditors outside Bolivia (Fernández Terán 2009, 47). The political conditions were ripe. Hyperinflation had created a generalized desperation for economic stability. Sánchez de Lozada had carved out some breathing room with his decentralization and land reform. Neoliberal reforms and a heavy-handed state had weakened the unions. Sánchez de Lozada's own vice president, the Aymara leader Víctor Hugo Cárdenas, had co-opted a segment of the Aymara political and intellectual classes. Much of the middle class was loyal to Sánchez de Lozada because they were employed by the state or by NGOs, then implementing a wave of projects tied to development aid (Gill 2000; Gustafson 2009c). The coca growers, the most cohesive site of opposition, were targeted for violent containment by the US-backed drug war. When it came to gas, Sánchez de Lozada operated largely in secret, and with some speed, to push the privatization vision forward.

The World Bank set up a division on energy sector management called the Energy Sector Management Assistance Program (ESMAP), which worked worldwide to promote privatization, discourage or limit government-run fossil fuel companies, and, in the case of Latin America, reduce Indigenous resistance (World Bank 1996).[6] This included promotion of debt-financed public investment in infrastructure, of interest to the World Bank and other banks, who were hoping to make money off the boom. Reminiscent of the 1920s, governments would take on debt and risk to help private capital find returns through fossil fuel infrastructures. In all these arrangements, governments are pressured to first pay back the debt, and then think about where to spend whatever fiscal surplus remained. A 1996 ESMAP report sketched out the privatization plan for Bolivia (World Bank 1996). Aware of the political implications of dismantling national oil companies in Latin America, where the idea that oil and gas belong to the people is deeply rooted, the ESMAP study recognized that it could not do away with the government-owned YPFB altogether. As with Gulf Oil in the 1950s, the idea was to allocate enough space to YPFB to assure its survival as a residual firm while opening up the most lucrative exploration and extraction rights to foreign companies. In the language of the oilmen, who calculate projects based on how much land they can access for exploration and drilling, this meant leaving "sufficiently attractive acreage" to foreign investors (World Bank 1996, 6). Even as a residual firm, YPFB would become a virtual private company (as in the Argentine case), such that it would also be capitalized with private money and subject to some non-Bolivian shareholder control. Its social and redistributive potential would thus be severely curtailed as it would have to compete with foreign investors for access to Bolivian exploration blocks. Khelil and the World Bank recommended the creation of "investment packages" (41) that included gas exploration blocks with Guarani names like Aguaragüe, Caigua, and Camatindi, once again converting Indigenous Guarani territory into something to be auctioned off to the oil- and gasmen. The World Bank plan would allow the Bolivian government some revenue. Indeed, the government was not viable, nor could it pay its mountainous debt, if the bank did not account for this. Yet the law sought to please investors by offering them generous conditions such as lower taxation (50 percent) and royalty rates (12.5 percent). The idea was to keep the government and YPFB on minimal fiscal life support, and to prioritize the return to foreign investors and creditors. The whole scheme was one of private capital accumulation and repatriation accompanied by the public assumption of debt and risk. It was also a systematic plan, underwritten by the World Bank, aimed at dispossessing Indigenous peoples of their land and livelihoods. Sánchez de Lozada and the MNR, as with experts like Carlos

Miranda Pacheco, saw this as an intelligent geopolitical strategy, indeed the "most advanced" ever, and enshrined the plan in the 1996 hydrocarbons law, written by and for fossil capital. And the capitalists came.

Eventually YPFB was broken up and sold off. The biggest parts, including existing oil and gas infrastructures, went to Chaco S.A., owned in part by Amoco (US), whose share was later purchased by British Petroleum (BP) and Argentine capital operating as Bridas. The other largest part went to Andina. New companies, including Brazil's Petrobras and Spain's Repsol (then Repsol YPF), stepped in. The long-standing vision of building a pipeline to Brazil materialized when Sánchez de Lozada signed a deal with Enron to invest in it, with the World Bank providing loans. Enron would team up with Shell (Hindery 2013). Knowing well that such deals would not be politically popular—nor were they technically legal, since presidents cannot sign contracts—Sánchez de Lozada operated much like President Enrique Peñaranda had in 1941 when he quietly approved a compensation check for Standard Oil (Fernández Terán 2009). Petrobras (Brazil), Repsol YPF (Spain), and Total (France) also teamed up to build a new gas pipeline to Argentina. The government reserved some shares that would be managed by Bolivian pension funds so that Bolivians could be told that they were also shareholders and partners (socios) of the foreign firms. British Gas (UK), Dong Won (S. Korea), Maxus (US, later bought by YPF), Pluspetrol (Argentina), and Vintage (US) secured other concessions. Another private firm took over storage. A division of British Petroleum (Air BP) got the concession to provide jet fuel in Bolivian airports. The law forbid YPFB from exploring or producing hydrocarbons, except in shared risk arrangements with foreign firms. Thus YPFB was left with some domestic petroleum sales and was charged with expanding the domestic gas market by installing household gas access infrastructure. Sánchez de Lozada's government also sold off public utilities (electricity and telecommunications) and transportation infrastructure (bus terminals, airports, and railroads).[7]

Investments in gas and oil exploration grew in the late 1990s, yet neither privatization nor the giveaway to foreign firms ameliorated the economic and fiscal crisis. Nationalists saw this as a sacking of the country (saqueo). Inequality, poverty, and unemployment were stagnant or rising. The state, on a neoliberal agenda, was gutting its own sources of income. With little tax base to fall back on, the government engaged in a new round of austerity. As this old regime was crumbling apart, lacking its bases for distributing patronage and rapidly losing popular support, the valves on the gasoducto to Brazil were opened up and gas started flowing in 1999. The gas pipeline tightened "lock-in"—the asymmetrical infrastructural, legal, and political-economic interdependence between the two countries. By that time the old general Hugo Bánzer was back in office. The little old dictator never met justice but he wanted some credit for the pipeline. To commemorate the moment, he had himself put on a postage stamp hugging then Brazilian president Fernando Henrique Cardoso. The stamp read "Gasoducto—1974–1999—The Most Important Energy Project on the Continent."

Though the export of gas to Brazil and Argentina moved forward, the plan to export Bolivian gas to Chile, and then to the United States as LNG, was deeply unpopular. Initially, the idea was to sell gas to Chile for electricity production. Reportedly, President Sánchez de Lozada's own mining company, Comsur, hoped to strike a deal with an associated firm in Chile, Río Tinto Zinc, suggesting that his own financial interests motivated the gas-to-Chile option. Yet an even bigger market was to the north, in California. Leading a consortium called Pacific LNG, the US company Sempra Energy was to be the main investor. Once the gas got to the Chilean coast, Sempra would liquefy it and ship it on supertankers to Baja California, Mexico. There another Sempra facility would regasify it and inject it into the regional pipeline system for sale to electricity utilities in Mexico and the United States. Backed by loans and private capital, the pipeline would be another huge infrastructural apparatus generating debt on one end and returns to capital (and carbon dioxide emissions) on the other. At the time, gas prices were high, fracking had not yet taken off in the US, and Bolivian gas would add supply for the world's most voracious energy consumer. The Chile pipeline plan also reaffirmed Sánchez de Lozada's personal and financial orientation toward the United States and Chile. It would also have geopolitical implications, suturing Bolivia more firmly into the orbit of Chile and US efforts to bolster free trade arrangements around the Pacific.

Gulf's oil pipeline, built under a dictatorship in the 1960s, had also gone through Chile. But by the 1990s, opponents of Sánchez de Lozada, and privatization generally, rallied around Bolivians' long-standing resentment over the late nineteenth-century loss of the sea to Chile. Some argued against exports to the US altogether. Others argued that the gas should go through Peru. Nonetheless, Sánchez de Lozada's government stubbornly pushed forward. When Bánzer returned to office in late 1997, he moved the plan forward. When Bánzer succumbed to cancer, Tuto Quiroga, his vice president, a favorite son of the Washington, DC, foreign policy circles and an alumnus of Texas A&M University, took over. He moved the plan forward. Sánchez de Lozada returned to office in 2002. By then he had little popular support and relied mostly on the backing of the US government, the financiers, the gas companies, the conservative sectors of the military, and the economic elites of Santa Cruz. With characteristic hubris, he moved the unpopular plan forward. It would be his undoing.

Villamontes, 2002

About halfway between Camiri and the Argentine border is the city of Villamontes, the heart of the Bolivian Chaco. Villamontes was the site of Bolivia's heroic stand against the advance of the Paraguayan army in 1935. Like Camiri, it is also an epicenter for remembrances of the Chaco War. Though the oil boom of the 1960s and 1970s largely bypassed Villamontes to favor Camiri, by the time of the gas boom, Villamontes appeared to be better positioned as a key transit and commerce hub. In 2002 its still somewhat sleepy streets and plazas were like most provincial Chaco towns with local particularities. The cattlemen claimed the rural scrub country. Weenhayek from the rural margins sold crafts in the market. Trotting horses clip-clopped down dusty streets, pulling Mennonites in their buggies, plying cheese and milk. The Pilcomayo River, which flows toward Paraguay just south of the city, attracted fish merchants from Santa Cruz and Tarija. The precariat with no stable employment dedicated themselves to fishing for these merchants, setting up long nets or pulling them through the river with heavy wooden rowboats. As gas development increased monetary circulation, a booming informal market sprung up alongside the highway on the outskirts of town. Kollas, Andeans of Quechua and Aymara origins, dominated the market. Merchants bought goods in Argentina and resold them here for further resale north in Santa Cruz. Other clandestine goods like cocaine moved south through Villamontes. Contraband liquor and other goods made their way up from Paraguay through the dusty backroads of the Chaco. Small farmers from the Andes were also seeking land, entering into tensions with local peasants and the Guarani and Weenhayek. Through it all, another legacy of the Chaco War and Cold War military expansion remained— the military bases all up and down the eastern borderlands, from Abapó to Camiri to Boyuibe and Villamontes and on to the border at Yacuiba. Just an hour south of Villamontes is Sanandita, site of an old oil refinery, and now a training center for the Condors, an elite Bolivian special forces unit created by one of the more notorious dictators, Luís García Meza, in 1981.

FIGURE 4.1 Petrobras, marking territory in Villamontes, 2004. Photo by the author.

Since getting to the huge gas fields of Tarija from Santa Cruz means passing through Villamontes, it is a crossroads of the new gas industry (see maps I.1 and I.2). Brazil's Petrobras was at San Alberto and Sábalo. Spain's Repsol, which employed many Argentines, was at Margarita. The gas industry expanded, maintained, and safety-patrolled what was once a treacherous winding dirt road into the region. Brazil was such a presence that Petrobras even paid someone to put up Petrobras-branded street signs in the plaza of Villamontes (figure 4.1). Further west, the tiny, dusty roadside town of Palos Blancos turned into a kind of rest stop for the new generation of petrolero gas workers. Wood-shack bordellos sprang up. Jokes about Brazilians, *negros*, *gauchos*, and their sexual preferences started circulating. The Guarani community of Puerto Margarita and towns like Carapari were overwhelmed by gas operations. And that was just the beginning.

In July 2002, Bolivia was in turmoil. Gonzalo Sánchez de Lozada— remembered by supporters and detractors alike as "Goni"—had been re-elected but had yet to take office. Indigenous movements, laborers, and the MAS were calling for a new constitution. In the small towns and cities of the southeastern Chaco, the upheaval was of a different sort. Everybody was talking about gas. That month I was en route to a meeting of Guarani communities who were discussing compensation issues tied to the work of Repsol at Margarita. My companions and I stopped in Villamontes to attend a public forum on the Chile pipeline question. The event, in hindsight, offers important insights on the complex and contradictory political forces that were converging.

In a country where I had long learned to be skeptical of the military, the gas forum was being held in the Casino Militar, the officers' club just off the main square of Villamontes. It was a typical public *salón* in Bolivia, with concrete floors and bad acoustics, in which the denunciations of imperialism later echoed off the laminated tin roof. Styrofoam letters covered with gold foil spelled out *Casino Militar* on one wall. On another was a picture of Simón Bolívar. Attendees included some local Guarani leaders as well as urban townsfolk and NGO employees, all of whom sat in rows of white plastic chairs. An environmental NGO called Foro Boliviano sobre Medio Ambiente y Desarrollo (FOBOMADE, Bolivian Forum on the Environment and Development) had organized the event, called "Advantages and Disadvantages of Oil Activity in the Bolivian Chaco" (the term *petrolera*, for oil activity, increasingly meant gas as much as it did oil). Co-sponsors included Centro de Investigación y Promoción del Campesinado (CIPCA, Center for Research and Promotion of the Peasantry), a national peasant and Indigenous rights NGO; and Villamontes's civic committee and a nationalist organization called the Comité de Defensa del Patrimonio Nacional (CODEPANAL, Committee for the Defense of National Patrimony). The speakers included a legendary former head of YPFB, Enrique Mariaca Bilbao; a university professor of engineering, Carlos Villegas; and a rear admiral in the Bolivian Navy, Gildo Angulo. Given that the military was generally dominated by conservative interests, and NGOs like CIPCA were increasingly being targeted by the conservative opposition, it struck me as a curious array of social actors in an incongruent space. But at the end of the day, it was less about environmental or social issues like Indigenous rights, and more about resisting the Chile pipeline and nationalizing the gas.

Gildo Angulo, the navy man, was a representative of those sectors of the military who embraced a long and deep tradition of resource nationalism. His speech struck the tone of Latin American anti-imperialism. Bolivia's history, he said, was one of "theft [*avasallamiento*] and sacking [*saqueo*] of natural resources" by foreigners led by a government that was "corrupt and deficient" and had given away so much of the state. By this he referred to the privatization policies during Sánchez de Lozada's first term but also to the whittling away of the state's economic role more generally. Now, he went on, "these foreign gas companies are going to lead us to millions and millions of dollars in losses." To feel the language of military nationalism one must absorb it at length.

They are creating great illusions for the gas markets but we have to avoid the model of theft [*avasallamiento*] that happened with gold and silver of the past. Gas is life for the countries that have it. It takes millions of years to form. Almost everything one needs comes from the industry of gas. We should repeat as a mantra, "The Gas Is Ours." The market economy is a fraud. What kind of patriotism is that of those who invented capitalization [the privatization of state industries]? Our national business class did not even participate. The state should be the only valid interlocutor, but now it is shrunken, inept, corrupt. The US is the first to protect its industries but here in Bolivia the US is pushing the free market and poverty. The worst thing is that we are turning into those who think "save yourselves whoever you can, the poor don't matter." We need to get used to speaking with valor [*valentía*]! They lie to us. Gas is the pillar of development, but now we see railroads and oil falling into foreign hands. No country lets this happen except Bolivia, which gave away its oil because of the hydrocarbons law [passed under Sánchez de Lozada, in 1996]. The government is acting as if Bolivia were a colony. We need to act like a nation, not a colony![8]

Over many years of work in Bolivia I had never heard a military man speak in such a register of anti-imperialism and antineoliberalism. Yet Angulo, rear admiral in the marine branch of the army, that is, in sealess Bolivia, the branch that patrols Lake Titicaca and the riverways of the Amazon, was a long-standing actor in CODEPANAL. It was a left-leaning nationalist organization that had fought privatization and was now fighting for renationalization. Angulo himself was no socialist. He was a military nationalist, a representative of that longer tradition within the Bolivian military, now seeking to mine the deep surplus "reserve" of nationalist and revolutionary memory and sentiment in Bolivia.[9]

Guido Villegas, the engineer, followed with an analysis of the proposal to export gas through Chile. The gas pipeline to Chile, and from there the LNG ships to California, would, Villegas said, "strengthen Chile and allow the USA to exhaust our reserves within ten years." The alternative proposal? Reconstruct the state oil company, YPFB. Demand that the government get 50 percent of all contracts. Negotiate firmly with Chile. Resist the political parties that have weakened the nation. We need a "sovereign and dignified energy policy!" he said. Both Villegas and Angulo, with significant experience, gave technical arguments about prices, volumes, and markets that illustrated how much Bolivia stood to lose under Sánchez de Lozada's plan to export gas to Chile. Smatterings of applause interrupted the speakers.

Enrique Mariaca Bilbao was the final speaker. Mariaca Bilbao was a legendary defender of YPFB. He had gone off to the Chaco War at age seventeen and served on the front lines here in Villamontes in 1935. He studied oil engineering in Argentina, became a leader on the nationalist left, and ended up as a director of YPFB. In 1966 he published a five-hundred-page history of YPFB called *The Myth and Reality of Bolivian Petroleum*, in defense of its nationalization. In 1970 he served as minister of hydrocarbons under Juan José Torres, the military socialist who oversaw the Gulf nationalization. He was a key figure in CODEPANAL. Now going on eighty-five years old, here in Villamontes again, he was Bolivia's nationalist hydrocarbon history in the living flesh, one of the last of the great intellectual leaders of the Generation of the Chaco. His were the ideas that Sánchez de Lozada and his free market backers sought to ridicule and eliminate.

Mariaca Bilbao began by attacking the "thinning" out of the state under neoliberalism, referring to Sánchez de Lozada's policies and the gutting of YPFB. Invoking the Chaco War, which, he reminded the audience, had created a "new oil consciousness" (*nueva conciencia petrolera*), he called for an "oil and gas policy that is progressive and nationalist" (*progresista y nacionalista*). Mariaca Bilbao reminded the crowd that Enron was part of the Chile scheme too, and he explained how Enron had "manipulated prices to create a crisis and exploit the people [*explotar el pueblo*] of California." What followed was an indictment of a crooked government and the sell-outs (*vendepatrias*) of the privatizing regime. Setting aside for the moment what we know about climate change and fossil fuels, this valiant voice for government control of gas and the demand that it be used for the amelioration of poverty, amid what seemed to be the heyday of neoliberalism, was both historic and impressive. The Casino Militar reverberated with applause.

The speakers then took questions from the crowd. Should we export gas through Peru instead? Villegas: No, we have to have a public debate on this. What do you mean by the shrinking state? Angulo: I mean it's like a colony and not a nation. Is Sánchez de Lozada's hydrocarbon law neoliberal? Mariaca Bilbao: Yes, because it does not benefit the country. And so it went. The positions could not easily be distilled into a singular ideology, although what they shared was pretty clear: Gas should be exported, but there must be a national debate. The current government is antinational. The gas should be nationalized.

In those days the event was one of many in the country being held in universities, at NGOs, or at sites like this one. These public *foros* are part of the Bolivian political landscape, and have been for decades. They might be organized by some ideological group, whether Trotskyites or feminists, or, as in this case, by representatives of NGOs or political factions currently excluded from power. As with the gas forums of 1967, and years later, like a wrinkle in time, much of what Bolivia had gone through in the 1930s, and then again in the 1960s, was here again being mobilized as a shared discursive position, a mantra: The Gas Is Ours.

Forums like the one in Villamontes were not simply public shows. They reflected a broad-based groundswell of organizations coming together to envision forms of counter government and to diffuse, as Angulo said, a new way of speaking about gas, a new consciousness. This mantra, "the gas is ours," thus took on a transportable quality, one that could be inserted alongside other social movement agendas and serve as an articulating device, given its national scale. Indigenous organizations had already demanded a rewriting of the constitution and real territorial rights. Soon they would also demand gas nationalization. The Aymara resistance, with its heartland at Achacachi, had virtually seized control over much of the region outside La Paz and were also saying "the gas is ours." Coca growers stood up to the US-backed militarization of their region with road blockades and picked up the mantra. Landless peasants were occupying lands that had been illegally doled out by right-wing parties in the east. Among their demands? Nationalization of gas. The MAS, under Evo Morales, was trying to bridge divides between these movements. At one point, the MAS even declared the existence of the "Estado Mayor del Pueblo Boliviano." The "Estado Mayor" refers to the military high command. Here the point was that an alternative state, with backing by some military officers who shared sentiments like that expressed by Angulo, was being envisioned. Its glue was part-Morales and part-"the gas is ours," with everything that that entailed for resistance to the neoliberal logic of privatization. For Jorge Lora, it was at this moment of nationalist effervescence against the Chile plan that Sánchez de Lozada's government was already toppled (Petras and Lora 2013, 62).

Gas War, 2003

By late 2003, after a series of other conflicts and political crises, a mass movement emerged, centered in El Alto and La Paz. The protests had grown after the killing of eleven-year-old Marlene Rojas in Warisata, in September

(Gustafson 2009c). A variety of factors came together that ultimately coalesced around the nationalization of gas. Thousands marched over several weeks in October 2003, shouting "the gas is ours" and "no gas to Chile." Though some have interpreted the gas demand as a kind of spontaneous articulation that agglutinated people with diverse grievances, events like that in Villamontes, only a few months prior, illustrate that sustained political work had brought the issue of gas nationalization to the foreground in public consciousness. Sánchez de Lozada, increasingly isolated and brimming with disregard for the darker-skinned citizens he was supposed to represent, refused to budge. He ordered the army into the streets. Over several days, soldiers killed sixty-seven civilians. As the mass movement took strength, the killing spurred ever wider repugnance and his allies abandoned him. He finally resigned and fled to the United States. The events are now known as the Guerra del Gas (Gas War).

The bloodiest day was Columbus Day, October 12, 2003.[10] The Bolivian army killed twenty-nine unarmed civilians that day, most of them residents of El Alto. The army had been using force for some weeks, ostensibly to break road blockades. Increasingly the soldiers seemed to be firing indiscriminately. On October 10, the movement intensified after the funeral of a student killed while he was riding his bicycle home. To fuel its cars and its military vehicles, La Paz depends on a gasoline distribution center at a plant called Senkata, in the city of El Alto. Marchers had shut down access to Senkata, and gasoline was scarce. On October 11, a convoy of military vehicles broke through civilian blockades to move a single tanker truck of gasoline into the city. As the trucks slowly moved down the main avenue of El Alto, the army used tear gas, rubber bullets, and live ammunition. They killed a five-year-old boy, Alex Mollericona, shot in the face while standing on the rooftop terrace of his house watching the convoy roll by. Another bystander, Walter Huanca, was killed when he was hit point blank by a tear gas canister. October 12 was worse. Sánchez de Lozada deployed two more military operations to El Alto. The first, attempting to clear a blockade of the Rio Seco bridge, led to the death of twenty civilians. The second involved another army caravan to escort gasoline tankers from Senkata down to La Paz. The line of tanker trucks moved slowly through the main thoroughfare of El Alto. It was a fossil fuel convoy flanked by military troop carriers bristling with weapons. The military again fired indiscriminately as the convoy rolled toward La Paz. One of the victims was Lucio Gandarillas. He had peeked out from behind the closed kiosk of a street vendor and was shot in the stomach. Sánchez de Lozada's soldiers wounded more than ninety people and killed thirty more that day. The dead included an improbable hero: a young army recruit from eastern Bolivia was shot by his own commanding officer. The brave young man had turned his hat around backwards, a sign of open rebellion, a refusal to fire on civilians. A newspaper later referred to the convoy of gasoline tankers as the "Caravan of Death."

In an attempt to justify the use of lethal force on that particular day, in relation to that particular stretch of road, and that particular supply of gasoline, President Sánchez de Lozada and his entire cabinet signed a decree the night before (Gobierno de Bolivia 2003). The decree declared a national state of emergency tied to gasoline supply. Never mind that the conflict was limited to a single avenue in El Alto where the tankers needed to pass. The decree proclaimed the duty of the military to be "to guarantee the normal supply of liquid fuels to the population, through the securing of storage facilities, the securing of fuel transport in tanker trucks or other forms, and the distribution in service stations for ninety days." The tragic ironies pile up. Sánchez de Lozada had privatized the Senkata plant, along with gasoline filling stations during the heyday of privatization in the 1990s. They were no longer under government control. Now, through an arbitrary act of lawmaking, the government conjured up wording that basically declared state control over private fuel infrastructures, and deemed the route between Senkata and La Paz a free fire zone. It was a neoliberal state of exception that granted special killing power to the state to allow private gasoline transport guaranteed by the military, killing power deployed to push forward the gas pipeline plan. Only a few weeks earlier, and despite widespread opposition, Sánchez de Lozada met with the head of Sempra Energy in Mexico. There he assured the CEO that the plan to export gas through Chile would be moving ahead.[11] Doing so meant using the violent force of the state, which one political cartoonist aptly represented as creating a gas pipeline cemetery (figure 4.2).

This led to a calculus of death played out in the moment, for gasoline, but on the wider scale, for the natural gas pipeline. At one point, witnesses said that then minister of defense Carlos Sánchez Berzaín had discussed how many deaths it might take to stop the protests and export the gas. "Maybe not 999," he reportedly said, "but 1,000 would do." Sánchez Berzaín, called "Zorro," also allegedly declared on the night of October 11 "that there will be deaths, but there will also be gasoline" (*va a haber muertos, pero va a haber gasolina*).[12] Several years later, in 2009 this "gasoline protection decree" was cited as justification for indicting all seventeen of the cabinet members who signed the document. Sánchez de Lozada and Sánchez Berzaín were declared *en rebeldía*, since they had fled to the US (Sánchez de Lozada, a mining mil-

FIGURE 4.2 Gas cemetery, 2003. Trond, *La Razon*, October 2003.

lionaire, lives in Bethesda, Maryland; Sánchez Berzaín deals real estate and works with right-wing Cubans and Venezuelans in Miami).[13]

The events reveal the arbitrary mix of legalism and violence deployed by the neoliberal regime as it sought to construct a fossil fuel export apparatus linked to the political and economic interests of US-centric fossil networks. I document part of the events here as a form of necessary inscription, given that the victims' families are still seeking justice.[14] Sánchez de Lozada's allies, both in Bolivia and in the United States, have argued that Sánchez de Lozada is innocent. In their story, repeated by Sánchez de Lozada's lawyer in the US courts, the killing was done by rogue military officers over whom Sánchez de Lozada had no control. In more imaginative versions, and without evidence, these apologists argue that the Gas War was planned by Evo Morales and funded by Venezuela, and the rogue officers were actually engaged in a false flag tactic. In other words, the story goes, sectors of the military intentionally ordered the killings, not to repress the movement but to incite the nationalist turn further.[15] In fact, court documents point out that Sánchez de Lozada's government had ordered the transfer of troops from Santa Cruz to La Paz, calculating, again, that those of the east would be more likely to obey orders to fire on Andean Bolivians of the west (the young hero of the east who refused notwithstanding). The narrative of a rogue military seeks to absolve Sánchez de Lozada, who has allies in the US political and academic world. The absolution of Sánchez de Lozada also seeks to erase the role of the political and structural conflicts over Bolivian gas, conflicts sparked by the failure of neoliberal policy. In a country riven by deep poverty and dependence on foreign aid and capital, the free market regime had no viable social or political agenda. Its primary purpose was to facilitate the expatriation of Bolivian gas, as much as possible, as fast as possible, along with most of the financial surplus it would generate. I return to this calculus of political death and the gaseous state in chapter 7.

From "Goni" to Mesa to Morales

"Mesa is like yogurt," one of my Guarani friends joked in early 2004, "because he has an expiration date." My friend was talking about Carlos Mesa, the historian and vice president who took office after "Goni" Sánchez de Lozada fled to Miami. Mesa managed to salvage some credibility by rejecting violence and distancing himself from Sánchez de Lozada as the government unleashed the army against the people of El Alto. Yet scarcely six months later, Mesa himself was under intense pressure. Political parties were in disarray. Congress was divided. Alongside the more conservative military nationalists of the Nueva Fuerza Republicana (NFR, New Republican Force) party, the MAS was pushing for a radical revision of the relationship with the foreign gas companies. The "agenda of October"—the gas is ours—was divided between those who called for expropriation and outright nationalization and those who pushed only for the revision of existing contracts. Others opposed the Chile plan outright. Some said the Chile plan should be negotiated in exchange for a sovereign outlet to the sea. Others pushed for Peru. President Mesa spoke progressively in public. But in private he leaned against nationalization and toward the interests of the oil and gas companies and the United States, all of whom were trying to stave off real change. To Mesa's right, the hardline elites of Santa Cruz pressed for the status quo. To his left, the mobilized people said "the gas is ours." Some of the capitalists in the country, and gradually the MAS itself, were leaning pragmatic. In the midst of the Mesa moment, the private bankers' association was consulted on its position and responded, "We're going to have to export the gas and with that we may generate the capital to industrialize." This was the discourse of fossil capital, but it was, increasingly, the discourse of the MAS as well. As conservative economists would later recognize, the reality was that there was no viable export project that was not, in some way, seen by the vast majority of Bolivia as a nationalist project. What that would look like was the question. The battle played out over the writing of a new law to reshape the relationship between the state, the gas, extractive capital, and the surplus money.

The Mesa government sought a buffer amid the polarization by calling a referendum vote, in which the people would decide. Or rather, people would feel like they decided something, at least for a minute. As with most referendum votes, this was a tricky spectacle that aimed to temporarily calm a polarized society through the semblance of the expression of collective democratic will. But the questions favored the private fossil fuel industry. Each was designed to produce yes answers, all of which would facilitate the export of gas and give the appearance of a state asserting more control over the industry and the money, without actually securing real power.

1   Are you in agreement with the abrogation of Law 1689 that was promulgated by Gonzalo Sánchez de Lozada?

This question captured the disgust with the Sánchez de Lozada regime, represented by the 1996 hydrocarbons law. A yes vote would legitimate the insurrectionary will of October 2003.

2   Are you in agreement with the recovery of the property of all hydrocarbons at the well mouth for the Bolivian state?

This issue had been widely internalized by the Bolivian public. Since Sánchez de Lozada's last decree had handed over commercialization rights to the industry (that is, they could sell gas directly themselves), and companies were booking Bolivian gas as "their" reserves to boost their stock price. A yes vote here would seemingly recover this "property" for the Bolivian state, and hence the people.[16]

3   Are you in agreement with reestablishing YPFB, recovering the property of the shares of Bolivian women and men in the capitalized [privatized] oil companies, so that [YPFB] can participate in the entire hydrocarbon production chain?

A yes vote here would support the reconstitution of the national hydrocarbons company and restore its potential role across the spectrum of activities—exploration, drilling, transporting, and selling. This was not expropriation. It simply meant that the new YPFB would assume a share of ownership in the private companies that had been formed by its breakup, that part that had heretofore been transferred to the pension funds.

The MAS, the social movements, and the Mesa-industry bloc (with some reticence) sought a yes vote on all three of these. Even though it did not speak of expropriation, the language of "recovery of property" appeared to restore a sense of ownership to the Bolivian people. More significantly, the referendum enrolled the entire nation into a hegemonic affective consensus that the gas should be extracted and sold. How could anyone say no?

The final two questions sought to salvage the Chile pipeline project of Sánchez de Lozada and his predecessors. Radical critics argued that the whole "referendum" was a *tramparendum* (trap-arendum), which held within it significant flexibility.[17] Here the trap was particularly seductive.

4 Do you agree with the policy of President Carlos Mesa to use the gas as a strategic resource to achieve a sovereign and useful outlet to the Pacific Ocean?

Bolivia's long-standing hope to recover an outlet to the sea offered an emotional trigger to support the export of gas to the US via Chile and the Pacific. Although the idea of exporting through Peru had been offered to the public as an alternative to Chile, none of the investors saw Peru as a viable alternative. If one voted no, they might feel as if they betrayed the nation's aspirations for the sea. If one voted yes, they basically accepted the strategic orientation toward the United States that the neoliberal bloc had long pursued. The MAS pushed for a no. Mesa and the industry wanted a yes.

5 Do you agree that Bolivia should export gas in the framework of a national policy that covers the consumption of gas for Bolivians, foments industrialization of gas in national territory, charges taxes and/or royalties on the oil companies that reach 50% of the value of gas and oil production in favor of the country [and] uses the resources of exportation and industrialization of gas, primarily for education, health, roads, and jobs?

Here again was a trap. The entire nation was interpellated as a potential gas consumer and beneficiary of an export-oriented program. Who could say no? But a yes vote would only endorse a modest proposal, one close to that of Sánchez de Lozada himself: a 50/50 split. This is still low in the world of oil and gas, where countries often take as much as 90 percent of the profit. And, in Mesa's plan, it would be attained not through ownership or production shares but through taxes and royalties. It was a business-friendly proposal. The MAS said no, aiming to push for a larger government share if not outright nationalization. Mesa, of course, wanted a yes.

Discursive Lock-In

The referendum unfolded amid intense advertising and lobbying by the government and its private backers. The Corporación Andina de Fomento (CAF, Andean Development Bank) gave money to the government to support a yes vote across the board. The decree that moved CAF monies into a state account for the campaign justified it as a way to "inform the Bolivian population about natural gas with the purpose of achieving a response from the population that is adjusted to reality." In effect, "reality" was deemed to be that of the hegemonic interests of the fossil networks. The World Bank, ever intent on maintaining a system of fossil fuel–based surplus extraction that would reduce state control, sustain debt burdens, and return capital northward, also funded a publicity campaign in support of "yes" votes. In the program, also supported by the Canadian embassy, the slogan was "*te toca a ti, el gas está en tus manos*" (it's up to you, the gas is in your hands). Note that this has a different feel than *the gas is ours!* The campaign director said the hope was to reach every single Bolivian and "involve them in the issue of gas . . . and that we speak in only one language." The IMF, the World Bank, and the CAF went a step further, seeking to sway middle-class opinion with fear, saying that if the referendum vote came out negative, the viability of the country would be at risk. The Bank, as before, worried about payments on the foreign debt. The IMF said the country had to "monetize the reserves," meaning export the gas to convert it into dollars, otherwise there would be no more aid to Bolivia. The distance between "monetize" to pay the debt (the fossil capitalists' urge) and "nationalize" (urged by the movements, for addressing poverty) was vast. Yet both embraced extraction. As such the referendum was both about interpellating Bolivians as gas consuming and extractive subjects, and doing so in ways that challenged the deeply nationalist sentiment while cultivating support for the private industry bloc advocated by Mesa.[18]

Amid what appeared to be chaos, for some a civil war brewing, more mundane processes unfolded. One of these could be seen in the men digging up the cobblestone streets of Camiri and other provincial towns, laying down

FIGURE 4.3 A new gas meter outside a house in Camiri, Bolivia, 2006. Photo by the author.

gas lines to hook up the domestic supply to people's homes. By January 2004, there were already more than forty-two thousand households hooked up to the gas supply. Most of these were in larger cities. Slowly the infrastructural work trickled down to places like Camiri, important because it was, of course, the Oil Capital of Bolivia. This was not coincidental. Behind the battles over political power, the industry, in the form of YPFB, was literally laying the infrastructural groundwork for a deepened public commitment to gas exports. Men chewing coca, wielding picks and shovels, and sweating in the heat tore up streets and buried pipes to establish connections, a single line under the sidewalk, up through the concrete floor of the house and leading to the kitchen stove. After the men chipped through the frontispiece of Camiri households, they installed a meter on the street side. A metal grate topped it off, with the word *gas* welded into the cage door, as if to drive home the point (figure 4.3).

By April 2004 the country was experiencing a test of strength (*medida de fuerzas*) between the right wing of eastern Bolivia, the middle-class backers of Carlos Mesa, and the social movements aligned with the MAS. In such moments, each political faction, and the state itself, seeks to assess or "measure its power"—its ability to put people in the streets or deploy legal or de facto violence and get away with it. Indigenous peoples of eastern Bolivia, peasant settlers in Pando, and the Guarani in the Chaco were all on the highways, where the blockade was the key instrument of pressure (Gustafson 2011). The demands revolved around land titling, a new hydrocarbons law, a constitutional assembly, and resources for Indigenous peoples. The Guarani were threatening to occupy gas facilities across the southeast, demanding a law with at least 50 percent royalties for the government. School teachers in Santa Cruz initiated a seventy-two-hour strike. Miners organized in cooperatives threatened to seize mines owned by the former president, Sánchez de Lozada. There were blockades across the country with people saying "the gas is ours" and demanding a "true" nationalization of gas.

Evo Morales was with the movements, but he was also maneuvering within the party system structure. Many accused him of being too close to Mesa. Others were more radical. Felipe Quispe, the fiery Aymara leader and longtime rival of Morales, was quoted as saying of Mesa, "We've got to overthrow that asshole" (Hay que tumbar a ese pendejo) (La Razón 2004d). The often funny Quispe summed up a sentiment largely shared by the movements: "It's like a milk cow, when the milk is inside the body of the cow, when they talk about the wellhead [la boca], they should be talking about where the milk comes out [the whole body], which we use to make butter, cheese. But who has that? The transnational firms still have it. We want all of it" (La Razón 2004a). Oscar Olivera, one of the leaders of the 2000 Water War in Cochabamba, was quoted as saying he would participate in the referendum but would mark an "X" in all the boxes, since "nationalization" was not in the questions. Indigenous leaders of the east also demanded to write "nationalization" on the ballots. In the Congress, divisions over the referendum led to fistfights.

The stakes were national and international. Venezuela, then led by Hugo Chávez, supported a counterhegemonic regional alliance that involved uniting Brazil, Argentina, Bolivia, and Venezuela through a supranational oil and gas consortium called "Petroamérica." On the other side was the United States, the multinational private oil and gas industry, the Bolivian agro-industrial elite, and the traditional political parties, now near tatters. This conservative bloc was desperate to prop up Mesa and avoid a Bolivian government takeover of the gas industry. The reactionary right of the Bolivian east, Santa Cruz and Tarija, where most of the gas was, was calling for autonomy, with some demanding radical federalism or outright separatism. Some rightist pundits in the United States im-

TABLE 4.1 Questions and results of the 2004 Referendum on Gas Nationalization (Political Database of the Americas 2004).

	Sí (%)	No (%)
Do away with Gonzalo "Goni" Sánchez's law?	86.6	13.4
Recover the gas at the wellhead?	92.2	7.8
Reestablish YPFB?	87.3	12.7
Negotiate gas for a sea outlet?	54.8	45.2
Export gas with up to 50% take?	61.7	38.3

plicitly endorsed the break-up of Bolivia, using that possibility to suggest that federalism was the answer to Morales and the nationalist resurgence.[19] The World Bank also preached federalism, hoping to stave off a real nationalist project.

To Mesa's credit, the tumultuous weeks of *bloqueo* and *paro* were not answered with state violence, despite calls from the rightists of Santa Cruz for *mano dura* (a strong hand). The referendum was held. While MAS called for a vote of "yes-yes-yes-no-no," Mesa urged "yeses" all the way down. Mesa was also clear that there was no possibility to read nationalization or expropriation into the outcome. Abstention and null vote percentages were high but the yes votes held the day (table 4.1).[20]

The referendum's outcome was a victory for Mesa and extended his expiration date by almost a year. But the tumult continued as Congress and other actors, from the gas companies to the social movements, pushed and pulled over the new hydrocarbons law. The social movements demanded that the gas industry be nationalized and existing contracts be transformed into shared operations with a newly rebuilt YPFB. Against the existing law that allowed foreign companies to book underground oil and gas reserves as their own, the left demanded that the country recover control over the reserves at the wellhead. Finally, critics demanded the revision of existing contracts so that rents and royalties to the state would increase.

Those who sought to maintain private industry dominance deployed a familiar argument: a nationalist approach would doom Bolivia to financial ruin. Horst Grebe, another of the preferred interlocutors of the United States, was Mesa's minister of the economy. He met on occasion with the US ambassador to share information about the debate over the new hydrocarbons law (Embassy La Paz 2004). Their positions were similar: that Bolivia had to increase exports of gas, that private industry investment was the only way to do so, and that nationalization would lead to the loss of aid and investment. The discourse of this right-leaning sector also stoked fears of "losing the market," that is, losing access to the market in California and Mexico. Along with close associations between figures like Grebe and the international banks, the gas firms were injecting money and influence into Mesa's circle of advisors. With echoes of the days of Standard, the gas companies were channeling money to those charged with negotiating the terms of the new law and contracts with the companies themselves. One of these key players, Francisco Zaratti, was having his travel expenses and per diems paid by the gas companies while he was using presidential decree power to set up legal obstacles to a radical nationalization process. There had long been a revolving door between working for the Bolivian state and working for private oil and gas companies, with close kinship ties and exchange of personnel between ministries and companies like Shell, Petrobras, Maxus, and Chaco. This created a fossil network that blurred the lines of interest between the state and the fossil fuel industry, much like we have long had in the United States (Solíz Rada 2001). Mesa's government was consulting with the World Bank to hire experts who could, as in the past, help Bolivia write the new hydrocarbons law. Private industry representatives and right-wing party leaders, including Mario Cossío and Hormando Vaca Diéz, were also sharing information with the US Embassy. All were pushing for a hydrocarbons law that would favor the interests of private investors and weaken the push for nationalization. As Ambassador David Greenlee wrote at the end of one cable, "The Embassy will continue to emphasize the sanctity of contracts and the importance of a business-friendly (or at least business-acceptable) law for Bolivia's economic future" (Embassy La Paz 2004).

In the background, throughout this period, was the possibility that fascist and rightist segments of the Bolivian military would stage a coup. Early during Mesa's time in office, the media reported on a supposed intelligence report that revealed a right-wing military plan to assassinate Mesa, to be carried out by a group called the Consejo Boliviano de Defensa y Seguridad del Estado (COBODESE, Bolivian Council of State Security and Defense) (La Razón 2004c). As the law entered final stages of approval, and the possibility of a constitutional assembly became real, the military ousted a conciliatory general, and an older fascist political instrument emerged, called Transformación Democrática Patriótica (TRADEPA, Patriotic Democratic Transformation), which had strangely troubling echoes of RADEPA, the fascist secret military society born out of the Chaco War. This organization demanded a political role for the military in any future constitutional convention (Lemoine 2006;

Agüero and Fuentes 2009). On the left, some labor union leaders argued that Bolivia needed a Chávez, like Venezuela, and they hoped for a nationalist military intervention that would oust Mesa and nationalize the gas. These cadres of younger officers, with echoes of the days of Torres, leaned toward restoring an older form of pact between the social movements and the military.

Talk of coups and military intervention intensified given that the US was extending its own military reach and US government actors were agitating further. The US Air Force sent a medical mission to El Alto in early January 2004, just after the Gas War. After the referendum, the US Southern Command gave a new crowd control vehicle, a Neptune, to the police force in El Alto. The Neptune is equipped with water cannons, a clear signal that the US was offering support for the repression of future protests. Meanwhile, the United States Agency for International Development (USAID) launched a new food-for-work scheme in El Alto, to deepen its networks of influence in the city. The conservative orientation of humanitarian work and crowd control was clear.[21] Roger Noriega, a hardline rightist from the Reagan era, also came to Bolivia in the wake of the referendum to meet with Mesa and US ambassador Greenlee. Along with offering US support for Mesa's hydrocarbons law and the "free market," the US was pushing the Bolivian Congress to grant immunity to US troops. Ostensibly this was to protect DEA agents from prosecution for their own role in repressing civilians. Critics saw this as preparation for US military intervention. At the time, there was a clear position in US foreign policy circles that, given high oil and gas prices, Latin American fossil fuel infrastructures should be oriented toward exporting to the United States, for the sake of "energy security." The right-wing leaders of Santa Cruz staged massive mobilizations with increasingly virulent anti-Indigenous rhetoric. The racist and reactionary elite of Santa Cruz were bolstered by the United States with a visit by a top US diplomat to Santa Cruz.[22]

Back in the United States, these conflicts revealed the limits of our own fossil-fueled two-party system. The fossil networks linked Democrats and Republicans—bankers, fossil fuel businessmen, lawyers, lobbyists, and even an ex-ambassador to Bolivia, Manuel Rocha. They were tied to both the Bush and Clinton administrations and united in their effort to protect Sánchez de Lozada from prosecution, prevent the election of Evo Morales, and push, at all costs, for the export of Bolivian gas to the United States via Chile. Even *before* Morales was elected, Thomas McLarty and Richard Klein, former aides to Bill Clinton and associates of Henry Kissinger (via the Kissinger McLarty law firm), wrote an editorial that complained of the "out of control nationalism" in Bolivia and pushed for more US involvement in Venezuela, Mexico, and Brazil, all aimed at undermining national oil companies and opening the doors to US fossil fuel capital and firms (McLarty and Klein 2004). The fossil capital bloc on the side of empire was wide and deep.

The Fourth Insurrection

By May 2005, the movements were again on the highways and in the streets, demanding nationalization. Roberto Fernández Terán (2009, 79) called this the fourth insurrection (after the Water War [2001], Black September [2002], and the Gas War [2003]). One lighter-skinned, middle-class acquaintance of mine, once sympathetic to Indigenous organizations, was expressing frustration at the ongoing blockades. "Maybe the Santa Cruz project is a coherent response," said this former state functionary, referring to the demands for autonomy for the eastern region of Santa Cruz. "All the blockades are financed by Hugo Chávez and the drug traffickers," complained another wealthy landowner in the eastern region. Anti-Morales discourse went hand in hand with anti-Indigenous racism. The landowner went on to say that "these Aymara are irrational, they want to create *ayllus* everywhere. It's absurd." The same white cattleman ended up telling me that someone should have assassinated Morales in the Chapare long ago. "It's too late now," he added. "You would rile up six million Indians if you did it now." I heard much overt racist talk about killing Indians. At an outdoor supply store in Santa Cruz, where I stopped in to buy a duffle bag, the clerk answered my question on gun sales by saying, "Yes, we're selling a lot, *muchos, muchos*." A bookstore owner in Santa Cruz remembered the days when men from the civic committee were coming around telling them to get weapons prepared (for the coming conflict with the indios of Evo Morales). "I don't have a weapon," the older woman recalled telling the man. "Then sharpen a broomstick, *señora*," he reportedly told her, "sharpen a broomstick."

Friends of a more critical bent were voicing concerns of many in the progressive sectors. It was rumored, one said, that the big landowners of the East who had roots in Yugoslavia were bringing in ex-military men as paramilitary recruits. "My [right-wing] friends from high school," one leftist cochabambino told me, "are ready for violence. They say, 'a los indios hay que meterlos bala' [you've got to put a bullet in these Indians]." Alfredo Rada, then an employee of the NGO Centro de Estudios Jurídicos e Investigación Social (CEJIS, Center for Legal Studies and Social Research) and until the 2019 coup a high-level functionary of the MAS government, responded to my question about rising violence from right-wing gangs in eastern Bolivia this way: "It's not yet paramilitary," he said, "since it's not coming from the state. But it is private violence. We are not to the point of Colombia, where the [paramilitaries] have unified into a coherent force. Nor, do we yet have in Bolivia any form of revolutionary violence. The strategy of the movements is to pursue [their struggle] through legal means."

As I discuss further in the following two chapters, by invoking the law, even while putting people into the path of this "private violence," the social movements pursued a nonviolent, sacrificial strategy to galvanize their struggle in support of the MAS. Such was also the outcome of the Gas War. In fact, in October 2004, as tensions rose over the new gas law, twenty-nine bodies of the victims of October 2003 were exhumed and moved to a mausoleum, and they were deemed "Heroes of National Dignity." It was a bit of the Chaco War in miniature, since their heroism and sacrifice was tied once again to the defense of fossil fuels. Marches and blockades again filled the streets and highways.

The MAS and the movements demanded revision of contracts, absolute state ownership of hydrocarbons, the state recovery of the privatized firms (formerly YPFB), and state control over all facets of transport, storage, and commercialization. Detractors pointed to the fact that existing foreign gas infrastructures would require some $3 billion to expropriate from an array of large firms such as BP, BG, Total, Exxon, and Repsol. It was much more complicated than the nationalizations of Standard Oil (in 1937) and Gulf Oil (in 1969). The neoliberal turn had created a sociotechnical and legal apparatus that made change immensely difficult. This was lock-in at work. On May 5, 2005, both houses of Congress passed a hybrid law that watered down the demands of the MAS and the movements. President Mesa refused to sign it because it allowed for the revision of existing contracts, which went against an agreement signed with the IMF. But nor did he veto it. The law went back to congress for de facto approval, which took another six days. Carlos Mesa's expiration date came when he resigned on June 6, paving the way for an interim president and new elections.

While the country was largely locked in to export the gas somehow and somewhere, the hegemonic struggle over the conditions through which that would happen was waged in the streets and in the congress, combining to tip the scale of power to the side of popular nationalism. On December 18, 2005, the country again went to the polls and Evo Morales won the presidency with 54 percent of the vote. He was sworn into office on January 22, 2006, for a five-year term. Throngs of people cheered in the streets. It was historically unprecedented in Latin America. Not only was he Indigenous; but he had a truly popular mandate that appeared to destroy the system of pacted democracy controlled by the elite parties. Morales's party, the MAS, also dominated Congress. In March, Congress passed legislation to convoke and schedule a Constitutional Assembly. Morales used a supreme decree (*decreto supremo*) to increase taxes and royalties and push for YPFB to regain control of the privatized firms. In May, he announced the nationalization decree named after the "Heroes of the Chaco" (Gobierno de Bolivia 2006 [DS 28701]). In the cities, and out in the backwoods corners of the country, in houses built of mud and thatch, with diesel oil lamps or candles flickering in the night, and the radio playing the news, many more also cheered for Morales. And for the gas.

5 bulls and beauty queens

THE RESURGENCE OF POPULAR NATIONALISM AND INDIGENOUS MOVEMENTS reflected in the election—and the actual physical body—of Evo Morales constituted an existential challenge to the dominant territorial, institutional, and discursive order of the state. The newly emboldened government of Morales appeared to be determined to use gas royalties, rents, and taxes for an ambitious program of social, if not socialist, redistribution. Yet in the Bolivian east and southeast, where most of the gas reserves were, elites conjured up an array of strategies to claim regional ownership of gas and to undermine the government of the MAS, led by this "indio." Much like racists in the United States, who transformed their animus for Barack Obama into antigovernment rhetoric, whitish elites in Bolivia pointed to Evo Morales to conjure up racist fears that Andean Bolivians and other Indigenous peoples would now seek revenge for centuries of colonialism. In Tarija and Santa Cruz, conservative elites began to retreat from the centralized state from which they had reaped great reward for many decades. The reactionary turn was strongest in Santa Cruz, where so-called civic elites wanted more gas rents and police power and opposed land reform, among other issues. They encapsulated their regionalism in a demand for autonomy (*autonomía*).

In progressive political discourse, autonomy refers to individual or collective autonomy from oppressive entities—capitalism, patriarchy, racism, political parties, or the state. Indigenous movements in Bolivia had begun to speak of autonomy as a demand for territorial self-determination. Although the elite appropriation of autonomy now mobilized the word's affective and liberatory urge, it was not a progressive political project. It was a demand for something closer to state-like power at the regional scale. The emphasis was on the autonomy *of* and *for* regional capitalist interests, not freedom from them. Its internal cultural content was saturated with racist and, in some cases, fascist meanings that further distanced it from anything remotely progressive.

Focusing on the period of instability between the ouster of Gonzalo Sánchez de Lozada in 2003 and the election of Evo Morales in 2005, this chapter examines the role of public spectacle in the constitution of autonomy claims in the eastern Bolivian city of Santa Cruz. The spatialization of political sentiment and claims to rights emerged out of a longer history of regionalism and fossil fuels in eastern Bolivia. During the battles over Gulf Oil, regionalism intensified over the demand for the royalty of 11 percent. In the age of gas, regionalism, refigured as "autonomy," was a renewed tactic to counter the popular push for the nationalization of gas. Autonomists conjured up the specter of a racial threat emanating from the Andean state center: the MAS (and Morales) at the national level; and those deemed to represent them locally—Andean migrants in the city-region, MAS political supporters, and lowland Indigenous organizations. Autonomists were responding to the political-economic crisis faced by elites, a crisis rooted in the structure of the regional economy and, with the rise of new actors, the MAS and the social movements. Theirs was a crisis of racial privilege under threat, one familiar in decadent colonial and commodity-dependent economies (Stoler 1989; Apter 2005). Facing the erosion of traditional forms of political control, regional elites used spectacle to conjure up displays of power and shore up gendered, racial, social, and spatial boundaries that were unraveling. These spectacles had a festive and a violent face, illustrating the regional schisms that were intensified during the age of gas.

Carnivals of Autonomy

In January 2005, Carnival in Santa Cruz heated up amid cruceño protests demanding autonomy. These were led by the Comité Cívico (Civic Committee) or Comité Pro-Santa Cruz (Pro–Santa Cruz Civic Committee), a body of business and professional organizations. An increase in the price of government-subsidized diesel sparked the protests, allowing the Civic Committee to speak of regional interests that united the elites (agro-industry depends on diesel subsidies) and the public (whose transport costs would rise). Yet diesel prices were a convenient pretext that set into motion a plan to display regional strength and assure that a referendum on departmental autonomy preceded the election of a national constitutional assembly. The Civic Committee staged a series of spectacles—hunger strikes, work stoppages, the naming of a "pre-autonomous" council, and the physical occupation of state institutions. The violent occupations were carried out by the Unión Juvenil Cruceñista (UJC, Cruceño Youth Union), a junior men's age-grade organization and the strong arm of the Civic Committee. The events escalated over ten days, eventually forcing the resignation of the moderate departmental governor, an appointee of President Carlos Mesa. Mesa did not intervene in what was essentially a regional coup against him. (Another joke I was told in Santa Cruz during those days was that Carlos Mesa was no longer yogurt; he was a tampon. He was hanging by a thread and trying to prevent bloodshed.) The show culminated on January 28 with a massive *cabildo* (public assembly). Perhaps a hundred thousand cruceños gathered in the streets around the towering statue of Christ on Monseñor Rivero Avenue. Waving green-and-white flags of Santa Cruz, the crowds celebrated "autonomy" as a new way of imagining themselves in relation to the Bolivian nation-state.[1]

The protests and the cabildo coincided with Carnival preparations and reflected the overlap between civic regionalism, street politics, and festival. Carnival is a time of raucous exuberance, music, and dance staged in the streets by upper-class men's social clubs called *comparsas* (fraternities). Comparsas select a queen and then dance (or "jump" in local parlance) around their queen in the main procession of the carnival floats. Like Carnival elsewhere, festivities were marked by occupations of public space with heavy alcohol consumption, sexual license, and violence. Amid the autonomy moment, Carnival transgressions were now layered over with talk of a particular kind of right to control public space in resistance to the national government. Institutional and social synergies linked folkloric display with political tactics. The Asociación de Comparsas (Association of Comparsas), one of the constituent members of the Civic Committee, had declared its formal support for autonomy. Comparsas touted their loyalty to the autonomist project by hanging large banners in the city streets. The sometimes violent UJC was also represented in a folkloric dance troupe called the *kerembas*.[2] These groups, linked by kinship, friendship, and economic exchange, overlap with political parties and professional institutions, such that prominent cruceño men invariably participate in several such organizations (professional organizations, social clubs, and comparsas). The leaders of the Carnival association that year were large landowners engaged in ongoing struggles against rural peasants. While not unique to Bolivia or Santa Cruz, the point I want to make was that there was a tightly interwoven network of upper-class interests that expressed itself in political, economic, and, here, spectacular cultural forms. With the perceived threat of a government led by Evo Morales and the MAS, these elites mobilized public spectacle to cultivate wider popular support for their own political project.

With tensions heightened over the occupation of public buildings, media calls for regional pride, and civic leaders on hunger strike, the Huasos comparsa led the last of three precarnival, or *preca*, parades that year. Their queen had been elected the queen of all Carnival, and it was their antics that were attracting attention. As reported by *El Deber*, "When they got to Monseñor Rivero Avenue, the Huasos started demanding autonomy [and] they had the bull's balls [*cojones del toro*] and the pants to do it" (Barba 2005). The bull's testicles, or semblances thereof, hung from green-and-white placards that proclaimed "Autonomía!" With this bovine claim to virility in tow, the young men jumped and shouted: "Autonomy! Autonomy!" (The word's five syllables in Spanish create quite a chant. Imagine hearing deep-throated shouts of AU-TON-O-MÍA! repeated over and over.) As the men danced around their queen, the parade traced a route from the central plaza, the heart of the city, to the Christ statue on tony Monseñor Rivero Avenue. This set the festive and political tone for the huge cabildo staged there a few days later.

After the cabildo, the fraternities danced again on the day of Carnival. The parade moved from the periphery toward the center, traversing more popular barrios of the southern part of the city. Even though the fraternities were represented by distinctly urban and lighter-skinned cruceños, the floats displayed rural and Indigenous claims to tradition, with faux Indigenous warriors and maidens, faux peasant farmers, and faux natural exuberance. The Huasos fraternity, escorting the queen, was dressed in the white pants and straw hats of the prototypical cruceño peasant. These motifs blended with icons of power like Egyptian pharaohs and Greek gods. Fraternities danced around the floats as the queen of each group waved to the crowd from on high. At the fore were the Huasos and their uber-queen, the Queen of Carnival. The reporter imagined the affective experience of the crowd as she passed: "The sovereign gave the public all of her splendor, dancing and blowing kisses without pause. Undoubtedly, Maricruz Ribera is the Queen of Autonomy. . . . The public clamored for the sovereign; especially the children who asked for her attention. The beautiful blonde sent thousands of kisses to those present. . . . Entire families stood on their chairs to show their affection shouting 'Maricruz, my love!' 'Long live the Queen of Autonomy!' 'Strength Maricruz!' " (*El Deber* 2005c). Protected by her "vassals," the "beautiful blonde" was imagined as an object of public desire, the symbol of Santa Cruz and the Queen of Autonomy. Cruceño men who danced around her were said to have exerted the "force of the bull" (*la fuerza del toro*) to protect the queen and demand "autonomy" (Barba 2005). Between the beauty queen and the bull's balls, Carnival in Santa Cruz echoed the elite imaginary behind the urban-centered regionalist putsch. Its terms were not complex. This was a means of making claims on both city and region and privileging certain kind of bodies, beautiful white(ish) women and manly white(ish) criollo men who were suited for its defense.

A Regional Landscape

Although it arose as a frontier town and is often neglected in Andean-centric writing on Bolivia, the city of Santa Cruz always played a central role in national dynamics. Relatively rich compared to the Andes, Santa Cruz leads the country in gross domestic product (GDP), exports, and living standards. This wealth is spatially and socially concentrated among urban middle and upper classes of the city and its immediate environs. Eighty-seven percent of the department's production is concentrated around the city and its agro-industrial periphery, which represent only 14 percent of the department's territory. Amid Miami-style opulence in some neighborhoods, poverty rates in the early years of the twenty-first century reached 50 percent in the city and 80–90 percent in some rural provinces (PNUD 2004, 24). Cruceño boosters speak of this wealth as a sign of the region's economic independence and *pujanza* (entrepreneurial spirit). Yet growth has relied on the state. Starting in the 1950s, with the US-funded Bohan Plan, state investment (via debt to the US banks) led to infrastructural expansion, credit, and a large-scale boom in land grabbing and speculation (Gill 1987). Oil and gas royalties and cocaine dollars cycled in and out of the mix through the 1970s. As a result, migration to Santa Cruz increased from the poorer Andean regions as well as from rural hinterlands. By the early twenty-first century, more than 25 percent of the department's two million people were of Andean origin (PNUD 2004). Reactions to this influx of kollas, as Andean Bolivians are known, included the intensification of racist and regionalist sentiment (Stearman 1985). A popular joke ran that the Christ statue on Monseñor Rivero Avenue, facing north to the Andes with arms raised, meant "Stop! No more kollas!"

Against this perceived kolla threat, cruceños assiduously cultivated their own icons of identity, which crystallized around the reconfiguration of the word *camba*. The word *camba* in much of southeastern Bolivia was once a derogatory term used for Indigenous peasants. In the 1930s, regionalists preferred a more explicitly white supremacist identity as cruceño, to distinguish themselves from both the Andean kolla and the lowland camba peasant. Mid-century demographic changes, including the expansion of what might be called a mestizo middle class, began to undermine this sense of racial purity. In the Andes, the whitish classes (criollos) eventually responded by acquiescing to expressions of mestizaje and widening the definition of *kolla* while maintaining a racist orientation toward rural indios and urban Indigenous peoples, called *cholos*. In Santa Cruz, the whitish elites similarly rehabilitated the word *camba* in the 1950s, allowing for an embrace, at arm's distance, of some mestizaje (Prudén 2003; Lowrey 2006). As with most hegemonic meanings of mestizaje, camba still contains a white supremacist logic. In local terms, whatever Indigenous "blood" one might have "mixed" in, it is subordinate to the "whiter blood" derived from European heritage. The reclaiming of the camba label also involved culturally appropriating peasant and Indigenous symbols, a practice assiduously cultivated by urbanites of Santa Cruz. By the age of gas, camba alternated with the older purist term cruceño. Both were made synonymous with "autonomist" (*autonomista*), that is, someone loyal to the elite-backed autonomy agenda. This set up a binary set of political positions for those deemed authentic and local (the cruceño-camba) as opposed to those deemed representative of the Andean kolla invader. If you were a real cruceño or camba, you were an autonomist. Even in Carnival, cruceños shout, "If you don't jump [i.e., dance], you're a kolla!" If one was not cruceño or camba, and thus autonomist, then they were probably an indio, a kolla, or a MASista, and you did not belong, or at least you had no rights to claim rights in this place.

Autonomists celebrated the cruceño-camba identity through the exaggerated use of markers of the regional Spanish dialect (like using local colloquialisms and dropping the final -s) and intensified attention on the consumption of regional foods, music, dance, and folkloric costumes. In editorials and political speeches, autonomists celebrated the aesthetic order of the colonial city. Autonomists expounded on the importance of symbols like the Christ statue and the plaza in the city center. These symbols, such as the depart-

FIGURE 5.1 Santa Cruz's coat of arms. Symbols are of Christianity, colonialism, and purity.

ment's coat of arms, supposedly created by the Spanish crown in 1638 but only converted into an official department symbol in 1985, invoke nobility and conquest with a cross potent (Christianity), the lion and the castle (the patriarchal monarchy), and the crown (royal hierarchy) (figure 5.1). The colors green and white from the departmental flag were ubiquitous in Santa Cruz, gracing taxis and buses, flooding civic assemblies, and marking logos for cruceño businesses. As cruceños learn in school, green evokes natural abundance and the riches of the frontier region. White symbolizes purity of lineage (*la pureza del linaje*) and nobility (*hidalguía*), a transparent invocation of racial distinction inherited from Spanish colonialism.[3] These symbols are encapsulated in representations of ideal cruceño-camba bodies, the virile men and beautiful women, all implicitly "white" in relation to Andean Bolivians and local Indigenous peoples.

Against the rise of Evo Morales and the resurgence of Indigenous peoples claiming rights to territory and autonomy, elite cruceño-cambas increasingly spoke of themselves as mestizos who shared the heritage of lowland Indigenous peoples of Santa Cruz. This included Guarani, Besiro (colloquially, Chiquitano), or Guarayu but never the destitute Ayoreo, who are treated with revulsion by most cruceños. Cruceño-cambas view Indigenous peoples of the east as "our ethnics" (*nuestras étnias*). Here the history of indigeneity is subsumed into the cruceño story of their own mestizaje, a racial mix seen as culturally and biologically superior to Andean mestizaje. Cruceño regionalists argue that Andeans, whether white or not, are, by virtue of their contact with the Aymara and Quechua, trapped in a culturally conservative irrational collectivism. They say this is derived from pre-Colombian and Spanish religious and bureaucratic centralism and the geographic and racial constraints tied to the Andes mountains themselves.[4] In contrast, the idealized cruceño-camba emerges from a fusion of the defense of agrarian patrimony; control over natural and cultural property, including traditions, land, peasants, Indians, and, of course, oil and gas rents; as well as the acquisitive power and political stance of the cosmopolitan individual consumer and capitalist. Agrarian wealth sustains the elite class, but public identity displays cast them as mestizo subalterns resisting the Andean-dominated state.

Cruceño-camba men claim to embody a modernizing pioneer of Spanish origins, a tad mestizo and imbued with the masculinity of Indigenous warriors. The male camba identity is performed by men wearing straw hats, sandals, white pants, and shirts, and carrying a slingshot, a machete, and a water gourd. Sometimes cambas dress as imagined Indigenous warriors with lots of feathers, loincloths, masks, and spears, and are imagined resisting not the white settler but the invading Andean hordes. The male cruceño-camba thus claims the warrior blood of the Indian or the hardiness of the peasant to defend his patrimony against usurpers.

On display, the female camba wears a white dress (as a peasant) or a stylized *tipoi*, a dress said to be typical of Indigenous women. She is sometimes called *kuñatai* (the Guarani word for young woman), to appropriate the supposed authenticity and the allure of the Indigenous maiden but not her physical appearance.[5] Increasingly, beauty queens and carnival queens have intensified the use of faux-Indigenous symbols, including motifs from weavings and also feathers, which few if any native peoples of eastern Bolivia actually wear. The queen's float in 2005 represented a giant Guarani warrior wearing Santa Cruz's cross potent on a necklace. In 2006 the autonomy-themed Carnival appropriated Guarani symbols en masse, declaring carnival the search for the "land without evil," a trope from Guarani history.[6] Yet, even when dressed as Indians or peasants, cruceño-cambas tend to emphasize their urban, cosmopolitan whiteness as an expression of their participation in middle-upper-class consumer society.[7] Commonly heard phrases like *camba neto* (pure camba) and *cruceño de verdad* (true cruceño) evoke whiteness, social power, and racial purity.

This cruceño-camba identity is projected outward from the city and seeks to establish itself as territorially congruent with the Department of Santa Cruz in alliance with bordering departments of eastern Bolivia (see map 5.1.). Yet the city is surrounded by diverse, conflicted regions rather than orderly satellites. The Valles Cruceños (Cruceño Valleys) to the west, three provinces tied to the provincial city of Vallegrande, comprise an area marked by rural poverty. The Norte Integrado (Integrated North) is largely dominated by Andean settlements organized as unions, a bastion of the MAS. The Chiquitanía, named after the Chiquitano (i.e., Besiro) people and also home to Guarayu and Ayoreo, is shaped by territorial conflicts between smallholder and Indigenous claims and forestry and cattle interests, an expanding soy frontier, mineral extraction, and the gas and rail corridor to Brazil. The Chaco of Cordillera Province to the south, as I have described earlier, is the traditional territory of the Guarani, today the stage for land tensions, hydrocarbon conflicts, and its own "chaqueño" regionalist project.

At the hub of this regional polity lies the Plaza 24th of September in the center of Santa Cruz. The plaza is a familiar arrangement of religious and secular power distributed around a main square (cathedral, municipality, social club, police, and prefecture). Surrounding the plaza is the *casco viejo* (old center). Beyond the old center, the city is surrounded by a series of ring boulevards called *anillos* (rings). Traditional cruceño power is associated with the casco viejo. Prominent traditional families are referred to as *cambas del primer anillo* (first-ring cambas). Much like a frontier fort, as described by Allyn Maclean Stearman (1985, 42–45), this center has historically been seen as needing "protection" from outsiders. Andean (and poor camba) migrants were segregated into areas beyond the outer rings. With urban growth, wealthy and first-ring cambas began to move to residential areas to the north, like Equipetrol, near

MAP 5.1 Santa Cruz and its surrounding regions. Map by Patty Heyda.

the Christ statue, with the wealthiest moving to the gated exurb called Urubó. Spaces like Equipetrol, which originated as an oil workers' neighborhood, and streetscapes such as Monseñor Rivero, dotted with coffee shops, evoke wealth and elite leisure even though they are clogged with cars and noxious diesel exhaust. Marginal satellite cities on the southern and western sides of Santa Cruz are marked as poor and dangerous spaces. As in the pre-Carnival parades and various instances of civic and violent spectacle, the plaza is spoken of as a site to be defended by elite regionalists as the aesthetic and sociopolitical template for order in the region.

Centered on the ideal of power and order emanating from the plaza, Santa Cruz projects itself as a model to be emulated by peripheral regions in its orbit through various forms: the spatial and symbolic template (the aesthetic tranquility of the plaza and associated symbols), institutions (provincial civic committees and UJC), and rituals (beauty pageants, Carnival, Day of Tradition, and civic anniversaries). For example, Santa Cruz's federation of fraternities was charged with replicating the department's "Day of Tradition," which followed a formal ritual calendar "year after year in more than thirty-five municipalities . . . constituting a great cultural contribution to the region, since *in all these places it is performed maintaining the same format as the capital city*" (FFC n.d., emphasis added). Provinces were convoked to pay homage to the center, which incorporated subregional symbols of music and indigeneity into departmental ritual. In return, the center promised status, resources, and security for provincial elite interests.[8]

Gas, Territoriality, and Economic Dependency

By now the reader may be wondering how all of this relates to the age of gas. The question revolves around the material and territorial politics created around the location of the gas reserves. The gas lands are on the rural periphery, not only of the nation (in the Chaco) but of two departments, Tarija and Santa Cruz (see maps I.1 and I.2). Indigenous claims to territorial rights, as well as provincial and municipal claims to rents in the places where gas extraction happens, are a threat to these elites in the department centers, the cities. Efforts to weaken the idea of Indigenous autonomy and centralize the production of political identity away from provincial loyalties were central to this camba autonomist effort to monopolize a claim on gas rents, present and future. Conversely, provincial tensions and Indigenous demands can be mobilized by the national government if needed to counter this elite urban opposition. Evo Morales was able to do this when he spearheaded passage of special legislation to grant more gas rents to the Gran Chaco province (as opposed to the department center at Tarija) and help the Guarani recover lands held by reactionary landowners (allied with the Santa Cruz autonomists), as I describe in the following chapter. More generally, the cultural performances I describe here were a key mechanism (another being rent circulation itself), through which the urban-centric claim to authority over gas rents was constructed not only against internal rivals but also against the national state.

Against the nationalist cry of "the gas is ours" heard in the streets of El Alto during the Gas War, the claim to regionalist "camba" rights to territory (and gas) was a powerful counterweight. In the case of Santa Cruz, this regional-national tension has long revolved around the production of political loyalties through cultural means as well as material exchange (Whitehead 1973). In this particular moment, as in the 1970s, the stakes were defined by the battle over gas. This cultural regionalism was mobilized over and over, and would again express itself in claims of radical federalism that underlay, in part, the coup that toppled Evo in 2019.

This is not unique to Bolivia. In Nigeria (Watts 2004b; Apter 2005), Venezuela (Coronil 1997), Russia (Rogers 2015a), and throughout the Middle East (Mitchell 2001), oil and gas industries have used the production of cultural spectacle as a way of making people think and act in terms of subnational and regional space. The US is no different. Texas and its cultural hyperboles are largely tied to the production of a vehement regionalism against possible national claims on control over oil wealth (or demands to leave it in the ground). At times, as described by Douglas Rogers (2015a) and Fernando Coronil (1997), this involves cultural work aimed at transforming the meaning and value of oil itself into other things, such as blood, soil, or a deep historical linkage between regional space (and people). In other places, it is not the oil or gas but the rents, or the aspirations for rents, that are behind cultural projects that seek to craft particular identity positions in support of particular political regimes. In Nigeria, these have been both national, as with the efforts to craft a pan-African and nationalist idea of race (Apter 2005), and regional, as oil struggles have also mobilized ethnic identities of various sorts (Watts 2004b; Labban 2008). Cultural production is part of a wider toolbox—including violence and money—through which oil and gas industries, and the elites supporting them, seek to evade strong states and exert hegemonic control over regional territory, narrow claims on the circulation of rents, control transport routes, and access the fossil fuel itself.

Like all cultural politics, these dynamics had a specific structural base, a political-economic order that helps explain both their form and the material stakes and interests. The economic model underlying the urban autonomist project was dominated by large-scale agro-industry (primarily soy) and natural resource extraction (primarily gas). Both relied on continuous frontier expansion in pursuit of new lands and resources. Both channeled flows of wealth from rural peripheries to the urban center. In the early years of the twenty-first century, soy and hydrocarbons comprised 80 percent of Santa

Cruz's exports. Neither generated broad-based employment or economic diversification. By 2016 the soy-hydrocarbon export complex was about the same: soy products (46 percent), natural gas (26 percent), and crude and fuel oil (6 percent). Most of the large export players were multinational firms, making cruceño elites the junior partners of transnational capital. In 2005 nine out of the top ten businesses in Santa Cruz were soy or oil and gas related. Eight of these were foreign-owned (PNUD 1995, 2004; IBCE n.d.). Cruceño elites were thus tied to a very narrow export and national market, relying on access to state patronage or speculative unproductive landholding as insurance against cyclical downturns. This agrarian pattern and attendant dependence on transnational export sectors reinforced the autonomist's opposition to redistributive land reform and the nationalist policies for deepening government control over natural resources. The narrow-based extractive model (Gray Molina 2005) also concentrated wealth among a thin middle and upper class. This created a shared elite interest in containing political pressure from below while waging their own intra-elite competition over access and control to state patronage and oil or gas rents. This unstable economic model created the illusion of growth and wealth when commodities surged. Yet in the period between 1950 and 2000, the GDP of Santa Cruz had been flat in relation to population expansion (PNUD 2004).

The autonomist projection of regional cultural order and the illusion of economic prosperity for all cultivated a vision of unity despite a real and imagined sense of economic, political, and social instability. Autonomy talk sought to redirect the public sentiment and discourse on the crisis against the national government and against what were interpreted as the region's internal threats. With now unveiled racism, the autonomists portrayed the national government as threatening because of the rise of Evo Morales and the MAS party. Internally, this constructed threat of Morales and the MAS was represented in the threatening bodies of Andean Bolivians who had moved to the region and city from the west. They were increasingly referred to as "invaders."

Migration and *Avasallamiento*

Andean Bolivian settlement in Santa Cruz since the 1950s was both state-sponsored and spontaneous, as poor farmers sought land in the lowland tropics (Stearman 1985). Andeans established themselves as rural smallholders, urban merchants, and laborers during the boom of sugar (1960s), cotton and oil (1970s), and coca-cocaine (1980s). North of the city, Andean migrants established communities that are vibrant farming and trading municipalities. These migrant farmers organized *sindicatos de colonizadores* (settlers' unions), replicating the labor union structure of peasant-Indigenous mobilization in the Andes. Against the cruceño ideal of sociospatial, aesthetic, and racial order represented in the tranquility of the colonial plaza, these Andean unions were alternative centers of power seen as threats to cruceño hegemony. For example, in October 2003, Andean farmers marched into Santa Cruz from the north to oppose the crumbling regime of President Gonzalo Sánchez de Lozada. The regionalist reaction highlighted the elitist notion of social order and "principle[s] of authority" while conflating Andeanness with political unrest and threats to private property.

> Even if the municipalities of Buenavista [cruceño dominated] and Yapacani [largely Andean] are only separated by 20 kilometers, the differences between them are great. The first has appealed to its cultural patrimony to generate income and prefers to project itself as a calm tourist town. One needs only to observe its imposing church, the tranquility of the plaza, the covered walkways of the traditional houses and the typical foods it offers. [In contrast] in Yapacani the majority of the population and authorities are of Andean origin and their economy is principally based on commerce that extends through a large part of the town and provokes daily agitation. . . . [Civic Committee vice president] Germán Castedo [said that] Yapacani is the entryway of the west [i.e., the Andes] and at this moment [they] are the majority there. They have come to invade private property; that is why we asked the government to put an end to this. . . .

> REPORTER: Do you think the Andean is conflictive?

> CASTEDO: The people of the west [the Andes] manage their affairs with unions, and that is due to the lack of a principle of authority and the Cruceños are not accustomed to that. We are more objective. (*El Deber* 2003a)

Andean migration also reshaped urban Santa Cruz. Excluded by camba resistance and their own poverty from the city center, Andeans established migrant enclaves that have now become part of the city's fabric. Andean cruceños, many now second and third generation, also occupy multiple professions in the urban economy. Nonetheless, cruceño autonomy discourse sought to stereotype all urban kollas as migrants exclusively involved in informal commerce. Like the unions of the rural farmers, urban Andean merchants organized *gremios* (guilds) to defend their interests in the city. Gremios and their members, called *gremialistas*, and the large urban markets they occupy were all coded as kolla spaces in everyday talk in Santa Cruz. Gremios eventually came to occupy a political niche in the municipality. Yet, like the rural farming unions, gremialistas were also spoken of as a threat to the city and region.

The discourse of *avasallamiento*—spatial invasion, usurpation, subjugation—characterized talk of both the rural and urban Andean. In the city, autonomist cruceños spoke of kollas with terms like "a flood," "a hemorrhage," and the *indiada*, or "Indian horde." In one conversation with me, the brother of a prominent politician exaggerated a moment of the recent past, saying, "By then, we had five-hundred thousand more kollas on top of us." The problem of urban public hygiene and sanitation was often said to be caused by Andean migration and street merchants (Kirshner 2011). Autonomists collapsed rural and urban Andeans into a multifaceted threat—spatial, social, racial, hygienic, and aesthetic—to cruceño order, beauty, and property. In an editorial titled "Santa Cruz Is Beautiful, But . . . ," one of the more radical autonomists wrote: "These [are] kollas who do not respect our customs, who think they can do whatever they want here, who rob us, who kill us, who convert our city into a market crushing onto the sidewalks, who close the streets without our consent to celebrate festivals that are not ours, who invade our lands" (García Paz n.d.).

In the rural areas, avasallamiento was imagined as an "invasion" of cruceño territory by violent, racially distinct, peasant hordes. Given highly unequal land distribution, peasant and Indigenous movements demanded land through legal proceedings. These demands were bolstered by the 1996 land reform, which called for redistribution of unproductive, untitled, or ill-gotten lands, but the law was never robustly implemented. With the land reform stalled, in the early twenty-first century, small farmers started occupying land seen to be illegally held. (Much of the land *was* of suspect legality, handed out under de facto military regimes of Bánzer Suárez [1971–78] and García Meza [1980–82].) Against the prospect of land redistribution, the Andean migrant and the MAS became useful targets of racist demonization, viewed as a threat to cruceño resources. In one political cartoon, Andean farmers, with exaggerated aquiline noses and monstrous, enraged faces, are portrayed shouting "land, land!" (in bad Spanish) as they hack away at trees marked "forestry reserve." These animal-like characters are wearing "MAS" armbands (see Gustafson 2006).

Civic Regionalists

As described near the beginning of this chapter, the Pro–Santa Cruz Civic Committee was the primary booster of the autonomist agenda. Civic committees exist in most Bolivian cities. They are generally unelected entities, dominated by business elites with a long history of resisting control of, or demanding subsidization by, the central government (Prudén 2003). Civic committees are a parallel arena for asserting elite power, especially when whichever political party in office was deemed to be against business interests. In Santa Cruz the Civic Committee included the private chamber of commerce, the cattlemen, the agro-livestock chamber, the industrialists, the forestry chamber, the soy-producers chamber, and professional organizations (doctors, lawyers, architects). Other members included representatives of provincial civic committees, Carnival fraternities (comparsas), and social clubs. The departmental labor union and the transport workers' union were the only nonelite members. Neither union was radical. In 2004 a leader of the Isoso Guarani organization, a part of the wider Guarani People's Assembly, was invited to join the committee in a nonvoting status. The move sought to weaken Guarani unity in eastern Bolivia and demonstrate cruceño support of "our ethnics." Civic Committee officers are chosen from within the organization and invariably rotate between doctors, cattlemen, and agro-industrialists. A parallel entity for women, the Feminine Civic Committee, reflected the explicitly male character of the Civic Committee.

New generations of men were groomed for leadership in the committee through their activism in the sometimes thuggish, sometimes folkloric, Cruceño Youth Union (UJC), the strong arm of the Civic Committee. While the UJC engaged in street actions, the Feminine Civic Committee staged acts of public charity and sought to replicate itself through the creation of similar entities in the provinces. There is no structural counterpart to the UJC for young women, although participation in the beauty industry and its attendant expression in the spectacles of Carnival and beauty pageants was one passage into civic protagonism for women.

At the extreme edge of this "civic" autonomy agenda was the ostensibly pro-secession group, which called itself Nación Camba (Camba Nation)

(Lowrey 2006). The Camba Nation was a group of intellectuals led by a septuagenarian fascist, a historian, a doctor, and an architect. They were at once editorialists, former Civic Committee leaders, and right-wing political figures. In addition to their labor rewriting cruceño history in opposition to that of "Upper Peru" (i.e., Andean Bolivia), the Camba Nation's radical position of separatism allowed Civic Committee leaders to cast their calls for "autonomy" as a moderate political demand. Though it would be generous to call it a movement, the Camba Nation voiced its views in cruceño television and newspapers, a website, marches, and manifestos.

These elite social networks outlined a narrowly construed and controlled expression of "civil society" marked internally by rigid boundaries of age and gender and marked on its borders by excluding, containing, or appropriating racial, spatial, and class differences. The prototypical committee member was a middle-aged, non-Indigenous man with intellectual inclinations; a zeal for public oratory and writing; ties to landed wealth and/or a profession; experience in party politics, generally of the right; a past role in the UJC; and an association with Carnival groups and social fraternities. These actors historically wielded control through state institutions and elite-controlled party politics. Against those construed as MAS supporters, eventually called the "sociales" (for social movements), the "civics" of the committee struggled to maintain power through the deployment of mass spectacle, media control, and violence, to which I now turn.

Prosperity and Crisis, Beauty and Violence

In those days the autonomist discourse pervaded virtually every spectacle in Santa Cruz's annual ritual cycle. But it was particularly intensified in September. Surrounding September 24, the founding anniversary of the department, the month is marked by folkloric festivals, an homage to the flag, the selection of the Queen of Santa Cruz, and the yearly agro-industrial fair called Feria Exposición de Santa Cruz (EXPOCRUZ, sometimes FEXPOCRUZ, the Santa Cruz International Trade Fair). In 2005 September was also a time of political tension over upcoming elections and the prospects of a MAS victory. Peasant land seizures had accelerated in the north. Regional tensions over gas royalties and expectations pit the civics of the exemplary center against their unruly peripheries. As if this were not enough, in the midst of festivity and tension, smoke darkened the skies like a solar eclipse. Santa Cruz, the cosmopolitan aspirant, was suffering the effects of annual burning in its agrarian hinter-lands as farmers prepared for planting.

"Autonomy!" was also in the air. After the spectacular January cabildo, media chatter favored the autonomist Rubén Costas (a cattleman) for the first-ever election of departmental governor. Cars, houses, and storefronts displayed green-and-white flags. Green-and-white taxis and buses crowded the streets. Green-and-white bumper stickers proclaimed "Autonomy: Yes or Yes!" and "Santa Cruz Owes Nothing to Bolivia." Newsstands were filled with tabloids promoting autonomy. One of these was called *Cash* (the title, in English, highlighted the appeal to cosmopolitan prosperity). The cover story that month, with a picture of an imposing Brahma bull, was on the "Cattle Elite" at the EXPOCRUZ fair. Another magazine, named *Catarsis*—catharsis, perhaps an outlet for cruceño nervous tensions—was rife with advertising for natural gas companies. The cover that month was the bikini-clad, German-descended Miss Santa Cruz, not to be confused with the Queen of Santa Cruz or the Queen of Carnival. The lead story was titled "Santa Cruz Is Betting on a Change in Its History."

The dance festival called Elay Puej (a cruceño colloquialism) started the month with the theme *lo nuestro primero*, "what is ours [e.g., our culture] comes first." Two thousand dancers from colleges, high schools, and dance troupes paraded on city streets costumed as "our ethnics" (Indigenous peoples) and "our traditions" (rural folklore and music). Young cruceños danced as faux Guarani and Guarayo. These imagined Indians nurtured the warrior-maiden complex: men were bare-chested and body-painted. Women wore feathers and stylized two-piece *tipois*, presumably better than the real thing, which is a one-piece frock. "Our traditions" refigured rural folklore for urban space with dance genres from the department's subregions: *coplas* (Vallegrande); *chacarera* (Chaco), and *taquirari* and *chovena* (Santa Cruz). Andean dances were notably absent. Taken from their original producers, contexts, and ritual moments, these performances were spatially and temporally recontextualized as tokens of cruceño unity under the control of an urban middle-upper-class ritual calendar.[9]

Around the same time, an annual gathering of provincial civic commit-tees paid homage to the departmental flag. Expressions of loyalty to Santa Cruz as the exemplary center were rewarded with medals of cruceño merit. In 2005 distinguished hosts included the editor of *Green and White* magazine and the president of the provincial civic committees. This notable happened to be the same man who kicked and beat an Andean Indigenous woman during a

UJC attack on peasant marchers in 2003 (*El Deber* 2003b). One participant, dressed in green and white, recited a poem called "Autonomía." The expression of regional loyalty and fraternal ties was marked by the cultivation of nostalgic sentiment. The press reported that the recipient of another award wept with emotion when the ex-paramilitary, self-declared fascist, and founder of the Camba Nation, Carlos Valverde, gave him his medal (*El Deber* 2005f).

On the night of September 23, the Queen of Santa Cruz (not to be confused with the Queen of Carnival, since beauty queens are everywhere in Santa Cruz) was crowned in a ceremony in a park inside the first ring. A few days earlier, talk shows buzzed with interviews of the candidates. Men dressed as camba peasants serenaded the candidates with camba music and offerings of camba food. Papers described the women's measurements, with height of prime importance, followed by hair color, skin tone, and bodily characteristics. The crowning spectacle, called the "serenade," represented the masculine courting of, and homage to, the beautiful city-region embodied in its "sovereign" queen. The musical and allegorical extravaganza again marshaled forth "traditions" and "ethnics." Invoking the language of empire, nobility, and regional sovereignty, the queen was presented as Gabriela I and adorned with a sash reading "Queen of Santa Cruz and Ambassador of Autonomy." She received kisses and the crown from the mayor and Civic Committee leaders.

Elite-controlled newspaper and television also embraced the Month of Cruceñidad. On September 24, *El Deber* ran a special anniversary insert. The headlines reinforced the illusion of prosperity amid the uncertainty of crisis ("The Economic Bonanza Has Not Stopped the Growth of Poverty" and "A Bet on the Future"). These merged with calls for order and continuity in the extractive model ("Santa Cruz Wants Autonomy, Work, and Security" and "The Future Is in Agriculture, Forests, and Oil") (*El Deber* 2005a). Green-and-white borders framed pictures, stories, and ads analyzing and celebrating Santa Cruz (figure 5.2). Opinion polls represented the camba public as pie charts in the shape of the Camba straw hat (2.3 percent support separatism), bar graphs drawn as the outstretched arms of Christ (56 percent support autonomy), and photos of the January cabildo (*El Deber* 2005a). The tenor of reportage recognized the threat of poverty but called for autonomy from bureaucratic centralism as the solution.

The authorities and the queen gathered again on the twenty-fourth for the civic parade through the 24th of September Plaza. There were representatives of the municipality, the prefecture, the electricity and phone cooperatives (both elite-dominated utilities long controlled by the secret societies, or

FIGURE 5.2 Marketing autonomy, 2005. Fidalga is one of Santa Cruz's supermarket chains. Christ as a camba (in peasant pants) liberates himself for autonomy against the backdrop of a green-and-white flag. The ad reads: "Rise up, Cruceños. Let us make history!" Below the logo it says, "True Cruceños!" *El Deber* (Santa Cruz), September 24, 2005.

logias), the neighborhood watch committees, the department of sanitation, the municipal botanic gardens, the traffic light division, and so forth. To the music of a military band, marchers passed the reviewing stand, where they were applauded by the "civic" and political authorities, the queen, and the Bolivian president. By that time Carlos Mesa had resigned. Eduardo Rodríguez Veltzé, the third president in two years of instability, made the trip from La Paz.

Civic parades usually pay visual tribute to the state, replicating its component parts and hierarchies through an aesthetic of order and allegiance (marching lines, national flags, and martial music). Yet the regionalist fervor added a subversive (and fascistic) twist. Interspersed among the green-and-white flags of Santa Cruz were green-and-black flags of the Camba Nation. These were symbols of the secessionist stance sprinkled amid marchers of various institutions. The effect was to demonstrate the infiltration of the separatist ideology into official spaces like the municipality. The Camba Nation also marched as its own block. Members passed the reviewing stand shouting "*Au-to-no-mía! Au-to-no-mía!*" as the master of ceremonies read over a loudspeaker: "The Camba Nation affirms that true autonomy would be that of a free state associated with Bolivia!" One marcher held up a giant 100 cruceño bill (there is no such thing), as a demand for sovereign currency. A banner quoted a passage of the Charter of Human Rights of the United Nations: "All Peoples Have the Right to Self-Determination." Another appropriated an Indigenous slogan: "Territory, Identity, and Power: Bases of Camba Nationalism." Most marching in this block were heavy-set, middle-aged, light-skinned cruceños with solemn faces. A few in the crowd also held Camba Nation flags. I heard a smattering of applause. Most viewers watched silently with arms crossed. Against this expression of cruceño specificity, the viewing public was a mosaic of Bolivian faces in all hues that reflected the reality of the population. At the rear, a black banner with white letters proclaimed: "The Camba Nation Is Unstoppable Because God Is a Cruceño" followed by a message to outsiders: "The Land Is Ours, Invaders Get Out!"

At the Fair

As the festivities unfolded, the EXPOCRUZ fair provided a spectacular ten-day backdrop. Since the 1970s, EXPOCRUZ has put cruceño economic power on display, drawing exhibitors from twenty countries and almost half a million visitors from Bolivia and beyond.[10] Spread out over a forty-block space of pavilions, stands, booths, restaurants, rides, and livestock barns, the fair is a middle- and upper-class social event as well as a site for deal-making, networking, and advertising. As one female colleague described the fair to me: "It's a microcosm of Santa Cruz: cattle, business, and women." The entry fee then (Bs 30, or US$3.70, then about two days' pay at minimum wage) acted as a filter against the urban poor.

The fair was also a regionalist platform. The cruceño industrialist Gabriel Dabdoub (a descendant of Lebanese immigrants) was the fair's director. He set the tone in his opening address by echoing the media celebration of cruceño economic prowess and "unstoppable" unity in the face of crisis and resistance to the national government. He invited those present to "gaze upon modernity with the eyes of peasants," and challenged opponents who dared to "blockade" Santa Cruz: "We [the fair's industrialist and agro-industry organizers] have allied with the civil society of the provinces and the barrios, and together with valiant congressmen, workers, neighbors, peasants, intellectuals, and original [Indigenous] peoples, led by the Civic Committee, we have planted in Bolivia the Mojón de la Autonomía, the landmark of autonomy."[11]

With the neon signs, banners, music, cars, tractors, motorcycles, food, and carnival rides, one could indeed "gaze upon modernity" with the eyes of "peasants" with aspirations to consume in the global market. On the nights I went to the fair, people could try out what it felt like to sit in a first-class seat at the Aerosur airlines booth. Others sampled cosmetics and hair gels produced locally and internationally. I stopped in to gaze at photos touting corporate responsibility at the pavilion of Petrobras, the Brazilian transnational that dominates Bolivia's gas industry. The telephone, cable, and electricity cooperatives dominated by cruceño elites interpellated passersby with bright lights: "You are Santa Cruz!" Over at the livestock corrals, one could see the latest advances of artificial insemination and genetic selection. Women in high heels and men in suits admired bulls to be sold at auction for thousands of dollars. One banner over a mellow bull touted its owners as dealing in the "best genetics for the development of the country." Over at the India pavilion, a new player in Bolivian natural resources, the stand was packed with women buying colorful clothes and scarves. The fashion craze that spring was Indian (the country, not "our ethnics") motifs. Down the way, a person dressed as a US$100 bill handed out flyers at the stand of the Banco Ganadero (Cattlemen's Bank).

I stopped in at the Civic Committee booth, where one could pick up an "Autonomy" bracelet. On the back wall of the booth, a video monitor replayed nonstop scenes showing masses of cheering people from the January cabildo. The booth offered T-shirts that read *Autonomía Sí o Sí* and coffee cups with the cross potent and the coat of arms, reading "Departmental Autonomy Now!" Pine-scented car air fresheners were also available. They were, of course, green and white, and shaped in the outline of the Santa Cruz department. They read "Autonomy Now!" Next to the booth, a huge wooden post was erected. This was one of the *mojones* (landmarks, or boundary markers) of autonomy, referenced in Dabdoub's speech.

Similar mojones were used to mark land boundaries since the colonial era. Autonomists put up mojones like this around the city and in contested spaces like the public university, where regionalists saw a hotbed of traitors among the sociologists, leftists, and nationalists sympathetic to the MAS (see figure 5.3). The UJC and Civic Committees also put up mojones in the provinces (*El Nuevo Día* 2005). Here in the context of the city amid the fervor of the civic autonomy project, these mojones stood in ideological opposition to the MAS and the social movements. To celebrate these phallocentric and colonial mojones was to express loyalty to the elite project. The mojón erected in the center of Camiri was later burned to ashes by MAS supporters.

At each of the business stands, *azafatas* (hostesses) handed passersby brochures for whatever was being touted—wines, textiles, glasses, gas, electricity, perfume, tourist resorts, tractors, cattle, designer clothing. Amateur models competed for these positions as azafatas to break into the beauty industry. Con-

FIGURE 5.3 A mojón of autonomy, in the central plaza of Santa Cruz, 2005. Photo by the author.

versely, the beauty industry supplied the most coveted and expensive professional models to the larger businesses. This was accompanied by much media commentary. Businesses competed for established models, especially those of an agency group called the Magníficas (Magnificents). As with the competition for queen of Santa Cruz, and an endless annual cycle of pageants and queens, *El Deber* ran daily spreads on the azafatas detailing their measurements, their agencies, the products promoted, and their aspirations. Logically, in the cruceño way, the fair culminated with the selection of *El Deber*'s "Azafata of the Year."

Like the beauty queens, azafatas are commodified and racialized icons of cruceña beauty and productive power. They are cultivated and assessed like the latest technology or stock animal. Amid the fervor of autonomy, these stagings of feminine beauty and consumer desire articulated with the regionalist project and cruceño claims to technological, even genetic, superiority. The *Cash* magazine article on the fair's cattle elite included an interview with Luis Fernando Saavedra Bruno, one of the region's wealthiest landowners and ex-head of the Private Businessman's Association. His bulls included Mr. Gladiador, slated to fetch a high price on the *pasarelas ganaderas* (catwalks of cattle). He described his cattle by comparing them to the Magnificents, the "top" models of Santa Cruz: "An example of high [quality] genetics cannot be made, it is born. Just like a Magnificent [fashion model], good food and exercise is not enough. These animals respond to a genetic code that year after year is improved through technology to show in the fair the best exponents of their races" (Quiroga Castro 2005, 31).

Unruly Subjects

After the fair's first weekend, *El Deber* celebrated the fair's financial success with the headline "EXPOCRUZ Moved Almost US$1,000,000 in Two Days" (*El Deber* 2005b). Sales of cars, silos, and cattle were considered "encouraging." Yet an image of brutality had been placed just below the headline. Riot troops armed with tear gas were pictured kicking a man in a drainage canal, his hands raised to protect his head. Tear gas floated in the air. The image was snapped the day before, as troops were sent to disperse a Guarani blockade on the highway south of Santa Cruz. While cruceños dressed up and danced as if they were Guarani in urban ritual time and space, the real Guarani on the poor southern periphery were disrupting regional order, demanding a larger share of gas royalties for the country's Indigenous population.

A day later the juxtaposition of regionalist fantasy amid the image of "ugly" disruptions was repeated. The front-page photo was labeled "Festive Atmosphere in the City" (*El Deber* 2005e). A family held hands as they walked toward a market where a green-and-white banner read "*Viva Santa Cruz.*" The family passed two Indigenous Andean Quechua women sitting with their children in the grassy median. Hats, braids, and pollera skirts marked them as migrants, or kollas, "people of the interior." In the photo, one of the Quechua children approaches the family with hand outstretched. The message that impoverished Andean masses were threatening cruceño prosperity is driven home in the headline for a separate story: "Another Land Seizure Unsettles the North." The lede of the article positioned the landless movements as agents of violence and the elite as upholders of legality: "The *sindicalistas* [peasant unions] are armed with sticks, machetes, and shotguns. The private landowners are going to court" (*El Deber* 2005e). The talk shows that morning interspersed broadcasts from the fair with invitations to viewers to call in and respond to a survey: "Should force be used against the land invasions in the north?" Random callers were selected for prizes. Chatter on the fair and the azafatas continued as votes tallied on the screen. Eventually, votes in favor of force won out. Four days later, the prefect sent troops to remove the peasants.

Despite the attempts to portray the civics as responding to law, and the movements as acting through violence, autonomists led by the Santa Cruz Civic Committee were intensely violent themselves. In the 1990s, violence against rural farmers and Indigenous leaders was largely hidden. But armed resistance to land reform, even during the neoliberal era, brought the reality of growing paramilitary-style organizing to national visibility. From 2003 forward, now emboldened by the virulent racism of Santa Cruz's public leaders and media outlets, young men organized by the Camba Nation and the UJC staged public assaults on those seen as threats to Santa Cruz. During the conflicts of October 2003, MAS and lowland Indigenous organizations marched into Santa Cruz to join the national protest against the decaying MNR regime. The UJC and the Camba Nation attacked them in the plaza. It was then that a provincial civic leader (the same who hosted the 2005 homage to the flag described earlier) attacked an Andean woman wearing a traditional pollera dress, kicking her repeatedly when she fell to the street in the main square. The civic leader also struck a cruceña woman who intervened, reportedly shouting, "If you are with these people, you are my enemy." Both the Andean woman and her cruceña defender embodied the antithesis of the posing, silent, desirable figures of Magnificents, Queens, and Azafatas. This challenge to gendered and raced codes for the legitimate occupation of public space was met with male cruceño brutality. The vice president of the Civic Committee justified the violence, saying, "The plaza is a symbol and it had to be taken [from the peasant marchers]" (El Deber 2003b). Peasant and Indigenous marches into Santa Cruz were routinely met with physical attacks by groups of young men, armed with sticks and bats. In January 2005, a peasant march backed by the MAS was attacked at the fourth ring north of the Christ statue. The UJC sought to enforce the figurative boundary of autonomy (like the mojón landmark erected there as well). At the same time, another protest march against the autonomist project came from the MAS stronghold of El Torno to the south of the city. The marchers were attacked at the fourth ring to the south. The media described the marchers as violent "outsiders" while their attackers were called lawful "citizens" (El Deber 2005d; Ondarza 2005). In videos you can find on YouTube, the UJC members, marked by cultures of weightlifting, soccer hooliganism, or common thuggery, looked like fraternity boys with baseball hats. They can be seen chasing down and attacking clearly less well-nourished Bolivians dressed in worn-out clothes. These forms of protofascist street violence proliferated in Santa Cruz during the early years of the age of gas.

From Autonomy to Civic Coup

As fossil capital sought access to Bolivian gas amid the failure of neoliberalism to secure unfettered control, the autonomy project sought to carve out a regional space of hegemony distanced from the regulatory and electoral pressures of the national state. The cruceño autonomists reveled in locality and faux authenticity but their localism was a transnational effort supported by outside forces and interests, from multinational gas companies to Spanish and USAID advisors supporting the "autonomy" agenda.[12] Claiming civil society legality while enacting racist violence, the autonomist project was a new configuration of tactics for securing access to extractive spaces, pushing back against efforts to democratize resource distribution.

In December 2005, when Evo Morales was elected to the presidency, voters also elected departmental governors. In Santa Cruz the victory went to Rubén Costas, a cattleman and prominent leader of the autonomist movement. The elections highlighted the strength of the autonomist turn in Santa Cruz, where Costas took 48 percent of the vote. The autonomists and their backers in Beni, Pando, and Tarija departments also won governorships. This set up the anti-MAS opposition block that would call itself the *media luna* (half moon), in reference to its crescent shape on the map. The autonomy project had secured a majority consensus in urban Santa Cruz and in eastern Bolivia. Nonetheless, Evo Morales took the presidency with 54 percent of the national vote, the highest of any presidential candidate in Latin American history. Morales even took 33 percent of the vote in Santa Cruz. The MAS won a majority in two of Santa Cruz's northern provinces. Autonomy had fueled the emergence of a new political force on the right, one that came out of the ashes of the Gas War and Gonzalo Sánchez de Lozada's defeat. The most radical autonomists would intensify their efforts to topple Morales, leading to the civic coup of 2008 and more eruptions of violence, as I explore in the following chapters.

6 just a few lashes

ON THE NIGHT OF APRIL 13, 2008, IN A MISTING RAIN AMID THE CHAOS OF shouts and gunshots, armed cattlemen at a road blockade dragged a young Guarani lawyer named Ramiro Valle Mandepora into the plaza of the eastern Bolivian town of Cuevo. They pulled him from a larger contingent of Guarani who, in a caravan of trucks and buses, were trying to get through Cuevo to enter a Guarani territory called Alto Parapetí. The cattlemen, among them a well-known hacienda owner and a local schoolteacher, beat and kicked Valle Mandepora. He later wrote in the police report that he felt "like Jesus [on his way to the cross]." Once in the plaza, the men tied him to a telephone pole. Racist insults and beatings continued with belts, whips (*chicotes*), fists, and sticks. In local parlance, they were giving him *la huasca* (the whip).[1] "My body could no longer breathe for the beating received, and I was on the point of dying; I was only thinking of death," he wrote. Pictures and video of his body, bare back exposed to show the signs of the lash, circulated on the internet in the days afterward.

Crowd violence has targeted alleged criminals in the Andes and elsewhere across Bolivia, events that have attracted both sensationalist and academic attention. On this rainy night, though, Valle Mandepora was no criminal. The whipping was a colonial spectacle of punitive control. Outside wider public view, such whippings of Guarani peons persisted well into the contemporary era. Bolivian criollo or white ranchers have long used the whip as a means of disciplining indebted Guarani laborers, a reality set deep in the memory and experience of Guarani today. One of the attackers may have in fact whipped his own laborers. He was Mario Malpartida, a cockeyed, potbellied fellow, one of the dominant landowners of the region. As he reportedly beat and choked the lawyer, threatening to castrate him, Malpartida cursed the Guarani for allying themselves with the MAS party of Evo Morales. Local schoolteachers, also part of the regional power structure, joined the attack, shouting, "You want to be educated? This is how we will educate you!" This patriarchal and racist language of colonial subjugation was directed toward Guarani who were now deemed traitors to the region. As in Santa Cruz, these local elites were claiming impunity and sovereignty that defied the laws and agents of the MAS government.

The violence erupted when a contingent of around one hundred Guarani (women, men, and children) riding in a convoy of trucks and buses sought to accompany state land-reform officials to initiate a survey of the territory called Alto Parapetí. The convoy was traveling from the provincial city of Camiri to a rural community named Itakuatia (see map 6.1). The plan was to rendezvous with another Guarani contingent. Together, the Guarani and the land-reform technicians, including the vice minister of lands himself, were to initiate surveying to demarcate the area and assess the effective use of the land in preparation for the establishment of a juridically recognized collective Indigenous territory. To enter Alto Parapetí and carry out what was in fact the official labor of the state, the convoy had to pass through the little town of Cuevo. Cuevo has long been a bastion of criollo settler occupation in Guarani country, and it was there that the convoy was attacked.

Both the government, and their Guarani allies, as well as the ranchers, organized by the federation of cattlemen, had been preparing for some time. The cattlemen had taken up the strategy of Bolivian social movements, setting road blockades to shut down all road access into and out of Alto Parapetí. The Guarani and the authorities knew this but intended to bypass the blockade. There was no police escort. When the convoy reached Cuevo, the ensuing violence was brutal. A video shows the retreat, in pitch blackness, with a light drizzle; shouts and gunshots are heard as the Guarani made their way out. Many are nursing head wounds. Pictures show bruised hands and legs from sticks and stones. Video released by the Guarani and their allies in government put these bloodied and bruised bodies on display. It was an attempt to make visible the violence of the local powers, those opposed to Evo Morales, the MAS, and the promise of a new plurinational Bolivia. The Guarani were protagonists of a national transformation.

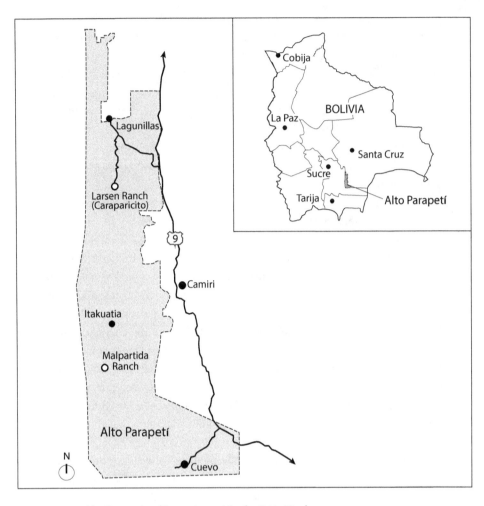

MAP 6.1 Alto Parapetí and its environs. Map by Patty Heyda.

At stake in this brief moment was a wider struggle over a piece of disputed land, the area known as Alto Parapetí. Beyond Alto Parapetí there was a broader territorial struggle over power and sovereignty in the southeastern Chaco region of Bolivia, an area of core concern for the regime of the MAS government. Almost eighty years ago, the Bolivian Chaco was the setting for the oil-fueled war that I described in chapter 1. During the age of gas, with immense gas reserves underground, the Chaco was at the center of the geopolitical conflict that pit regional interests against the nationalist project. The state sought to establish hegemony nationally and secure unfettered control over gas regions. This process entangled itself with prior histories of struggle, like that of the Guarani, who had for decades been struggling for territorial rights. In the gas-rich Chaco, state, regional, and Indigenous claims to sovereignty, resource rights, and control over reterritorializing processes all collided.

In this chapter I revisit this event to remember, as my Guarani friends do, the past and present forms of colonial violence that intensified during the age of gas. The events continue to be borne as a collective trauma, trauma that was folded in with prior memories of violence. Second, it is important to understand this event in the context of the wider struggle against the re-actionary backlash that Evo Morales and the MAS faced between 2006 and 2010. The ways in which the Guarani mobilized, and were mobilized by the state, shed light on what seemed then to be a revolutionary tactic. Yet revo-lutionary and decolonial aspirations would later dissipate as these liberatory efforts gave way to the expansion of the gas industry across Guarani lands. Echoing recent scholarship on the domestication of land reform (Garcés 2011) and the limits to decolonization (Anthias 2018), the case illustrates the subsumption of Indigenous political trajectories to those of the gas as-semblage. Finally, the case sheds light on the longer struggle over Indigenous territory and what, if anything, these territories mean in political terms dur-ing the age of gas. What we see is neither national liberation nor Guarani self-determination but the retrenchment of deeper patterns of state forma-tion that continue to invisibilize and erase Indigenous territorialities, utiliz-ing Indigenous bodies as available for maiming, when politically convenient, while the government selectively distributes rents to put salve on the wounds (Puar 2017).

The Demarcation of Alto Parapetí

Bolivia's 1996 agrarian reform law granted Indigenous peoples the right to claim collective lands called *tierras comunitarias de orígen* (TCOs, originary communitarian lands). Over the next decade, Indigenous organizations and their NGO collaborators engaged in long, conflictive processes to achieve real titles to these territories. Several Guarani TCOs exist, although the 1996 re-form, created to promote land markets, not self-determination, never offered any real rights to economic or political autonomy. Even so, the TCOs were a hard-won victory. Nonetheless, Alto Parapetí, because of the ranchers' fierce resistance, had never entered into the process. It was still known as a "captive" or "slave" territory.

With Morales's election in 2005, expectations intensified for a new land reform and consolidation of Indigenous territorial claims. In 2006 a new law to "relaunch the agrarian revolution" modified the 1996 legislation. Invoking the unfinished revolution of 1952, the 2006 law expanded provisions for acceleration of titling. The law also centralized control over key components of the process, since implementation of the earlier law was often hijacked by local landowning interests themselves. In particular, the new law identified criteria through which lands could be made subject to redistribution through expropriation (with payment) or reversion (without payment). Coupled with the new constitution, which spoke of Indigenous autonomy, the new law promised to convert TCOs into "Indigenous territorial autonomies." As is now clear in hindsight, the law was not as radical as supporters hoped, in terms of both Indigenous autonomy and constraining the growth of large-scale agro-industry. However, the new land reform was a potential instrument for transforming relations of power in the East, where de facto power had long been held by large-scale farmers, whose lands were largely illegally held or, at best, of murky legality. As with gas nationalization, the agrarian "revolution" also pursued a transformation of the temporal and spatial narrative of the nation-state. In MAS descriptions of the law, the Andes were said to have undergone a revolutionary shift dating to the 1952 Revolution, while eastern Bolivia, as evidenced in the feudalism of places like Alto Parapetí, was never fully integrated into this national and revolutionary time-space. In Alto Parapetí, a regional Guarani agenda for the reconstitution of ancestral territory was thus convergent with a new state project for reimagining and restructuring the nation.

The presence of natural gas and modern slavery in Alto Parapetí both facilitated and complicated this articulation. Gas exploration in the 1990s led to the identification of the Incahuasi gas field, a "megafield" granted in concession to the French company Total. The Incahuasi field intercepts Alto Parapetí at its northern end. Under existing laws, royalties from Incahuasi would largely benefit local municipalities and the department of Santa Cruz, given that "producing departments" have rights to the 11 percent. The assumption that many had on the ground then was that declaring the land an autonomous Indigenous territory might undercut these claims and position the Guarani as direct beneficiaries. The ongoing Guarani struggle for territorial autonomy most certainly sees local access to, and control over, gas rents as a key component of their vision (Anthias 2018; Morell i Torra 2018). Even before drilling had started, gasified expectations had intensified the stakes on all sides.

Since before the arrival of Total, the Guarani had been trying to free several communities in the area from the feudal relations of debt servitude that persisted on the haciendas. The zone was notorious. Guarani living and working as indebted peons were called "slave" (*esclava*) or "captive" (*cautiva*) communities. Both words have a long colonial history, littering Spanish colonial chronicles as well as twenty-first-century human rights documents. Captive communities had no lands of their own and were bonded by dependence, violence, and debt. Even as many other Guarani regions began to organize in the 1980s, the challenge of the slave zones was always a pending issue for leaders and their NGO allies (Gustafson 2009c). A map drawn by Guarani leaders showed how Alto Parapetí was still, by the time of Morales's election, lived and politically understood by the Guarani as a cartography of "consolidated" communities (*comunidades consolidadas*, i.e., liberated or free) and "captive families" under the control of various haciendas (see Gustafson 2010).

It is important to situate the events of April 2008 within the wider context of the most intense moments of the MAS government. Parapetí was one of the first in a chain of events that eventually culminated in the civic coup attempt carried out by the "autonomist" elites of the city of Santa Cruz in 2008. The following months saw racist attacks on Quechua farmers in Sucre and the illegal autonomy referendum in Santa Cruz (May 2008), attacks on public buildings in Santa Cruz, and the killings in Pando (September 2008, as discussed in the following chapter). The tensions on the ground were electric, with growing clashes, as I discussed in the previous chapter. My friends later told me that those who "looked indio" (as they did) were afraid to go to the city squares and plazas for fear of being attacked as a supporter of "Evo." What was brewing was a deeper effort in the east to destabilize the MAS government to the point of collapse or military intervention. In May, Hugo Chávez, then Venezuela's president, weighed in, suggesting that if the Bolivian right-wing forces and its US backers wanted "one, two, or three Vietnams," Venezuela would support Bolivia in giving it to them. He was, of course, channeling Che Guevara's famous challenge to the US made in a speech to the UN in 1966. For its part, the US government was also still fanning the flames. In June, the Bush State Department sent envoy Derek Shearer to Santa Cruz amid the rising fracas. He gave a public speech that compared Evo Morales to Zimbabwe's Robert Mugabe, which was not subtle, considering that his Santa Cruz audience had already mobilized intensely racist attacks on Morales. Shearer suggested that federalism was the answer for Bolivia.[2]

Parapetí was a flashpoint, one of many in eastern Bolivia, where local histories were transformed into powerful political instruments amid the wider clash between the MAS and the opposition. Alto Parapetí was tactically situated because of the gas fields known as Incahuasi. Yet Alto Parapetí was also shaped by the intersection of Indigenous claims, latifundist agrarian relations, contested natural resources, entrenched and violent local powers, morally potent reserves of social drama (such as Guarani struggle and human slavery), and contested national narratives (revolution, gas, and the Chaco War). In tactically engaging the east from what was then a position of relative weakness, the MAS mobilized around these flashpoints as part of its effort to consolidate hegemony and exercise sovereignty. It did so in part, and this is an important point, through *putative* control over a state apparatus, including all the *putative* force of the law and the armed state itself. Yet this was a state apparatus that was embedded in local relations that were dedicated to the opposite purpose: that is, the state, exercised by local police, judges, army officers, and cattlemen, had long existed to ensure Indigenous subjugation by endorsing the de facto sovereignty of local elites, like the landowners of Parapetí. Evo Morales was president, but the state was neither him nor his.

As such, the strategy of the MAS involved conceptualizing feudal relics like Alto Parapetí as spaces of (pre)capitalist relations that had to be dismantled to carry out a revolutionary transformation. Juan Carlos Rojas was then director of the Instituto Nacional de Reforma Agraria (INRA, National Institute of Agrarian Reform). He told me later that these were moments that were, "for us, moments of absolute political clarity. This was a natural consequence of the struggle for land, and we were absolutely convinced about what had to be done." Rojas would know. He spent his youth working alongside the Guarani pursuing rights to land in the 1990s, when I first met him. By 2005 he had risen in prominence as part of the MAS movement and took over what might have been the most difficult job in the country: overseeing land redistribution in a state founded on the logic of settler coloniality. Along with other places where landholders had been particularly vociferous in their attacks on the MAS, such as the Guarayos region dominated by Santa Cruz's Marinkovic clan, Parapetí was a place where land reform could be deployed as a liberatory instrument and a means of dismantling counterrevolutionary forces. Rojas, a humble agronomist, was at the vanguard of what to him and his comrades felt like revolution.

This was not merely political fabrication. The public, and to my mind empirical, justification for the focus on the area converged on the conjoined issues of Indigenous rights and human slavery. Laws and rights, not natural gas, shaped government and Guarani discourse on the case of Alto Parapetí. Debt slavery had long characterized labor relations in Guarani country. The oil novelist, diplomat, and oil seeker Adolfo Costa du Rels set his novel *Tierras hechizadas* ([1932] 1943) in the region. There, his white protagonist encounters the thuggishness of the ranchers in the figure of his own father and tries to pursue a modernizing change, in part signified by the potential discovery of oil. First documented for the academic world by Kevin Healy (1982), debt slavery in the canyons of Ingre, Guacaya, Huacareta, and Alto Parapetí involved a range of violent forms of labor control, from rape, to public whippings, to a range of sadistic tortures dating from the colonial era through much of the twentieth century. In the 1990s, we encountered conditions of violence and debt slavery, called *peonaje,* across the remote hinterlands of Guarani territory, especially in the hard-to-access canyons where the *karai* (white and mestizo) ranchers had long been the law of the land. After the events of 2008, I sat down with Lucrecia, a Guarani woman who was then a leader of the Asamblea del Pueblo Guarani (APG, Guarani People's Assembly). The attack was still fresh, and her account showed how colonial violence folded together from past into present. Her grandmother had been from Parapetí, a captive community, though she and her parents had managed to flee the region. Now, as a leader, she tied the histories together: "They have gotten rich off of our backs," she said, voicing a commonly heard refrain of Guarani discourse about the karai, "the landlords, the *hacendados.*" She illustrated her point with her own story, recalling her grandmother, who had been a house servant for a large landowning family. These women are locally referred to as *internas,* those who live inside the big house. Her grandmother had been brought to work in the Parapetí area from a community farther north, and she was subjected to repeated rape by the patriarch of the family: "Whenever the wife traveled to Sucre to visit her children, the *patrón* [boss] stayed with the [Guarani] interna, [her grandmother]." These relations of sexual violence live on in crude racist jokes, contemporary folkloric music, and treatment of domestic labor. Landowners and their sons raped Guarani women. Veritable slave owners with absolute power, the men often visited each other on different ranches to assault other women. Or, as I was told, the men waited for women in the forest as they went out each day to take food to the Guarani men working in the fields. "Women went out with clay pots full of hot stew on their heads, and the patrones waited for them along the trails," she recounted. Now with tears in her eyes, she said telling it always made her own grandmother weep as well. With the understatement of one who has suffered, she said, "It is a sad and difficult history [*Es una historia triste y fuerte*]."

It was against this backdrop of ongoing violence and coloniality that the Guarani and their state backers pursued a twofold struggle: first, to make visible the social relations and forms of physical and structural violence heretofore normalized, such as the whipping of Valle Mandepora; and second, to hold these up for public judgment to support the robust intervention of the state and reparations to the victims, through land redistribution. Despite the trauma of the confrontation, the mobilization of memory was a tactical political action aimed at injecting the notion of state sovereignty with new moral content, that of the liberation of subjugated peoples. At least aspirationally, as Rojas, the agronomist-turned-land reformer said, there was political clarity: we were hoping for a structural, social, and geopolitical transformation of the state itself. Or, as Lucrecia concluded, switching to Guarani, this is "so that our land can return to our hands, so that we can unify our territory again [*ipuere vaerä ñande ivi oyevi ñandepope, ñamometei vaerä ñande iviye*]."

The Guarani had long demanded government attention to these areas. Through community organizing and NGO support, they had made some progress in whittling away at debt peonage, sometimes resettling families in other communities or on land purchased by an NGO. But this was a gentle, reformist evasion of the fact that they were slaves on their ancestral lands. With the collapse of the MNR regime after the Gas War of 2003, Guarani increased their pressure on the presidency of Carlos Mesa. This led to an investigation sponsored by the International Labour Organization (ILO) (Bedoya Garland and Bedoya Silva Santiesteban 2005). The ILO report detailed three foci of debt servitude in eastern Bolivia: Alto Parapetí, the Amazonian Pando (as discussed in the next chapter), and the sugar cane fields of Santa Cruz. Carlos Mesa's government, firm in its free market convictions and its inability to address real power relations, tried to resolve the issue by offering credit to individual Guarani farmers. The Guarani rejected the offer. The demand was for territorial rights.

With the election of Evo Morales, the issue of Guarani slavery became much more visible in the Bolivian and transnational media. The MAS government invited a human rights team from the Inter-American Court of Human Rights (IAHCR, or Comisión Interamericana de Derechos Humanos [CIDH] in Spanish), an agency of the Organization of American States (OAS). This was unprecedented. Indigenous peoples must usually seek redress before this body against the opposition of their own governments, and often with their own governments as the target of complaints. That team's report further substantiated allegations of forced labor, as did reports of national NGOs (CIDH 2007; Defensoría del Pueblo 2007). The then United Nations (UN) Special Rapporteur on Indigenous Peoples, Rodolfo Stavenhagen, also traveled to Bolivia in 2007. Stavenhagen's report made explicit reference to Guarani slavery and the racist actions of the civic autonomists (United Nations Human Rights Council 2009).[3] In late 2007, the Bolivian congress voted to adopt the UN Declaration on the Rights of Indigenous Peoples as national law.[4] In the midst of the rising tensions, Guarani leaders themselves visited IAHCR offices in Washington, DC, performing the more conventional ritual of petitioning the court to make recommendations to the Bolivian government. The government representative was also present and formally accepted the petition (CIDH 2008a, 2008b). Even the German development agency Deutscher Entwicklungsdienst, active in the region, produced a report on debt servitude (DED 2008). This international vetting of state and Guarani claims laid out solid documentary evidence of debt labor and situated the issue in a wider purview of human and Indigenous rights.

These transnational acts of "seeing" (such observers are called *veedores*, "seers") were redeployed in defense of land reform. Vice Minister of Lands Alejandro Almaraz, at a press conference held in the main plaza of Camiri just four days before the attack, asked rhetorically, "Why do these landowners resist the application of the law, precisely in a site where the international community has identified the existence of Guarani peons reduced to relations of servitude? . . . Through their blockade, they reveal [their] guilt." His phrasing illustrated the mediated position of the state, attempting to construct legitimate hegemony bolstered by local movements and transnational publics against a hostile array of traditional powerholders in these rural regions. He linked the work of the government to the effort to reestablish the national oil and gas company YPFB, and bring jobs and prosperity back to Camiri, a message the local audience was eager to hear. The effort was aimed at appealing to a more populist-minded public, both Indigenous and not, who would side with the MAS against the landowners who were simply, in Almaraz's terms, "holding a blockade to defend *latifundia*" (Vilca 2008).[5] That Almaraz was the son of the famous socialist intellectual Sergio Almaraz, strategist of the defense of oil and gas during the 1950s and 1960s, added historic and political weight to the moment, as well as fuel to the fire of the reactionary opposition.

The mobilization of transnational witnessing was accompanied by national legal measures (Supreme Decrees, or Decretos Supremos [DS]) that identified Alto Parapetí as a territorial exception to existing agrarian law. While DS 29215 (August 2007) laid the regulatory framework for the agrarian revolution, establishing forced labor as a criterion for nonfulfillment of social function (Article 157), DS 29292 (October 2007) established the interministerial plan to address the specific issue of Alto Parapetí, and DS 29354 (November 2007) declared a vast area of the Guarani region subject to expropriation for reasons of public utility. These decrees radically altered the decrees issued by Carlos Mesa two weeks before his resignation in 2005 (DS 28159, May 16, 2005). The Mesa decree sought to consolidate individualized landholding in Alto Parapetí by offering credit to "captive" families to buy land (fifty hectares per family). This treated the Guarani as rural laborers under existing labor laws. The strategy of individuation included delegating powers to departmental elites to control land distribution. Mesa was clearly in the grip of the Santa Cruz elite. Yet the 2006 agrarian reform law and the 2007 decrees invoked collective Indigenous rights legislation (international and national) and the category of "pueblo" (people) and gave the executive (Evo Morales) the power to determine public utility. Here a state that many saw as leaning socialist deployed a space of exception but inverted the expected exercise of state power by focusing on the social meanings of land rather than the biopolitical utility (or uselessness) of laboring subjects. These measures privileged collective Indigenous demands rather than individual rights. It was indeed, as Rojas said, a moment of radical potential.

Through this series of resolutions, decrees, and technical reports, the government authorities laid the legal groundwork for implementation, down to the detailed steps of posting newspaper announcements about lands under study, declaring the process legal, certifying the authenticity of the Indigenous claim, holding public meetings, distributing pamphlets and flyers around the region, and notifying potential claimants. A complex scaffolding of transnational public discourse and national legal inscription was in place. With reason, Almaraz, sitting in the plaza of Camiri before the attack, reminded his audience that the government had an "unbreakable will to impose the law."

The ranchers were also mobilized. They had strengthened alliances with the autonomist Civic Committee of Santa Cruz (see chapter 5) and the Federación de Ganaderos de Santa Cruz (FEGASACRUZ, Federation of Cattlemen of Santa Cruz). This led to the highly publicized creation of "provincial land defense committees" (comités de defensa de la tierra). Some readers will recognize in this language the seeds of Latin American paramilitarism. Less publicly, these actors were in fact organizing armed gangs of young men. In early 2008, I was told that ranchers in Parapetí were already hiring members of the Unión Juvenil Cruceñista (UJC) as well as common criminals. Later accounts by the Guarani reported sightings of encampments of armed men on ranchers' farms in Alto Parapetí.

Amid rising tension, on February 26, 2008, the government land-reform office issued a resolution to initiate surveying. The action authorized the physical entrance of a survey team into Alto Parapetí from the INRA office in Camiri. Before this could happen, the cattlemen and UJC men attacked the office. The cattlemen escorted the surveyors to the outskirts of Camiri and forced them to retreat to Santa Cruz. Having expelled the agents of the state, the cattlemen claimed authority for their own acts in a written resolution declaring that an upcoming referendum on departmental autonomy, the illegal Santa Cruz autonomy vote of September 2008, would give them, not the central government, legal control over the land (FEGACAM 2008). Connecting land, gas rents, and the right-wing autonomy discourse, it read in part:

CONSIDERING

That the National Government intends to invade [*avasallar*] productive lands, amputate [*cercenar*] municipal territories, and seize [*arrebatar*] the [gas] royalties of the municipal governments, through illegal processes, and with political intentions. . . .

RESOLVES

To prohibit any surveying by INRA because it intends to apply unconstitutional norms. Thus we have decided to close the offices of INRA. We make it known that if there are confrontations and blood is spilled because of the illegal acts of INRA, the functionaries of INRA and the agrarian authorities will be responsible.

The Guarani were caught between a government with limited power over local judicial and police apparatuses and local elites' increasing claim that *they themselves*, rather than the government, had legitimate right to decide the law and use violence. The Guarani issued a counterresolution declaring the "territorial reconstitution of the Guarani nation." Distinct from the cattlemen, who fashioned themselves as local bearers of de facto law against an illegal state, the Guarani invoked national law and international treaties, from the UN Declaration all the way down to the technical resolution RA-ST 0034/2008, to start surveying. They went on to denounce the "NEOLIBERAL OLIGARCHS OF THE RIGHT" and the "violent actions" of the "latifundists," pronouncing themselves bearers of "INDIGENOUS AUTONOMY" in defense of their "constitutional and human rights to access to land and territory" (APG 2008).

Two days after the expulsion of the surveying team, Almaraz, the vice minister of lands, traveled from La Paz to Camiri like a general or, perhaps more aptly, a guerrilla leader, heading to the front lines. With Guarani leaders he attempted to lead a surveying crew into Alto Parapetí through a northerly route (see map 6.1). The public road crossed the property of Ronald Larsen, an American rancher. Larsen met them with a blockade. Brandishing a pistol as if he were in the Old West, he shot out their tires, threatened them with death, and, assisted by other ranchers, held them captive for almost twelve hours. At one point hired men of another rancher arrived with ropes and sticks, threatening to lynch them all. Rojas, part of the sequestered team, recalled that the issue was clear. The cattlemen accepted neither the rights of the Guarani nor the legitimacy of the government and the land-reform law. It was here, face to face, that the hegemony of the state was disputed.

Then Guarani leader Daniel Kañandiri was also held captive that day. A few months later, he recalled for me the tension of the moment. The conflicts still raged nationally and the outcome was still uncertain. As with many others, his trauma was palpable. The fear was real. It was August 2008, and there was a sense that Morales might actually be toppled. Colleagues in Camiri told me that they were experiencing fear as yet unparalleled, as threats and rumors circulated that their offices would be raided and Guarani leaders would "see what would happen to them," as the frequent threats they heard intimated. I suggested that it sounded like the times of Bánzer, referring to the military dictatorship of the 1970s. Another longtime Guarani leader said quietly, with clear concern in his voice, "No, this is worse. If Evo falls, our leaders are dead." The Guarani confronted the uncertainty with pain and defiance. In our conversation, Kañandiri, having been seized along with the state officials, recounted what it was like being held hostage in Larsen's house, by the hired thugs of "the gringo." His words bear extensive quoting: "What I saw in the house of, this, this" (he paused and looked at my own gringo face, chuckling), "this gringo, was that there were people from elsewhere, from outside of the region. We saw young men with their faces scarred, with their arms scarred, like with a knife, like this." He drew his finger across a forearm to illustrate, and continued:

And we said to ourselves, "These people aren't from here, these aren't Guarani. We know who we are." Well, sure, there were some Guarani there, the peons, the brothers that have been working there for a long time, enslaved, for [Ronald Larsen], but there were these other people as well. We saw this when they detained us, took the truck, cut the four tires, with knives, stole our phones, our cameras, tore up the truck. When we went back later, after things had calmed down . . . we saw a group of fifty, maybe eighty men, and again they came to threaten us. . . . They said another group is coming from Santa Cruz, they will be here soon, and we knew again these were outsiders, simply from their appearance, and we said, "These are the killers [*matones*] of Santa Cruz." But we weren't afraid. . . . They [looked] like gang members [*pandilleros*], drug addicts [*pitilleros*], or escaped prisoners, killers, hired people; we know in Ipati [nearby] they were being paid fifty dollars a night, brought from outside. . . . If they are bringing in people, killers, from elsewhere, I think the government has to apply the law, it has to make itself respected as the maximum authority. . . . The government has to act with a firm hand [*mano dura*], against those who have always been subjugating and denying the rights of the Guarani people.

An Indigenous leader asking the state to act with a firm hand sounds paradoxical but then seemed absolutely right to me as well. The Guarani, long subjected to the iron fist of the state, demanded that the same now be applied to these violent landowners. And the state was putatively on their side. This was indeed a remarkable moment.

For his part, Alejandro Almaraz, known for his revolutionary commitments, scoffed when I asked him what it was like to be held at gunpoint by a North American gringo in his own country. Channeling the deep commitment to change then held by these MAS authorities, he said the landlords were social groups undergoing a process of disintegration. "They acquired their lands through violence, and the only way they know how to defend them is through violence." He went on to detail the "unstoppability" of land reform and the rule of law. For his part, the gringo Larsen engaged the curiosity of the *New York Times*, to whose reporter he and his son represented themselves as legitimate property owners facing off against an ignorant Chávez-style socialist (Romero 2008). Scarcely a month later, there was another confrontation between Larsen's son and Almaraz's team. Images and accounts of the events entered a viral world of internet reportage full of terms such as *liberation*,

Guarani slavery, American ranchers, landlords, and *latifundia* (Comunica Bo-livia 2008c).

The battle over authority and lawmaking was thus reduced to a physi-cal struggle over the presence of certain kinds of state actors in the region. Almaraz began holding evening news conferences in Camiri's main square. Establishing a presence in town squares, whether for a press conference or for whipping a Guarani lawyer, was a claim to de facto authority. There Alma-raz called for dialogue while attacking the cattlemen's embrace of violence. The UJC toughs and representatives of the autonomist movement besieged his hotel, forcing his retreat to the local military base. In response, the cattle-men blockaded the entire region, hoping to stall cadastral activities until after Santa Cruz had held its illegal autonomy referendum. At these roadblocks, ranchers demanded identity cards of all who tried to pass, reportedly interro-gating Guarani, in particular, about their comings and goings. These statelike forms of spatial and bodily control had long characterized the techniques used by ranchers in Guarani country to keep the Guarani in their place while tacti-cally rejecting or embracing state authority (Healy 1982, 144–58).

In the rural areas of Alto Parapetí, Guarani were subjected to threats to guarantee their silence. Those labeled agitators were expelled from the haci-endas. In provincial towns like Camiri, Lagunillas, and Cuevo, the cattlemen harassed and intimidated urban Guarani leaders. Guarani friends told me that this was a time when leaders moved in groups and slept in the organization's offices for fear of attack. Urban Guarani who had, over several decades, won a modicum of acceptance as fellow citizens were now questioned as MASis-tas or traitors to regional interests. One TV commentary portrayed a Guarani teachers' school as a training center for guerrillas said to be allied with Co-lombia's Fuerzas Armadas Revolucionarias de Colombia (FARC, Revolutionary Armed Forces of Colombia) guerrillas, an absurd if oft-heard accusation from the right. Guarani changed the way they dress, removed the logo of the organ-ization from their trucks, and feared going out at night. The local phone com-pany, whose owners were allies of regional elites, was thought to have tapped the cell phones of leaders. "They were breaking into conversations," said one Guarani friend. Our "president [the Guarani leader] was constantly switching cell phones," added another. Threatening calls were received with voices say-ing, "Watch yourself!"

In later interviews, I learned that the land-reform technicians were also operating in a space of fear and uncertainty. While Almaraz's bravado was on the surface, unbreakable, Rojas told me that nobody knew what would happen. He recalled a time of legitimate fear of reactionary violence, with no guarantee that the police, or even President Morales himself, would step in to support them: "It was a complicated moment. We could have done the land measurement by satellite, and avoided the conflict. But we would not have been able to count the cattle that way. In any event, we decided to go in by land. We had to organize a special team to take on the risks, one that could do good technical work in a short time in difficult conditions. Many on the staff backed out of the brigade, because of the [fear] of violence."[6]

After the first skirmishes, when the brigade, under Almaraz's leadership, retreated to the army base at Choreti, Rojas recounted how these urban land reformers from La Paz were given the option to withdraw. Some did. The feeling was, he said, of "an epic moment." Almaraz later explained to me that the attempt to implement land reform was not a technical or legal problem or simply a problem of civil society opposition. It was, he said, fundamentally a problem of state structure.

> The mayor [of Cuevo] is married to the regional army commander. The local military leader is also a landowner. The district attorneys are controlled by the landowners. The landowners are ready to defend their lands with bullets, since that's how they acquired them. The police are pissed that they now have to serve the Indians. Sure, they do not earn much, but their pockets are filled thanks to these local powers. [Despite the fact that we are attempting to support Indigenous claims] we are working from within a state structure that was designed to do the absolute opposite.

It was an open question: If called on to deploy, would the local army officer answer to the mayor (who was on the side of the cattlemen) or to the indio president in far-off La Paz? Almaraz made numerous phone calls to La Paz to ascertain whether or not Morales and Álvaro García Linera, and the main intermediary on these conflicts, Alfredo Rada, would back them up. It was not altogether clear whether the national tug-of-war, with the MAS against the right wing, was worth this additional point of conflict. The land-reform technicians were unarmed pawns. For better and for worse, they enlisted the Guarani as their equally unprotected ground forces—which returns us to that dark, rainy night where this chapter began.

The plan was to enter the zone in a convoy of trucks and buses, Guarani and land surveyors alike. The convoy reached the outskirts of Cuevo at nightfall. A makeshift toll gate had been set up on the outskirts of town. On a later return visit with me, Kumbay Kañani, who had been there, walked me through the attack and recalled the scene.

> We entered [the town] normally, here in the entrance to Cuevo there at the gate, [and] there were a few guys there and just a few rocks. So what we did is get out of the trucks and move the rocks. They threatened us, but we said, "We're just passing through." And they told us, "It's not permitted." And about that time one of them grabbed a *cohete* [a large Roman-candle-like firework], and—*¡paaa!*—set it off. We passed on by, but then the others came with sticks and stones, and that's when the stoning [*pedrada*] began. Then the thing was to race forward, and the stones rained down upon us. In truth, they took us on with stones and sticks from the town gate all the way to the place of the ambush.

The trucks pushed through this point and headed around the edge of town, where the highway leads to the bush. There the road had been blocked by a tractor. It was a ruse to let the convoy through to a more difficult spot on a curved incline. There the pincer caught the Guarani vehicles from three sides. Scores of people had lined the sides of the road and stones rained down on them. The Guarani were forced to get out. Their vehicles were sacked and windows and tires destroyed.

> So there we were, and we wanted to talk, and there were women, men, there with machetes, and we said, "Let us talk," and they were threatening us with machetes, and there was a woman shouting, and by that time it was rocks from here, rocks from there, and women were bringing rocks in baskets. They had the rocks ready for us; they were piled up and waiting. It was raining stones. And there was a creek on one side and barbed wire on the other, and we couldn't get out. And it was drizzling. Finally, the trucks got turned around, [but by then] they had sacked and destroyed them.

Almaraz recalled the moment as well: "This was not a confrontation [*enfrentamiento*], though I expected it might be. We hoped to elude the blockade, but they cut off our retreat. It was a cruel humiliation [*escarnio*] and a punishment [*escarmiento*] by the landlords. They took [the Guarani] off the vehicles and beat them. It was there that we saw heavy weapons, rifles and shotguns."

At this point Ramiro Valle Mandepora, the Guarani lawyer, was seized and whipped. An Argentine solidarity journalist, Tanimbu Estremadoiro, was also seized, although some local townspeople managed to free her. Guarani fled on foot or in crippled vehicles that managed to turn around and head back toward the highway, as did the land-reform team. As they made their way out, they were confronted again by groups of men along the road. Forced out of their crippled vehicles again, my friend Kañani recalled that they were "made to put our hands up, like criminals" and walk. Out on the highway, suvs and pickup trucks filled with young men again drove back and forth harassing them, shouting, "We're going to fuck you over [los vamos a cagar]." Some walked twenty or thirty kilometers before finding rides back to Camiri. Guarani friends who received the news in Camiri recall a night of wailing and lament.

At this retelling we had stopped at the site of the stoning. My guides pointed out a barbed-wire fence that lined the road and Kañani waved his hand in an arc. "This is where we turned around, and as the trucks turned, the headlights shone alongside the road, [and] we saw these guys lined up there in the brush, behind the barbed wire. Those guys did not just have stones; they were armed. I recognized a kid, we used to play soccer together in Cuevo, no? He had two weapons in his hands as the headlights lit him up. That's the saddest thing; these were people we know, schoolteachers, district officials. . . . They were involved in this." No one was killed, but a score or more of Guarani were severely injured, as was the national director of land reform, Juan Carlos Rojas.

Cuevo's mayor, Sonia Gutrie, a schoolteacher, later claimed that the Guarani had assaulted the city. Civic leaders of Santa Cruz, in support of the provincial elites, also referred to the Guarani attempt to pass through Cuevo as an act of "armed aggression" (El Deber 2008). In fact, the Guarani offered no resistance. There were no reported injuries on the side of the ranchers. Though some of Almaraz's land-reform team reportedly carried pistols, they had fled the scene.

It was a clash foretold. When my friends and I went back to Cuevo, they took me to the house of an acquaintance. "He's one of ours," they said. I was led behind a curtain to talk with a young boy of around sixteen. With the bedhead of a teenager and a pierced ear, he was neither chaqueño nor Guarani but the son of migrants from the Andes. His family had been marked as dissidents, as MASistas. During the ambush, he reportedly helped the Argentine journalist flee. Now, he acceded to giving an account from the inside. He turned up the radio, to hide our voices from passersby. I jotted down notes as he spoke. In order to emphasize both the intensity of the moment and the seeds of planning for extralegal violence that united local landowners and the wider autonomist project of Santa Cruz, I paraphrase his words extensively here.

In the days before the conflict, the town had filled up with outsiders. These were people from Santa Cruz; some were UJC they said were paid fifty bolivianos per day [about US$7, the equivalent of what Guarani farm workers make in five days]. A truck would go around the town with loudspeakers on the roof, announcing that the government was going to bring "people from another place" to occupy their lands and "inhabit the territory," that the government was going to "bring kolla [Andean] people to live here." They set up vigils at the entrance road points and used the loudspeakers to continue these announcements. I saw with my own eyes the preparation of Molotov cocktails, at each blockade. They had slings, machetes, and shotguns. These outsiders, the hired ones, were also doing drugs and drinking at night. They would fight among themselves, since some were just *maleantes* [ne'er do wells] and others were the wealthy kids of the UJC, who arrived in luxury SUVs. Malpartida [one of the landlords] came back to town [after the attack] because he still owed money to these people. Later, there were threats to our family and to others. The schoolteachers who were involved said that anyone who betrayed the pueblo would fail their exams. In the end, this is all in favor of the cattlemen, but they do not even work their lands and there are a lot of poor people here. And a lot of fear, a lot of fear.[7]

Although the Guarani were local people, well known to these karai, the cattlemen had stoked up fears that what was really happening was an Andean invasion spurred by the election of Evo Morales. Many who may have had no interest in defending cattlemen, and indeed no land at all, were coerced into joining the blockade against the Guarani.

In the following months, Almaraz himself returned to Cuevo to confront the town's mayor. By now those involved had been subjected to judicial proceedings, and the law was slowly being deployed against the aggressors. The mayor was defiant. A video captured the conversation between her and Almaraz.[8] Almaraz, with his cochabambino accent, can be heard off-screen, a calm yet angry voice, "[You're talking about after Valle Mandepora] was tortured?" The mayor responded in the rapid-fire Spanish of the southeastern Chaco, snapping back, "Well, I don't know." In the brief second or two as she collected her words, she raised her right hand out of her lap almost unconsciously. "Well, sure," she went on dismissively. Her hand moved ever so slightly, palm upward, and made a nearly imperceptible chopping motion. It was the ubiquitous Bolivian body language for a beating, to *dar huasca* (give the lash).[9] "They gave him just a few lashes [*chicotazos*]. But that is not torture."

The spectacular form of punitive violence was explicitly characterized by the Guarani and government officials in terms of historical colonial relations (rape, captivity, massacre, humiliation, punishment). References to being treated like "criminals" and "foreigners" illustrated how local power constituted Guarani subjects as deserving of violence because they occupied a space of exception, outside of or "prior to the institution of law" (Das and Poole, 2004, 12; see also Krupa and Nugent 2015). Yet these violences were now revealed through the sign of the lash and became crucial to enacting a new politics of sovereignty aimed at dismantling local power. The lawyer Ramiro Valle Mandepora said later that his own suffering allowed him to really "see" what his poorer rural kin had long dealt with on the haciendas. "It was there that I understood the reality lived by my brothers. I felt in my own flesh what the Indigenous people on the haciendas suffer." At the end of the day, Valle Mandepora and other Guarani had become exhibits themselves, caught in the paradoxes of nonviolent struggle, transformed into a story aimed at producing moral outrage and political leverage elsewhere.

The Aftermath, Part I

The ambush brought to the surface the uncomfortable truth that several years of organizing had not yet dismantled the deep-seated coloniality of race and class relations between the Guarani and their others. The Guarani were not only traumatized but deeply conflicted. Had their own long-term strategy of crafting a new place in local politics been hijacked by Morales and the MAS? Or had the state played its role as a trusting supporter of their local struggles? The strategy of the convoy was critiqued by some Guarani as poorly planned, a feint that had made them cannon fodder. One Guarani friend suggested later that the land reformers had a bit of a "guerrilla complex," wanting to be like Che Guevara, heroic and martyred. But it was the Guarani who had suffered. These debates will continue. But the tactic was successful if seen in the wider context of the conflicts that would intensify in the coming months. The stories and bodies of the Guarani were transformed into emotive and forensic evidence deployed to indict the local powers (see Vice Ministerio de Tierras 2008a, 2008b, 2008c). The ranchers played their part perfectly, enacting a colonial script that attracted public scorn and entered human rights list-servs connecting the United States,

FIGURE 6.1 Juan Carlos Rojas, delivering an eviction notice, 2009. Rojas, former director of INRA (*standing left, with cap*), delivers the papers of *desalojo* to Duston Larsen (*right*). Larsen's lawyer stands to his left. Photo courtesy of Juan Carlos Rojas.

Bolivia, and Europe. Quietly, the government began making overtures to medium-size landowners, suggesting that the surveying would benefit them as well as the Guarani, thus weakening the reactionary alliance. Legal proceedings were started against Larsen, the gringo, and Malpartida, the landowner who had led the ambush.

A new decree was issued declaring any lands where forced labor was documented subject to expropriation. Almaraz returned to the Larsen ranch, this time with police in tow. Arrests were made and weapons were confiscated. Ronald Larsen, the father, targeted for arrest, fled the country. Almaraz was quoted saying, "Now there will no longer be sedition, nor obstruction of the law. . . . We are going to survey every last millimeter of this country" (*Bolpress* 2008). In early 2009, the then director of INRA, Juan Carlos Rojas, traveled back to the region from La Paz with another brigade. This time there were no roadblocks and the team drove right up to the front gate of one of the contested properties, that of the gringo Larsen himself. Rojas put on his official khaki vest and a white baseball hat. Flanked by his staff and a

FIGURE 6.2 Guarani march into Caraparicito, 2009. After the eviction, several hundred Guarani, the former captive communities, march onto the lands seized from the Larsens. Photo courtesy of Juan Carlos Rojas.

handful of police, he walked onto the Larsens' ranch to deliver the papers of eviction. Four properties where human servitude was documented were slated for expropriation, including two properties of the Larsens and one of Malpartida. Fifty Guarani families were to receive these lands, totaling some thirty-six thousand hectares (*Erbol* 2009). Outside the wooden gates waited several score Guarani from the local community, families who had grown up as peons under Larsen.

Recounting it in 2015, Rojas shook his head. "We still did not know what the reaction would be." In the wake of the violence, it was still unclear whether the Larsens would again try to cowboy their way out of it. By that time, though, the events of 2008 had ended in favor of the MAS. "When we arrived," he said, "the trucks full of cattle were already leaving." Larsen was moving his stock to other properties in eastern Bolivia. Rojas shared a photo of the moment. Larsen's son, Duston, a former Mr. Bolivia—yes, you read that right—muscular, and well over six feet tall, towered over Rojas (figure 6.1).

Duston Larsen angrily took the papers and, as remembered by Rojas, voiced one last moment of defiance. "This is an *abuso*," he shouted, an abuse of power. He was silenced by his lawyer, the Bolivian woman standing next to him. "She used to work for the land reform too," Rojas said wryly. It was not uncommon. The land-reform agency had long been saturated and infiltrated by the landowners and their lawyers, who worked the system to their favor. Finally, however, here was a small victory for the Guarani. Larsen the father had left for the United States. Now Larsen the son had to leave too. Juan Carlos said, "It was a very emotional moment, watching the Guarani march in after all those tensions." The Guarani were playing flute and drum (figure 6.2).

By March 2009, President Evo Morales himself flew to the Larsen Ranch, now a Guarani community called Caraparicito. In a grandiose ceremony, Evo handed over the official titles to the Guarani. It was a decolonizing reconquest, of sorts (*Bolpress* 2009).

The Aftermath, Part II

When I first wrote about this case, the story ended with the titling of the territory. My optimistic assessment was that a social movement state was emerging, one in which the organic social forces of the people were reconstituting state power from below (Gustafson 2010). By way of Guarani protagonism, I surmised, the state was able to "seat sovereignty" (*sentar soberanía*) and implement the law in favor of the Guarani. I suggested that Morales's reelection in 2009 meant that a new order was unfolding in eastern Bolivia. Nonetheless, another order was unfolding as well, that of the rapid expansion of Total's gas operations in the area.

The gaseous state has now overtaken the social movement state. Morales returned to the region in early 2010. He was no longer speaking the language of Indigenous liberation but that of gas. He went back to Caraparicito for the inauguration of the first well drilled by Total. In 2018 when I returned to Caraparicito, the whole region of Alto Parapetí was the epicenter of Total's operations. As the story goes, most of the former workers on what was Larsen's ranch received cash payments from the gas companies and have acquiesced to a new form of dependence. The paradoxes of fossil fuel economies are such that many Guarani have bought used cars and are putting them to use as rural taxi drivers. Some envisioned a new kind of communal land system rooted in the old ways, but the legacies of servitude and internal tensions have yielded the individualization of smallholdings, with ongoing conflicts over disputed properties. To be sure, they also have access to land. When I visited, the community leader said that many relatives were coming back from the city, since there was land available. "Thanks to Almaraz, we have land," he acknowledged. Looking out the front door of his house, the view is one of Total's immense gas plant, flaring gas (figure 6.3). But "the plant only brings us problems," he said. Larsen's old house nearby, once lavishly built in the style of the colonial hacienda, is in ruins.

Meanwhile, the area is now most frequently invoked in public media as "Incahuasi," the name given to the gas field (see map I.2). It has been taken

FIGURE 6.3 Total (France) Incahuasi gas plant, Caraparicito, 2018. The immense gas plant now rises over the "liberated" community of Caraparicito. Photo by the author.

up as a new kind of political instrument by the right-wing opposition, in rent-seeking political battles that largely make the Guarani invisible. Situated along the border between Santa Cruz and Chuquisaca departments, Incahuasi has been determined to lie wholly in, or rather under, the Santa Cruz department. This guarantees royalties to Santa Cruz, as the "producing department." Chuquisaca wants a portion of the royalties, claiming that some of the gas lies under their side. Santa Cruz does not want to concede. The regionalist political sentiments that I described in the previous chapter have once again been put into motion over gas rents, now fought over by urban elites in far-off Sucre and far-off Santa Cruz over lands once deemed insignificant or left to rural overlords. Other than constantly asking Total for compensation or handouts for one thing or another, and fighting about dusty roads, polluted water, and 24/7 noise, the Guarani have no formal right to rents.

To be sure, newish houses, electricity, and water have come to the region. And the Guarani do have land. But the MAS had shifted away from a revolutionary and Indigenous politics of liberation to a politics dominated by the gas complex. This is state-developmentalist thinking, not decolonizing practice. Both Alejandro Almaraz and Juan Carlos Rojas, ideologically committed land reformers, left the MAS party in 2010 because it had shifted to the right. Both told me that the government owed a debt to the Guarani, one that is still unpaid. Maybe one day that debt, too, shall have its due. By late 2018, Alejandro Almaraz was on hunger strike in Cochabamba, in opposition to Evo Morales, who was seeking reelection in the upcoming elections, a moment I refer to in the postscript.[10]

excess
part three

7 requiem for the dead

THE FARMER'S BODY LAY ON A SLAB IN A DAMP MORGUE. IT LOOKED LIKE A shower room: cold tile walls, a tile-covered table. A camera's flash brightened for an instant what must have been a dark place. The man's torso was exposed, his pants soiled. A pale hand hung limply to one side. Blood pooled on the tile by his head. His anonymous face was out of view. The photo arrived in my inbox in the days after September 11, 2008. It was part of a PowerPoint file circulating on the internet. The slides detailed, with forensic clarity, an armed assault on poor farmers marching across the Amazonian backwater of Pando department in northern Bolivia. The picture of the dead man—and scores of other graphic images of bodies, wounded and dead—circulated widely in the following weeks and months. Who was this dead man? And why and how did his dead body come to matter in relationship to the wider politics of territory and gas in Bolivia?

Images of peasants marching, guns firing, and young people being beaten rippled across Bolivian news sources as well as YouTube, Indymedia, and email. Young women and men, bodies hardened by rural life, posed sadly with bloodied faces. In one scene, a camera panned over a charred body. On the wrist was a red, green, and yellow bracelet—the colors of the Bolivian flag. Another shot showed gleaming white coffins flanked by a portrait of Simón Bolívar. In yet another, there were bodies lying helter-skelter on a flatbed truck. That photo made the front page of Santa Cruz's newspaper, *El Deber*. The headline read "Baño de sangre" (bloodbath). Other bodies under sheets were pictured laid out on wooden tables and flanked by neatly arranged candles. An impromptu wake became a stage, as rubber-gloved health workers gingerly raised the cloth to reveal bullet holes for government cameras. In one scene, a Bolivian flag, black bunting of mourning attached, hung from a wall. A printout on A4 paper read *Masacre del Cacique* (Massacre of the Bossman), referring to Leopoldo Fernández, the opposition governor of Pando, deemed the intellectual author of the attacks. Another labeled the dead "Martyrs of Democracy."

This chapter explores how, culturally and politically speaking, certain forms of political violence and death were central to the constitution of the body politic, and to the construction of state hegemony in the age of gas. Along with the following two chapters, this one grapples with a wider phenomenon of the extractive, gaseous state, that of the politics of the excess. I have already raised this question in relation to the Chaco War of the 1930s (chapter 1) and the Gas War of 2003 (chapter 3), epoch-changing moments of violence that produced bodies said to have been made dead because of, or "in defense of," oil or gas. I extend these reflections here. I ask, on the one hand, how the surplus meaning produced through spectacular exercises of violence or, as with the Guarani, subjection to it was also a form of gaseous excess, a surplus that became a terrain of political dispute over and through which the state was imagined and contested (Aretxaga 2003). In short, as with rent itself, what was the value of these dead bodies and who had the right to claim it and to what end? Though we might see this as an enactment of sovereignty through the expenditure of human life, the killings were politically productive. They were productive not merely as disposal of surplus bodies or wanton destruction of the enemy, that is, necropolitics, in Achille Mbembe's terms.[1] Rather, the production of a hegemonic state apparatus for relative control over fossil fuel extraction relied on bodies whose deaths could produce symbolic, affective, and juridical effects, what Townsend Middleton (2018) has deemed thana-topolitics. Dead bodies contain raw emotive power, which is precisely the point. They force those who contemplate them to confront their own mortality, blurring, Katherine Verdery (1999) suggests, the particularities of the moment with the absolutes of life, existence, the order of the cosmos, and the political order. For Verdery, dead bodies "enliven politics with a richer sense of what it might consist" (1999, 26), suggesting, it seems, that death makes politics more real. But political killings and the bodies they produce are ambiguous, generating not forensic clarity but narrative ambiguity (Verdery 1999; Middleton 2018). And since they can no longer speak for themselves, with "their stubborn will to mean, to signify something," dead bodies are subject to endlessly being made to speak by others (Mbembe 2003). And this is the point, that dead bodies are productive terrains for waging political struggle. Even if individual victims are forgotten, or conversely when they are incessantly remembered, political killings live on through stories that continue to animate the political field. These exercise their own form of lock-in to a particular political-economic order. Indeed, once one has died for oil or gas, whether we admit it or not, how could we ever think to leave it in the ground? Or maybe that is why we precisely should.

In what follows I draw on conversations, events, media, images, and memories. The connections with gas may not be immediately clear. This book's initial reviewers saw the chapter as a bit of excess itself, something that is surplus, extra, that somehow did not fit. The events are indeed disjointed. But much like the incongruous images and people that appear in dreams, which we later try to make sense of, these stories appeared and reappeared in my notes and conversations on gas. I suggest that the story of Bolivia's age of gas cannot be told without saying something about these bodies, even if they produce more meaning than an ethnographer can hope to access or capture. At the risk of self-righteous denunciation, death porn, or melancholic remembrance, and, most troubling, participating in the logic of state death itself, I offer a requiem for these dead, an attempt to grapple with the ambiguity of excess death as it relates to the wider politics of resources and the making of the gaseous state.

Bolivia's 9/11

As with much of Bolivia's hardscrabble eastern lowlands, Pando is a rough place. In 2004 researchers from the International Labour Organization documented cases of debt slavery tied to Brazil nut extraction (Bedoya Garland and Bedoya Silva Santiesteban 2005). The system is frightful, relying on the subjugation of labor to brutal working conditions. Beyond Brazil nuts, there are also rubber, cattle, and timber—all extractive industries that concentrate wealth, power, and landholding, with land claims frequently relying on illegal and fraudulent titles, many secured during the era of the dictatorships. The atmosphere of brutal illegality was compounded by other kinds of shadowy operations, particularly cocaine, contraband, and the dollars these move, flowing downriver from Bolivian forests, across isolated borderlands to and from neighboring Peru and Brazil. Politics here was old-fashioned, with bosses—or caciques—controlling the law and exercising rule through a combination of money and violence. In months and years prior to 2008, landowners and local civics had already harassed and attacked peasant and Indigenous leaders and their NGO advocates, beating and threatening them for demanding rights to land. The arrival of migrants and students from the Andes had also sparked a racist backlash as these "kollas" came to be seen as invaders of the MAS.

Leopoldo Fernández, then governor of Pando, had a long political history with the right-wing Acción Democrática Nacionalista (ADN, Nationalist Democratic Action) party in Bolivia. He had been minister of government overseeing state security under Tuto Quiroga (2001–2), during which time state and paramilitary killings in the Chapare and the Chaco went unpunished. After the Gas War of 2003 and the demise of the ADN, Fernández retreated to his home region of Pando and won the governorship under Quiroga's new party, Poder Democrático y Social (PODEMOS, Social and Democratic Power). There he sat at the top of a backwater political machine with an iron grip over the region. He supported Santa Cruz's autonomist movement, comprising, along with Tarija and Beni, the junior partners of the so-called half-moon (media luna) alliance against Evo Morales (the half moon referred to the shape of the departments when traced on a map of Bolivia). As I discussed in chapters 5 and 6, Fernández and other governors of the east sought to claim their own kind of de facto sovereignty. As in Santa Cruz, and with the media behind them and no other logic other than racism as a means through which to transform those who challenged their power into enemy subjects, these politicians replayed arguments suggesting that the MAS and their social movement backers (as Indians, implicitly) were outside the law.

The MAS government characterized these backwater regions as feudal holdovers where local or de facto powers (poderes locales or poderes fácticos), rather than the state, exercised sovereignty. Local powers operated in legal and extralegal gray areas on the margins of law but often in coordination with, or enacting, the state itself, albeit for private reasons (Das and Poole 2004; Krupa and Nugent 2015). Securing hegemony, let alone some ideal vision of democracy, decolonization, plurinationalism, and the possibility for equitable development, would require dismantling these local powers. Throughout 2008, the local powers were trying to topple the MAS government. They were mobilizing in the buildup to a civic coup attempt, trying to precipitate a crisis. Tensions were high. Just two days before the Pando killings, Evo Morales ousted Philip Goldberg, the American ambassador, for allegedly conspiring with the regional elites.[2] As in Santa Cruz, in Cobija, Pando's capital city, groups of men organized by the governor had also seized state offices like that of the land reform agency, INRA. Pando was a flashpoint where the MAS sought to dismantle the local powers one by one.

In other revolutionary times and places, this might have been carried out with revolutionary troops dispatched to drag feudal caciques like Fernández and his henchmen before a firing squad. Yet Bolivia's revolution, if it ever was one, was subject to a global audience and its judgments. The keyword was "democracy," not revolution. Of more importance, the MAS had no revolutionary troops and no effective control over the military, the police, or the judiciary in these regions. Furthermore, the opposition sought to produce violence, rage, and instability by provoking the state to produce dead bodies that could be attributed to Morales, something Morales could ill-afford given the active opposition of the urban middle classes of the east. So whether Morales wanted to use state force or not, the MAS could not call on the army or the police to stop these illegal actions. So it called on the only bodies it could mobilize, the social movements. Rural farmers and students took to the roads as a collective political instrument, part of a push for a historic transformation to be carried out through nonviolent action.

In the early morning hours, two caravans of farmers, including women, children, and men, converged on the town of Filadelfia.[3] The marchers' objective was to hold a meeting there, bringing together pro-MAS unions from throughout the department. Students from the local teachers' college, most of them recent arrivals from La Paz, also marched alongside the farmers in solidarity. Intent on preventing the farmers from gathering, the governor sent out a road crew with bulldozers to dig a trench across the dirt highway. The governor and his agents also mobilized townspeople and other functionaries, with estimates that these included some sixty armed men. Out on the highway, in the first encounter between the two sides, a representative of the governor's office was shot, in conditions that remain murky. The march continued. A few hours later, at noon, at the little crossroads town called Porvenir, the two sides collided. In what followed, twenty rural farmers and two more functionaries of the opposition governor were killed.[4]

Video taken that day from behind the armed men of the governor's side offers a look down a dusty highway just before noon. A hundred yards or so down the road, the farmers backing the MAS stand calmly, a tractor at the fore. There are no signs of aggression. There is no sign that they are armed, save a few sticks and slingshots. Later reports suggested a few may have had old shotguns. Seeking some protection from violence, the farmers had seized a group of functionaries earlier that morning and were holding them as a guarantee. Yet as truckloads of armed men arrived from the provincial capital of Cobija, the police negotiated the hostages' release. After that, the police withdrew to a distance. Some said this showed the complicity between the governor and the police. Others said the police withdrew under MAS orders, to let the killing proceed. Suddenly shooting erupted from the side of the governor's men. The farmers scattered into the bush lining the road, fleeing as the rapid-fire staccato of weapons is heard on the video. Angry cursing and shouting surround the camera. *"Métele bala a los hijos de puta* [give the sons-of-bitches bullets]!" Gunshots sound in the video, *pop-pop-pop-pop-pop* (Comunica Bolivia 2008b). With the police retreating, the peasants, some running, some in pickup trucks, also flee to avoid the gunfire.

The farmers and students bore the brunt of the attack. Some fled into the jungle. Others jumped into a nearby river, where they were also subject to gunfire. When wounded peasants were transported to hospitals for treatment, men in the city dragged many from the ambulances and beat them. Groups of thugs entered the hospital to prevent their treatment. Others were seized and taken to the main plaza of Cobija. There they were beaten and whipped with barbed wire, yet another restaging of plantation-style punishment. Three of the students from the teachers' college were seized, beaten, killed, and mutilated. Gangs of men dragged others into the city and kicked, beat, and interrogated them. It is all, painfully, on video. The supporters of the right-wing governor, calling themselves civics, shout, "Who sent you here?" Rifle butts slam into heads; fists and kicks fly. "For this shitty people, there is no compassion," shouts one of them, invoking local prejudices against Andeans. "You have to make him suffer!" "Tell us who sent you or you're going to the firing squad [*el paredón*]." "Kill the shitty kolla," shouts another. The violence sought submission, stripping the marchers of humanity. "They killed us like pigs, like dogs," said one survivor, his head bandaged and eye covered. "They have no pity for their fellow beings. They wanted to finish me off. I was not seen as a person in that moment; I was treated like a beast." The fact-finding mission sent later by the Unión de Naciones Suramericanas (UNASUR, Union of South American Nations) declared the killings a "massacre in the sense employed by the United Nations": carried out in organized form, with a "chain of command and with functionaries and materiel of the departmental governor in service of this criminal enterprise" (UNASUR 2008, 58).

Bolivia is a place known for public spectacles that fuse Indigenous and Catholic customs into fantastic folkloric parades, merging with a long tradition of combative union politics and mass marches that fuel a democracy of the streets (Lazar 2008). These spectacles turn collective bodies into visual vehicles of voice in a country where formal "democracy" and "rule of law" have long worked against the effective exercise of any semblance of equal citizenship. Such is unsurprising in a country marked by colonial racism, where the aesthetics of the body—skin color, dress, features, and ways of speaking— were symbols that dictated whether one had the right to public voice. Against this aesthetics of exclusion, mass mobilizations of dark-skinned bodies always offered a challenge, a clamor for visibility and recognition that could bring down governments or prop them up. Rights, like rule, are frequently exercised physically, manifest in collective corporeal movement. Yet when these bodies were deemed threatening—as in 2003, and now again here—they sparked responses ranging from mass violence to corporal punishment and submission. As the governor Leopoldo Fernández, by then imprisoned, later told the UN-ASUR commission, "What were those students doing there?" as if to say they had neither reason nor right to assemble, and their very presence justified the violence against them.

Bolivia, 1967

Another dead body, that of Che Guevara, and the mythos of revolutionary sacrifice surrounding "el Che," as he is remembered, have long occupied a central place in the Bolivian political imaginary. His image, especially the silhouette derived from Alberto Korda's famous photo, is known (and cheapened) globally. Korda's photo of live Che has been most lasting in Cuba and the world. But it is the lesser-known image of dead Che, from a photograph by Freddy Alborta, that seems to be the one that is most commonly visible in Bolivia (figure 7.1). Of course, Bolivia is where Che was killed and that moment fuses Bolivia, forever, to his truncated revolutionary struggle. If memories of live Che predominate in Cuba, the image of dead Che did something for Bolivia. It bore resemblance to a martyr, a saint, an icon, a call for future generations to emulate revolutionary sacrifice, a call to fearlessly confront death through revolutionary struggle.

Alborta's dead Che popped into my head when I first saw the picture of that dead farmer on that tile slab.[5] Could the similarities be coincidental or might their staging have been intentional? Or is it just (my) political imaginary? Che Guevara was similarly displayed more than fifty years ago. After

FIGURE 7.1 Che Guevara's body on display at Vallegrande, 1967. Photo by Freddy Alborta. Bride Lane Library / Popperfoto via Getty Images.

he was executed in the little village of La Higuera, Bolivian Rangers tied his body to an American helicopter and flew it to Vallegrande, the nearest city. There the soldiers put him on display for the press. He lay on a stretcher—which looks like US government issue—placed on top of a laundry room sink behind the hospital. In one of those photos a military officer lays a hand on his tangled hair. Another points to one of his wounds. Che stares into eternity, his right fist clenched. The Bolivian army later allowed townspeople to parade past the body. Incidentally, making a spectacle of the death was probably not the best decision. Today the laundry room is a revolutionary pilgrimage site. In death, Che is as powerful as ever.

Che's body was quickly disappeared, though this did little to tame the power of its image. In 1997 Argentine and Cuban forensic anthropologists arrived in southern Bolivia to look for him. After several months scouring

FIGURE 7.2 Hugo Bánzer Suárez's commemorative statue dedicated to the Bolivian soldiers who fought against Che Guevara in 1967. Camiri, 1997. Photo by the author.

the airstrip of Vallegrande, the team unearthed the bones of Che and several comrades. His protruding brow was clearly visible on the skull. His hands, removed at his death, were still missing. The mass grave was left open. Now covered with a tin roof, at the bottom of the hole are several white stones, each painted with the name of a dead *guerrillero*. As Verdery (1999) points out, reburials often spark monumental transformations. In Che's case, his reburial and monumentalization happened far away, in Santa Clara, Cuba. Bolivia was left with the laundry room sink and an open grave. Yet even in its absence, Che's body was still unsettling. In 1997, after the bones were dug up, then president Hugo Bánzer, the former dictator trying to close the gas pipeline deal with Brazil, was so perturbed that he staged a huge military demonstration in Camiri. Commandos from the special forces base at Sanandita marched through the town, faces painted black, hefting huge machine guns. Meanwhile, just over the mountain, around that laundry room sink in Vallegrande, thousands of global revolutionaries, backpackers, hippies, and wannabes gathered to commemorate the thirtieth anniversary of Che's death. In a fit of pique, Bánzer commissioned a monument to the soldiers who killed him, ensuring again that both Che and his mythos would live on. The statue is Iwo-Jima-esque, with roughly sculptured Bolivian army heroes, chests and arms rippling like the oil worker, brandishing machine guns and wearing bandoliers. It still stands in Camiri (figure 7.2).

Bolivia, 1980

The rediscovery of Che Guevara's bones added fuel to the fire of memories about another body that was also in the news throughout the age of gas, that of Socialist leader Marcelo Quiroga Santa Cruz. Quiroga Santa Cruz, cited in chapter 3, was one of the defenders of gas who oversaw the nationalization of Gulf Oil in 1969. In July 1980, as he was leading opposition to the right-wing military coup of Luís García Meza, armed paramilitary gangs burst into the national labor union office in La Paz and assassinated him in a hail of machine-gun fire. His body was disappeared. Despite the ongoing pressure by the Association of Families of the Detained, Disappeared, and Martyred for the National Liberation of Bolivia (ASOFAMD, Asociación de Familiares de Detenidos, Desaparecidos y Mártires por la Liberación Nacional de Bolivia), Quiroga Santa Cruz's is but one of many whose bodies are still missing. In obeisance to the military, and in return for their loyalty, ever fickle, not even Evo Morales was willing or able to unearth it. As such, Quiroga Santa Cruz's missing body bears within it the deepest contradictions of the nationalization of gas, once again revealing the limits of change in a country where ultimate power is still mediated, more and less publicly, by military forces rooted deeply in society. It is as if the MAS and the military made an exchange—Evo Morales rules and we take more control over the gas, but the military gets to keep the secret of Quiroga Santa Cruz's body underground.

For his part, Che Guevara wrote of sacrificial death so much that most say he was fixated on it, fetishized it, and even worshipped it as the ultimate end of true revolutionaries. Bolivian movements also often speak of the "mystique" and "sacrifice" of struggle, the push to the "final consequences" and "final victory." To me, the association between revolutionary sacrifice and the later representation of the dead of Pando was clear. Or at least that is the way the MAS spoke of them, as "martyrs for democracy." In the age of gas, the consolidation of hegemony over the extractive project relied on this revolutionary mystique, and it needed the movements—and their bodies—for revolutionary sacrifice.

Bolivia, 2015

In 2015 I sat in conversation with one of the ideological minds behind the rise of the MAS, a former member of the government, once close to Vice President Álvaro García Linera. He had become one of the dissidents on the left, like Alejandro Almaraz and Silvia Rivera Cusicanqui, by then all outspoken critics of Evo Morales and the MAS. We were talking about gas, the state, and histories of struggle. My interlocutor, lamenting the direction that the MAS government had taken, was questioning the revolutionary credentials of the vice president, García Linera. "They were never radical," he told me. "Álvaro said if we do something radical [like seizing land] we won't even last three days in power." Speaking of revolutionaries, the conversation turned to the ill-fated armed guerrilla movement of the 1980s led by Álvaro García Linera alongside the Aymara leader Felipe Quispe and the Mexican revolutionary intellectual Raquel Gutiérrez. García Linera and his comrades organized the Ejército Guerrillero Túpac Katari (EGTK, Túpac Katari Guerrilla Army) and sought to create an interethnic alliance between Indigenous and mestizo militants (Escárzaga 2012). The movement was named after Túpac Katari, the Aymara rebel of the late eighteenth century whose body was dismembered by the Spanish and who, like Guevara, still haunts, energizes, and activates political imaginaries in Bolivia (Dangl 2019). The EGTK brought together other movements, some armed, some not, that represented ideological lines tied to neo-indigenist, neo-Marxist, and Trotskyite factions. After its first armed action in 1992, a bungled attempt to blow up a power line, the group was dismantled by the state. The three leaders were jailed and tortured. After their release in 1997, it was only eight years later that Álvaro García Linera took office alongside Evo Morales, through the ballot box, not the gun.

As we discussed these ill-fated struggles, other dead bodies kept popping up in the conversation. My host, one cheek full of coca, remembered another moment with some sorrow: "They were three young, beautiful people." He was talking about Luís Caballero, twenty-two, and Oswaldo Espinoza, twenty-four, two Bolivians shot down in 1990 in a La Paz safe house alongside an Italian comrade, Miguel Northtufter, twenty-eight. It was one episode of many in Bolivia's recent past of ill-fated guerrilla struggles: Che in 1967, the resuscitated Ejército de Liberación Nacional de Bolivia (ELN, National Liberation Army of Bolivia) at Teoponte in 1970, and this one, of a group called the Comité Néstor Paz Zamora (CNPZ), whose fleeting struggle preceded that of the EGTK. Like wrinkles in time, they all seemed to fold together with similar stories and sacrificial bodies, along with political contradictions. The government of Alfredo Ovando, who in 1970 oversaw the systematic annihilation of fifty-three ELN guerrillas in the jungles of Teoponte, was the same government that nationalized Gulf Oil (and for whom Marcelo Quiroga Santa Cruz served as minister until he resigned in protest). The government of Jaime Paz Zamora, which in 1990 oversaw ongoing neoliberal reforms and called itself the Movimiento de Izquierda Revolucionaria (MIR, Movement of the Revolutionary Left), ordered the killing of these young leftists, whose cell was named after the president's own brother, Néstor Paz Zamora, who had died at Teoponte. To confuse things further, the putatively leftist MIR was then in alliance with the far-right ADN party of Hugo Bánzer, whose largely Santa Cruz–rooted political base was in control of the state military and intelligence apparatus.

As part of their strategy for financing their revolutionary cell while targeting representatives of imperialist domination, in 1980 the CNPZ militants—those three beautiful young people remembered in our conversation—kidnapped Jorge Lonsdale, the CEO of Coca-Cola Bolivia. When troops discovered their location, the three young people were summarily executed and Lonsdale was also killed, most likely by state forces. Amnesty International (1996) reported that the government troops had carte blanche orders to kill from the Ministry of the Interior. My interlocutor interwove his memories of that day with our conversation about the MAS having strayed from its revolutionary path. What I heard in his voice was pain and sadness. "I remember," he said again of the CNPZ group, "they put their pictures in the newspaper, beautiful young people. The [state forces] who did the killing were *tipos desalmados* [men without souls]."

The heroicization of revolutionary violence and revulsion at the soul-less qualities of state violence is an affective and discursive part of the guerrilla mystique on the left. I sympathize with the position. Yet the point of my story-telling interlocutor that day was that the myth of the revolutionary hero had become part of the MAS political theater but was being carried out by those who had never been in combat. For him, it was not that revolutionary sacrifice had no meaning but that it was now being illegitimately appropriated by those in power, actors who had no true revolutionary authority themselves. They were impostors.[6]

It's the Oil (or Gas), Stupid

After Venezuelans elected Hugo Chávez, the wheels were set in motion to create a regional anti-imperialist alliance in Latin America, the Bolivarian project of twenty-first-century socialism. Oil was crucial to this vision, as was gas in Bolivia. Oil was also of central concern for the gringo foreign policy hawks and their fossil fuel industry backers. Without exaggeration, almost everything revolved around fossil fuels. In May 2008, with conflicts in Bolivia intensifying, several Latin American countries joined to create UNASUR, a counterweight to the US-dominated OAS). While UNASUR replaced an older body called the Council of South American Nations, it also spawned the Consejo Energético Suraméricano (South American Energy Council), which was founded to promote and coordinate energy policy within the framework of counterhegemonic regional integration (Rigirozzi and Tussie 2012). Venezuela and Bolivia were joined by Brazil under Luiz Inácio Lula da Silva, Ecuador under Rafael Correa, and Argentina under Cristina Fernández de Kirchner., All had oil and gas reserves coveted by the international private oil companies. Venezuela and the UNASUR sought to consolidate itself as a counterhegemonic regional alternative (Rigirozzi and Tussie 2012). On the other side stood US efforts to promote "hemispheric energy integration," a euphemism for borders open to capital and fossil fuels (but closed to people) and dominated by interests of the US-based private oil and gas companies.

Earlier that year, UNASUR's Energy Council, composed of ministers of energy from its twelve member countries, met in Caracas, Venezuela. Flush with high oil prices, Chávez hoped to defend the fledgling political transformations in Ecuador and Bolivia. Those gathered at the meeting included representatives from more right-leaning countries like Colombia and Peru. Despite the ideological divides, when it came to energy, UNASUR, both left and right, shared a commitment to the expansion of fossil fuel infrastructures in the region. Oil, gas, and even coal were promoted for a more solidary, sovereign, and cooperative UNASUR. This included expanded infrastructure, petrochemical plants in Venezuela, the Colombia–Venezuela gas pipeline, and the possible creation of a gas exporters' alliance. The most radical proposal was for the return of state participation in ownership and investment in these industries.

Most concerning to the US fossil capital and militarist alliance was that any subregional effort might marginalize US private oil companies and financial interests, closing doors for US companies and opening doors to China or Russia. This became visible in one small disagreement, when Evo Morales and Hugo Chávez spoke out against ethanol as a sugar-cane-fueled machine of devastation that undermined food production and food sovereignty (Pereira de Lima 2010). Ethanol was then being hyped by George W. Bush and the United States as a way to make inroads with the agro-industrial elite in Brazil. Yet in Bolivia, at least at that moment, ethanol was a mainstay of agro-industrial power behind the autonomists trying to topple Evo Morales.

As the violence in Bolivia intensified, Chávez argued at the UNASUR meeting that the right-wing plots in his own country were being cooked up by Venezuelan reactionaries in Miami. "We have information," he said, "because they drink a lot and start to talk. . . . We know we are the target of a great international machination directed by the empire." For its part, the empire was also meeting and worrying. In the months before the killing at Pando, the US ambassador was trying to assess whether the military would obey orders from Morales or if a coup was a possibility. Bolivian military officers loyal to the US Embassy were routinely offering information to the Americans, even telling the embassy, to wit of the argument herein, that Morales would not use military force against opposition protests, since he knew that "deaths would lead to the loss of political support." After Pando, pro-MAS social movements surrounded Santa Cruz in a show of strength against the opposition's civic coup. Hugo Chávez, now a prime backer of Morales, spoke again, holding up the dead farmers and students of Pando as victims of right-wing fascism, as indeed they were, arguing that the Bolivian army had allowed "fascist paramilitaries to massacre the Bolivian people." By September, with its ambassador sent packing, the US Embassy was planning for emergencies such as "a coup attempt or President Morales's death" and worried that a confrontation in Santa Cruz might lead to a "bloodbath."[7] The dead bodies of Pando had been scaled up into an international tug-of-war over fossil fuels.

The Bodies of Pando

Back in Bolivia the battle over the bodies played out in glossy media on the internet, which multiplied displays of the dead and intensified the political struggle over their ownership. In the days and weeks after the event, the farmers' dead bodies were figuratively pulled between the government and the opposition. Were they "humble" people, of the pueblo, slaughtered by a criminal and fascist elite? Or were they government cannon fodder, people manipulated into a confrontation, used by the MAS to topple an opposition leader?

The right-wing opposition media waged its own interrogation of the dead, as the civics had done to the young people seized in Pando, asking, "Who sent you? Who paid you?" For the opposition, these rural people were MAS puppets, paid off or forced to march. This colonial logic replicated the logic of the boss man, who buys, sells, and kills indios as if they were property. Thus, the victims were denied the possibility that they could act of their own accord (Soruco Soluguren 2011). The most prominent outlet of the right was the powerful UNITEL (Universal de Televisión) network of Santa Cruz, something like Fox TV in the United States. One of its key anchors was Jimena Antelo, former beauty queen, once selected in a newspaper poll as the most beautiful woman of Santa Cruz. Antelo projected what some must have seen as sensuality but what struck me as sadistic pleasure. Through her whiteness, she established authority over the truth and the darker-skinned Bolivians she brought on her show. On one show, she beckoned visitors to come and see "what really happened on the 11th of September" and to hear the "truth of the dead at Pando" (UNITEL 2008).

Antelo spun all the angles, offering her own body as a lens through which the dead bodies of Pando could take meaning and speak their truth. The peasants had been armed, she told the viewers. They had killed first. The government provoked the violence and planned the confrontation. The peasants were manipulated. The killings were the responsibility of the MAS. It was a MAS operative who had orchestrated the whole thing. Those doing the beating on the autonomist side were infiltrators of the MAS, backed by Chávez and the Venezuelans. See here in this video, this tall, dark man, he is clearly a Venezuelan. And on and on it went. Pando was a montage, an image, a show, Antelo reminded the viewer with a smile. As the viewer confused fantasy with reality, real life with a show, one became the other. Antelo beckoned the viewer, invariably that heteronormative whitish masculine viewer assumed to be the one that mattered, to consume her and her truth.

The MAS government waged its own video campaign with scores of postings on YouTube. Videos were slowed down and labeled with the intent of showing forensic clarity. These videos decried the killings as the actions of the racist and fascist autonomists of the right. The government gave detailed attention to authoritative legality, voiced in the language of the righteous struggle of humble people. The minister of health, reporting on state TV, described the injuries with a doctor's attention to detail and a revolutionary's commitment to justice: These were "humble peasants," of the pueblo. The civics were not autonomists defending themselves against government aggression but grand assassins (*grandísimos sicarios*) and criminals (*maleantes*). Just witness, one video asked a viewer, the evidence of the dead bodies. It was through death, as Walter Benjamin wrote, that the storyteller sought authority (Benjamin 1968; see also Martel 2018).

In the days after, the opposition autonomists in Pando seized the airport at Cobija and the government finally sent in troops loyal to Morales. Public opinion shifted toward the MAS. Leopoldo Fernández, the governor, was seized and placed under arrest, the only person jailed. Several score of the governor's partisans fled to Brazil. While the names of the dead are largely forgotten, the deaths were politically consequential. The farmer on that slab in the morgue did not go out that morning to kill or die, but his and the other deaths were productive even if their meaning is ambiguous. At least at the moment, it seemed revolutionary to me. The cacique was brought down. As one leader said later, speaking of the dead, through tears: "We are going to tell their truth, but we are not going to tell it with arms, with beatings." Another bandaged survivor added, "We are still on our feet, because we are carrying out the total transformation of our country" (Comunica Bolivia 2008b).

Terrorist Cell?

The local powers of Santa Cruz were a bit more difficult to bring to heel. But my conversation about the CNPZ, the revolutionary limits of the MAS, and the soul-less ones who did extrajudicial killing jumped from Pando in 2008 to La Paz in 1990, and then back again to Santa Cruz in 2009, where the conflict between the MAS government and the reactionary opposition led to the production of three more dead bodies. After the failed civic coup attempt of September 2008, somebody hired a group of mercenaries to come to Bolivia. Their aim was allegedly to generate violence, destabilize the country, and perhaps kill Evo Morales himself. At one point, the group spent the night in the Hotel Las Américas, in Santa Cruz. In the early morning hours of April 16, 2009, a Bolivian commando unit called Unidad Táctica de Resolución de Crisis (UTARC, Tactical Unit for Crisis Resolution) burst into five rooms on the fourth floor of that hotel. In a hail of gunfire, they killed three of the five alleged mercenaries. The leader, now dead, was Eduardo Rosza, a Hungarian Bolivian who of late had fought for the Croatian army during the wars in the Balkans. The other two were Arpad Magyarosi, a Romanian; and Michael Dwyer, an Irishman. Two others survived. A score of alleged conspirators, most of them part of the business elite of Santa Cruz, were imprisoned, exiled to Paraguay or Brazil, or put into judicial purgatory. The three dead bodies have been laid to rest but the story most certainly has not.

On a whim, perhaps macabre, I checked in to the hotel in mid-2015. Standing at the front desk, I asked about the events. "We'll put you in the same room if you want," said the front desk attendant.

"What about ghosts?" I asked, trying to lighten the implications. "No, no worries," she assured me. "They've done exorcisms and blessings in there. And the mattresses were full of holes, but all of them have been replaced." After some discussion about which specific rooms had been involved, other stories emerged. Sure, some guests come to the hotel out of curiosity, I was told, but those who were working here that night were traumatized: "The troops came in. They pointed their guns at those who were on the night shift and said get down on the floor [*bocaabajo*]. They took control of the hotel, and then the bombs went off, to open the doors. There were three [dead]. It was an execution."

The whole story was politically troubling. The first impulse of Morales's supporters (and, I confess, myself at the time) was relief: a dangerous right-wing plot had been dismantled. The killings were justified. This finally showed that Morales had harnessed the power of the state to great and brutal effectiveness. Instead of murdering peasants, miners, and Indians, finally the forces of the state had been turned against right-wing terrorists plotting against Morales. Having been following and writing about the violent racism of the right in Santa Cruz, I was not surprised that it had come to this. I have to say, at least initially, that I had to repress a bit of satisfaction myself.

As the official story emerged, a rapidly escalating investigation began to snare some of the prominent figures in Santa Cruz's autonomist movement. It appeared that Santa Cruz's agro-industrial elites, or some shadowy subset thereof, had hired the team of European mercenaries to foment unrest. True or not, the operation was clumsy. It seemed as if it was a plot played out in the style of Cold War intrigue. The would-be mercenaries took a number of selfies with their guns and their collaborators as they moved around hotels in Santa Cruz and traveled in the rural areas, photos that later circulated as evidence for their conspiracy. Seen shirtless and smiling in fancy hotel rooms, the men, who came to be called the Rosza Group or the "terrorist group," seemed as much macho poseurs with guns and bluster but little sense. The government arrested more than a score of alleged plotters. The operation sparked the flight of several right-wing leaders, including one of the most extreme, the Croatian Bolivian cooking oil baron Branko Marinkovic, to Brazil. The Croatian connection seemed to make the whole thing come together (Vicepresidencia de Bolivia 2009).

The opposition argued again that the whole thing was a montage, a government plot. Carlos Valverde Bravo, a former right-wing politico and now a talk-show radio journalist in Santa Cruz, is a useful exemplar. Valverde Bravo's father, Carlos Valverde Barbery, was a founder of both the UJC (the group that led the battle for the 11 percent oil royalty in the 1950s and were the shock troops of the autonomist movement during the early twenty-first century) and the FSB (a fascist party that was distinctly not socialist and that led early opposition to the 1952 Revolution). At one point the FSB even started a right-wing guerrilla movement in the east to destabilize the country and pave the way for the military coup in 1965 (Almaraz 1964). The FSB and the Valverdes were allied with the Bánzer dictatorship throughout the 1970s (Field 2014). By 1990, when the fascist party had dissolved, Valverde the son became an intelligence chief in the Ministry of the Interior under the government of Jaime Paz Zamora, in alliance with the ex-dictator Bánzer. Valverde the son was in charge of the division that interrogated and tortured the young revolutionaries of the CNPZ in 1990. In the first decade of the twenty-first century, as the MAS ascended, both Carlos Valverde Bravo and his father became mouthpieces of the Santa Cruz autonomist movement. As the Santa Cruz autonomist movement started unraveling, Valverde the son took it upon himself to write a book, ¡Maten a Rosza! (Kill Rosza!) (Valverde Bravo 2012). In it, he accuses the MAS and its operatives, including the vice president's brother, Raúl, of having conjured up the entire operation, from contracting the mercenaries in Europe, to planting arms in various strategic points in Santa Cruz and convincing local Santa Cruz elites of joining the plot against Evo Morales. Raúl García Linera himself, Valverde argues, drove an ambulance to the Eighth Army Division to get the weapons that would later be planted on the dead.

It is hardly believable that the struggling MAS government had the capacity to infiltrate the right-wing elite and trick unwitting businessmen of Santa Cruz into financing an operation. Evidence to the contrary is abundant. There were donations to a shadowy ring called "The Tower." Somebody at the Cooperativa de Telecomunicaciones Santa Cruz (COTAS, Santa Cruz Telephone

Cooperative), long a bastion of Santa Cruz's elite secret societies, had allowed their facilities to be used to store arms. Receipts and phone calls showed links between the mercenaries and high-level Santa Cruz political and business figures. Businessman and former government official Zvonko Matkovic even hosted the mercenaries on his remote hacienda. Among the implicated were former members of the paramilitary organization created by the United States to repress coca farmers in the Chapare. Even Gary Prado Salmón, a former army officer who played a role in the killing of Che Guevara, was allegedly involved. The circles of bodies kept going around and around.

In the internecine world of Bolivian political factionalism, and longer histories of political violence, betrayals, and vendettas, much of what really happened is unknowable, especially for a gringo anthropologist. The details of what is in fact known are too complex to address here. And veracity, even were we to rehash these details, would be elusive. But in the gaseous state, feeling was as important as knowing. Acquaintances on the left who may have had some sympathy for Morales were taken aback by the brutality of the killing. These were extrajudicial executions, they argued. Yes, they *were* right-wing mercenaries, yet their apparent execution evoked repudiation of state terror, the hooded commandos, the bursts of machine-gun fire, the work of the *desalmados* (soul-less ones). This brought back memories of the dictatorships, of other extrajudicial killings, of other bodies of the past. Indeed, in my conversation with that former supporter of the MAS, it was the killing of Rosza in 2009 that brought to his mind the killing of those young people of the CNPZ in 1990. Evo Morales, whether entirely willfully or not, was exercising the sovereign claim to decide who could live and who must die. This is what the gaseous state had wrought. But it brought Santa Cruz to heel. In December 2009, Morales won reelection with 64 percent of the vote.

Looking for Dead Bodies

As Begoña Aretxaga wrote of the phantasmagorical and fantastic effects of state violence and terror, the "boundaries between fiction and reality become indistinguishable, endowing encounters between the state and terrorism with a phantom quality" (2003, 402). Back at the Hotel Las Américas, where the Rosza Group had met its end, the staff waffled when I asked what they thought had really happened that night. In hindsight, my curiosity must have come off as an interrogation of its own. "Was it an execution?" I asked.

"Who knows?" they replied. Shaking their heads, they said, "The doubts, the doubts [*Por las dudas, las dudas*]." The desk agent handed the key to the bellhop.

"Which room was it?" the bellhop asked the desk agent again.

"That's it," she replied, pointing to the key fob, room 458. Taking the key, he escorted me upstairs. "Was this it?" he muttered to himself. "I think so, yes, this was it," he said, definitively. He put the key in the doorknob, pushed the door open, and showed me in. There I saw the tile floor; there was a bit of dampness in the air, a window AC unit, wooden doors with flimsy locks and handles, and a tiled bathroom.

THE BODIES OF CHE GUEVARA AND THE FARMERS OF PANDO, AND THAT OF Eduardo Rosza and his mercenary group, and those of the CNPZ and that still missing body of Marcelo Quiroga Santa Cruz—among many others whose stories I have not told—are all tangled up with the politics of gas and a changing valuation of political death in the country. The political killings were productive. They dismantled much of the apparatus of the most reactionary elements of the right wing, removed two of the most recalcitrant opposition governors, and brought to heel virtually the entirety of the autonomist movement. From the calculus of the state, the heavy hand of the UTARC was needed in this most spectacular and excessive way.[8] As polarization surrounding the MAS government intensified in later years, each social conflict led to speculation. Was the opposition looking to create a dead body (*buscando un muerto*)? Or was it Evo Morales who was "*buscando un muerto*"? That a death might be tactically useful was clearly part of a crude political calculus. This was not new to the age of gas, nor are such calculations unique to Bolivia. But grappling with a seeming mutation, or a distortion of more familiar ways of writing Bolivian history, there was something unsettling about what seemed to be happening in the gaseous state that surpassed representation.

In what ways might the meanings of political death—that is, dying for the state, or dying at its hands, or in resistance to it—have shifted in the age of gas? René Zavaleta (1977) argued that it was only with the Chaco War that Bolivians realized that power, by which he meant the power of the state, was something worth killing and dying for. Whereas in the US one must not say that our soldiers died for oil or that we kill for it, although they did and we do, in the case of the Chaco War, in Bolivia one *must* say that the soldiers died for the oil. That notion of sacrifice for an energy resource entails a number of other commitments, to masculinity, militarism, and oil itself, all of which generate their own secondary effects. After the US-backed regime of General Juan José Barrientos turned the army against protesting miners in 1967, soldiers and officers in La Paz faced mass public repudiation. Zavaleta argued that it was in this context that the military factions began to rethink their Cold War allegiances to the national security doctrine pushed by the United States and to take up the issue of natural resource sovereignty and nationalization, leading to the 1969 expropriation of Gulf Oil. In exchange for legitimacy, the military offered up support for nationalization of the oil. In an essay originally titled "The Worst Enemy of Gulf [Oil]," which served as a requiem for Sergio Almaraz as well as a review of Almaraz's book *Requiem para una república* (1976b), Zavaleta (1970, 645–46) argued:

> Almaraz went, in the *Requiem*, even further because he formulated an articulation between the defense of natural resources and military nationalism, which in that moment appeared to be fading. "Some variation of military rule would be acceptable" [Almaraz noted], "if nationalist soldiers displaced the group committed to the Pentagon." But he argued that the "precondition would be that such mobilization be backed by a popular movement." This penetrated profoundly into the army, which had become so confused about its triumph over the guerrillas [of Che Guevara] and could do little else than live suffering the collective hostility of the people for their massacres of miners and guerrillas.

Part of that calculus in the past revolved around the linkage between the moral status of the military, the issue of nationalism and natural resources, and the ethico-political status of the dead, all factors whose meanings are produced in struggle. When the left was out of power, the left relied on convincing the public and some sectors of the military that the moral compass pointed toward the pueblo. Yet some deaths mattered more than others. Crudely put, killing twenty peasant farmers—Aymara or Quechua—had a smaller value than executing a leftist son or daughter of the whitish political classes. On the other hand, killing "communists"—whether leftists of the universities or Trotskyites in the mines—was, for a time, politically palatable to the ruling classes and their North American backers. But even those killings had a limit in a country in which the urban classes were not so distant from their rural kindred and many families raised both revolutionaries and reactionaries. There is also a deep revolutionary spirit of martyrdom inflected by Catholic images of Christ's own martyrdom and Andean understandings of sacrifice and reciprocity.

In the wake of the 2003 Gas War, during which sixty-seven civilians were killed by the troops under the command of Gonzalo Sánchez de Lozada and Carlos Sánchez Berzaín, the killings galvanized the indignation of a wide spectrum of the population. Those killings were beyond the pale. And once again, they were directly equated with the question of fossil fuels. The victims, this time women, children, and men, all civilians, were also deemed martyrs of gas, whether gas was the motivation that took them to the streets or not. But against this story of sacrificial death, the political calculus carried out by Sánchez de Lozada and Sánchez Berzaín in 2003, like that of colonial orders of rule more generally, was one based on bare life: How many dead bodies might it take? What kinds of dead bodies can be produced without the killing being turned into political sacrifice (Agamben 1998; Mbembe 2003)? It back-fired. As in 1967, the killings brought public repudiation against the soldiers. The pendulum shifted toward support of Evo Morales and the nationalization of gas. At least while he was president, Evo seemed to have brought the military to the side of the people. During much of Evo Morales's time as president, the main task of soldiers each year was handing out the Juancito Pinto payment to schoolchildren, suturing the image of the Bolivian soldier with the distribution of the gas rents.

What underwent a reversal during the ascent of the MAS, up to a certain point, was a certain revaluation of the lives of the pueblo, the Indigenous, the worker, and the peasant. Right-wing regimes exploited racism (or "communism") to pre-criminalize such victims as bodies deserving of death, whether as savages or subversives. Yet in Pando, Parapetí, Sucre, and elsewhere, a decolonial calculus inverted the formula, making of these bodies the representatives of the true pueblo. The indios who could in the past be killed because they did not matter were remade into political bodies whose deaths revealed and brought into question a colonial power structure that was—at least ideally—being dismantled. Yet this revaluation of Indigenous lives did little to change the underlying calculus, the instrumentalization of their deaths as the axis on which sovereignty rested. As with the notion of heroic sacrifice for oil, this did not really challenge the underlying truth: they were cannon fodder for the state. Dying for the state—or accepting the heroic status of such deaths—meant subjection to a particular expression of militaristic and patriarchal sovereignty. It required intensifying a masculinist incitement to resist the oppressive power of the state, or die fighting it, as Che did. Or, with Evo Morales in the presidency, and the uncomfortable proximity between the MAS government and the special troops trained to kill—the "soul-less ones"—it meant that one was expected to embrace this militaristic state.

In the end these are the limits of a certain way of talking about revolutionary sacrifice in the age of gas, a point to which I return in chapter 9 and the postscript. The language of heroic revolutionary struggle mobilized thousands, but when oriented toward sustaining the fossil fuel complex it became a thanatopolitical trap. Fossil capital benefited from the fact that indios were now sacrificed not because they were resisting the extractive state but because they were defending it. It was a struggle that increasingly devolved from one rooted in ideology to one trapped in a crude calculus of power. Certain bodies were exchanged for gas. A certain relation of power was exchanged for bodies. But just as one is not supposed to say that US troops died for oil, certain things are hard to say in Bolivia as well. What really happened in all these cases?

8 gas work

BY 2015 SANTA CRUZ HAD CALMED DOWN A BIT, POLITICALLY SPEAKING. Evo Morales and the ex-guerrilla fighter vice president, Álvaro García Linera, had come to a détente with the agrarian elite of the east, declaring a shared interest in economic growth and the expansion of the soy-based agricultural frontier. In the soy regions, smaller farmers were working as semiproletarian labor, underemployed on large farms or scrambling on smallholdings to produce and sell to the soy buyers, despite low prices and high debt. Those who had no land or jobs went to the city. The MAS and the latifundist elite had come to a pragmatic relationship, which is to say the MAS abandoned its aggressive efforts to redistribute land and kept the diesel and credit subsidies flowing to large-scale farmers (Webber 2016; Farthing 2019). The elites, in turn, desisted from open opposition to Morales. There was wealth to be had. Sectors like banking and construction always boom when hydrocarbon rents flow through an economy, and Santa Cruz was no exception. At the macro level, inequality and poverty were decreasing. But formal jobs were scarce. The so-called informal economy of the precariat, the underemployed and unemployed doing day-to-day survival work, still comprised 60–80 percent of the workforce (Webber 2017, 1870). Though statistics are hard to come by, there seemed to be an increase in reporting on criminality. Most disturbing was the rise in violence against women, a topic I return to in the next chapter. Gang-related activity, including some spectacular assaults on armored cars and banks, suggested an expansion of Brazilian drug trafficking organizations. On an almost daily basis, papers reported on a drug lab discovery in the region's hinterlands or an *ajuste de cuentas*, a killing related to trafficking disputes, especially in border towns through which cocaine paste moved east to Brazil or south to Argentina. On the other hand, consumption was on the rise: washing machine, TV, and air-conditioner imports were skyrocketing. Automobile imports were also up. The number of cars in the country doubled between 2005 and 2015. And that is counting only the legally registered ones. Sales of *chutos*, black market cars, were also hot. The already-clogged streets of the cities entered into a near permanent gridlock of horns and exhaust. The age of Morales and the age of gas had fueled a consumption boom.[1]

A new bypass—the G-77, named and built for the meeting of the G-77+China, held in Santa Cruz in 2014—now connects the airport to the city, bypassing much of the clogged north-south highway. The airport is also newly redone, having reaped the benefits of the renationalization of the airports and the rents from the gas. Along the G-77, billboards touted perfumes, tennis shoes, smartphones, and Bolivia's aspiration to be the "Energetic Heart of South America." Another celebrated a new solar power plant in Cobija, in Bolivia's far Amazonian north. Another announced the new thermoelectric (gas-fired) power plant on the southern Argentine border, set to export electricity. Pope Francis had also visited Bolivia and passed along this route. Another billboard showed his smiling image, saying, "I like this phrase, the 'process of change,'" referring to the slogan of Morales's government. (Evo Morales had returned the favor by offering him a wooden carving that combined the crucifix with the hammer and sickle.) Bolivia was a clash of contrasting symbols and icons, communism and hyperconsumption, fossil fuels and renewable energy, opulent wealth and grinding labor on the streets.

Heading south to the gas lands of the Chaco takes you through the bus station, once again. As one waits to board for interprovincial travel, the vendors of the street economy remain, much as they were in years past. The one novelty is the ubiquitous smartphone. Otherwise, daily work means selling to the travelers who pass through. On one day, two women offered *cuñapés* (a sweetish cheese and cassava flour muffin) and a Coke. The soda woman's basket, well worn, had a handle wrapped in plastic tape. Heavy layers of plastic bags were used as a makeshift cooler. The women would have had to navigate social ties, and maybe offer kickbacks, to get permission to sell here on the loading platform, because it is a prime spot. Everyone knows each other. The vendors know the drivers and the young men who load the buses, the fellow who sells newspapers, the one shining shoes, the employee who checks tickets, the private security guard who circulates. Near the bottom of the gas economy were jobs like these, women eking out a living selling home-cooked food to passengers. But gas rents bring liquidity, and more money circulating means that more trickles down, at least for now. Eavesdropping as usual, I watched as the soda woman, wearing flip-flops, a thin dress, and an apron, set down her heavy basket. She examined her hair, pulling at it like a college student plucking split ends during a lecture. She turned to her friend. "Look, it's falling out. They say it's because of stress."

In the bus, another monument of the Bolivian highways is also at work. This is the welcome-aboard salesman. For some exchange with the driver, these vendors perform well-rehearsed infomercials on board. Usually they are pitching a natural remedy. As you leave the bus terminal, the pitch begins, sometimes with a small portable megaphone: "Ladies and gentlemen, please forgive me for interrupting your journey, I'll only take a few minutes of your time, to offer you this little thing that is going to change your life." And so it goes. He puts a sample into everyone's hand—no obligation to buy, he assures you—as he moves down the aisle, eloquently, and with humor, invoking ailments that everyone has and offering the daily solution. On one day, it was *sábila*, a medicine allegedly used for two thousand years, long before the time of Christ, he said. Another day it is an herbal remedy that cures burns and scars, clears the skin, and will take away your pimples. Another cures exhaustion, tiredness. Another is a blood purifier; it burns fat. Outside the streets are crowded and diesel fumes waft in through the bus windows, burning the eyes. A woman sits on a curb, selling melons. A truck has opened a makeshift ceviche stand. In the newspaper, the MAS has moved forward with launching the effort to change the constitution and allow for Morales's reelection. A national referendum vote will be held on the question, scheduled for February 2016.

"Hold out your hand, try a little bit of the lotion," the vendor urges. The salesman gives his spiel. "This is not an expense," he says. "This is an investment in your skin. The lotion is thirty for one, fifty for two, and the information brochure is free." The bus driver moves up through the gears as the traffic lightens toward the edge of the city. The diesel engine knocks and makes a familiar gargling noise, black smoke pouring out behind the bus. As usually seems to be the case, sales were brisk. Maybe this is because travelers for the provinces usually go with extra money. "Give me two, give me two," say some of them. The vendor moves through the aisle collecting his samples and closing his sales, with mellifluous courtesy. A lady across the aisle tries the new lotion. Another tucks it into her bag. We arrive at the toll booth on the highway heading south. The lotion vendor descends. He will catch another bus back to the terminal and do it again. New food vendors board for a last quick chance at a sale: grilled corn, chicken, sodas, oranges, crackers. Coins change hands, and the economy trickles some more. The driver honks and hurries them out. And the bus heads south to the gas lands.

Thinking about work is another way to think about the excesses and contradictions of the gaseous state, the theme of these final chapters. I am not centrally concerned with labor in the gas industry, though I describe a bit of that below. The focus is on other kinds of work that people do to try to position themselves into a place where they can capture a bit of the money that circulates as excess. Though only 0.1 percent of the formal labor force is directly employed by the gas industry, the circulation of rents and royalties through public spending and investment created a situation in which almost everybody seems to be working in the name of the gas. Some of this is political work, done by those who maneuver and strategize to occupy public office, where gas rents flow through and control of budgets and allocative power is fought over. Some of it is government work, like that done by some of my Guarani friends now working as state functionaries in new teacher-training programs, universities, and language institutes.[2] Here I juxtapose a particular kind of political work—Guarani leaders negotiating with a gas company—with that of formal labor for the industry and the circulation of underemployed labor that surrounds it. In the Guarani case, I point out how the gas assemblage has wreaked some considerable havoc on Indigenous organizing, despite the influx of monetary resources for some leaders and communities. This unfolds, as I describe, through largely male-centric relationships between Guarani communities and the gas industry, while women are relegated to lower and unpaid support work. Through juxtaposition with formal and informal labor for the industry, I consider both the political limits of labor organizing as a means of transcending gas dependency or transforming wider political orders and describe how hierarchies of labor and dependence are reproduced by the gas assemblage. As scholars of hydrocarbon economies have argued, labor in and around the fossil fuel complex offers some capacity to pursue redistributive gains but ultimately limits the capacity for thinking politically outside and beyond it.[3] Expanded consumption and redistribution of surplus value or excess is in one sense the positive hallmark of the age of gas. Yet it also works to flatten Bolivian political horizons and generates its own secondary and often violent social excesses.

Since the 1990s, the Guarani region had been transformed into ground zero for the expanding gas apparatus of exploration, pipelines, processing plants, and related infrastructure. The setting for the story that follows is a subregion of Guarani country, a place of rugged hills and valleys that I will call Irenda, or water place. One of a dozen zones that make up the wider Guarani region, Irenda is composed of twenty-three communities, each with their own leadership. These leaders, almost invariably male, are called *mburuvicha* or *capitán*, the latter a term inherited from the Spanish colonial period. Irenda itself is called a captaincy (*capitanía*) and also has an elected leader, called *mburuvicha guasu* or *capitán grande* (big leader or big captain). Historically all Guarani captaincies were united, at least discursively, in a single organization called the Asamblea del Pueblo Guarani (APG). But with the rise of gas exploration and pipeline building, and efforts by the MAS party and the opposition parties to capture Guarani support, gas politics and party politics have created deep divisions within and between the captaincies. Communities struggle and quarrel internally as they try to wrest some bit of excess from the industry or the state. Irenda is one such area, now grappling with gas companies both state and foreign.

In 2017 a gas company that I will call Big South (BS) gained a concession to explore an area that intersected the eastern portion of Irenda's territory. The exploration had the most direct impact on three of Irenda's twenty-three communities. Though companies always try to negotiate with only the local communities, Irenda, for the moment, was unified.[4] As part of its exploration work, BS hired a subcontractor to do seismic. Doing seismic involves carving one-meter-wide trails in a grid across the entire exploration zone, setting explosive charges at intervals of several hundred meters and detonating these charges to generate an echogram of the underground in pursuit of geological signs that might mean gas or oil is present. Seismic in a neighboring region was blamed by communities for its impact on water supplies. Guarani theorized that the explosions diverted underground waterways. Game was also dispersed. Even more impactful was the arrival of lots of men from elsewhere. The men in the work camps would clear the bush, lay the charges, and operate the surveying and measuring devices. The presence of several hundred outside workers, invariably male, has been the source of more and less direct forms of violence against women in hydrocarbon landscapes globally.[5] The gas company would subcontract other firms to set up these worker camps and yet others to feed the workers (*catering*), wash clothes, and move equipment. The capture of a "catering" bid (the word in English is used) is seen as a lucrative opportunity for local aspiring entrepreneurs. These were all coveted jobs and contracts, though most were not obtained by Guarani.

The gas company stumbled in its initial dealings with the Guarani of Ïrenda. Initially BS met with Ïrenda's leaders, then led by a captain I will call José, and signed an initial agreement with José and other community leaders. While I was not privy to the exchanges that characterized this first signing, BS considered this document to be permission to carry out the entire project. Apparently, though, the signature was achieved with some promises made that the Guarani would have rights to participate in catering contracts and a certain allotment of jobs in the camps. After signing the initial agreement, BS initiated work on three seismic lines and an access road.

In 2018 the Guarani of Ïrenda put a stop to the work, alleging that BS had begun operations without permission. The stoppage led to interventions that reached up to the national ministry of the environment, which sided with BS. However, on the ground it was still unresolved. A meeting was called between BS and the leaders of all twenty-four communities of Ïrenda. That was the point at which I became aware of the process. By this time, the communities had ousted the captain, José, who had become embroiled in allegations of corruption and was in some legal trouble. (Apparently, the initial signature had also been had with some financial incentive allegedly captured by José.) The new captain, Vicente (a pseudonym), invited me to come to the meeting with BS. Early on a Saturday morning, we convened in the central area of the zone. Vicente, his advisor, other local leaders, and I loaded into two pickup trucks and slowly made our way up a bumpy dirt road over steep mountain ridges and down toward the community closest to the gas operation.

On our drive in, Vicente asked his advisor, Marcos, another old acquaintance of mine, to explain the situation to me. Marcos recounted what I detailed here and pointed out that the Guarani had only given their permission for the company to do preliminary work, including surveying a site for a communications antenna. The Guarani had not given BS permission to begin the project as a whole. Marcos deemed the access road and initial seismic lines an "infraction." "Had there been a prior consultation?" I asked, referring to the right to prior consultation enshrined in international and national Indigenous rights legislation. Researchers have detailed the problems inherent in prior consultation processes in Bolivia, which have been weakened, along with environmental impact oversight, despite Evo Morales's stated commitments to Indigenous rights (Schilling-Vacaflor 2014; *Página Siete* 2019). For example, Carlos Villegas, the nationalist I described in chapter 4, who became the director of the reconstituted YPFB under Evo Morales, suggested once that prior consultation was a waste of time. For Indigenous peoples, prior consultation is an important space for claiming rights. Yet the government and the industry frequently draw Indigenous communities into other political situations and relations that can intentionally blur the formal procedure or evade it altogether. State decrees in recent years have further limited consultation or done away with it as an attempt to accelerate gas projects. Internal schisms generated by the company or the government itself contribute to this, such that prior consultation is as apt to be reduced to prior or ex-post facto compensation, which involves the passing of a bribe or the transfer of money or a project to the community.

So was there a consultation? "Well, sort of," answered Marcos. But, he explained, it was only a preliminary consultation. It was not permission (*permiso*) for them to begin work. The definition of consultation, as well as its application, was deeply ambiguous. Here permiso, a local colloquialism of great significance, is not enshrined in any law. No prior consultation rights confer a veto right to communities. Permiso here was about a social license to operate, that is, a negotiated form of informal consent to industry access. As we bumped along, I commented on the recent antipipeline struggle in the United States, the #NoDAPL battle waged by the Oceti Sakowin at Standing Rock. "What happened in the end?" my friends wondered. "They sent in the police," I said, "and the pipeline went through." After some silence, Vicente responded, "We know we cannot say no, because if we do they will bring in the *fuerza pública* [the public force, i.e., the police]. What we hope for is that they recognize us [*que nos reconozcan*]."

Recognition is also a politically useful colloquialism. *Reconocer* is to recognize one's political status. Even more than the issue of consultation itself, this political recognition of the entire territory and its leadership structure was a crucial issue. But reconocer can also refer to the payment of a wage for some labor or compensation for some damage. It entailed an economic recognition via redistribution, a collective claim to a rightful share.[6] The Guarani hoped to be able to get something out of the company. Far from circuits of gas rent circulation that went through white-dominated department and municipal capitals, and not enjoying the benefits of natural gas consumption as in urban areas, the Guarani had to wage their own political labor to quarrel directly over the excess.

Leaders from other communities arrived on foot and in other vehicles. About one hundred Guarani were there. All but two were men. The BS team of three men and one woman, the community relations coordinator, arrived in their own pickup truck from the east, where Ïrenda's territory abuts a larger municipality where BS had an office. The meeting unfolded like many others I observed. The Guarani men sat in desks brought out from the school, lined up under a large shade tree. The local leader leaned a whiteboard against the tree while Marcos wrote out the agenda. Vicente and Marcos sat in the front, on the left side. Vicente motioned for me to sit next to him. I was a silent bit of excess myself, giving the Guarani something extra, a gringo observer assumed to have some weight in this encounter with Big South. (The BS team did eye me curiously, and later asked what I was up to in the region.) Waiting, the Guarani men chewed coca, chatted, and laughed, always joking, as Guarani are invariably doing.

The BS representatives huddled in a group on the right side. The BS men—Guarani would call them white or karai—sported woven Guarani shoulder bags and also chewed coca. The BS woman was smiling and vivacious. In classic male Guarani style, Vicente and Marcos made quiet jokes about whether she might marry one of them, upending gendered racial hierarchies that generally yield marriages between karai men and Guarani women but not the reverse. The BS men also joked with the Guarani, using words like "friends" (*amigos*), and later made their own sexist jokes amid the tension of the negotiation. It was a masculinist scene, like most in the world of gas.

To add incongruity to the situation, many of the Guarani men wore the distinctive blue denim shirts and jeans of one or another gas company. This was a signal of a distinctive male experience, that of having been employed by the gas apparatus, probably as temporarily contracted manual labor, clearing roads, driving trucks, or opening trails for seismic crews. Not a few of the Guarani also wore heavy leather boots, also icons of the gasmen. To top it off, my friend Vicente, the regional grand captain, was wearing a bright red nylon jacket emblazoned with "Halliburton," the US gas services company that works in drilling and well-cementing in Bolivia. (Far from the matter at hand, the Halliburton logo took my mind wandering to Dick Cheney, oil, and the Iraq War.[7]) So as the BS white men were sporting Guarani woven bags and chewing coca to try to fit in, the Guarani men were engaged in their own mimicry, with their own tokens of gaseous masculine authority and labor in the service of gas.

This scene lent itself to a sense of masculine confrontation but also one of back-slapping and deal-making. The two Guarani women who had accompanied our group sat quietly to one side and did not speak out during the meeting. The women of the local host community sat on logs and benches set up at a bit of a distance, off to one side. There they cradled children, spun yarn from wool, and watched and listened quietly. None spoke publicly. Other local women were working, preparing the lunch that would be served to all present. Women had clearly labored beforehand too. Two plastic buckets full of *kägui*, chicha, a sweet corn drink, were set on a small table between the men's chairs and the whiteboard. Making kägui takes several days of women's work. As the meeting progressed, men took turns serving themselves cups of kägui. The scene mirrored the wider patriarchal form of the gaseous state, a political space dominated by men jousting over the excess with the work of women largely invisibilized and unpaid. Recall, again, the picture of Standard's oilmen paying Guarani laborers in 1924 while the women watched (figure 1.1).

The meeting got underway. After greetings, Vicente stood up to explain first in Guarani, and then in Spanish, that the meeting had been called to discuss the fact that BS had started work without permission. Trying to defuse the tension, he joked in Spanish for the sake of the BS reps, saying that he hoped that, as in the selection of a new pope, "white smoke would go up" after they were done. Vicente asked the BS team to retire to the schoolhouse on the other side of the soccer field so the Guarani could discuss the "infraction." Then, mostly in Guarani, Marcos made the case to all that an infraction had happened, since the document signed by the ousted captain, José, was only to allow them to survey an antenna site. The conversation quickly turned to money. Many of the Guarani had experience with seismic and they, like the BS crew, knew there was a calculating metric used by the industry to determine compensation for damages. But Vicente argued that this was not compensation for impacts of the seismic work. It was, as we had discussed in the truck, a *multa* (fine), since this was an infraction. Before anything else could be discussed, this had to be settled. They decided to calculate the fine based on local land values. So, they estimated the length and width of the road and trails already cut, and set a price by square meter. The Guarani calculated a negotiating window with a high (2.50/m², about 240,000 bolivianos) and a low (1.50/m², about 140,000 bolivianos). They would start by demanding the high number, about US$35,000. The quarrel was a way of enacting sovereignty, of sorts. With the vocabulary of permission (permiso), infraction (*infracción*), recognition (*reconocimiento*), and fine (*multa*), the Guarani were appropriating the language of state authority.

The BS reps were called back to the tree. Vicente explained that BS had committed an infraction and that they would have to pay a fine. On the whiteboard, Vicente wrote out the calculations that the Guarani had worked out. When the final figure was announced, the BS crew shook their heads in disbelief. One of the BS engineers abruptly stood up. In a loud voice, he said, "There has been no infraction and that has already been determined by the Ministry!" In contrast to Vicente's measured tone, the engineer spoke in a register familiar to the Guarani, that of a boss (*patrón*). Vicente had a poker face but he turned and quietly whispered to Marcos, in Guarani, "They are already starting with us [*Omboipima ñandeve*]." It was akin to "here we go." The engineer went on, recounting that the dispute had been resolved by the Ministry, which said there was a miscommunication but not an infraction. He rattled off dates and places where BS and the Guarani made various agreements. It would be illegal, he suggested, to make any payment to the Guarani.

Unperturbed, Vicente stood up calmly and spoke to his people in Guarani while the BS team looked on with no apparent understanding of what was said: "We are here to argue with our enemies because of the damage they have done. We did not give them permission. We should help ourselves here by staying united. If they are going to get angry with us, then we too will get angry." Skilled in dealing with white people, though always doing so from an asymmetrical disadvantage, the Guarani listened with no overt emotional reaction. Well aware that bribes may have circulated backstage to some of the Guarani gathered there, Vicente sought to show the local community that their best option for dealing with BS was by maintaining territorial unity. Then in Spanish, Vicente turned to the BS team and asked for calm and mutual respect. He said again that the permission given was only to come in and "look," not to carry out the project. With quiet assurance, he told BS that if they could not reach an agreement, "I will be the first one here to blockade the project."

Still overheated, the engineer repeated that any payment would be illegal. Marcos, the advisor, then stood up, equally taciturn. He said that if BS wanted to talk about legality, "We can all go back and talk about how the first agreement was reached," making reference to José, the former leader who was now in the courts. This bold play abruptly shut down any more BS discussion of legality. Marcos went on to say that the Ministry knows that in order for the work to get done, sometimes the Guarani and the companies have to resolve things themselves. "Resolving this" was another euphemism for the transfer of money. Another BS man, Carlos, clearly more astute than the engineer, stood up. "Yes, my friends, we must recognize that whether the government says so or not, there was a transgression here. And we need to be flexible." At that point he made a sexist joke about the struggles of a man with three wives and asked for time to call his boss. The BS team retreated to the schoolhouse while the Guarani waited, chewing coca, smoking, and drinking kägui. The women sat quietly on the margins.

When BS came back to the tree, the Guarani asked for them to be straight. Just tell us, Carlos, what do you have to offer? Carlos played the role of someone whose hands were tied by budgets. Shrugging his shoulders, and acknowledging the BS mistake, he was apologetic. "I'm sorry, I understand your position, but all I can offer is 35,000 bolivianos [about US$5,000]." This was well below the Guarani's low ask and a fraction of their high. Yet Marcos, sitting next to both of us, whispered quickly to Vicente, "That's good [*Jae ikavi*]." I was taken aback. We had spent all that time calculating the amounts on our phones and this seemed like rapid acquiescence. The Guarani again asked the BS team to retire while they discussed the counteroffer.

Here the affective lure of money began to be clear. Another leader, to my eyes a bit too cozy with BS, stood up to suggest that this was a reasonable counteroffer given the reality of budgets and the need to maintain good relations. Indeed, the Guarani just over the mountain, he said, had already given their permission. If Irenda did not make a deal, they might get left out. Another leader stood up defiantly to say they should ask for 100,000 bolivianos. Another said 50,000. Yet another said, take the 35,000 and ask them to fix the road. The consensus seemed to be 50,000. The BS reps were called back. The scene was repeated again—looks of surprise, claims of having hands tied, concern for the Guarani. The BS team left and came back again with 42,000 and road repair, less than a third of the Guarani low ask. Again, Marcos whispered "That's good." The Guarani, with Vicente's guidance, nodded in consent. It had come down to being able to capture a small bit of excess from the company budget. Vicente reported to all present that the money would be used for a potable-water supply project.

The discussion continued about the catering contract. Supposedly BS had promised the contract to the Guarani, or at least had promised that the Guarani could decide who got the contract. This was another fuzzy extralegal means through which the Guarani could reap some excess. By claiming political authority, the Guarani in other areas had demanded some right to decide on subcontracting, meaning they could extract a payment from some white petty capitalist to whom they channeled the contract. But BS had already given the catering contract to a national firm. The BS man, Carlos, again apologetic, said that there were corruption cases already tied to such kickbacks on catering contracts, indirectly offering a warning to the Guarani. He said BS could not afford legal problems. This returned some tension to the scene. Marcos gave a rousing statement, in Spanish, about the fact that the Guarani also had a right to do businesses like catering, because "as Guarani, are we not also Bolivians?!" This was directed to the reps of BS, three of whom were not Bolivian. Carlos, again apologetically, promised that any local opportunities for Guarani to be involved in the work camp economy (washing clothes or baking bread) would be encouraged. The Guarani conceded defeat.

Then the discussion turned to actual jobs. Out of four hundred jobs for the various weeks of the seismic phase, forty-five were reserved for the Guarani. Twenty of these were unskilled, men who would carry equipment or hack through the bush with machetes and axes, just like the Guarani peons hired by Standard Oil a century ago. Twenty-five of the jobs were skilled—chainsaw operators, drivers, medics, crew chiefs, and survey assistants. The Guarani began discussing how these jobs would be allocated.

As day wore into night, the encounter was transformed from a confrontation with the gas company to an intense discussion between the Guarani men themselves. Vicente acknowledged that the local community would get more jobs than other communities because it was directly impacted. But who would get to fill the other slots? Each of the community leaders sought some recognition of their status, which would come from their ability to allocate a job. This was a space of internal conflict. The effort to generate a list of names in public did not prosper. As with the contracts, the capacity to allocate was also the right to demand payment. In Bolivia, a well-positioned political actor might get a job for a friend but will do so at a price, a one-time payment or a percentage of the salary. On this level, the Guarani-gas relationship had devolved into a job-selling venture. In Guarani politics, this expressed itself as a claim to a political right. As with the Guarani demand to let them decide who got the catering contracts, a Guarani leader had to give his *aval* (imprimatur) so that Guarani individuals could take a company job. This aval had a price, which a captain might receive in cash, kinship obligations, or some other return. (If at this point the reader has the urge to call this corruption, digress here.[8]) They were talking about tough short-term jobs like hacking through the bush. These were small stakes compared to real industry jobs and the profits reaped by the multinational firms. Even so, in hardscrabble communities, the Guarani coveted any access to the cash wage that manual laborers earned on gas projects. But hashing it out was an internal issue that generated intense conflict and jealousy. The BS crew said, "Just send us a list," and loaded into their truck and left. To avoid public argument, Vicente astutely cajoled the men to think with love (*mboroaiu*) for each other. The list of names would be "resolved" in other venues.

As the Guarani prepared to depart, the capitán of the local community thanked all the leaders for coming. He announced that the following Friday there would be a ritual to ask permission of the *iya*, spiritual beings who have dominion over the bush. The iya are a quintessential expression of what Marisol de la Cadena (2015, 14–23) has termed a kind of excess of its own, a surplus knowledge and experience that operates beyond both the legal and the extra-legal spaces that conjoined the Guarani and the gas industry. What is revealing is that this Guarani knowledge, also a form of work and exchange, albeit with supernatural entities, was also aimed at working for the gas. But as with the sorting out of jobs, Guarani dealings with the iya are internal matters. So here this part of the story ends.

The 0.1 Percent behind the Fence

Back in Camiri, the former oil capital, the YPFB jobs that once made oil workers kings were largely gone. A few families formerly connected to YPFB were able to parlay their experience into employment for the new YPFB or one of the multinational firms. Elana Shever (2012) traces a similar history in Argentina in the 1990s where family ties and class position were determinants of whether workers would find a niche after privatization. In the foreign firms that dominate gas extraction, Bolivian engineers now labor for Brazilian, French, or Spanish managers, or for one of several service companies, including Chinese, American, and Argentine firms. Nonetheless, direct employment by the big multinational firms is small. And overall, work in the oil and gas industry is only 0.1 percent of the nation's work force, a minuscule yet privileged minority.[9] For Bolivians in the gas lands, this labor force becomes visible when crews come into town in their pickup trucks, with steel-toed boots, heavy blue denim shirts, and jeans. All such workers are referred to as petroleros (oilmen), though most are looking for gas. A handful employed at the upper levels of YPFB and the foreign firms are women. Marisol, whose dad worked for the old YPFB, is one of them.

Following a divorce from the oil worker, Marisol's mother cobbled together a living in Camiri working to put her kids through school. With the husband gone and YPFB privatized, the postbonanza era was lean. She knitted sweaters to sell, washed clothes, made bread, and prepared lunches for pensioners. Given the ways of the oilmen, such women-led families were common in Camiri. While her sisters ended up in early marriages with kids, Marisol dedicated herself to studying petroleum engineering like her dad. She had an eye on the gas boom on the horizon. When the foreign firms started to arrive, many ex-YPFB technicians used their connections, as Marisol's father did, to land jobs for their children in the new *empresas extranjeras* (foreign companies). Marisol's brother ended up as a driver for Halliburton and even had a stint of training in Oklahoma. One of her sisters married a taxi driver who later got a job driving trucks servicing one of the big gas plants. For her part, Marisol landed a job at one of the big multinationals based in Santa Cruz. I will call it BM, for short. From being a family largely dependent on the state oil company, they transitioned into a family immersed in multinational gas.

In the early twenty-first century, Marisol and her family, who were decidedly *not* Indigenous, were ambivalent about Evo Morales and nationalization. By 2006, when the right wing was besieging Morales's government, Marisol told me that anti-Morales and antinationalization emails were daily fare circulating among company employees, all of whom were based in Santa Cruz, the bastion of anti-Morales sentiment. Indeed, many of the gas companies were firm backers of the right-wing autonomist project, since Morales threatened to put more national demands on companies and their excess profits while Santa Cruz hoped to carve out its own privileged relationships with the industry. Though Morales came out on top, his less-than-radical program also evolved into a partnership with the firms, which Morales referred to as *socios*. When BM's CEO visited Bolivia to announce new investments, Morales, wearing an oil worker's helmet, much like an employee himself, posed for pictures with him.

Marisol worked in BM's office in Santa Cruz. She told me sexual harassment was rife but she was doing well, with a mortgage on an apartment and a note on a midsized SUV, as well as meeting commitments to help out her mother and sisters. This formal job among the 0.1 percent working in the hydrocarbon industry was one of the most coveted in the country. For Marisol, though, it was as if she were working to support four or five people despite not having children of her own. When she flew out to the gas plant for two-week stints, she sported the steel-toed boots and the denim workshirt emblazoned with BM's logo. Marisol regaled me with stories of life inside the enormous BM plant, facilities surrounded by tall chain-link fencing that marked a stark divide with the rural world outside. Everything was a marvel to which she was becoming accustomed, despite her modest upbringing. Marisol said it was like a five-star hotel: "We've got catering. We've got a buffet at every meal. Or you can have a la carte. There's even an outdoor running and bicycle track for exercise. There's a gym too, but women are somewhat uncomfortable there. It's all air-conditioned. And there's cable TV and internet of course." These are not conditions faced by the roughnecks of old, the workers who shared their drilling stories with me. Nor were these the temporary crews, like those Guarani men quarreling over the hard manual labor in Ïrenda. These were engineers and technical staff who monitored the flow of gas out of the ground and into Bolivia's pipeline networks. Given the poverty outside the fence, the relative luxury inside the fence was a form of excess of its own.

It was not only the luxury of the living conditions but the discipline that seemed new and different. "It's not like YPFB," she said, referring to the oil and gas company her father had worked for. "There is a lot of discipline." In one conversation, her brother-in-law chimed in to comment that the place was "immaculate." He told of strict rules for workers, who must all wear steel-toed boots and a hard hat. No alcohol is allowed. Chewing coca while working, seen as a near sacred birthright in Bolivia, is forbidden. There were tight regulations on drivers with speed-control technology and instant dismissal for accidents. Everything was tightly controlled. Marisol came to appreciate it, embracing a discourse of professionalism and modernity. Order and control were associated with the foreigners in charge. During another of our many conversations, Marisol's mother sat listening and shook her head as she remembered the old days, embodied in her drunken philandering husband. "It's not like it was before [Ya no es como antes]," she said a bit thankfully.

Gendered to the core, as one might expect, most of the well-paid jobs are held by men and all involve university education, itself limited by class position heavily mediated by a longer history of racial exclusion. At the bottom, cleaning and catering services are largely staffed by women. The Guarani and other poor rural folk who live around the plants are largely relegated to doing piecemeal labor like clearing brush, washing clothes, or doing basic construction. What this sets up is a privileged labor force, largely male and urban, socially and economically enclaved in the cities or in periodic stints at the remote plants, safely ensconced inside the fence.

Outside the fenced-in enclave of the plant, there are neither air-conditioning nor buffets. The Guarani have seen their lives upended by gas without the benefit of territorial rights or great economic gain (Anthias 2018). Those inside the fence see those outside as a threat, poised for blackmail. For Marisol, the fenced-in areas were "high security," she said. "We've got forty cameras" to monitor inside and out. But "we're surrounded by Guarani communities, and they'll blockade you for anything. So BM is always paying. We paid for a cow that drowned on the road. We paid for someone's bull that died, though it wasn't our fault. We buy baskets, artisanry, everything." Here the excess trickles out to Guarani workers to stave off more intense protest. As is the case nationally, there is a latent sense that the indios are always there, threatening the flow of gas and surplus. "They can blockade us at any time [*Nos pueden bloquear*]," she says. I had come to see the gas apparatus as a behemoth that the Guarani, like my friends at Irenda, could scarcely resist. But Marisol's complaint betrayed a sense of anxiety that characterizes an industry in a hurry in a highly unequal—and sometimes volatile—country, an industry that wants to make the gas flow as fast as possible, with little delay, because time is money. That is why consultation rights and environmental impact regulations had been weakened, to save time.

If BM sought to keep disruptions outside from coming in, daily life outside the fence was subjected to social and ecological disruption that came out. For Guarani and their neighbors, this entailed first a visceral, aural, and visual transformation of daily life and landscapes. Around processing facilities a constant, mind-numbing roar of machinery has altered the natural audible space. Airplanes and helicopters ferry in engineers to inspect operations. Trucks roll in and out. Dust roils up along new roads now maintained by and for the industry. Gas flaring lights up the sky. "There is no night-time where a gas plant is," said one leader, referring to the gas flaring and bright lights that burn 24/7 at these plants. Sex work and its similars spread. Women with few options seek boyfriends connected to the gas payroll in some way. Brothels, of sorts, emerge on transit points where labor, truck drivers, and engineers circulate, from makeshift tents in the hot and dusty environs of work camps to the more elaborate economies of sex in provincial cities like Villamontes and Yacuiba. Much like the fracking regions of North Dakota, where excess cash is tied to excess masculine desire, the gas region has become a sex-trafficking hotspot (Zabala and Ramírez Quiroga 2016).

The heyday of Latin American oil nationalism saw the growth of oil workers' unions like that of the old timers I talked to in Camiri. Despite their flaws, these unions represented a structural component of a redistributive state and wider space for making demands. With the neoliberal eruption of the 1980s and 1990s, these unions, along with the state-owned industries on which they depended, were dismantled or greatly diminished, marking a significant shift away from an era of labor protagonism, albeit one of a rather privileged sector of labor. Though the YPFB has been reborn, and its workers are unionized, organized labor offers little impetus for change (Haarstad 2009a, 2009b; McNelly 2018). The private multinational firms, like BM, are not unionized, and subcontracting is still the dominant model, reducing costs and weakening organizing capacity. The result is that in and around the gas plants, as Stephen Reyna and others have observed in the urban and peri-urban margins of oil operations, groups of the unemployed, mobilized by the possibility of jobs, proliferate (Behrends, Reyna, and Schlee 2011). But neoliberalism could not do away with the spirit of collective claims-making and organizing. So, in ever-organized Bolivia, even the unemployed create unions, such that one can find groups like the Federation of Unemployed Workers of Yacuiba or the Association of Skilled Manual Laborers of Yacuiba, who may compete with workers of a neighboring town's Association of Skilled Manual Laborers of Pocitos. Seeking catering jobs has yielded in another place an Association of Gastronomic Workers. These assemblages, usually tied to criollo rather than Indigenous organizations, represent provincial urban efforts, ever fragmenting into localist spaces, to demand some form of employment. Frequently they threaten to blockade the operations themselves, if enough money or jobs are not released to calm the expectations. At this writing, for instance, the BM plant where Marisol sometimes worked was confronting a conjoined protest of local Guarani communities and local groups of the "unemployed," all seeking jobs where there were none to be had.

Seen from the extractivist's-eye view, a phrasing I borrow from Macarena Gómez-Barris (2017), the Guarani and their territory are merely sociogeographic obstacles to "rescuing"—as the industry says—the gas that is "trapped" underneath Guarani lands. Pipeline transects sketch new trails out of the region and toward the cities, east and then south to Argentina, west to Tarija, north toward La Paz and Santa Cruz, and from there across the hinterlands to fuel the industrial behemoth at São Paulo, Brazil. A giant web of gas flowing out generates gas rents flowing back to the country, but only with some difficulty does this excess trickle down to rural backwaters, and only then through hard-fought struggles and quarrels that absorb the political and affective energies of daily life.

Movement Work

Back on the ground out in the Guarani gas lands, the impacts of two decades of gas industry expansion are visible in the state of the Guarani movement. In 2018 I stood on Camiri's main avenue waiting to greet Guarani leaders gathered for an assembly. As I waited, I watched a local man—a city resident—his legs doubled up against his chest, come scooting down the street. His legs, it seemed, were permanently locked into a bent position. He ambulated, sort of, by rocking forward onto his fists and then dragging his bottom behind. Reaching forward and leaning onto his fists, he lifted his buttocks and legs off the ground, at least enough to drag them forward, and set them down again. He was on the cobblestone street. Why was he not up on the sidewalk, I wondered? His head no higher than a truck tire, he must have been barely visible to the drivers of taxis, cars, and tractor trailers that were rumbling down Camiri's main avenue, which connects the thoroughfare between Santa Cruz, in the north, and Argentina, to the south. Diesel exhaust hung in the air. The crawling man made his way to who knows where, perhaps a spot to seek coins from passersby. Scenes like this have long been common in Bolivia. It was at once heart-wrenching and normal. As Guarani gathered for their meeting inside the assembly hall to quarrel over rents and compensations, the crawling man continued his fist-to-bottom ambulation, down the street. Clearly the democratic cultural and political revolution had a long way to go.

In the two decades I have worked with the Guarani, things have changed dramatically. The leaders are younger. They are still mostly men, many less fluent in their language than the captains of just a few years ago. The older leaders lament the state of the organization. Young women increasingly lament the male-dominated fields of negotiation and struggle with the gas companies and the government. "Ninety percent of the men are useless," said one young Guarani woman, inspired by a recent trip to Chiapas, Mexico, to visit Zapatista communities where things seemed to be better. The problems are familiar: men are said to be more easily corrupted by the gasmen and government men, who play up, in a guffawing way, the need to "get the job done." Visits to bars, brothels, nice hotels, and nice restaurants have long characterized the venues where gas companies have tried to cajole a signature from a Guarani leader. The corruption of the fossil patriarchy is evident, and clearly so to women. Yet, against the internal critiques that some Guarani have sold out to the MAS, others stand firmly by the government, in acquiescence to a process of gas industry expansion that, at least from here, appeared unassailable.

Based on scores of conversations with Guarani friends, there was a generalized assessment that the "gas business screwed us up [*empresas ore roikomegua*]." In Isoso, a friend tells me, "We're divided between the greens [those behind Santa Cruz's governor] and the blues [the MAS]." In Irenda, as detailed previously, leaders had fallen to corruption charges and divisions grew between communities. In another zone, the battle over jobs had led to blows between community members. In yet another, domestic violence against women was on the increase. Some men were complaining after women started appealing to the judicial system, paradoxically aided by a gas company–funded center for women. The word for jealousy, *motarëi*, or *envidia* in Spanish, litters my notes on these conversations. Friends who worked at different public entities were no longer speaking, divided by party politics. Another longtime leader blamed the right-wing opposition, the Verdes, for doing everything it could to split the movement against the MAS. Those more closely aligned to the government of the MAS were embittered with other Guarani communities who dared take money from the opposition governor of Santa Cruz, Rubén Costas. If, in other contexts, the coming to ground of the structural realities of gas or oil extraction generates a pervasive sense of fear (Reyna 2007), here the dominant sentiments combined aspirations for capturing some of the excess coproduced with unsettledness and internal tension.

Another longtime ally lamented that it was prebendalism, the consequences of political patronage, that was tearing everyone apart. "We're not able to take advantage of this great historical moment," he said, referring to the political shift underway in the country. "We don't know who the enemy is anymore." Another young Guarani, on the fact that many karai (white people) who were once their enemies were now acting like they were friends, agreed. "They're taking advantage of the MAS to take our space away, those who were our enemies." He was referring to the fact that many of the right-wing of Santa Cruz had by then been converted into MAS supporters. A more militant leader suggested that the Guarani had lost sight of what was going on. Many young Guarani teachers were using their relatively stable salaries to take on debt. Teachers and some communities who received large compensation payments from gas companies were buying cars. The microlending boom evolved in the early twenty-first century to medium-scale loans, given the excess circulation of cash. Debt was widespread. Grifters traveled through rural communities, hawking appliances and furniture on installment plans, seeking to extract from the poor only to disappear before the last payment and the furniture showed up. Others commented on the arrival of Colombians in the Camiri market. With more cash circulating, Colombians sought clients who would deposit money for them as a means to *blanquear* (whiten, or launder) drug money. Sex labor and trafficking, and even kidnapping, were on the rise. The daughter of a colleague disappeared temporarily, the victim of express sexual trafficking. Other young people without employment became runners or hiders of drugs. The militant said, "Capitalism seeks to find a way in, and to trap us. It has totally perforated our organization. We need to figure out how to activate our organization, as it was before." Another lamented that there were more red light bulbs in Camiri than there were in the days of the YPFB. He was referring to the motels or brothels. Another longtime friend known for his acerbic humor countered those criticizing the MAS by saying:

> Yes, we've got corrupt leaders. And Evo tells us to get our act together, but the government doesn't prosecute these corrupt leaders. And we don't either, because they are our relatives. So maybe there will be a punishment when they get to heaven. Maybe God will make [a former leader] get a whipping for that deal he made, and maybe [another corrupt leader] will have to weed God's fields for all eternity. But look at the MAS, what they've done. Projects, investments, schools, jobs. And the [right wing]? All they talk about is entrepreneurs; they want every woman to have a cart selling in the street. That's not a vision of the country. But it's true. We're divided. Maybe the right wing needs to return to power so it shakes us up, so that we can unify once again.

Between money, jobs, and party politics, and new forms of violence, especially against women, the tenor of discourse was summed up by a Guarani word, *oikomegua*—everything is messed up. Against the rather constrained space from which Vicente and the Guarani of Irenda were able to carve out a bit of recognition from BS, thus constituting a particular kind of limited self-determination, this array of conflictive, anxious quarreling revealed the deeper dislocating effects of gas work.

It is true that the Guarani are trying to reconstitute their organization through other means. Some are organic and internal, including informal gatherings between second-generation leaders trying to rekindle an ideological base for redirecting the organization. Another trajectory is territorial autonomy. Autonomy—that word with so many valences—here refers to the possibility that municipalities with Guarani majorities might be able to transform themselves into autonomous territorial entities, or, "Indigenous Municipalities." In Charagua, where autonomy is most advanced, community members rewrote the municipal statute to transform the town from a white-dominated city council into a political configuration that mirrors the more organic social and spatial configuration of Guarani captaincies (Morell i Torra 2018). In Guakaya and Kaipependi, Guarani communities were also gearing up to start their own process of autonomy through a referendum. Latin America has seen a number of utopian projects tied to the discourse of autonomy, most notably that of the Zapatistas in Mexico. Yet here in the gas lands the Guarani process might not be so radical. The reconfiguration of political representation at the municipal level may allow for some democratization of economic and political power, that is, access to decision-making processes and budgets that impinge on local needs, from roads to water systems to housing. On the other hand, rent and royalty circulation—the politics of the percentages—has created high political stakes. Guarani autonomy, with men generally as the main protagonists, will yield new masculine-centric circuits for the quarrel over the excess, legal and otherwise. This might marginalize traditional mestizo and white elites, a pyrrhic decolonial victory. As long as it depends on gas work, it will be something less utopian than a world otherwise.

9 quarrel over the excess

SIMILAR TO THE GUARANI, WHOSE EFFORTS TO EKE OUT A SEMBLANCE OF local self-determination by quarreling over jobs and cash against the dominance of the state-backed gas company, the country as a whole quarreled over the excess while situated in a position of subordination to fossil capital. The foreign companies and the national treasury reaped great reward with the higher prices of oil and gas from 2005 to 2014. In macroeconomic terms, the economy was doing quite well. This meant that the government was also able to distribute more, giving the appearance of a bonanza. Flushing huge amounts of gas royalties into the system—whether as public works, public-sector jobs, direct cash transfers, massive contracts, monumental stadiums, or various forms of subsidies—the gaseous state had managed to deliver by spending the surplus, the excess. With all its warts, the MAS government and Evo Morales, at least if relative stability and reelection mean anything, were successful at mediating the unwieldy assemblage of interests spanning eastern Bolivian capitalists, urban Aymara and Quechua merchants, rural coca growers and farmers, and a range of others who had become materially and affectively dependent on the circulation of the excess.

If Sergio Almaraz could ask in 1967 what should be done with so much gas, the political debate during the late 2010s was largely over whether the excess had been squandered and when the gas might run out. As prices began to decline in 2014, with uncertainty about the Brazilian and Argentine markets and much polemic over how much gas was left in the ground, critics and opposition parties hoping to oust Morales started talking more and more about wasteful spending. The government borrowed more money and implemented financial incentives for the foreign gas and oil companies. The hope was to spur investment and exploration for new gas and oil reserves. The MAS was also strategizing to allow Morales to run for a fourth term. The MAS called for a national referendum to abolish term limits, as written into the constitution. The referendum vote was scheduled for February 21, 2016. Having handily won every vote ever taken, Morales was confident. The right-wing opposition had no real alternative policy agenda other than to get rid of Morales and seize the reins of the gaseous state for itself. So going in to the referendum vote, the opposition had one strategy: destroy Morales's charismatic image through an affective politics. The question of gaseous excess was at its center. Recognizing that much of Morales's support was tied to his capacity to perform a range of affective roles—landlord, caregiver, Indigenous leader, revolutionary, nationalist icon, antiracist liberator—the opposition's tactic was to heighten a generalized state of abjection and moral revulsion and make it stick to Morales. There was plenty of excess to work with. Corruption was seemingly everywhere, as it always had been. As has been true since the 1970s, the problem of drug trafficking implicating people in positions of power was also front-page news. Yet little of this stuck to Morales. The state made a show of punishing those caught, or at least some of them. But then came the torrid story of a president's mistress, a dead love child, and Chinese construction contracts. It was a juicy story indeed.

Just prior to the referendum vote, Carlos Valverde Bravo, the ex–intelligence chief and cruceño purveyor of the fable of the innocent mercenaries from chapter 7, launched a bombshell story in the media: Morales once had a mistress, a beautiful woman who had access to the inner halls of power. The mistress had given birth to a child. Morales had not legally recognized the child as his own. Yet tragically, the child had died in infancy. What is more, the former lover worked for a Chinese construction company. She had used her proximity to Morales to reap no-bid contracts for her employer, which had almost $500 million in state-funded jobs. At least, that's how Valverde's story went. The ex-lover publicly confirmed the story and demanded that Evo Morales acknowledge the truth.

Pointing out Morales's machismo—along with numerous offensive comments about women and homosexuality—had already been seen to be an effective way to erode his image among some segments of the population. In addition, the issue of debt to the Chinese and the proliferation of Chinese companies in Bolivia had also sparked a growing anti-China discourse coming from the Bolivian right. Here both stuck to Morales in a perfect storm of sexual, moral, and political dirt. Morales bungled in his responses, saying at one point that the woman seemed familiar (as if he had forgotten about her). And then, he first denied, then confirmed, the existence of the child, all of which made him out to look like a typical chauvinist *mujeriego* (womanizer). Just four days before the vote, those playing thanatopolitics and looking for useful dead bodies were also at work. In unclear circumstances, a march in El Alto led by a political boss loosely tied to the MAS turned violent when some of the marchers lit fire to the municipal building, then controlled by an opposition party. Again the police were absent. Six city workers died. Were those who started the fire rogue agents working for the MAS? Or the opposition? Or some other forces seeking destabilization? First the dead love child and now charred dead bodies. Neither favored Evo Morales. The media was saturated with images of abjection, death, and disgust. As the voting unfolded, a third opposition strategy was waged on Twitter and Facebook, using doctored images to argue that the government was rigging the voting. It was not true. At the end of the day, Morales lost the referendum by a slim margin of 1.5 percent.[1]

In the days and weeks following, the story continued festering and morphing. The child had not died, the woman said, but was alive. Morales and the courts demanded that the child be presented in public. So the woman presented the little boy to the cameras. A relative of the woman told the press that the child's name was Ernesto Fidel Morales, after Ernesto "Che" Guevara and Fidel Castro. The country reeled.

But then the story collapsed. There was an affair but there was never a child at all. The lover had borrowed a child from her aunt to present to the press. The Chinese contracts were very real, though it was not clear that Morales was involved. It was mostly fake news. The ex-lover was arrested, tried, and sentenced to ten years in jail. Carlos Valverde, facing prosecution, took a hurried vacation to Argentina. But the damage was done. True or not, it was all just too much: excessive, corrupt, sordid, a waste. A friend at a progressive NGO told me that Morales was *spent*, in a situation of *desgaste*.

As corruption cases mounted and disaffection grew, the word *derroche* also became commonly heard in the battle to discredit Morales. *Derroche*, from *derrochar*, means to squander, waste, or spill. The word was used to talk critically about government waste of gas wealth. The new gondola system (Mi Teleférico) that crisscrossed the city sky was for some a sign of hypermodern progress. The gondolas also had a baroque quality, each line of a different color from red to orange to purple, almost Disneyesque in their incongruence over the earthen hues of La Paz. In 2018 a cab driver answered my query about the state of Bolivia by saying, "The Teleférico is great, but the national soccer team still sucks." But critics attacked the system for moving few passengers and absorbing much money: derroche. The government built new skyscrapers for YPFB and for the Ministry of Finance. Officials argued that these were symbols of the success of the Chuquiago Boys, using the Aymara name for La Paz as a label for the homegrown economists of the MAS, as opposed to the free-market Chicago Boys who advised Gonzalo Sánchez de Lozada and created the economic crisis of the 1990s. Detractors sniffed again: derroche. Gas money had flowed into an Indigenous Fund (Fondo Indígena Originario Campesino; Indigenous, Peasant and Originary Peoples Fund) to channel a special tax on hydrocarbons to local communities. Yet in 2016 those running the Indigenous Fund were caught spending money on phantom projects, reaping kickbacks, and siphoning off dollars. Several went to jail. Indeed, constant invocations of Morales's indigeneity were now met with charges coming from the whitish opposition that Indigenous peoples had no moral qualities at all: derroche.

But derroche is double-edged. One can also derrochar love, money, or joy, pouring out emotional or financial excess to express and celebrate personal pleasure or economic abundance. In Bolivia, exuberant public festivals are marked by the embrace of derroche. For instance, dancers in the Gran Poder festival of La Paz, which celebrates economic prosperity derived from devotion to a particular Andean icon of Christ, speak of their exuberant once-a-year expense on costumes, beer, food, and bands as derroche, a joyful celebration of abundance in the most baroque way possible. To spend, in the Andes, is to look forward to earning. There is also a baroque embrace of style as derroche, a celebration of acquisitive power put on display in expressions like the cholet architecture of late trending among the merchant classes of El Alto. What the whitish bourgeoisie sniffed at as derroche can also be seen as constitutive of life lived at its fullest. Indeed, why would one engage in political struggle, if not to benefit from economic well-being, and even wealth? Morales's new presidential palace, the Casa Grande del Pueblo (Great House of the People), encapsulated this quarrel.

The twenty-nine-story tower of shining glass rose up behind the old colonial-style building that used to be the presidential palace. The name echoed China's Great Hall of the People, as did its pretensions. It had grand halls with huge brightly colored murals and motifs drawing on Andean archaeological designs. At night, colored lights dance across its upper floors. In mid-2018 the government inaugurated the building with great fanfare while TV ads showed Bolivians of all dress and hues entering freely, suggesting the access of the once excluded to the halls of power. On opening night, social movement leaders celebrated its grandeur. A former leader of the national workers' union, the Central Obrera Boliviana (COB, Bolivian Workers Central), sublimated the architecture and the state, saying, "The building was up to the heights of the plurinational state [*a la altura del estado plurinacional*]." Another invoked revolutionary sentiment, saying, "We feel full of power and joy to enter into our house of the people, and to see the magnitude of the work. This is from the sacrifice of the struggle." A miners' leader added a Marxian economic interpretation, telling the audience that "in the past, the surplus was robbed [*fue saqueada la plusvalía*], but the new policies of the state have captured the surplus and now benefit the workers!" Racial equality was also cheered. Another speaker compared his own brown (*moreno*) skin to Morales's, celebrating the fact that one did not need a necktie, the symbol of the white colonizer, to get into the building. He explained, "These are stingy critics [*críticas mezquinas*] who want us to keep living in the past, but what better patrimony are we creating [than this palace], thanks to the Process of Change?" Spoken of in the language of social struggle, the palace was celebrated for exuberance and grandeur, derroche in its positive sense, all achieved by Morales and the nationalization of gas.[2]

Critics saw the excess as repugnant. The building, where the president would live on several upper floors, also had a sauna (reportedly fitting eight), massage room, discotheque, karaoke, and helipad on the roof. The sauna? "It's to fuel Evo's thirst for young women," said a friend, highlighting Morales's alleged sexual excesses. The helipad? "That's so he can escape, like Goni," said a cab driver, "because when he leaves [office] they are going to put him in jail." María Galindo (2018), the fearless leader of the anarcho-feminist collective Mujeres Creando, wrote that the building was a "phallic monument . . . a fascist vision . . . closer to a Las Vegas casino . . . a high-class brothel . . . or the big house of the master."[3] It did not help that during the same week the palace was inaugurated, one of the presidential guards lost the presidential sash and medallion that Morales wore in state ceremonies. No small deal, this one. It was the same sash and medal worn by the liberator Simón Bolívar in 1825. Thieves stole it from the guard's car after he left it parked outside a brothel in El Alto. Luckily for the medal, the thieves balked when they discovered what they had stolen and left the loot in a nearby church. In defense of their reputation, the Unión Sindical Única de Trabajadoras Sexuales de la Avenida

12 de Octubre (Union of Sex Workers of the 12th of October Avenue) released a public statement "clarifying to their clientele and to public opinion" that the president's medallion was not lost inside their establishment but in the street (Chávez 2018). Despite the political humor generated, the event reminded critics of Morales's sometimes vulgar machismo, the masculinist excess of those who surrounded him, and his apparent indifference to rising levels of violence and sex-trafficking impacting girls and women. The 12th of October Avenue, where the guard lost the medallion, is known for sexual trafficking of minors (Zabala and Ramírez Quiroga 2016). Amid the scandal and the jubilee, an opposition senator deemed the new palace a symbol of everything that was wrong with Morales, "a monument to *derroche*."

Reading Redistribution and Excess

Though precise figures are hard to come by, between 2007 and 2017, state and multinational firms received as profits and recoverable costs approximately US$15 billion from operations in Bolivia, about 42 percent to YPFB and its subsidiaries and 58 percent to private multinational firms. Not including YPFB earnings, the Bolivian government take, in special taxes and royalties that accrued to both the national and departmental governments during that period, was approximately US$22 billion. We can roughly read this $22 billion as the *excedente* (surplus), or the excess (YPFB 2017, 17–18). Economists have long been preoccupied with the distortionary effects that surplus expenditure can have during resource booms, often, as in Bolivia's recent past, leading to stagnation rather than growth.[4] Here, however, I read excess more anthropologically. I offer readings of the material and affective politics of the excess through three lenses.[5] First, I consider Bolivian social expenditures through the lens of recent work on the anthropology of redistribution. Drawing on Tania Murray Li (2017) and James Ferguson (2015), I ask whether and how cash transfers or a universal basic income might resolve the contradictions of fossil fuel extraction. Second, drawing on the Bolivian theorist René Zavaleta, whose phrase *querella del excedente* (quarrel over the excess) is the source of this chapter's title, I consider what the circulation of the excess tells us about the making and remaking of the Bolivian state. Zavaleta saw in the capture of the excess the potential for sovereignty, democracy, and popular hegemony, a way to free the nation from subordination to foreign capital and its feckless Bolivian lackeys (*lacayos* in his terms). Understanding what the excess has wrought, in one sense, entails consideration of whether Zavaleta's vision has been achieved. Third, anthropologists have also read the excess symbolically, inquiring into the ways that money or the objects that it can be used to make produce cultural meaning and conjure up images of the state (Coronil 1997; Apter 2005; Rogers 2015a). Building on this approach, I explore how expenditure of state wealth, largely made visual through the body of Evo Morales, generated secondary affective senses like derroche, both positive and negative, that saturated the political field during the late 2010s. By focusing on the quarrel over material and affective expenditure, I seek to capture the political dilemmas and ambiguities of the gaseous state, many of which contributed to a generalized disenchantment with Evo Morales, especially among the middling and urban classes, and even among some who once saw the revolutionary potential of the process of change.

On Redistribution

The issue of surplus and its redistribution raises questions of concrete relevance to the alleviation of poverty and the prospects for more equitable development. Though more orthodox free market economists generally push for market-based redistribution, of late even right-leaning economists have offered support for some form of direct payments to the poor. In anthropology, Li (2017) and Ferguson (2015) have recently joined in the discussion of the structural limits of economies that produce surplus accumulation (profits) but do not produce jobs. Nor do these economies effectively redistribute wealth. Structurally speaking, as Li writes, there is simply a surplus population of under- and unemployed people, many living in poverty amid great wealth and inequality. It is important to emphasize, as Li does, that this is not a demographic surplus. There are plenty of resources, but they are not distributed. It is a surplus from the perspective of the dominant capitalist system, which reproduces itself first by exploiting labor, and second, through automation, by making labor redundant (Li 2017, 1251). Like the precarious labor in Bolivia—the street vendors and the bus hawkers—who will likely never have formal jobs, in many countries capital has either displaced people from land or has no need for their labor in cities, or both. This fact, exacerbated by climate change, explains much of the massive global migration we are seeing, as people made surplus by capital in their home countries flee elsewhere looking for a means of survival. This is structurally intensified in extractive economies that are not labor intensive or industrialized, like Bolivia. It is even increasingly characteristic of highly industrialized but highly automated societies, where gig work or "bullshit jobs" prevail (Graeber 2018). Indeed, the idea of a universal basic income has taken hold in seemingly unlikely places, like Silicon Valley, given that those working there are actively trying to find new ways to put people out of work.

In response, Ferguson has argued for thinking about a politics of redistribution based on acknowledgment that all people have a "rightful share" (2015, 24). Ferguson considers the forms through which some of the surplus generated by mineral extraction in South Africa is redistributed as direct cash transfers to the poor. He develops a sophisticated defense of the idea of a "rightful share" in collective public goods (against the idea that one only gains rights and personhood through wage labor) and develops an argument for a universal basic income. Li (2017) asks more generally how the conditions for demanding a share are necessarily the task of political struggle. Beyond cash transfers or universal incomes, Li suggests that what is needed, rather than continuing to believe in the myth that "imminent development" will eventually raise all boats, is a renewed politics of distribution, one that is largely class-based and pro-poor, a "struggle over who will have access to global wealth and income." This might entail cash transfers but could just as well also involve collective restrictions on the wealthy, redistribution of property, higher taxes, and so forth. If, as Li says (2017, 1258), a "robust sense of entitlement and lively practice of critique" are lacking in places like Indonesia, they are most certainly not lacking in Bolivia. As I further explore later in this chapter, and recalling only the recent history of "the gas is ours," Bolivians maintain a powerful understanding of the "rightful share" and are more than willing to fight for it.

In Bolivia, the government of Evo Morales instituted a number of cash transfer programs and subsidies for low-income housing, jobs programs, and access to credit. One annual payment (about fifty dollars per year), named for a hero drummer boy of the war with Chile, Juancito Pinto, goes to schoolchildren. The government claims it has reduced desertion. The Juana Azurduy payment (named for a heroine of the independence wars against Spain) guarantees pre- and postnatal care for expectant mothers. The Dignity Rent (Renta Dignidad), about forty-three dollars per month, goes to elderly who have no formal pension. Other government programs subsidize loans for housing. The Indigenous Fund transfers monies to communities and municipalities for local projects. A universal health insurance plan is in the works. Other department-level programs, like Tarija's Prosol (Solidarity Project), provided short-term jobs through community-initiated work projects such as roads or bridges. Something less than a universal basic income, these conditional cash transfers and state-backed loans were a positive aspect of the expenditure of the excess, embodied in images of a caring state led by Evo Morales (Farthing 2019).

Such policies are popular but not radical. Many have been endorsed by the World Bank. Direct cash transfers have also been endorsed by Bolivia's free market economists. Under the libertarian notion that individuals know best what to do with surplus money, it was hoped that gas rents would be distributed directly to citizens rather than used, as Evo Morales had, to create a larger state apparatus (Morales 2008). (Alaska does this with some of its oil revenue, and its public infrastructures leave much to be desired, as individuals tend to consume and only capitalists or the state can invest at a productive scale.) Must we concede that Bolivia will never industrialize and should only accept its place in the global division of labor as a provider of raw materials? Will 60 to 70 percent of the population always be under- or unemployed? If so, following Ferguson, structural relations of inequality, such as the deeply unequal access to land, might be ameliorated by cash transfers or a basic income but they will never be radically changed. It is a rather conservative political vision.

For these reasons, the argument for cash transfers or universal incomes is convincing in some ways, but limited in others. Ferguson has little to say about the social and ecological problems inherent in relying on rent derived from nature, and especially specific forms of rent derived from fossil fuels like gas. Designing social policy around unstable mineral economies seems short-sighted. Ultimately, the modesty of his proposal seems designed to appeal to those who hold power. To link mineral extraction (or, as in Bolivia, gas drilling) to redistribution via cash transfers is primarily a means of securing consent to keep drilling, with the social and ecological toxicities that entails.

Li's approach is more appealing, given that it invokes a wider politics of redistribution that is not simply about receiving a small payment but about transforming economic and political relations. If we are to demand a "rightful share," people have to organize and imagine themselves as having rights, and demand something be taken from the rich, not just asked of them or extracted as rents from the earth. And, in some ways, this is what Bolivians were able to do during the government of the MAS. But "progressive extractivism" also has its limits, as many have argued and I have pointed out here. What is the alternative? For some, anti-extractivism or postextractivism have been keywords, suggesting the pursuit of a new economy, whether of services or small-scale organic farmers or tourism that is somehow not dependent on exporting raw materials. Yet as Matt Huber (2019) has argued, even if we get to an ecosocialist future, the world is going to need some form of mineral extraction. It is hard to imagine, in Bolivia, that any political future, utopian or otherwise, will be a postextractive economy. Whether and how those industries are organized to sustain livelihoods and radically reduce ecological and social toxicity, ideally under worker control, seems to be the main political question. But fossil fuels are different. We may not need fossil fuel extraction and nor does the climate. Should we endorse a universal basic income dependent on fossil fuels? Should Bolivians acquiesce to gas dependence simply because Evo Morales offers cash transfers?

On one level, then, this is what the politics of redistribution entailed in Bolivia during the 2000s and 2010s: securing the hegemony of fossil capital. On the right wing, whether technocratic neoliberal or unabashedly fascist, the so-called natural workings of the market and the rational individual congeal in a bourgeois theory of inevitable fossil fuel consumption (Malm 2016, 271). Yet in Bolivia, amid the amalgam of left-sounding affect and right-leaning policy, other sentiments were deployed through the language of "the gas is ours." While that held within it a powerful claim to a collective rightful share, it also held within it the inevitability of fossil fuel extraction, achieved through a different means.

Zavaleta's *Querella del Excedente*

From another perspective, the excess can be considered through the work of René Zavaleta (1984), for whom the quarrel over the excess (*la querella del excedente*) was central to his thinking about Bolivian state formation. Zavaleta's concern was that the bourgeoisie and oligarchic elites of the past had failed to capture the excess and use it to suture Bolivia's fragmented social formation into a modern nation. Most of the wealth, for instance, of silver, guano, or tin, was shipped overseas. Zavaleta's writing hews closer to Li's Gramscian reflections on the politics of distribution. He saw in political and revolutionary struggle and the capture of the excess by the people a means to build democracy in ways that were not subordinated to the interests of foreign capital. Zavaleta's concern was with the disposition of the surplus, not simply in redistribution but with the ways that the state spent the surplus (or not) as a constitutive political force, that is, as a transformative power. In his view, the revolutionary ideal was to transform Bolivia from a feudal semicolony in the hands of an inept and antinational bourgeoisie into a democratic and industrialized sovereign nation. His was, in broad strokes, a vision of popular nationalism and socialism shared widely across Latin America.

In 1967 Zavaleta spoke about gas and the surplus to a forum at the University of San Simón, in Cochabamba. With Bolivia's gas reserves then controlled by Gulf Oil, he warned that the future of Bolivia was at stake. He argued that the bourgeoisie had subordinated themselves to the United States. In contrast, what Bolivia needed to do was to "make a national State, that is, to achieve internal articulation, achieve democratization and the ascent of the masses that cannot be achieved without the growth of consumption through industrialization on a national base, which will also achieve cultural identification and what is called sovereignty, or the disposition of oneself . . . [but] because of the economic and human poverty of the bourgeoisie, Bolivia cannot achieve these goals without socialist methods under the political direction of the workers and peasants" (Zavaleta 1967b, 142).

Zavaleta knew that gas wealth was double-edged; like a "machete, it could serve to open roads, but also to kill." If Bolivia was to be a nation, it would have to accumulate the excess internally to industrialize and democratize consumption, a means of integrating the fragmented (*abigarrado*) nation. But if used incorrectly, the excedente would cause the "breakdown [*dislocación*] of the economic structure of the country" (1967b, 157). The quarrel over the excess would determine what kind of development Bolivia would have, and what kind of nation it would be.

The MAS project of nationalization in the late 2000s and early 2010s spoke in similar terms of the need to capture the surplus, industrialize the gas, and encourage economic democratization through consumption and redistribution. This, presumptively, for both Zavaleta and the MAS, was a means of economic democratization and a "prerequisite for future industrialization" (McNelly 2018, 916). In macroeconomic terms, consumption has been democratized, to an extent. The government has also used gas wealth to expand the state apparatus, creating public institutions that have sought to incorporate social difference into the state while passing progressive legislation in some areas, such as the law against racism and laws in support of Indigenous language rights (Gustafson 2017b). At least in the early years of the MAS government, the sense was also that gas wealth would contribute to the building of a sovereign, decolonizing, plurinational state. Yet as Zavaleta himself pointed out, the excess is a form of mediation between the state and the (subjugated) citizens that can be liberatory and democratizing but can also turn the "fury of the oppressed into part of the political program of the oppressor" (1984, 177). Thinking further about what the excess has wrought, and how it compares to Zavaleta's vision, requires returning to consideration of how Evo Morales himself came to embody both the state and the surplus, producing affective responses that suggested both revolutionary change and decadent subordination to fossil capital, something other than the democratic socialism Zavaleta envisioned.

Morales's Affect(ations)

Despite the love child scandal and the referendum defeat (later remedied when the Constitutional Court ruled that term limits were an infringement of human rights), Morales continued with his daily labor reminding Bolivians that thanks to gas nationalization, they were in the midst of a revolutionary process of change. In late 2017, he was giving a speech as he delivered a round of development funds to the relatively poor department of Potosí. As he did several times a week, traveling the country making gas wealth visible and exercising sovereignty through the expenditure of the excess, he again refreshed the memory of his audience.

> The battle, the struggle, is permanent. And I want you to know, sisters and brothers, that as long as imperialism exists, as long as capitalism exists, the struggle will continue, not just in Bolivia, not just in Latin America, but across the planet, wherever there are human beings. And we should remember as well, the Russian Revolution, November 7, 1917, after so many uprisings among workers and peasants in Russia, against the Czar Nicholas II, against the tyranny of the monarchy, finally the rebellion of the people, of the social forces of Russia [triumphed] in revolution. It was another uprising of the peoples because, sisters and brothers, uprisings don't just happen in Bolivia nor in Latin America, but around the world, we can talk about the French Revolution, we can revisit the grand uprisings of many countries, of Africa. That is to say, where there is inequality, where there is injustice, the people rebel, the peoples rise up, the peoples organize. (Ministry of Communication 2017a)

FIGURE 9.1 Revolutionary Evo Morales delivering checks in Potosí, November 2017. Ministry of Communication 2017a.

It happened to be the one-hundredth anniversary of the Russian Revolution, so his message was fitting. Yet it was also a moment of state ritual during which the revenues generated by gas, transformed into a material object, were delivered to the people. Usually these transfers involved some public works project: a new soccer stadium with Astroturf field for a small rural community, a local hospital or new computers for a school, an electrical transformer station, a new gas-line installation, or a new gasoline filling station. The list was endless. That day he was handing out checks, hand delivered to one hundred or so municipal authorities, monies theoretically destined to fund local projects like bridges and irrigation systems. That day Morales delivered 140 million bolivianos, about $2 million worth of projects. The funds came from the newly reborn Indigenous Fund (in the wake of its collapse in a corruption scandal, as mentioned above). Morales was not spent and, in fact, had more spending to do (figure 9.1).

His rousing speech repeated what he said often. The conquests of the gas and the goods and resources being delivered to the people by the state were the result of a longer history of struggle against neoliberal capitalism, military dictatorships, and US imperialism. As he said that day, and frequently said, "we have to refresh our memory," to recognize how much better off we are today. In a country in which the historical memory of anticolonial struggle is so powerful (Hylton and Thomson 2007; Dangl 2019), Morales worked to articulate a longer temporality of resistance with the current temporality of fossil fuel extraction. The implicit message was that the struggle was over, even though it could be continuously evoked to maintain vigilance against the right wing. I call this register *revolutionary affect*, a sense that when he spoke, at least judging from the enthusiasm of the crowds, people felt a spontaneously produced intensity, the hard-to-define "impulses, expectations, sensations" that "catch people up in something that feels like something" (Stewart 2007, 2). It did not hurt, of course, that the enthusiasm also came with a check in hand. But though the crowds were enthusiastic, critics saw all this talk about revolution in its absence as lacking sincerity, as a "simulacrum" (Petras and Lora 2013) or a "revolutionary parody" (Rivera Cusicanqui 2013). As such, we might also consider these discourses as a form of *revolutionary affectation*, a routinized form of speaking that spent the affective coin of revolutionary struggle without actually waging one.

Even in his revolutionary role, Morales was doing a form of political labor for the gas industry. Morales represented the landlord president, presiding over a landlord state that redistributed some of the rents it received from its tenants, the foreign gas companies. Making sure that the gas continued to flow, and the rents kept getting paid, was one of his main tasks as landlord president. Eventually, though, the tenants had more power than the landlord, who increasingly made concessions to try to get them to stay. Critics like Raúl Prada (2013) preferred the image of "manager," since Morales was also like the manager (*gerente*) of an armed apparatus at the service of fossil capital. For others, Morales was like a small-town mayor. Some colleagues called him *Evo alcalde* (Mayor Evo). In a country where building *obras* (works) is seen as the job of political leaders, obras were a means of evaluating political performance. The more obras the better. Like a mayor who inaugurates a new town plaza, Morales showed up to dedicate schools, stadiums, and the like, always connecting these obras to the nationalization of gas. Still others remarked on Morales's ability to change outfits so often and called him *Evo Barbie* (after the doll, not the Nazi war criminal). Morales could hang out with the whitish fossil fuel–loving fans of off-road car racing at the noxious spectacle of the Dakar Rally (figure 9.2). He could also don Aymara clothes to participate in a ritual for the Pachamama (Mother Earth).

Yet Morales was also like a worker. He often wore a YPFB oil worker's hard hat when he went to inspect a gas field or turn on the gas supply in somebody's kitchen. For example, in a modest neighborhood of Oruro Mo-

FIGURE 9.2 Evo Morales at the Dakar Rally, 2015. Vice President Álvaro García Linera and his partner (*first and second from left*) and Morales (*center*), with Chavo Salvati-erra, a Bolivian driver, coca-leaf wreaths, and models. The off-road race, a spectacle of motorcycles, dune buggies, and trucks, tore across the Andean high plateau four times between 2014 and 2018. Started in 1979 as a race from Paris to Dakar, Senegal, it is a festival of fossil fuels. In 2020 it was held in Saudi Arabia. Photographer unknown. *Página Siete*, September 15, 2015.

rales posed for a picture beside a gas meter recently installed in the exterior wall of a humble abode. Then, inside the kitchen, at the stove (and wearing his helmet), like the local utility employee he turned on the gas while festooned with a wreath of flowers and the ubiquitous confetti that accompanies public ritual in Bolivia. He lauded the process of nationalization that allowed the government to "attend to the demands of the people" and reduce their gas costs to around two dollars per month. All of this, Morales argued on one occasion, was because "thanks to Mother Earth" Bolivia has "cheap gas." On another occasion, as in many such events, he visited Beni department to inaugurate a new public water system. There, again in a hard hat, he was received by local authorities and flanked by local women dressed in faux Indigenous bikinis, classic Bolivian forms of cultural appropriation and commodification of women (figure 9.3).

In Villamontes in 2017, I hired a taxi and asked for a tour of the gas-related spots. The driver started me off at the Museum of the Chaco War,

FIGURE 9.3 Evo Morales inaugurates a new water system in Pando, October 2017. Ministry of Communication 2017b.

drove me down the street past the (unmarked) brothel where he takes many petroleros, and then drove past the Mennonite farms to see the British Gas plant flaring gas out of its processing and pumping station. Along the way, we bounced down a dirt road on the outskirts of town, the highway leading across the vast expanse of the Chaco. Here is where the drug smugglers, the narcos, go by, he said. It sparked his memory a bit and he got excited to tell me the story of a truck driver who had discovered a mine (*mina*) of his own. The fellow had made himself quite rich digging up streambed gravel in the outskirts of Villamontes and smuggling it across the Chaco to Paraguay. He was lucky (*tenía suerte*). But eventually, the fellow's luck ran out when he ended up getting caught and put in jail for running contraband. Even so, the mina had made him rich.

A doctor friend from Potosí used the same phrase—he was lucky—to describe Morales. The discovery of a new gas well had just been announced in the news. She exclaimed, *"Evo tiene suerte!"* suggesting that the discovery would add to his political capital. Her phrasing, like the taxi driver's, was laden with Andean notions of extraction as yielding treasures that are something other than the outcome of geological study and prospection. It was the outcome of luck, but in a Bolivian sense: not of chance but of a metaphysical propensity that some people have but not others. Tales of the lucky are invariably about men who discover some underground treasure and brave the threats of some often but not always feminized threat—a snake, the china supay, a gringa. These stories are laced with excitement, told with widening eyes, and shaped by a bit of fear of the chtulian spirits or "earth beings" that mediate one's access to these treasures (de la Cadena 2015). At another point a Guarani friend and Morales supporter reinforced this image, telling me that Morales was always "working." Here working did not mean gas work or political work, at least directly. It meant metaphysical work. Working refers to the use of special knowledge to influence the course of events. In the Andes, burning ritual offerings is one way of working, as people seek to appeal to earth beings or the Pachamama. Or you could hire a yatiri, those who know, to work for you. My friend summed up Morales's luck and his labor by saying, "Evo has people burning for him all the time."

I bring this up not to suggest that Morales really did have yatiris "burning all the time," though he might. Nor am I suggesting that these ideas motivated Morales's politics. The point is that the extractive subjectivity is a powerful discursive domain in Bolivia, a subject position that is widely embraced. (Consider again the challenge for those pursuing anti- or postextractivist futures in such a context.) Somewhat like the poor farmer who finds oil and "strikes it rich," yet here laden less with chance than with spiritual luck, these ideas encompass a range of understandings about underground things, like oil, gas, or hidden treasure, and the creation of aboveground wealth, that is, money. As with the oilman who strikes it rich, it entails an embrace of the possibility of exuberant excess. Morales's Casa Grande del Pueblo, seen in this light, is nothing to criticize. Nor, seen in this way, does gas extraction contradict his embrace of the Pachamama, Mother Earth.

When June Nash (1979) studied Bolivian mine workers in the 1970s, she found that *pachamamismo*, practices and ideas that miners associated with the spiritual beings in the mines, seemed to have revolutionary potential. Miners' relations with the underground beings helped combat alienation and coexisted with radical Trotskyism in a potent combination that made miners the most militant of workers (save their inability to critique their own patriarchal relationship with their wives). Yet in the early twenty-first century, Morales's articulation of revolutionary affectation, gas extraction, and pachamamismo seemed to be devoid of this kind of militance, and in fact did little other than legitimate the foreign-dominated export of Bolivian gas. It might be read as a form of alienation itself. Since resistance was already embodied in the gaseous state, the struggles of the past were said to have been made complete with nationalization, and its most visible representation was Morales himself. Ergo, there is no more need for social mobilization and social change. If the neoliberal regime failed at exporting the gas, Morales's skills at playing landlord, manager, mayor, Barbie, macho, and Pachamámico all succeeded.

Begoña Aretxaga inquired into how the state becomes a social subject in everyday life: "we must ask about bodily excitations and sensualities, powerful identifications, and unconscious desires of state officials" (2003, 395). "The subjective component of the state," Aretxaga wrote, emerges around the "discourses, narratives, and fantasies generated around the idea of the state." I have sought to do that here by describing Morales's various personae. Similarly, Krupa and Nugent have argued that states come into being as something "real" only through their effects. This "state effect" in the Andes relies in part on state affect, that is, the production of a sentimental engagement tied into a cycle of hope that the state will fulfill its obligations to citizens, or despair when it does not (Krupa and Nugent 2015, 15). What is central to the state effect is not so much whether the state is materially present or effective but that this "affective bond" with all its internal contradictions is reproduced, helping make the state "real" again. At base there is a persistent understanding of the state that has survived the neoliberal onslaught—that the state is obligated to provide for its citizens, health, education, infrastructure, and care. To that extent, Morales's performances and works are indeed, as he suggests, a sign that he fulfills obligations. Through expenditure of the excess, *Evo cumple.*[6]

Yet this patriarchal figure—the mayor, the gas worker, the landlord, the revolutionary, the caretaker—merges revolutionary affectation and the sublimation of the extractive impulse to yield perverse outcomes and secondary affects of repulsion, abjection, and degradation. One of them emerged from the androcentric shape of the industry itself, which transforms masculinist desire into the commodification and consumption of everything, deepening existing forms of violence, especially against women. Morales's frequent habit of framing his politics in misogynist terms is merely an index of a wider characteristic of the extractive economy, which sees nature, women, and rent in similar terms. As embodied in Morales, revolutionary or otherwise, we see how the excess of the gaseous state intensifies an already patriarchal political system. Yet as opposed to the patriarchal force of the law under liberal regimes that "legalize" gendered inequalities under the guise of individual freedom, in the gaseous state revolutionary affectation is a form of "cathexis of the caudillo," in which desire is invested in Morales, and exudes from him, such that the logic of paternal care coexists with masculinist consumption of all things feminine).[7] And all of it relies on the mina, that is, the gas.

Against further fossilization of the economy, the MAS also spoke, in a limited way, of renewable energy. In 2014 the MAS coined a new slogan for Bolivia, that of "the energetic heart of South America."[8] The slogan first appeared in a campaign ad for Morales that represented Bolivia as the beating energetic heart of Latin America, with investments in lithium, solar, wind, hydroelectric, gas plants, and geothermal energy, all set to be exported as energy to its neighbors.[9] As an "energetic heart," Bolivia would continue to pump electricity as blood through the infrastructural veins connecting it to its larger, more industrialized neighbors. Energy transformed into wealth was at the heart of this vision of future exuberance. It was a step beyond the "gas hub of South America" that the right had floated back in the late 1990s. It suggested what might lie in store for the near future of Bolivia.

Morales's macho jocularity framed the vision of the energetic heart through the lens of desire for both women and money. In 2014, at a speech inaugurating a new coliseum for a technical training school in Cochabamba, he joked with the audience, saying, "My advisers say we can make even more money exporting electricity than exporting gas. I used to say I am in love with Bolivia. Now I say I'm in love with energy . . . not that there's a girl named Energy, don't be thinking bad things, rather [I'm saying] that we're looking into how to export energy, for example, [and] there will be a lot more money" (Ministry of Communication 2014, 13). The joke was similar to one told more recently by the head of the state mining company, COMIBOL, associating mines with minas, a slang term for young women. Here again was the other side of the energetic heart, that which rested on the exploitation and monetization of all things feminized. Once locked into the gas-pipeline infrastructures and the idea of the energetic heart, there is no easy way out of this material and affective dependence, which work to reproduce each other.

Meanwhile, the infrastructural deepening of fossil dependency went on. In 2017 the MAS government reversed its earlier stance on ethanol, passing a law that would encourage biofuel production, an attempt to address Bo-livia's stubborn dependence on imported diesel. Here Morales had to eat crow (*comer sapos*), since he and Hugo Chávez had questioned biofuels during the Bush era, when the empire was pushing biofuels as a way to get inroads in Brazil. In those years Morales and his ministers also denounced fracking, since it was then being pushed by the United States to undercut Russian gas and Venezuelan oil.[10] Morales's minister said fracking was an environmental scourge. Yet by April 2018, Morales announced his approval of initiatives aimed at experimenting with fracking in Bolivia (Angelo 2018). In the water-scarce Chaco, where the gas companies are already sucking up, poisoning, and reinjecting toxic flow water, fracking would bring an even deeper threat.

Political Futures

The government of Evo Morales was certainly more successful than prior governments at capturing and redistributing the surplus. Detractors say that this is just because the price of gas was high. Yet it is worth remembering that no matter what the price of export commodities are, free market capitalism has a poor track record in Bolivia when it comes to redistribution and poverty reduction. The MAS did far better. And, though far from revolutionary, the MAS government at least exercised a modicum of sovereignty against the entities that oversaw the country's economic decline during the 1990s. As Bolivian authorities reminded the IMF, which still "reviews" the country's finances each year: "Between 1985 and 2005 [meeting the conditions] of the IMF did not solve Bolivia's economic problems, expressed in twin deficits, important foreign reserve losses, high levels of foreign debt, and a large financial dependence. On the contrary, since 2006, Bolivia has implemented its economic policies with sovereignty and will not follow any IMF recipe" (IMF 2017).

Yet the structure of existing and new debt, and the dependence on capital investments, meant that Bolivia's financial sovereignty, its ability to spend gas rents the way that it wants to, was highly constrained (Macías Vázquez and García-Arias 2019). Critics on the left also argued that Bolivia is deeper in the grip of foreign (fossil) capital than it has ever been. Experts at the Centro de Estudios para el Desarrollo Laboral y Agrario (CEDLA, Center for Studies of Agrarian and Labor Development) have argued that the decision-making process about natural gas exploitation was largely determined by the foreign (private and semipublic) hydrocarbon companies, the three largest being Repsol (Spain),

Total (France), and Petrobras (Brazil). Carlos Arze Vargas (2018), CEDLA economist, pointed out that foreign companies still controlled more reserves and production and that government fiscal dependence on hydrocarbon rents was deepened during the 2010s, even as the MAS and Evo Morales spoke of economic diversification. As far as Zavaleta's vision goes, Bolivia had not freed itself from subordination to foreign capital.

In addition to creating a political field saturated as much by affect as clear ideology, the gaseous state destabilized and distorted progressive paradigms of struggle: popular nationalism, revolution, and indigeneity. The intellectual project of popular (left) nationalism represented by thinkers like Almaraz, Quiroga Santa Cruz, Solíz Rada, and others had several gaps and silences. Indigenous peoples were usually ignored or subsumed into assimilationist paradigms of mestizaje or class struggle. The gendered structure of extractive economies and politics was also largely invisible, which is to say, masculinity was centered as either heroic subject (the petrolero, the revolutionary, the honest customs agent) or political protagonist. And, of course, the question of global warming and environmental toxicity was nonexistent. This is meant not as a dismissal of the popular nationalist perspective but a way to recognize the conditions of its production and the highly militarized, hence masculinist and authoritarian, political field that shaped it. In the age of gas, this older form of nationalism occupied significant space within the state. Yet as the committed ideologues decamped, its content lost any ideological center, other than defense of the industry. Critics on the left, like CEDLA, waged a valiant struggle to point out the limits of Morales's form of nationalization. Even so, it is not clear that demanding more control over the gas industry would offer an improvement. Is there a progressive nationalism that can renew itself in the political and ecological terms of the twenty-first century? Or is popular nationalism inherently limited by its deep imbrications in the militarized extractivist and fossil-fuel dependent state?

Similarly, talk of class struggle is central to any project of political critique. The discourse of revolution invoked by many social movements in Bolivia helped bring Morales to the presidency. But it has undergone some bruising because of the ways that Morales kept "spending" it. Turned into something like a meme on Twitter or a Che Guevara T-shirt, the rhetoric of class struggle increasingly seemed to be deployed to justify subordination to foreign capital in exchange, as one revolutionary friend told me, for "*cañonazos de dólares*" (big cannon-shots of dollars). One may feel (as I did) the impulse to cheer Morales when he called out US imperialism, but most of Bolivia's true left had thrown up their hands in frustration. As such, Evo's revolutionary affect risked becoming kitsch.[11] The pink tide in Latin America, led by progressive movements in Venezuela, Brazil, Ecuador, Argentina, and Bolivia, reflected a longer legacy of revolutionary thought and praxis. In all those cases, an embrace of the fossil fuel apparatus was central to the building of left projects. Fossil fuels have also been central to bringing them down. If the left relies on defending state control of fossil fuels (the latest addition to this trend is Mexico's president, Andrés Manuel López Obrador), the right is equally devoted to extracting them, though for different reasons. So while divesting from fossil fuels and supporting a Green New Deal can mobilize the left in the US, it is hard to imagine broad-based social and political support for keeping oil or gas in the ground in Bolivia, Brazil, or Venezuela. Herein lies the structural trap, in which left and right do the bidding of fossil capital. The challenge for revolutionary thinkers is immense: how to imagine a class-based struggle against imperial capital in contexts of deep inequality and dependence that is also a struggle against the particularly toxic effects of fossil fuels.[12]

As for indigeneity, which was for many an anchor of moral value and political potential in the struggles against neoliberalism, it has been shunted, at least in public discourse, into a space that many associate with Morales's derroche. It is hard to imagine the emergence, for the foreseeable future, of a leader who might build on the discourse of indigeneity, as Morales did, and assume national protagonism. While struggles for Indigenous rights to territory and prior consultation will persist, the scope of being Indigenous is so politically heterogeneous that it is difficult to conceive of an "Indigenous" movement today having any similarity to what that phrase meant even as recently as the 1990s. Indigenous leaders like Victor Hugo Cárdenas and Rafael Quispe, who are among Morales's staunch critics, have joined forces with right-wing political forces. Pro-Indigenous NGOs, once aligned with a broader left politics, have also turned against Evo, but in some cases have even made troubling alliances with the right, which has discovered in environmentalist discourse a new point of leverage against Evo Morales. This is not to deny Indigenous peoples the right to any political stance, nor to suggest that all Indigenous leaders have lost "authentic" Indigenous politics. It is to say that indigeneity, once assumed to be a key component of popular, class-based nationalist struggle, has been transformed into a political instrument rent asunder by clashes between political parties. The underlying point is that nationalist, revolutionary, and Indigenous paradigms of struggle have also been "spent" during the age of gas.

In November 2018, just a few short months after its grandiose inauguration, the Casa del Pueblo was the site for a small guerrilla operation staged by members of the Mujeres Creando anarcho-feminist collective. Using balloons filled with paint—a Carnival tradition turned into a popular instrument of struggle—María Galindo and her compañerxs doused an outer wall of the building in red. Meant to symbolize the blood of women killed in the wave of femicides, the paint offered a stark disruption. Within minutes, police arrived and detained Galindo. As she was cuffed and taken away, she shouted a manifesto of denunciation of judicial corruption, government indifference, presidential misogyny, and revolutionary parody. The video went viral on Facebook. Such was the power generated by speaking pure truth against pure fear, Morales could not keep her in jail. To her detractors, some of whom shouted at her in the streets, she retorted, "The paint is water soluble; I'll wash it off" (*Página Siete* 2018).

While I have not emphasized ecological toxicities herein, I have attempted to highlight expressions of gendered toxicity emanating from masculine excess. I have documented these expressions of the gaseous state in order to highlight its gendered and raced structural contradictions. As in the photo of a Standard Oil employee paying Guarani men while women stand and watch (see figure 1.1), the gas industry also lined up Morales and his men to deliver rents while women were politically silenced, or used as objects and props. The photograph—in ways similar to the photo of Morales at the Dakar Rally (figure 9.1) or the dedication of the new water supply in Beni (figure 9.2)—metaphorically encapsulates the gaseous state. The growing violence against women and girls, including sexual trafficking, also has direct and indirect linkages to the gas boom and, for Galindo, to the machismo and indifference of Morales and his government. If the political bodies I discussed in chapter 7 were argued over in the terms of sovereignty, liberation, and the martyrdom for natural resources, the violences of the patriarchal order are creating dead, wounded, and trafficked bodies of women whose stories cannot be reduced to revolutionary myth. For this reason the critiques raised by Galindo and many others compose a powerful space of critique of the gaseous state, a space where political transformation would require unraveling all the prebendal masculine ties that hold the gaseous state together. At the forefront, of late, are the anarchist-inspired networks of queer, lesbian, feminist, and trans communities. Pride marches now occupy the streets of Santa

Cruz, as feminist and LGBTQIA organizations push back against the patriarchal orders of the state, society, and the Catholic and Evangelical Protestant Churches. As the right wing responds with its attack on "gender ideology," it is here that demands for abortion rights, the rights of sex workers, the defense of minoritized sexualities, and struggles surrounding violence against women all draw attention to what the fossil-fueled left and right share in Bolivia: a deep masculine commitment to a patriarchal state. One might imagine, at some point, an anarchist-inspired ecofeminist challenge to the gas assemblage, and it will likely work its way up from the underside through articulations with urban and rural movements, many whose livelihoods are already deeply impacted by ecological degradation and the violence of the extractive economy.

postscript
bolivia 2020

ON OCTOBER 20, 2019, BOLIVIANS WENT TO THE POLLS TO VOTE IN PRES-
idential elections. Evo Morales, already in office for thirteen years, was
running for an unprecedented fourth term. Many questioned his candidacy,
given that he had lost the referendum vote in February 2016 and that his
later appeal to the constitutional court pushed the limits of credible legality.
Even so, the court ruled in his favor. Several opposition parties participated in
the election, adding to the vote's legitimacy. The former vice president, Carlos
Mesa, whom I described in chapter 4, was seen to be the main contender, but
there were several other opposition candidates as well, which would disperse
the anti-Morales vote. Mesa needed to force a runoff with Morales to have a
chance to win. For Morales, avoiding a runoff meant having to secure a win
by at least a 10 percent margin in the first round. As returns began coming
in on the night of the vote, Evo's lead was significant. Then a preliminary
vote-counting system was temporarily shut down as the system switched over
to the official count. Opposition parties cried foul. As the official vote count
came online, Evo's lead moved past the 10 percent hurdle. The next day he
declared victory.

Opposition protestors took to the streets. And, while some saw this as
spontaneous indignation, many organizations had already announced their
intentions of protest if Morales won, whether or not there was fraud. In response to the protests, the MAS government immediately called on the Organization of American States to audit the vote. This did little to appease the opposition, some of which was peaceful, much of which was not. Somebody set

fire to offices of the electoral body in various cities. Street clashes broke out between organized opposition groups and supporters of Evo Morales. Those opposed to Morales began organizing neighborhood vigils and blockades, in what would later evolve into a national work stoppage that lasted more than twenty days. As the audit of the vote proceeded, the demand was no longer for a recount or even a new election. The demand being shouted in the streets was for Evo Morales to resign. Social media—especially Twitter, Facebook, and WhatsApp—was ablaze with new memes, slogans, and increasingly incendiary, often racially charged attacks on the MAS.

Though the vote count was disputed, it is clear that Morales was going to poll somewhere around 45 percent, a high vote for any presidential election. It must not be forgotten, therefore, that Morales maintained significant popularity. On the other side, the question of who made up the anti-Morales opposition is complicated. Many young people, frustrated at the lack of employment—and many too young to remember the social struggles that brought the MAS to power—were a key component. Urban middle classes, some of whom had supported the MAS in prior elections, were also frustrated with Morales's attempt to prolong his presidency. Many of these professionals, unless they professed loyalty to the MAS, had been marginalized from access to jobs in the growing public sector. Feminists, anarchists, and many committed leftists also opposed Morales's reelection, arguing that the government had taken a turn to the right and had been corrupted by gas wealth. Evo Morales's once revolutionary credentials had indeed been sullied by a range of compromises with the right, the gas industry, the agro-industrialists, and the military.

Yet the most powerful bloc arrayed against Evo was the old right wing of the Santa Cruz elite (see chapter 6). In the middle were the police and the military. And, as I have described at various points in this book, the police and the military can be a politically fickle and disloyal bunch. Here, too, the story is complicated. The economic elite of Santa Cruz had long been arrayed against Morales and the MAS government, but over the years had increased its own wealth, given that the MAS showed itself to be an able manager of the state and maintained stability and economic growth. Bankers and agro-industrialists had reaped great wealth during the long period of economic growth. Nonetheless, a vocal sector of the extreme right was at the center of the hard-core opposition to Morales. Hailing from the eastern Bolivian city of Santa Cruz, this more extreme sector of the opposition—recall the autonomists and hardliners described in chapter 6—seized the opportunity for a putsch. Now it seemed that the elite hoped to retake a state structure over which they had lost control during Morales's time in office.

Led by a relatively unknown civic committee leader named Luís Fernando Camacho, and allied with an Andean opposition figure named Marco Pumari, of Potosí, this "civic" opposition demanded that Morales resign. The language replayed the racist rhetoric of the autonomy struggle I described in chapter 6. Supporters of the MAS were referred to (and dehumanized) as "mobs" (*turbas*) and "hordes" (*hordas*), with Morales criminalized as a "narco-dictator." The opposition called themselves *pititas*, to refer to the thin cords used to block streets. Of primarily middle- and upper-class origins—though not without a significant presence of other social sectors also opposed to Morales—the *pititas* represented their side as the "civil" society fighting to "recover democracy." Evidencing the conservative Catholic and evangelical Protestant tenor of the reemergent right, they responded to Morales's secular turn and Indigenous symbols like the Pachamama by demanding that God and the Bible be returned to the national palace.

Clearly reflecting a premeditated plan with coordination and financing, organized gangs of young men took to the streets to violently confront pro-Morales supporters. One group in the city of Cochabamba, the Cochabamba Youth Resistance (RJC, Resistencia Juvenil Cochala), consisted of hundreds of men on motorcycles wielding sticks, bats, and shields. The RJC was clearly inspired (and likely coordinated) with the Santa Cruz–based Cruceño Youth Union (UJC) I described in chapter 6. Both groups circulated through the cities to confront supporters of Morales and occupy public buildings, much as they had done in 2005 and 2008. The hard-right Camacho, in a bid to provoke instability, traveled from Santa Cruz to La Paz with his own delegation of UJC bodyguards. His self-declared goal was to deliver a letter of resignation that he demanded Morales sign. (During a military coup in 1980, the army generals delivered a similar letter to then president Lidia Gueiler, demanding that she sign it.) As the otherwise moderate opposition clamored for political renovation and democracy, this more extreme and violent sector elbowed its way to the fore.

Clashes between pro- and anti-Morales forces intensified. The police did not deploy lethal force, but were increasingly subjected to public scorn from the opposition. With the electoral audit underway, and nearly three weeks into the protests, on November 8, 2019, police in major cities declared themselves *amotinados*, in mutiny. In effect, they refused to keep order. This was the first sign that a coup was coming. On November 10, 2019, the Organization of American States released a preliminary report on the elections, suggesting that there had been "irregularities" but failing to demonstrate any hard evidence that there had been a major miscount. In response, Morales, by then having retreated to an air force base in El Alto, announced that there would be new elections. A dialogue might have still been possible, but the more extreme opposition intensified its calls for Morales to resign. Later that day, the top-ranking general of the military high command went on television and "suggested" that Morales resign. Morales and his vice president, Alvaro García Linera, flew to the Chapare region, where his support was strongest, and from there he announced his resignation. The next evening a Mexican air force plane landed there and he was flown to exile in Mexico. The electoral fraud claims have not yet been substantiated, and may never be. But by any reasonable measure, given the police mutiny and the military intervention in the process, it was a coup.

With government figures resigning under intense threats and pressure, the chain of succession eventually made its way down to an opposition senator named Jeanine Añez, who proclaimed herself president despite the absence of a quorum in Congress (many MAS legislators were in hiding and under threat for their lives). Añez, who hails from the cattle-ranching region of the Amazonian state of Beni, belonged to a right-wing opposition party called the Democrats (*Demócratas*). The party had garnered only 4 percent of the vote in the elections.

The task of the coup regime would technically only be to call for and guarantee free and fair elections. Yet in the face of protests clamoring for Morales's return, Añez sent out the military, who killed more than twenty people. Many were killed at the Senkata gas plant, the same place that saw the murders of several score civilians in 2003. In Sacaba, outside of Cochabamba, ten more people were killed by the army. The CIDH called both events massacres. It was as if the country was returning to the calculus of death from the Gas War of 2003. In a bid for stability, the congressional representatives of the MAS party—still technically a majority in Congress—entered into negotiations to establish a procedure for new elections. The MAS conceded that Evo Morales, by then having flown from Mexico to Argentina, would not be returning to be on the ballot.

With the coup regime controlling the courts and the legal system, many figures charged with criminal acts during the MAS government began to return. Leopoldo Fernández, charged with organizing the killing in Pando (chapter 7), was freed from house arrest. Branko Marinkovic and other representatives of the most radical right-wing "autonomy" movement (chapter 5), some also charged with their involvement in the Rosza mercenary plot (chapter 7), returned to Santa Cruz from exile in Brazil. Opposition figures charged with corruption—including Tarija's Mario Cossío (who had been in Paraguay) and Cochabamba's Manfred Reyes Villa (who had been in the US)—also came back. Meanwhile, the coup government set about prosecuting some six hundred MAS officials for alleged corruption, and even began prosecuting social media activists, accusing them of sedition.[1]

The question of whether or not what happened was a coup is contentious. Many Bolivian intellectuals have argued that it was not a coup, but rather a peaceful citizens' uprising that led to Morales's resignation (after his electoral fraud) and constitutional succession. The fact that the regime that followed was revanchist and authoritarian is said to have been an aberration, a "truncation" of the democratic uprising against Evo Morales. Other noted critics, such as Silvia Rivera Cusicanqui, argued eloquently that the coup narrative too easily victimized Evo Morales, while obscuring how he and his government were at the height of a long process of political decay and degradation. In one impassioned presentation, Rivera Cusicanqui pointed out—as I have suggested earlier—that militarism and patriarchal conquest had thoroughly permeated the MAS. Many movement and union leaders had been drawn into an old style of boys' club politics—much influenced by the military and the gas industry—that not only entailed debauchery and excess, but also corrupted Indigenous organizational forms and involved organized sexual exploitation of women.[2] While these events will be debated for many years, the outcome signaled the resurgence of a right wing linked to the conservative factions of the US political system and its South American allies and was a blow to the progressive turn known as the Pink Tide.

Whichever government emerges after Bolivia's next electoral process will face a significant political and economic challenge. Income from gas revenues is flattening out while gas reserves are in decline. There are expectations about lithium being the next boom for Bolivia, although lithium also risks extending the extractivist system without yielding economic diversification. Iron ores in Bolivia's far eastern border with Brazil are also seen as a coming boom for steel, yet tensions between Brazil, eastern Bolivia, and the Andean political center will surely complicate efforts to develop that resource. Meanwhile the United States has shown signs of restoring an older form of soft imperialism, with the return of the United States Agency for International Development and the use of the coup in Bolivia to reconfigure the wider regional balance of power in favor of the neoliberal doctrine of the United States and the deeper militarization of politics. The coup government itself set about destroying symbols of Evo Morales—such as statues erected at the soccer stadium in Cochabamba—and dismantling the revolutionary symbolism that the MAS had attached to components of the state. For instance, the anti-imperialist officer training school named for Juan José Torres (the socialist general discussed in chapter 4) was renamed after the "heroes of Ñancahuazú," in reference to the Bolivian rangers who killed Che Guevara. It is as if both the left and the right are still fighting a Cold War–style struggle, at least in symbolic terms.

As I suggested in chapter 9, there lies ahead a new era of political organizing that must transcend the limitations of an older style of left politics—the patriarchal, vertical, and militaristic—while confronting a newly resurgent right. The right has been emboldened by the wider global turn toward authoritarian, protofascist (or outright fascist), xenophobic nationalism. In Bolivia, this new right politics is further shaped by conservative Catholicism and evangelical Christianity marked by homophobia, intense opposition to women's reproductive rights, and a paranoid fear of what is called "gender ideology," that is, the notion that gender is a social construct. The right-wing project in Bolivia will push for a more radical federalist style of government, one which concentrates wealth regionally and socially, and which will combine both neoliberal (free-market) and statist economic policies that will deepen the extractive model in gas, minerals, and soy. The return of a militarized politics shaped not by nationalism and a commitment to redistribution and poverty alleviation, but by a national security mentality that looks inward to find enemies, is also probable.

Yet beyond Evo Morales and the MAS, Bolivia's deep reserve of social and political struggle is also being transformed with new political actors and forms. Some of the most powerful are emerging around a critique of patriarchy conjoined with widening recognition of the ecological and social degradation caused by the extractive industries. New movements, especially queer, trans, and women-led, are focusing on the fissures and violences—such as the degradation of movement leadership and the violence against women—that underlie the foundations of the gaseous state together. Demands for abortion rights, the rights of sex workers, the defense of minoritized sexualities, and struggles surrounding violence against women all draw attention to what the fossil-fueled left and right share in Bolivia: a deep commitment to a patriarchal state. It will take some time for these movements, newer and older, to rearticulate in this new political moment, yet the rightward turn may provide some clarity. This might also require taking some distance from the political nostalgia that has hamstrung the left—from the heroes of the Chaco to the struggle of Che Guevara. A new generation of Bolivian movements—the post-2003 generation—has its own collective memories of struggle that will energize new political visions. Those of us from elsewhere might also take some lessons from Bolivia to rethink our own subordination to the interconnections between fossil fuels, racial capitalism, and militarized political and economic systems. As Sergio Almaraz wrote in 1958, "Tell me what you think about oil [or gas], and I'll tell you who you are."

NOTES

INTRODUCTION: GASEOUS STATE

1 That pipeline is the subject of Hindery 2013.

2 Quantities have fluctuated between 2005 and the present. These are approximations based on 2017 numbers.

3 The Otero family has ties to both the Gonzalo "Goni" Sánchez de Lozada regime (Jaime Aparicio Otero was his ambassador to the US and was again named ambassador after the November 2019 coup) and the Inter-American Development Bank (María Otero's father was a founding trustee).

4 I refer to the statements made by the US Department of Energy in May 2019 that sought to promote liquefied natural gas (LNG) exports and confront the rising tide of climate action by rebranding natural gas as "molecules of freedom."

5 For overviews, see Rogers 2015b and several edited volumes, including McNeish and Logan 2012; Appel, Mason, and Watts 2015. On the prior generations of energy anthropologies, see Nader 2010; Boyer 2014; Günel 2018.

6 Following Bolivian anthropologist Sarela Paz, Jeffrey Webber identifies the coca farmers, El Alto merchant classes, and cooperative miners as key segments of this petty capitalist base of MAS support. In Webber's terms, "the logic of big capital runs alongside the legitimating function of indigenous bourgeois class formation" (2017, 1866).

7 For an overview of the new extractivism, see the special issues of *Latin American Perspectives* from September 2018 and March 2019.

CHAPTER ONE: HEROES OF THE CHACO

1 I draw on J. H. Sawyer 1975; Cote 2016. For semifictional accounts, see Costa du Rels (1932) 1943; Peláez C. 1958.

2 The literature on militarism and capitalism is vast, but one might start with Luxemburg (1913) 2003.

3 The interviews cited here and the following two chapters were carried out between 2007 and 2009 by Ubaldo Padilla and the author. Author's archives.

4 The complex of nitrate (used for explosives), rubber (for automobiles), and oil (for energy to move ships, planes, and trucks) suggests that Bolivia's territorial losses were all tied to capitalist military expansion elsewhere and that Bolivia was a war resource colony, a pattern that would continue with the United States and tin.

5 Among numerous others, Zook 1960 offers an account of the Chaco War.

6 See Lora 1977 for a more detailed account of this period.

7 English version from Neruda 1991, 176–77; Spanish version from Neruda (1950) 2016, 341–42.

8 Galeano's status notwithstanding, the Braden connection seems largely coincidental. In his memoir, Braden accused "the Communists and others" of exaggerating the "influence of oil" in the war (Braden 1971, 150).

9 On the oil industry and its capture of the US government, see Painter 1986; Mitchell 2001. As I wrote this in 2019 and 2020, President Donald Trump's administration was intimately entangled with both the weapons and the fossil fuel industries.

10 Another indispensable literary reference imbued with this indignation is Augusto Céspedes's *Sangre de mestizos* ([1936] 2000).

11 The title translates roughly as *Cannon Fodder: "Now It's Burning, Kollitas!"* According to Guillermo Delgado-Peña (personal communication, June 19, 2019), his father Trifonio Delgado Gonzales explained that the subtitle was shouted by their officers in the intensity of combat in the trenches, roughly, "now things are getting hot." Kollitas was a diminutive form of *kolla*, to refer to Andean Bolivians.

12 For a treatment of this period in the Caribbean, see P. Hudson 2017.

13 Equitable Trust later merged with Chase, which also came under control of Rockefeller interests.

14 Revealing of the racial and class positions represented by the oil industry, Thomas Armstrong was the youngest son of a family of Texas ranchers whose vast Armstrong Ranch abutted the King Ranch, both enriched by cattle and oil. Armstrong's father was part of the Nelly's Rangers, a paramilitary militia known as the "Death Squad" that supposedly cleared south Texas of Mexican bandits but also waged a campaign of ethnic cleansing to rid the area of its original Mexican occupants. A laudatory piece on the ranch and on the "Death Squad" was published in Standard Oil's bimonthly magazine, *The Lamp*, in June 1935. Along with leading Standard's efforts in Bolivia, Thomas Armstrong also negotiated Standard's "entry" into Colombia and Venezuela. In the latter case, Armstrong worked with the dictator Juan Vicente Gómez,

as Standard under various company names vied for concessions against Royal Dutch Shell, Gulf, and others, dealings also shaped by the oil banks (Tinker-Salas 2009, 58).

15 Surface rental fees are paid to the government (like a landlord) for use of Bolivian land.

16 A similar arrangement unfolded with a Rockefeller National City Bank loan and the Barco oil concession in Colombia in 1930. After the new petroleum law was enacted and a pro–oil industry contract signed, President Enrique Olaya Herrera reportedly said, "We've done everything the Americans asked for [so can we have the money now?]." Standard later acquired the concession from Gulf Oil. Colombia later defaulted (United States Congress Committee on Finance 1931–32, vol. 1, pp. 849–80; J. H. Sawyer 1972). All participants denied any connection between the bonds and the oil industry (Randall 1976).

17 Figures are from the hearings of the United States Congress Senate Committee on Finance 1931–32, vol. 1, p. 752 (1928) and pp. 767–68 (1929). On 1929, see also Klein 2003, 176.

18 Among the cast of characters that circulated through Bolivia in those years and who testified before the Senate Committee on South American Loans was the enigmatic Lawrence Dennis (1893–1977), a former analyst for J. & W. Seligman, one of the Wall Street banking houses selling bonds for Peru. Dennis was African American and Ivy League educated. Said to have passed as white amid the racism of the day, he was seen by many as a fascist and later put on trial for sedition, allegedly because of connections to German agents. Nonetheless, his incisive critique of Wall Street corruption aligned him with the isolationist push of some progressives in those years. His testimony included details on the expenditures funded by the Bolivian loans, including contracts for US companies and military activities such as purchasing arms and building access roads to the Chaco. Fascist or not, Dennis was prescient. He predicted that in the United States, burdened by white supremacist imperialism, the middle classes were simply waiting "to follow a good [fascist] demagogue." See United States Congress Senate Committee on Finance 1931–32, vol. 3, p. 1703 (Johnson quote); vol 3, pp. 1579–1607 (Dennis testimony on Bolivia). See also Horne 2006, 44–47, 50.

19 Harry Elmer Barnes was a nexus between Marsh's work and *Merchants of Death*.

20 On Dorothy Detzer (1893–1981) and parallels with the contemporary "total war" economy in the United States, see Detzer's (1948) memoir; Coulter 1997.

21 Guillermo Delgado-Peña, Trifonio's son and editor of his memoir, recalled that his father often complained that they had been given secondhand surplus weapons (personal communication, June 12, 2019).

22 See United States Congress Special Committee 1934: on Remington and Winchester ammunition sales to both sides (2345); on "pygmy Indians" (2391).

23 The US politics of the time, as the country debated war and the New Deal, are too complex to explore here. But another character is worth remembering. The battle over Standard Oil and the Chaco War was also taken up by Louisiana's populist governor, and later senator, Huey Long. Long defended Paraguay as a victim of Standard-financed Bolivian aggression. Facing off against Standard Oil over taxation issues in his home state he railed against the criminality of Standard and the forces of American imperialist finance. Despite his often hyperbolic embrace of the "blame Standard" narrative, he echoed the indisputable facts about the oil-bank relationship. He was one of the few who made it clear that "Standard Oil is financing the Chaco War." Long also accused Standard Oil, rightfully, of opposing the arms embargo. He was assassinated in 1935 (United States Congress 1934, 10811; see also Gillette 1970).

24 On industry collusion with the Nazi regime, see Borkin 1978. Under the Marshall Plan for post–World War II European recovery, US taxpayers bought more than $1.2 billion worth of oil from Standard and other companies for Europe. By the late 1940s, company interests were increasingly aligned with the US military and the State Department, deepening the militaristic approach to oil in the Middle East. The vertically integrated oil companies were also gouging the United States, by charging overmarket prices, eventually leading to (yet another) federal lawsuit against Standard Oil of California in 1952 (Painter 1986, 157–61).

25 David Painter refers to this arrangement between US government, military, and private oil industry interests as the "corporatist foreign oil policy." The vision was one of "maintaining an international environment in which all U.S. companies could operate with security and profit" and to maintain "public support for private control of one of the most important natural resources of the world [which] facilitated control of the world oil economy by the most powerful private interests" (1986, 207–8).

26 For the Bolivian nationalist history, see, among others, Marof 1935; Montenegro 1938; Almaraz 1958; Orgaz 2005. On the Rockefeller Foundation's contemporaneous effort to use philanthropy as a political tool in the context of the Chaco War and the public health crises it unleashed, see Gotkowitz 2007. On the Paraguayan side, see Chesterton 2016.

27 I return to this question of excess, by way of Bataille and Zavaleta, in chapter 9.

28 On negotiations with Standard and relations with YPF in Argentina, see Almaraz 1958, 113–32; Wood 1961, 168–202.

1 Given demands of the war, and the lack of importance of Bolivia's small oil supply, as compared to Mexico and Venezuela, the compensation was small. The US State Department was unwilling to back everything that Standard Oil hard-liners like Thomas Armstrong wanted (Randall 1985, 91–96). Wood 1961 offers a fairly pro–Standard Oil account, which should be read against Almaraz 1958.

2 On price fluctuations and the pendulum of nationalization, see Klein and Peres-Cajías 2014.

3 Ambassador Irving Florman, cited in Dorn 2011, 110.

4 On the ways that racism shaped British and US justification for access to oil reserves in the Middle East, see Mitchell 2001 and Vitalis 2006. Huber 2013 details the interdependence between racism on the extractive end and on the consumer side of oil in the United States.

5 McCarthy's rise and fall is memorably preserved in the novel *Giant*, written by Edna Ferber in 1952 and made into a Hollywood film in 1956. *Giant* was a gently feminist and antiracist critique of the new oil rich of Texas, who were threatening the political-economic dominance of the northeastern United States. In the film, McCarthy, rendered as Jett Rink, was played by James Dean, his final role. McCarthy told Mike Wallace he thought the film was "unfair" to Texas (Wallace 1957).

6 I draw here on Lora 1977; Dunkerley 1984; Field 2014.

7 Declassified documents lay out how the secret "40 Committee"—a group of high-level security, military, and intelligence officials in the US government, led by Henry Kissinger—planned covert action in Bolivia. The CIA passed cash to military officers just days before the coup. By most accounts, US involvement in the Bolivia coup was a test run for Augusto Pinochet's coup in Chile. See, among others, National Security Council 1971 and accounts by Katzin 1974; Dunkerley 1984; Colby 1995, 693. On the battle of August 21, 1971, see Zavaleta 1972.

8 It bears emphasizing that Robert McNamara (1916–93) is another embodiment of what I call the oil-military-capital nexus, via his roles in the US Army, as secretary of defense; at the World Bank, as a servant of capital; and with Ford Motor Company, as a fossil-fuel man. For his role in firebombing Tokyo during World War II and in overseeing the senseless killing during the Vietnam War, he was also a war criminal (Weiner 2009). With the pipeline loan, the US was again sinking Bolivia into fossil fuel infrastructural debt and subordination, as it had in the past, and as it hoped to do with the Chile gas pipeline in the early twenty-first century.

1   Hugo Bánzer Suárez (1926–2002) oversaw the extralegal killing, imprisoning, exiling, and disappearing of hundreds of Bolivians. The later creation of his Acción Democrática Nacionalista (ADN, Democratic Nationalist Action) party and his return to electoral politics was primarily aimed at protecting himself and his allies from judicial action by the state. In the end, death took him before justice could (Dunkerley 1984; Field 2014). On the killed and disappeared, see the blog of the Asociación de Familiares de Detenidos Desaparecidos y Mártires por la Liberación Nacional (ASOFAMD), accessed December 12, 2019, http://asofamd.blogspot.com/.

2   The casing tong also demands another story. California inventor Web Wilson (ca. 1880s–1955) patented the tong that became a global standard and, with other inventions, made the Wilson family wealthy. Web Wilson–style tongs are still in use all over the world. By the 1950s, when this tong made its way to Camiri, Wilson Oil Tools was run by Web's son, William A. Wilson (1914–2009). William was a director at Pennzoil, a UC regent, a cattle rancher, and a real estate developer whose money helped Ronald Reagan become California governor and eventually president. Reagan made Wilson one of his informal "kitchen cabinet" advisees and later named the Catholic convert as special envoy to the Vatican. In late 1985, whether as oilman doing side business or as Reagan's representative, or both, Wilson went to Libya to meet Muammar Qaddafi. The Italian government, interested in Libyan oil, had set up the meeting hoping to calm tensions between the US and Libya. Outed by competing factions in the US intelligence community amid allegations that Libya was behind a recent terrorist attack, the visit cost Wilson his post. In April 1987, the Reagan administration's John Poindexter and Oliver North (of Iran-Contra infamy; the latter at this writing is head of the National Rifle Association) oversaw a CIA and US Air Force operation to assassinate Qaddafi. The US pilots killed Qaddafi's fifteen-month-old-daughter, Hana, and more than one hundred civilians but not Qaddafi. By 2003, when Bolivia erupted in the Gas War, Evo Morales was reportedly visiting Qaddafi in Libya. But that is another story (Maitland Werner 1984; *New York Times* 1986; Hersh 1987).

3   Ciro Bustos recalled with fondness the Italian food prepared at the Marietta. During his three-year imprisonment in Camiri, Bustos received support for legal representation from Sergio Almaraz and his Grupo de Octubre (Bustos 2013). Bustos remembered Debray as a pompous showman. Debray's partner, Elisabeth Burgos, the Venezuelan anthropologist-turned-revolutionary, went on to help Rigoberta Menchú write her testimonial. A third prisoner, the Bolivian known as León, got much less attention.

4 This chapter draws on several years of residence in Camiri, which included many hours of listening to oil stories from many sources, including Doña Teresa, who passed away in 2018, and whose stories I share here in tribute. The main corpus is based on a score of oral histories collected from retired oil workers that Ubaldo Padilla and I compiled between 2007 and 2009, hence the "we" in my recounting. I compensated Padilla for his work.

5 *Chiverío* (a goat fest), from *chivo* (a goat), refers to a generalized situation of cuckoldry. In Bolivia, colloquially, the chivo is also known as a *cornudo* (elsewhere, *venado*, deer), or someone who has horns (*cuernos*) because their partner has cheated on them.

6 I discuss the linguistic contours of this racist vocabulary of sexual violence in Gustafson 2009c. Cepek 2018 details a similar history of sexual violence against women in the Cofán territory of Ecuador's oil lands.

CHAPTER FOUR: GAS LOCK-IN

1 I refer to these fossil fuel promotion assemblages elsewhere as "fossil networks" (Gustafson 2012).

2 On integration, security, and cooperation from the fossil capitalist perspective, see work affiliated with the Baker Institute at Rice University, e.g., Mares 2006; or with the Center for Strategic International Studies, e.g., Weintraub 2007. For a critique, see Gustafson 2012, 2017a.

3 On carbon lock-in, see Seto et al. 2016. Kaup 2012 makes a similar point about the wider political-economic trajectory that constrained change under Evo Morales. Though the main line of tension in Bolivia was between the nationalist and the neoliberal perspectives, this lock-in, it is worth remembering, also entails locking in carbon-based energy consumption and CO_2 production over time until the source or the infrastructure is exhausted.

4 On the Bolivian side, it was seen as a giveaway to a subimperialist state. On the Brazilian side, unions and Petrobras feared it would undermine Brazil's own gas industry (Quiroga Santa Cruz [1978] 2013).

5 The incestuous world of oil experts, businessmen, functionaries, and officials has many revolving doors. Khelil, with a BS degree from Ohio State and a PhD in petroleum engineering from Texas A&M, was the World Bank's privatization strategist for Bolivia. After working in Bolivia for the World Bank, Khelil later returned to his native Algeria to serve as minister of energy; then head of Algeria's national oil company, Sonatrach; and eventually the president of the Organization of the Petroleum Exporting Countries (OPEC) between 2001 and 2008 (Fernández Terán 2009).

6 ESMAP designed strategies for the privatization of fossil-fuel-based energy industries worldwide, from Algeria to Zimbabwe. In Bolivia ESMAP had been working since 1983 on creating national energy plans and assessments of the utility sector as well as oil and gas. Because oil and gas development was pushing further into Indigenous territories, ESMAP also backed training of Indigenous leaders to engage in dialogue processes aimed at softening their attitude toward fossil fuel extractivism. See S. Sawyer 2004 for an account of these processes in Ecuador.

7 The wave of privatizations targeted nearly all (ninety-four) public (state-owned) enterprises, from railroads to fish farms, hotels, bus stations, airlines, and utilities, including the entirety of the nation's energy infrastructure. The Water War of 2001 stopped water privatization. For generally critical accounts of the privatization period, see Farthing and Kohl 2006; Fernández Terán 2009; Kaup 2012. For a sympathetic World Bank account, which touts gains in efficiency and profitability as well as the creative ways the private takeover was done, see Capra et al. 2005.

8 Paraphrased, from field notes.

9 Molina 2018 describes the reemergence of the military nationalist perspective and its break with both the national security doctrine and neoliberal orthodoxy, as sectors of the military and Evo Morales moved closer together during this period.

10 This section draws on descriptions provided by witnesses documented by the Harvard Human Rights Clinic. See Human Rights @ Harvard Law, "Mamani v. Sánchez de Lozada and Sánchez Berzaín," accessed May 25, 2017, http://hrp .law.harvard.edu/areas-of-focus/alien-tort-statute/mamani-v-sanchez-de-lozada -and-sanchez-berzain/.

11 United States District Court Southern District of Florida Miami Division (2013), §. 59.

12 United States District Court Southern District of Florida Miami Division (2013), §. 95.

13 Sánchez Berzaín, now exiled in Miami, created a nonprofit (501(c)) called the Interamerican Institute for Democracy (IID). The IID is aligned with hard-right Miami Cubans. On the real estate, which some say is money laundered from Sánchez Berzaín's days defending drug traffickers, see Gurney et al. 2016.

14 In Bolivia, a number of military officers were found guilty, and some are in prison. Despite Bolivia's request, the United States, under George W. Bush, Barack Obama, and Donald Trump, has refused to extradite Sánchez de Lozada and Sánchez Berzaín to Bolivia. With the help of the Harvard Human Rights Clinic and the Center for Constitutional Rights, the victims' families sued the pair in US civil courts under the Torture Victim Protection Act, alleging extra-

judicial killings, among other claims. In April 2018 a jury in Fort Lauderdale, Florida, found the pair guilty and awarded the victims' families ten million dollars. Yet, as one of the victims' lawyers wrote, "unfortunately, in May, a Judge [James Cohn] overturned the historic jury decision. The judge upheld the defendants' Rule 50 Motion for Judgment as a Matter of Law, which argued that there was insufficient evidence to support the verdict" (Becker 2018). At this writing (early 2020), the case is under appeal.

15 In these versions, the killings were carried out by supporters of Evo Morales—or some shadowy apparatus of military power—in order to damage the reputation of Sánchez de Lozada. The evidence to the contrary is overwhelming.

16 International oil companies (IOCs) have relatively little access to fossil fuel reserves in their home countries. Most reserves are now controlled by national oil companies (NOCs). But IOCs rely on documenting ("booking") reserves to establish their firm's value and convince capitalists to invest. Since NOCs often need capital and technology, in much of the world, these operate through shared risk agreements with private IOCs, allowing IOCs to book reserves. In cases where NOCs threaten to exclude IOCs, or seek to challenge the hegemony of the dollar or the terms of IOC involvement, US intervention ramps up. This was behind the push to open up Mexico and Pemex to private capital. This largely explains the forever wars in the Middle East. This is also behind the current effort to destabilize Venezuela, which challenged US fossil capital hegemony by trading oil for credit in Chinese yuan. The US ultimately seeks to weaken nationalist oil regimes, maintain dollar hegemony, open up access to reserves, and increase returns to Western fossil capital (Mitchell 2001). In all cases, calculating reserves is a political and cultural act of prestidigitation, the contours of which are discussed by Hughes 2017.

17 The term *tramparendum* was rendered into song by union leader Roberto de la Cruz. Information compiled from press reports, May–July 2004, author's archives.

18 On the CAF loan, see Gobierno de Bolivia 2004. On the campaign, "*involucrar a cada uno de los bolivianos . . . hablemos un solo código*," and the IMF, CAF, and World Bank positions, see *El Deber* 2004a, 2004c. On gas company support for the referendum, *Bolpress* 2004.

19 Regionalist putsches emerged in Ecuador, Venezuela, and Bolivia, all oil and gas producers where regional "autonomy" was being promoted by the right and backed by liberal (i.e., free market) think tanks of the United States (Gustafson 2009b, 2010). I take this up in chapter 5.

20 See Political Database of the Americas 2004.

21 On the Neptune, *La Razón* 2004b. USAID had long been involved in so-called democracy promotion in El Alto, part of US government strategy to cultivate a more docile population in a city deemed conflictive (see Ellison 2018).

22 Charles Shapiro was the undersecretary of state for Latin America under George W. Bush. The Bolivian Chamber of Hydrocarbons, which represents foreign and domestic oil and gas member firms, also supported the Santa Cruz elite.

CHAPTER FIVE: BULLS AND BEAUTY QUEENS

For comments on the original version of this chapter, I thank Marcelo Arandia, Guido Chumira, Hermán Fernández, Ana María Lema, Alfredo Rada, and Monica Sahonero for insights reflected herein. David Guss, Jean Muteba Rahier, and Christi Navarro offered editorial advice. On the chapter in its current form, two anonymous readers helped clarify the connections between the autonomy movements and the politics of gas.

1 January 28 marked another specious appropriation of indigeneity since it seized a date associated with the Guarani movement, January 28, 1892, when the Bolivian state executed Apiaguaiki Tüpa, a Guarani leader who rebelled against settler colonialism (Gustafson 2009c).

2 Keremba is another appropriation of a Guarani symbol, the word for warrior (*kereimba*).

3 See Gobierno Autónomo Departamental de Santa Cruz 2020.

4 One of Bolivia's liberal scholars, H. C. F. Mansilla (2004), elaborated this cultural racism, suggesting that high altitude and mentalities inherited from Spanish and Inca centralism contributed to Andean backwardness.

5 As in all colonial settings, discourses of cruceño masculinity suggest that white(r) men are licensed to sexually violate Indigenous women.

6 The search for the "land without evil" refers to the messianic pursuit of a paradise on Earth (Gustafson 2009c).

7 A well-worn anecdote is revelatory. While wearing Indigenous Guarani motifs, Miss Bolivia 2004 (a cruceña) declared during the Miss Universe pageant in Quito that in her region of Bolivia, people were not Indians but white, tall, and English speakers. Scorned in La Paz, the hapless queen was given a hero's welcome by carnival *comparsas* and civic leaders upon her return to the airport in Santa Cruz. She would go on to become the host of a popular morning show on the UNITEL (Universal de Televisión) network (*Economist* 2004; *El Deber* 2004b).

8 Santa Cruz's regional project, in its aspirations, if not in its actual capacity to exercise hegemony, echoes the imperial "galactic polity" surrounding an "ex-

emplary center" described by Stanley Tambiah (1976, 258–66). For Mexican parallels, see Alonso 2004; Poole 2004.

9 I use the word *ethnic* (*étnia*) as it is used locally. It is problematic because of the appropriations underway, and because it enacts minoritization and erasure, masking racialist and class structures at work and undermining the preferred categories of Indigenous peoples themselves: *pueblos* (peoples) or *naciones* (nations).

10 From the brochure distributed to visitors. See also http://www.fexpocruz.com .bo/ferias/expocruz/.

11 Translated from Dabdoub 2005.

12 The similarity between the autonomist movement and the "color revolutions" in Europe, aimed at regime change and led by middle-class urban "civics" who flattened ideology into flags and slogans, is not a coincidence. (As with "svoboda" in Ukraine or "otpor" in Serbia, "autonomy" worked similarly in Santa Cruz.) USAID funded autonomy workshops in eastern Bolivia. Transredes (the Shell-Enron-Prisma pipeline company) financed autonomy workshops and supported pro-autonomy media. Spanish advisors visited Santa Cruz frequently. Cruceños obliged by plagiarizing Catalonia's autonomy statute (compiled from press reports, 2003 to 2005).

CHAPTER SIX: JUST A FEW LASHES

This chapter benefited from feedback at the University of Toronto, the University of Chicago, and the University of Washington, with special thanks to María Elena García, Tony Lucero, Gastón Gordillo, Lucas Savino, and their students and colleagues. The account is compiled from video and print media and interviews with numerous Guarani colleagues who remain anonymous. Quotations from Valle Mandepora were obtained from the Observatorio de Derechos Humanos, the document presented by Valle Mandepora to the police, and a videotaped interview with town mayor Sonia Guthrie, all provided to me by the Vice-Ministry of Lands. I thank Alejandro Almaraz and Juan Carlos Rojas for recounting their perspectives in interviews in 2017 and 2018.

1 The huasca (or chicote) is a common accessory of ranchers. *"Dar huasca"* is a figure of speech that refers to patriarchal disciplinary violence against children, wives, and rural laborers. Public whippings and other punishments were also common on the haciendas.

2 Shearer, a former Clinton advisor, was part of the State Department speaker program, which sends academics or diplomats to give pro-US lectures in contentious places. The following month Shearer was in Syria. (Shearer quotes are from my field notes, as reported in the press June 16, 2008.)

3 Rodolfo Stavenhagen (1932–2016) was a Mexican anthropologist and a legendary figure in the history of Latin American anthropology and Indigenous rights movements.

4 See App Gaceta Bolivia, "Bolivia Ley No 3760 del 07 Noviembre 2007," http://www.derechoteca.com/gacetabolivia/ley-3760-del-07-noviembre-2007.htm.

5 Latifundia refers to the holding of large estates that concentrate wealth and power, as compared to minifundia, smallholdings at semisubsistence level. Getting rid of latifundia has long been a key goal of revolutionary struggle.

6 Landowners had to demonstrate ownership of a certain number of cattle per hectare, otherwise the property was deemed unproductive and subject to expropriation. Rojas recounted the tricks landowners used to defeat this rule. They fought the law itself. Then they borrowed cattle from neighbors when they knew the surveyors were coming. The land brigades called these "tourist cows" (*vacas turistas*). They were covered with so many different brands that Juan Carlos said they looked like they were wearing multicolored vests.

7 Anonymous interview, paraphrased, Cuevo, August 16, 2008.

8 Provided to me by Alejandro Almaraz.

9 The motion approximates the slight turn and snap of a wrist that would accompany the use of a short braided leather horsewhip with a wooden handle, a common accessory of ranchers. The gesture is used when voicing a threat of violence or recounting instances of it, whether husbands beating their wives, parents beating children, teachers smacking students, or, in this case, landlords whipping peasants.

10 The sacking of Almaraz and Rojas was related to a shift within the MAS party, as coca growers and peasant colonists began to demand individual land titles, as opposed to the collective titling approach sought by lowland Indigenous peoples. The shift also moved patronage jobs to Andean "peasant" leaders and away from the eastern Bolivian Indigenous movement, with which criollos like Almaraz and Rojas had long worked in solidarity.

CHAPTER SEVEN: REQUIEM FOR THE DEAD

This chapter includes material originally published in *Caterwaul Quarterly* (Gustafson 2009a). I thank Thea Riofrancos and Daniel Denvir for soliciting the piece, offering comments on it then, and to Thea for granting me permission to reuse portions of it for this book. Conversations with Claudia Chávez and comments from the anonymous reviewers helped me to clarify my arguments for this rewritten version.

1 On necropolitics and sovereignty as expenditure, see Mbembe 2003, 2005. There are shades of Georges Bataille in Mbembe's account, and in my own, a point to which I return in the following chapters.

2 Though evidence of coup-mongering would be hard to come by, it did not help Goldberg's case that he had been chief of mission in Kosovo (2004–6) and a participant in the US-led breakup of Yugoslavia. Some saw a parallel attempt to break up Bolivia or at least fragment the nationalist project by supporting the regional right wing. However, Schultz (2008) suggests that it was Goldberg's prior Colombia experience waging the drug war and militarizing politics that was more relevant to his Bolivian posting, not that that offers any consolation.

3 The narrative draws on UNASUR 2008; UN 2009. For another critical reading of the events at Pando, see Soruco Soluguren 2011.

4 Those killed among the Indigenous and farmers' organizations include Bernardino Racua, a well-known leader, great-grandson of a historic Indigenous leader of Pando; Wilson Castillo Quispe (19), Alonzo Cruz Quispe (20) and Johny Sarzury (25), students at the teachers' college, all of Andean origin, tortured and executed; Wilson Richard Mejía (29), Arnolfo González, Celedonio Bazoaldo García (53), Felix Roca Torrez (44), Ditter Tupa Matty (27), Nestor da Silva Rivero, Miguel Racua Chau, Ervin Villavicencio Chau, Vicente Rocha, Abdiel N., Atipe Tupamati, Luis Zabala, Elvis N. The functionaries of the regional government who were killed include Pedro Oshiro and Alfredo Robles Céspedes. Other sources note up to forty wounded and a number disappeared along with other killings in weeks prior (UNASUR 2008).

5 Freddy Alborta (1932–2005) and his photographs were the subject of Leandro Katz's documentary *El día que me quieras* (1997), which he produced during the search for, and subsequent exhumation of, Guevara's body in Vallegrande, Bolivia (1997).

6 Since past struggles continued to animate current politics, it is worth digressing to point out that the Peruvian revolutionary organization Movimiento Revolucionario Túpac Amaru (MRTA, Túpac Amaru Revolutionary Movement) assisted the CNPZ in the kidnapping of Lonsdale, events memorialized in *Der pfad des kriegers* (The way of the warrior), a 2008 film by Andreas Pichler. The Bolivian police tortured one of the Peruvians to death (after he revealed the whereabouts of the kidnapped Coca-Cola man). In revenge, the Peruvian MRTA kidnapped cement magnate Samuel Doria Medina in 1995, securing a $US1.3 million ransom for his release (Archondo 2017). By 2019, Doria Medina, by then also owner of Bolivia's Burger King franchises, was a presidential candidate and opponent of Evo Morales. Doria Medina complained on Twitter that among his kidnappers had been one José Pimentel, who directed the state mining agency Corporación Minera de Bolivia (COMIBOL, Mining Corporation

of Bolivia) under Morales and the MAS between 2010 and 2012. Pimentel, labor union leader and now college professor, had indeed served two years in jail for the kidnapping (1998–2000). For Pimentel's supporters, he was a revolutionary hero (Agencia de Noticias Fides 2000).

7 On Bolivian military informants to the US embassy and the Chávez statement, see Tellería Escobar 2016. On "bloodbath," see Embassy La Paz 2008.

8 The UTARC unit was accused of later abuses against two journalists and disbanded scarcely five months after the operation. In 2013 the ex-UTARC troops who carried out the Hotel Las Americas assault were awarded special medals of valor.

CHAPTER EIGHT: GAS WORK

This chapter draws on fieldwork between 2015 and 2018. Earlier iterations were presented at several conferences and at Washington University's Ethnographic Theory workshop, where it benefited from commentary by Kate Farley, John Bowen, and Talia Dan-Cohen. I thank Vicente and Marcos for inviting me to observe and document their meeting with BS, and Marisol, for sharing her experience in the gas industry.

1 Statistics are from the World Bank and the IBCE.

2 I discuss the expansion of public jobs for Guarani language activists in Gustafson 2017b.

3 Here I follow Mitchell (2001) and Watts (2004b) who argue that the socio-technical arrangements of the fossil fuel complex set both the possibilities and limits for pursuing democratic or more revolutionary transformations. Coronil (1997, 2019) makes a similar point about the particularly distortionary effects of fossil fuel dependence on Latin American politics, a question I return to in chapter 9.

4 As Suzana Sawyer (2004) described for Ecuador, the strategy of companies is to narrowly delineate their area of operation, thereby setting up divisions between communities. See Anthias 2018 for another Bolivian case.

5 Known as "man camps" in North America, in the US and Canada these temporary work settlements are rife with problems of drug use and sex trafficking, with an acute impact on native women (see, e.g., Deer and Nagle 2017).

6 The idea of the "rightful share" draws on Ferguson 2015 and Li 2017, a point to which I return in the following chapter.

7 Former US vice president Dick Cheney was an architect of the Iraq War and of the 2005 National Energy Security Act. Cheney had financial interests in Halliburton, which benefited greatly from both war and US energy policy. See, e.g., Rosenbaum 2004.

8 It is worth remembering that the Chinese and the Americans who loan money to Bolivia also decide on who gets the contracts those loans are spent on, such that he who spends exercises sovereignty, just as, on the Guarani scale, he who allocates jobs does. What makes one legal and one extralegal is a question of power, not law or morality.

9 Data from 2013 suggest that direct employment at the big operating firms was low: Repsol (208), Petrobras (846), and Total (31). Repsol had some 3,000 subcontractors, tertiary laborers associated with various service firms; YPFB employed substantially more, growing from 598 in 2002 to some 2,000 employees by 2017, still significantly lower than its 8,480 workers in 1985 (Gandarillas 2013). In 2018 approximately 11,000 people were directly employed by the oil and gas firms, which in one calculation suggests about 0.1 percent of the formal labor force (*Energy Press* 2018; McNelly 2018).

CHAPTER NINE: QUARREL OVER THE EXCESS

1 I describe these efforts in Gustafson 2016.

2 From the TV broadcast, August 9, 2018 (Bolivia TV).

3 Colonial-era plantations were referred to as the *casa grande* (big house).

4 For one such analysis of economic windfalls from mining and petroleum in Bolivia, see Auty and Evia 2004. On anthropological treatments of rent, Coronil 1997.

5 I have not taken a possible fourth path, that of philosophy. One of this book's readers suggested that engaging Georges Bataille might be productive. Given Bataille's arguments for exuberant expenditure without return (and a fair dose of death and eroticism for good measure), there is indeed some proximity between the excesses of the gaseous state and Bataille's reflections on "the accursed share" ([1947] 1991). Scholars have also taken up Bataille's specific ideas about surplus energy (Stoekel 2007). I have chosen to hew more closely to Bolivian political vocabularies.

6 Bolivia Cambia, Evo Cumple is the name of a state development initiative, which translates roughly as "Bolivia Changes, and Evo Fulfills [His] Obligations."

7 I thank Pamela Calla for this juxtaposition of liberal legality and the figure of Evo, as well as the phrase—"cathexis of the caudillo"—which she shared in conversation, February 28, 2014.

8 The slogan has a Facebook page, and scores of videos and references can be had by googling "corazón energético de Sud América."

9 Evo y Pueblo, "Bolivia, Corazón Energético de Sudamérica," September 22, 2014, https://www.youtube.com/watch?v=TLtGggQw_XY.

10 Fracking pursues the extraction of hydrocarbons that do not flow readily to the surface because the rock in which they are found is not porous enough. By drilling, injecting, and detonating explosives, and then pumping chemicals, water, and sand under immense pressure, tight oil and gas can be forced to the surface.

11 I thank Talia Dan-Cohen, who read an early version of this chapter and reminded me of Milan Kundera's critique of revolutionary kitsch in *The Unbearable Lightness of Being*.

12 In Brazil, Alexandre Arauja Costa (2017) has begun to articulate such a vision, suggesting that full government control over Petrobras and its transformation into a renewable energy company is the only way to address social development and climate change, ideas that overlap with the postextractivism debate (Svampa 2017).

POSTSCRIPT: BOLIVIA 2020

1 I base this account on press and social media coverage between November 2019 and January 2020.

2 See Rivera Cusicanqui in Awasqa 2019 and Prada 2020.

ABI (Asociación Boliviana de Información). 2013. "Morales entrega 1.600 instalaciones de gas domiciliario en el Distrito 3 de Oruro." February 7.

Adams, Richard. 1975. *Energy and Structure: A Theory of Social Power*. Austin: University of Texas Press.

Agamben, Giorgio. 1998. *Homo sacer: Sovereign Power and Bare Life*. Palo Alto, CA: Stanford University Press.

Agencia de Noticias Fides. 2000. "Corte rebaja a 10 años sentencia de militante del MRTA." December 19. https://www.noticiasfides.com/nacional/sociedad/corte -rebaja-a-10-anos-sentencia-de-militante-del-mrta-279786.

Agüero, Felipe, and Claudio Fuentes. 2009. *Influencias y resistencias: Militares y poder en América Latina*. Santiago: Facultad Latinoamericano de Ciencias Sociales (FLACSO).

Ahlbrandt, T. 2000. "US Geological Survey World Petroleum Assessment 2000; Compiled Power Point Slides." US Geological Survey Open File Report 99-50-Z. https://pubs.er.usgs.gov/publication/ofr9950Z.

Alonso, Ana María. 2004. "Conforming Disconformity: 'Mestizaje,' Hybridity and the Aesthetics of Mexican Nationalism." *Cultural Anthropology* 19 (4): 459–90.

Almaraz, Sergio. 1958. *El petróleo en Bolivia*. La Paz: Editorial Juventud.

Almaraz, Sergio. 1964. "Un minuto antes de la medianoche: La violencia en Bolivia." *Praxis* 3:22–28.

Almaraz, Sergio. 1967a. "Lo básico: No perder el gas y ganar el mercado argentino para Y.P.F.B." In FUL 1967, 253–84.

Almaraz, Sergio. 1967b. *El poder y la caída: Historia del estaño en Bolivia*. In *Sergio Almaraz Paz: Obra Completa*, pp. 297–448. La Paz: Plural.

Almaraz, Sergio. 1967c. *Requiem para una república*. La Paz: Universidad Mayor de San Andrés.

Amnesty International. 1996. "Bolivia: Awaiting Justice: Torture, Extrajudicial Executions, and Legal Proceedings." AMR 18/09/96. September 1. https://www .refworld.org/docid/3ae6a9c210.html.

Angelo, Andrea. 2018. "Evo abre las puertas de Bolivia al 'fracking.'" *El País* (Tarija), April 12.

Anthias, Penelope. 2018. *The Limits to Decolonization: Indigeneity, Territory, and Hydrocarbon Politics in the Bolivian Chaco.* Ithaca, NY: Cornell University Press.

APG (Asamblea del Pueblo Guaraní). 2008. "Pronunciamiento público de la Asamblea del Pueblo Guaraní." Camiri, Bolivia. Unpublished manuscript. Author's files.

Appel, Hannah, Arthur Mason, and Michael Watts, eds. 2015. *Subterranean Estates: Life Worlds of Oil and Gas.* Ithaca, NY: Cornell University Press.

Apter, Andrew. 2005. *The Pan-African Nation: Oil and the Spectacle of Culture in Nigeria.* Chicago: University of Chicago Press.

Archondo, Rafael. 2017. "¿Quién mató a Jorge Lonsdale?" *Noticias fides*, November 13. https://www.noticiasfides.com/nacional/politica/sshshshshshsh-383399.

Aretxaga, Begoña. 2003. "Maddening States." *Annual Review of Anthropology* 32:393–410.

Arrighi, Giovanni. 2010. *The Long Twentieth Century: Money, Power, and the Origins of Our Time.* New York: Verso.

Arze Vargas, Carlos. 2018. "Orientación de la política hidrocarburifera." Accessed January 11, 2019. https://cedla.org/sites/default/files/files/evn/pdgealyb /Energia-CArze-orientacion_politica_hidrocarburifera.pptx.

Associated Press. 1935. "'Tin Hermit' of Bolivia Has Quiet Paris Birthday." *New York Times*, June 3.

Auty, R. M., and J. L. Evia. 2004. "A Growth Collapse with Point Resources: Bolivia." In *Resource Abundance and Economic Development*, edited by R. M. Auty, 179–92. Oxford: Oxford University Press.

Awasqa. 2019. "Silvia Rivera Cusicanqui: What Is Democracy? What Is Being Indigenous?" https://www.youtube.com/watch?v=z-CjK7ZW6BA.

Bakke, Gretchen. 2016. *The Grid: The Fraying Wires between Americans and Our Energy Future.* New York: Bloomsbury.

Barba, Rildo. 2005. "Los huasos le pusieron 'huevos' a la última preca." *El Deber* (Santa Cruz). January 23.

Bataille, Georges. (1947) 1991. *The Accursed Share.* Vol. 1. Translated by Robert Hurley. New York: Zone Books.

Becker, Thomas. 2018. "After Fifteen Years, the Bolivian Struggle for Justice Continues in the United States." HumanRights@HarvardLaw blog, November 13. http://hrp.law.harvard.edu/staff-reflections/after-fifteen-years -the-bolivian-struggle-for-justice-continues-in-the-united-states/.

Bedoya Garland, Eduardo, and Alvaro Bedoya Silva Santiesteban. 2005. *Enganche y servidumbre por deudas en Bolivia.* International Labour Organization Working Paper. Geneva: International Labour Organization.

Behrends, Andrea, Stephen P. Reyna, and Gunther Schlee, eds. 2011. *Crude Domination: An Anthropology of Oil*. London: Berghahn Books.

Benjamin, Walter. 1968. *Illuminations: Essays and Reflections*. New York: Schocken.

Bolpress (La Paz). 2004. "Mesa se juega su futuro en un referendum pagado por las petroleras." July 18. https://www.bolpress.com/?Cod =2002081807.

Bolpress (La Paz). 2008. "Comienzan a sanear haciendas del Chaco Cruceño y el tco Alto Parapetí." November 21. https://www.bolpress.com/?Cod =2008112106.

Bolpress (La Paz). 2009. "Hacia la liberación de familias guaraníes cautivas en el Alto Parapetí." March 18. http://www.bolpress.com/art.php?Cod =2009031806.

Borkin, Joseph. 1978. *The Crime and Punishment of I. G. Farben*. New York: Free Press.

Boyer, Dominic. 2014. "Energopower: An Introduction." *Anthropological Quarterly* 87 (2): 309–33.

Boyer, Dominic, and Imre Szeman, eds. 2016. *Energy Humanities: An Anthology*. Baltimore: Johns Hopkins University Press.

Braden, Spruille. 1971. *Diplomats and Demagogues: The Memoirs of Spruille Braden*. New York: Arlington House.

Breglia, Lisa. 2013. *Living with Oil: Promises, Peaks, and Declines on Mexico's Gulf Coast*. Austin: University of Texas Press.

Bustos, Ciro. 2013. *Che Wants to See You: The Untold Story of Che Guevara*. New York: Verso.

Canessa, Andrew. 2012. *Intimate Indigeneities: Race, Sex, and History in the Small Spaces of Andean Life*. Durham, NC: Duke University Press.

Capra, Katherina, Alberto Chong, Mauricio Garrón, Florencio López de Salinas, and Carlos Machicado. 2005. "Privatization and Firm Performance in Bolivia." In *Privatization in Latin America: Myths and Reality*, edited by Alberto Chong and Florencio López-de-Silanes, 117–44. Washington, DC: World Bank; Palo Alto, CA: Stanford University Press.

Carmical, J. H. 1956. "Domestic Oil Producers Flocking Overseas." *New York Times*, April 1.

Cepek, Michael. 2018. *Life in Oil: Cofán Survival in the Petroleum Fields of Amazonia*. Austin: University of Texas Press.

Céspedes, Augusto. (1936) 2000. *Sangre de mestizos*. La Paz: Juventud.

Chávez, Gonzalo. 2018. "¿Patria o pieza? ¡Venceremos!" *Página Siete* (La Paz), August 12.

Chesterton, Bridget. 2016. "Introduction: An Overview of the Chaco War." In *The Chaco War: Environment, Ethnicity, and Nationalism*, edited by Bridget Chesterton, 1–20. New York: Bloomsbury.

CIDH (Comisión Interamericana de Derechos Humanos). 2007. "Access to Justice and Social Inclusion: The Road towards Strengthening Democracy in Bolivia." June 28. http://www.cidh.org/pdf%20files/BOLIVIA.07.ENG.pdf.

CIDH (Comisión Interamericana de Derechos Humanos). 2008a. "IACHR Concludes Visit to Bolivia." Press release, June 13. http://www.cidh.org/Comunicados/English/2008/26.08eng.htm.

CIDH (Comisión Interamericana de Derechos Humanos). 2008b. "Memorandum of Commitment: Hearing on Captive Communities." March 11. http://www.cidh.org/pdf%20files/cautivas_inlges_comunicado.pdf.

Colby, Gerard. 1995. *Thy Will Be Done: The Conquest of the Amazon; Nelson Rockefeller and Evangelism in the Age of Oil*. With Charlotte Dennet. New York: HarperCollins.

Comunica Bolivia. 2008a. "Bolivia: Testimonios de la masacre a campesinos." September 15. https://www.youtube.com/watch?v=cH8Y_FQAkuY.

Comunica Bolivia. 2008b. "Masacre en Pando." November 25. http://www.youtube.com/watch?v=-J-eBCmkYno.

Comunica Bolivia. 2008c. "Terratenientes atacan a funcionarios de Gobierno Boliviano." April 9. http://www.youtube.com/watch?v=QwCAnjvxZdQ.

Corbett, Charles D. 1972. "Military Institutional Development and Sociopolitical Change: The Bolivian Case." *Journal of Interamerican Studies and World Affairs* 14 (4): 399–435.

Coronil, Fernando. 1997. *The Magical State: Nature, Money, and Modernity in Venezuela*. Chicago: University of Chicago Press.

Coronil, Fernando. 2019. "The Future in Question: History and Utopia in Latin America (1989–2010)." In *The Fernando Coronil Reader: The Struggle for Life Is the Matter*, edited by Julie Skurski, Gary Wilder, Laurent Dubois, Paul Eiss, Edward Murphy, Mariana Coronil, and David Pederson, 128–64. Durham, NC: Duke University Press.

Correa Vera, Loreto, Tanya Imaña Serrano, and Martín Añez Rea. 2003. *Los laberintos de la tierra: Gasoductos y sociedad en el oriente boliviano*. La Paz: Programa de Investigación Estratégica en Bolivia.

Costa, Alexandre Araujo. 2017. "As the Earth Heats Up, Brazil Digs Deeper." *NACLA Report on the Americas* 49 (4): 444–51.

Costa du Rels, Adolfo. (1932) 1943. *Tierras hechizadas*. La Paz: Amigos del Libro.

Cote, Stephen. 2016. *Oil and Nation: A History of Bolivia's Petroleum Sector*. Charlottesville: West Virginia University Press.

Coulter, Matthew. 1997. *The Senate Munitions Inquiry of the 1930s: Beyond the Merchants of Death*. Westport, CT: Greenwood Press.

Curti, Merle. 1959. "Subsidizing Radicalism: The American Fund for Public Service, 1921–41." *Social Service Review* 33 (3): 274–95.

Dabdoub, Gabriel. 2005. Discurso de inauguración de EXPOCRUZ 2005. http://www.ibce.org.bo/eventos/discurferia.htm. Originally accessed January 30, 2006. Manuscript in author's collection.

Dangl, Benjamin. 2019. *The Five Hundred Year Rebellion: Indigenous Movements and the Decolonization of History in Bolivia*. Chico, CA: AK Press.

Das, Veena, and Deborah Poole, eds. 2004. *Anthropology in the Margins of the State*. Santa Fe, NM: School of American Research Press.

DED (Deutscher Entwicklungsdienst). 2008. *Familias guaraní empatronadas: Análisis de la conflictividad*. La Paz: Deutscher Entwicklungsdienst.

Deer, Sarah, and Mary-Kathryn Nagle. 2017. "The Rapidly Increasing Extraction of Oil, and Native Women, in North Dakota." *Federal Lawyer*, April, 30–38.

Defensoría del Pueblo. 2007. "Servidumbre y empatronamiento en el Chaco." *Derechos Humanos y Acción Defensorial* 2 (2): 219–32.

de la Cadena, Marisol. 2015. *Earth Beings: Ecologies of Practice across Andean Worlds*. Durham, NC: Duke University Press.

Delgado Gonzales, Trifonio. 2015. *Carne de cañón: ¡Ahora arde, kollitas! Diario de guerra, 1932–1933*. Edited by Guillermo Delgado P. La Paz: Plural.

Delgado-Peña, Guillermo. 1996. "La corografía de *En el país del silencio* de Jesús Urzagasti: El espacio estriado entre el Chaco y el Altiplano." In *Construcción poética del imaginario boliviano*, Estudios bolivianos 3, edited by Josefa Salmón, 61–74. La Paz: Plural.

de Onis, Juan. 1967. "Bolivia Finds Rich Gas Fields." *New York Times*, December 18.

Detzer, Dorothy. 1948. *Appointment on the Hill*. New York: Henry Holt.

Dinges, John. 2005. *The Condor Years: How Pinochet and His Allies Brought Terrorism to Three Continents*. New York: New Press.

Dorn, Glenn J. 2011. *The Truman Administration and Bolivia: Making the World Safe for Liberal Constitutional Oligarchy*. University Park: Penn State University Press.

Drake, Paul. 1989. *The Money Doctor in the Andes: U.S. Advisors, Investors, and Economic Reform in Latin America from World War I to the Great Depression*. Durham, NC: Duke University Press.

Dunkerley, James. 1984. *Rebellion in the Veins: Political Struggle in Bolivia, 1952–1982*. London: Verso.

Dunkerley, James. 2007. "Evo Morales, the 'Two Bolivias' and the Third Bolivian Revolution." *Journal of Latin American Studies* 39 (1): 133–66.

Economist (London). 2004. "Two Countries in One." 371 (8378): 46.

El Deber (Santa Cruz). 2003a. "Cambas vs. collas, un áspero debate en las provincias." October 20.

El Deber (Santa Cruz). 2003b. "Interés político en trifulca en la plaza." October 20.

El Deber (Santa Cruz). 2004a. "Arrancó la campaña sobre el gas, se extenderá hasta mayo." February 10.

El Deber (Santa Cruz). 2004b. "Gabriela Oviedo recibió atenciones de los comparseros cruceños." June 9.

El Deber (Santa Cruz). 2004c. "El referéndum definirá también la estabilidad y el futuro del país." March 29.

El Deber (Santa Cruz). 2005a. "195 aniversario: Una apuesta por el futuro." September 24.

El Deber (Santa Cruz). 2005b. "EXPOCRUZ movió casi US$1,000,000 en dos rubros." September 19.

El Deber (Santa Cruz). 2005c. "Maricruz lidió con la espuma y los globos." January 30.

El Deber (Santa Cruz). 2005d. "Montereños rompieron el bloqueo." January 29.

El Deber (Santa Cruz). 2005e. "Otra toma de tierras intranquiliza el norte." September 20.

El Deber (Santa Cruz). 2005f. "Santa Cruz tuvo un emotivo homenaje." September 3.

El Deber (Santa Cruz). 2008. "Gobierno frena intento de sanear; presión sube." April 15.

Ellison, Susan. 2018. *Domesticating Democracy: The Politics of Conflict Resolution in Bolivia.* Durham, NC: Duke University Press.

El Nuevo Día (Santa Cruz). 2005. "Mojones propagan la autonomía en provincias." March 30.

Embassy La Paz. 2004. "President Mesa and Congress to Work Together on New Hydrocarbons Law." Wikileaks Cable: 04LAPAZ2814_a. September 3. https://wikileaks.org/plusd/cables/04LAPAZ2814_a.html.

Embassy La Paz. 2008. "Emergency Action Committee Meeting—La Paz 9/23 1600." Wikileaks Cable: 08LAPAZ2083_a. September 24. https://wikileaks.org/plusd/cables/08LAPAZ2083_a.html.

Energy Press (Santa Cruz). 2018. "Trabajadores petroleros: La fuerza del país." December 21.

Engelbrecht, Helmuth Carol, and Frank Cleary Hanighen. 1934. *Merchants of Death: A Study of the International Arms Industry.* New York: Dodd, Mead.

Erbol (La Paz). 2009. "INRA revertirá diez predios en la TCO Alto Parapetí por existir relaciones de servidumbre." January 5. http://www.erbol.com.bo.

Escárzaga, Fabiola. 2012. "El Ejército Guerrillero Tupak Katari (EGTK), la insurgencia aymara en Bolivia." *Pacarina del Sur* 3 (11). http://www.pacarinadelsur.com

/home/oleajes/441-el-ejercito-guerrillero-tupak-katari-egtk-la-insurgencia
-aymara-en-bolivia.

Fabricant, Nicole, and Bret Gustafson, eds. 2011. *Remapping Bolivia: Resources, Territory, and Indigeneity in a Plurinational State*. Santa Fe, NM: School of American Research Press.

Falacci, Oriana. 1970. "Essere la moglie di un condannato." *L'Europeo* 26.

Farthing, Linda. 2019. "An Opportunity Squandered? Elites, Social Movements and the Government of Evo Morales." *Latin American Perspectives* 46 (1): 212–29.

Farthing, Linda, and Benjamin Kohl. 2006. *Impasse in Bolivia: Neoliberal Hegemony and Popular Resistance*. London: Zed.

FEGACAM (Federación de Ganaderos de Camiri). 2008. "Resolución de los ganaderos del Chaco boliviano." Manuscript in author's collection.

Ferguson, James. 2015. *Give a Man a Fish: Reflections on the New Politics of Distribution*. Durham, NC: Duke University Press.

Fernández Terán, Roberto. 2009. *Gas, petróleo e imperialismo en Bolivia*. La Paz: Plural Editores.

FFC (Federación de Fraternidades Cruceñas). n.d. "Día de tradición." Manuscript in author's collection.

Field, Thomas. 2014. *From Development to Dictatorship: Bolivia and the Alliance for Progress in the Kennedy Era*. Ithaca, NY: Cornell University Press.

FUL (Federación Universitaria Local), ed. 1967. *Gas y petróleo: Liberación o dependencia*. Cochabamba: Federación Universitaria Local.

Galeano, Eduardo. 1973. *Open Veins of Latin America: Five Centuries of the Pillage of a Continent*. Translated by Cedric Belfrage. New York: Monthly Review Press.

Galindo, María. 2018. "No es palacio de gobierno, es casa grande del amo." *Página Siete* (La Paz), June 27.

Galindo, María. 2019. "Empoderamiento-desempoderamiento." *Página Siete* (La Paz), June 5.

Gandarillas, Marco. 2013. "Empleo y derechos laborales en las actividades extractivas." *Petropress* 30:4–7.

Garcés, Fernando. 2011. "The Domestication of Indigenous Autonomies in Bolivia: From the Pact of Unity to the New Constitution." In Fabricant and Gustafson 2011, 46–67.

García Linera, Álvaro. 2018. "Construyendo la Bolivia posible, la Bolivia necesaria." *La Migraña* 28:12–17.

García Paz, Ricardo. n.d. "Santa Cruz es hermosa, pero . . ." Accessed February 12, 2004. http://www. nacioncamba.net/.

Giannecchini, Doroteo. (1898) 1996. *Historia natural, etnografía, geografía, lingüística del Chaco Boliviano*. Edited by Lorenzo Calzavarini. La Paz: Fondo de Inversión Social; Tarija: Centro Eclesial de Documentación.

Gill, Lesley. 1987. *Peasants, Entrepreneurs and Social Change: Frontier Development in Lowland Bolivia*. Boulder, CO: Westview Press.

Gill, Lesley. 2000. *Teetering on the Rim: Global Restructuring, Daily Life, and the Armed Retreat of the Bolivian State*. New York: Columbia University Press.

Gill, Lesley. 2004. *The School of the Americas: Military Training and Political Violence in the Americas*. Durham, NC: Duke University Press.

Gill, Lesley. 2016. *A Century of Violence in a Red City: Popular Struggle, Counterinsurgency, and Human Rights in Colombia*. Durham, NC: Duke University Press.

Gillette, Michael. 1970. "Huey Long and the Chaco War." *Louisiana History* 11 (4): 293–311.

Gledhill, John. 2011. "The Persistent Imaginary of 'the People's Oil': Nationalism, Globalisation and the Possibility of Another Country in Brazil, Mexico and Venezuela." In Behrends, Reyna, and Schlee 2011, 165–89.

Gobierno Autónomo Departamental de Santa Cruz. 2020. "Escudo de armas de Santa Cruz." Accessed January 8, 2020. http://www.santacruz.gob.bo/sczturistica/asies_historia_simbolos/contenido/433/300151.

Gobierno de Bolivia. 2003. "Decreto Supremo 27209: Declárase emergencia nacional en todo el territorio de la República para garantizar el normal abastecimiento de combustibles líquidos a la población." October 11. http://www.lexivox.org/norms/BO-DS-27209.xhtml.

Gobierno de Bolivia. 2004. "Decreto Supremo 27594: Establecer los mecanismos financieros para la ejecución de la Campaña Informativa del Gas que realiza el Ministerio de la Presidencia en el marco del Contrato de Préstamo de la CAF N° 2845." June 25. https://www.lexivox.org/norms/BO-DS-27594.html.

Gobierno de Bolivia. 2006. "Decreto Supremo 28701: Bolivia; Nacionalización de hidrocarburos 'Héroes del Chaco.'" May 1. https://www.lexivox.org/norms/BO-DS-28701.html.

Gómez-Barris, Macarena. 2017. *The Extractive Zone: Social Ecologies and Decolonial Practices*. Durham, NC: Duke University Press.

Gordillo, Gastón. 2014. *Rubble: The Afterlife of Destruction*. Durham, NC: Duke University Press.

Gotkowitz, Laura. 2007. *A Revolution for Our Rights: Indigenous Struggles for Land and Justice in Bolivia, 1880–1952*. Durham, NC: Duke University Press.

Graeber, David. 2018. *Bullshit Jobs: A Theory*. New York: Simon and Schuster.

Grandin, Greg. 2006. *Empire's Workshop: Latin America, the United States, and the Rise of the New Imperialism*. New York: Henry Holt.

Gray Molina, George. 2005. "Crecimiento de base ancha: Entre la espada y la pared." *T'inkazos* 15:95–101.

Günel, Gökçe. 2018. "Review Essay: New Perspectives on Energy." *PoLAR: Political and Legal Anthropology Review*, May 14.

Günel, Gökçe. 2019. *Spaceship in the Desert: Energy, Climate Change, and Urban Design in Abu Dhabi*. Durham, NC: Duke University Press.

Gupta, Akhil. 2015. "An Anthropology of Electricity from the Global South." *Cultural Anthropology* 30:555–68.

Gurney, Kyra, Anjali Tsui, David Iaconangelo, and Selina Cheng. 2016. "Suspected of Corruption at Home, Powerful Foreigners Find Refuge in the U.S." *ProPublica*, December 9.

Gustafson, Bret. 2006. "Spectacles of Autonomy and Crisis: Or, What Bulls and Beauty Queens Have to Do with Regionalism in Eastern Bolivia." *Journal of Latin American and Caribbean Anthropology* 11 (2): 351–79.

Gustafson, Bret. 2009a. "Bolivia 9/11: Bodies and Power on a Feudal Frontier." *Caterwaul Quarterly* 2:20–24.

Gustafson, Bret. 2009b. "Manipulating Cartographies: Plurinationalism, Autonomy, and Indigenous Resurgence in Bolivia." *Anthropological Quarterly* 82 (4): 985–1016.

Gustafson, Bret. 2009c. *New Languages of the State: Indigenous Resurgence and the Politics of Knowledge in Bolivia*. Durham, NC: Duke University Press.

Gustafson, Bret. 2010. "When States Act Like Movements: Dismantling Local Power and Seating Sovereignty in Bolivia." *Latin American Perspectives* 37 (4): 48–66.

Gustafson, Bret. 2011. "Flashpoints of Sovereignty: Territorial Conflict and Natural Gas in Bolivia." In Behrends, Reyna, and Schlee 2011, 220–40.

Gustafson, Bret. 2012. "Fossil Knowledge: Industry Strategy, Public Culture, and the Challenge for Critical Research." In McNeish and Logan 2012, 311–34.

Gustafson, Bret. 2016. "Bolivia after the 'No' Vote." NACLA *Report on the Americas*, March 7.

Gustafson, Bret. 2017a. "The New Energy Imperialism in the Caribbean." NACLA *Report on the Americas* 49 (4): 421–28.

Gustafson, Bret. 2017b. "Oppressed No More? Indigenous Language Regimentation in Plurinational Bolivia." *International Journal of the Sociology of Language* 246:31–57.

Gutiérrez, Raquel. 2014. *Rhythms of the Pachakuti: Indigenous Uprising and State Power in Bolivia*. Durham, NC: Duke University Press.

Haarstad, Havard. 2009a. "FDI Policy and Political Spaces for Labour: The Disarticulation of the Bolivian *Petroleros*." *Geoforum* 40 (2): 239–48.

Haarstad, Havard. 2009b. "Globalization and the New Spaces for Social Movement Politics: The Marginalization of Labor Unions in Bolivian Gas Nationalization." *Globalizations* 6 (2): 169–85.

Healy, Kevin. 1982. *Caciques y patrones: Una experiencia de desarrollo rural en el sud de Bolivia*. Cochabamba: Centro de Estudios de la Realidad Economica y Social.

Hersh, Seymour. 1987. "Target Qaddafi." *New York Times Magazine*, February 22.

Hindery, Derrick. 2013. *From Enron to Evo: Pipeline Politics, Global Environmentalism, and Indigenous Rights in Bolivia*. Tucson: University of Arizona Press.

Horne, Gerald. 2006. *The Color of Fascism: Lawrence Dennis, Racial Passing, and the Rise of Right-Wing Extremism in the United States*. New York: New York University Press.

Huber, Matthew. 2013. *Lifeblood: Oil, Freedom, and the Forces of Capital*. Minneapolis: University of Minnesota Press.

Huber, Matthew. 2019. "Ecosocialism: Dystopian and Scientific." *Socialist Forum*, Winter.

Hudson, Manley O. 1936. *The Chaco Arms Embargo*. Washington, DC: United States Government Printing Office.

Hudson, Peter. 2017. *Bankers and Empire: How Wall Street Colonized the Caribbean*. Chicago: University of Chicago Press.

Hughes, David McDermott. 2017. *Energy without Conscience: Oil, Climate Change, and Complicity*. Durham, NC: Duke University Press.

Hylton, Forrest, and Sinclair Thomson. 2007. *Revolutionary Horizons: Past and Present in Bolivian Politics*. New York: Verso.

IBCE (Instituto Boliviano de Comercio Exterior). n.d. "Estadísticas por departamento de Bolivia." Accessed June 15, 2018. http://ibce.org.bo/informacion -estadisticas-departamentos.php.

IMF (International Monetary Fund). 2017. "Bolivia: 2017 Article IV Consultation." IMF Country Report 17/395. https://www.imf.org/en/Publications/CR/Issues /2017/12/22/Bolivia-2017-Article-IV-Consultation-Press-Release-Staff-Report -and-Statement-by-the-45504.

Johnson, Lyndon B. 1968. "The President's Toast at a Luncheon at the LBJ Ranch Honoring President Barrientos of Bolivia." *The American Presidency Project*, July 5. http://www.presidency.ucsb.edu/node/236806.

Katzin, Donna. 1974. "Alliance for Power: U.S. Aid to Bolivia under Banzer." *NACLA Report on the Americas* 8 (2): 27–30.

Kaup, Brent. 2012. *Market Justice: Political and Economic Struggle in Bolivia*. Cambridge: Cambridge University Press.

Kirshner, Joshua. 2011. "Migrants and Citizens: Hygiene Panic and Urban Space in Santa Cruz." In Fabricant and Gustafson 2011, 96–115.

Klein, Herbert. 1964. "American Oil Companies in Latin America: The Bolivian Experience." *Inter-American Economic Affairs* 18 (2): 47–72.

Klein, Herbert. 1982. *Bolivia: The Evolution of a Multi-Ethnic Society*. New York: Oxford.

Klein, Herbert. 2003. *A Concise History of Bolivia*. Cambridge: Cambridge University Press.

Klein, Herbert, and José Alejandro Peres-Cajías. 2014. "Bolivian Oil and Natural Gas under State and Private Control, 1920–2010." *Bolivian Studies Journal* 20:141–64.

Klett, T. R., T. S. Ahlbrandt, J. W. Schmoker, and G. L. Dolton, G. L. 1997. "Ranking of the World's Oil and Gas Provinces by Known Petroleum Volumes." Open-File Report 97-463. http://pubs.usgs.gov/of/1997/ofr-97-463/index.html#Table.

Krupa, Christopher, and David Nugent, eds. 2015. *State Theory and Andean Politics: New Approaches to the Study of Rule*. Philadelphia: University of Pennsylvania Press.

Kundera, Milan. 1984. *The Unbearable Lightness of Being*. New York: Harper and Row.

Labban, Mazen. 2008. *Space, Oil, and Capital*. New York: Routledge.

Langer, Erick. 2009. *Expecting Pears from an Elm Tree: Franciscan Missions on the Chiriguano Frontier in the Heart of South America, 1830–1949*. Durham, NC: Duke University Press.

La Razón (La Paz). 2004a. "La entrevista: Gas es como la vaca lechera; nosotros queremos todo, no sólo de donde sale la leche." July 8.

La Razón (La Paz). 2004b. "Los militares tienen un carro antidisturbios." July 28.

La Razón (La Paz). 2004c. "Un rumor hace mención a un plan para matar a Mesa." August 6.

La Razón (La Paz). 2004d. "Sectores sindicales y sociales anuncian otro octubre negro." January 16.

Larson, Henrietta, Evelyn Knowlton, and Charles S. Poppe. 1971. *History of Standard Oil Company (New Jersey): New Horizons, 1927–1950*. New York: Harper and Row.

Lazar, Sian. 2008. *El Alto, Rebel City: Self and Citizenship in Andean Bolivia*. Durham, NC: Duke University Press.

Lehm, Zulema, and Silvia Rivera Cusicanqui. 1988. *Los artesanos libertarios y la ética del trabajo*. La Paz: Gramma.

Lehman, Kenneth. 2006. "A 'Medicine of Death'? U.S. Policy and Political Disarray in Bolivia, 1985–2006." In *Addicted to Failure: U.S. Security Policy in Latin America and the Andean Region*, edited by Brian Loveman, 130–68. Lanham, MD: Rowman and Littlefield.

Lemoine, Maurice. 2006. "Bolivia, the Military Plan and Wait." *Le Monde Diplomatique*, February.

Li, Tania Murray. 2017. "After Development: Surplus Population and the Politics of Entitlement." *Development and Change* 48 (6): 1247–61.

Limbert, Mandana. 2010. *In the Time of Oil: Piety, Memory, and Social Life in an Omani Oil Town*. Stanford, CA: Stanford University Press.

Lindquist, Sandra. 1998. "The Santa Cruz-Tarija Province of Central South America: Los Monos-Machareti (!) Petroleum System." Open-File Report 99-50-C. https://pubs.usgs.gov/of/1999/ofr-99-0050/OF99-50C/.

Lora, Guillermo. 1977. *A History of the Bolivian Labor Movement, 1848–1971.* Translated by Christine Whitehead. Cambridge: Cambridge University Press.

Lowrey, Kathleen. 2006. "Bolivia Multiétnico y Pluricultural, Ten Years Later: White Separatism in the Bolivian Lowlands." *Latin American and Caribbean Ethnic Studies* 1 (1): 63–84.

Luxemburg, Rosa. (1913) 2003. *The Accumulation of Capital.* New York: Routledge.

Macías Vázquez, Alfredo, and Jorge García-Arias. 2019. "Financialization, Institutional Reform, and Structural Change in the Bolivian Boom (2006–2014)." *Latin American Perspectives* 46 (2): 47–64.

Maitland Werner, Leslie. 1984. "Case of Vatican Envoy Unexplained." *New York Times,* June 13.

Malm, Andreas. 2016. *Fossil Capital: The Rise of Steam Power and the Roots of Global Warming.* New York: Verso.

Mansilla, H. C. F. 2004. *El carácter conservador de la nación boliviana.* Santa Cruz: Editorial El País.

Mares, David. 2006. "Natural Gas Pipelines in the Southern Cone." In *Geopolitics and Natural Gas from 1970 to 2040,* edited by David G. Victor, Amy M. Jaffe, and Mark H. Hayes, 169–201. Cambridge: Cambridge University Press.

Mariaca Bilbao, Enrique. 1966. *Mito y realidad del petróleo boliviano.* La Paz: Amigos de Libro.

Marof, Tristán. 1935. *La tragedia del altiplano: Bolivia y la guerra.* Buenos Aires: Editorial Claridad.

Marsh, Margaret Alexander. 1928. *The Bankers of Bolivia: A Study in American Foreign Investment.* New York: Vanguard Press.

Martel, James R. 2018. *Unburied Bodies: Subversive Corpses and the Authority of the Dead.* Amherst, MA: Amherst College Press.

Mbembe, Achille. 2003. "Necropolitics." *Public Culture* 15 (1): 11–40.

Mbembe, Achille. 2005. "Sovereignty as a Form of Expenditure." In *Sovereign Bodies: Citizens, Migrants, and States in the Postcolonial World,* edited by Thomas Blom Hansen and Finn Stepputat, 148–68. Durham, NC: Duke University Press.

McLarty, Thomas, and Richard Klein. 2004. "Latin America May Be Source of Energy Relief." *Miami Herald,* October 3.

McNeish, John-Andrew. 2013. "Extraction, Protest, and Indigeneity in Bolivia: The TIPNIS Effect." *Latin American and Caribbean Ethnic Studies* 8 (2): 221–42.

McNeish, John-Andrew, and Owen Logan, eds. 2012. *Flammable Societies: Studies on the Socio-Economics of Oil and Gas.* London: Pluto.

McNelly, Angus. 2018. "Labor Bureaucracy and Labor Officialdom in Evo Morales's Bolivia." *Development and Change* 50 (4): 896–922.

Menchaca, Martha. 2016. *The Politics of Dependency: U.S. Reliance on Mexican Oil and Farm Labor.* Austin: University of Texas Press.

Middleton, Townsend. 2018. "The Afterlives of a Killing: Assassination, Thanatos, and the Body Politics in South Asia." *Public Culture* 30 (1): 85–112.

Ministerio de Información y Deportes. 1971. "El extremismo escupía al rostro de la nación." La Paz. Pamphlet in author's collection.

Ministry of Communication. 2014. "Los frutos de la nacionalización son para todos los bolivianos." June 11. https://issuu.com/cambio2020/docs/discurso_presidencial_11-06-14.

Ministry of Communication. 2017a. "Discurso del presidente del Estado Plurinacional de Bolivia, Evo Morales, en la entrega de certificados de transferencia bancaria." November 7. https://issuu.com/cambio2020/docs/discurso_20presidencial_2008-11-17.

Ministry of Communication. 2017b. "Discurso presidencial No. 1337." October 10. https://issuu.com/cambio2020/docs/discurso_presidencial_11-10-17.

Miranda Pacheco, Carlos, and Javier Aliaga Lordemann. 2009. *Gas y política: Una geopolítica explosiva*. La Paz: Instituto Latinoamericano de Investigaciones Sociales / Friedrich Ebert Stiftung.

Mitchell, Timothy. 2001. *Carbon Democracy: Political Power in the Age of Oil*. London: Verso.

Molina, Fernando. 2018. "'Patria o muerte. Venceremos': El orden castrense de Evo Morales." *Nueva Sociedad* 278 (November-December): 119–29.

Montenegro, Carlos. 1938. *Frente al derecho del Estado el oro de Standard Oil (El petróleo, sangre de Bolivia)*. La Paz: El Trabajo.

Moore, Sally Falk. 1987. "Explaining the Present: Theoretical Dilemmas in Processual Ethnography." *American Ethnologist* 14 (4): 727–36.

Morales, Juan Antonio. 2008. "Distribución directa a las personas de la renta hidrocarburífera: Impactos macroeconómicos." *Documentos de Trabajo* 7 (2008). Instituto de Investigaciones Socio-Económicas. https://ideas.repec.org/p/ris/iisecd/2008_007.html.

Morell i Torra, Pere. 2018. "'Pronto aquí vamos a mandar nosotros': Autonomía Guarani Charagua Iyambae, la construcción de un proyecto político indígena en la Bolivia plurinacional." PhD diss., Universitat de Barcelona.

Nader, Laura. 1981. "Barriers to Thinking New about Energy." *Physics Today* 34 (2): 9, 99–104.

Nader, Laura, ed. 2010. *The Energy Reader*. Oxford: Wiley-Blackwell.

Nash, June. 1979. *We Eat the Mines and the Mines Eat Us: Dependency and Exploitation in Bolivian Tin Mines*. New York: Columbia University Press.

National Security Council. 1971. "Memorandum from Arnold Nachmanoff of the National Security Council to President's Assistant for National Security Affairs (Kissinger), August 19, 1971, 10:15 a.m." In *Foreign Relations of the United States, 1969–1976*, vol. E–10, *Documents on American Republics,*

1969–1972. https://history.state.gov/historicaldocuments/frus1969-76ve10
/d107.

Neruda, Pablo. 1991. *Canto general*. Translated by Jack Schmitt. Berkeley: University
of California Press.

Neruda, Pablo. (1950) 2016. *Canto general*. Madrid: Catedra.

New York Times. 1954. "Texas Oil Man in Bolivia." March 7.

New York Times. 1956. "Gulf Oil, Bolivia, Sign 40-Year Pact." March 27.

New York Times. 1957. "M'Carthy Disposes of Bolivia Oil Right." June 6.

New York Times. 1958. "Future of Bolivia Brightened by Oil." January 1.

New York Times. 1959. "New Bolivian Oil Well." November 27.

New York Times. 1963. "New Vistas Open in Bolivian City." August 12.

New York Times. 1986. "Envoy Admits Visiting Libya in 1985." June 19.

Ondarza, Gustavo. 2005. "Ciudadanos despejan vías a la fuerza." *El Deber* (Santa
Cruz). January 29.

Orgaz, Mirko. 2005. *La nacionalización del gas*. La Paz: Centro de Estudios y Documentación Latinoamericanos.

Otero, María. 2010. Email to Hillary Clinton, January 24. *Wikileaks Hillary Clinton
Email Archive*. https://wikileaks.org/clinton-emails/emailid/9356.

Página Siete (La Paz). 2018. "Detienen a Galindo por manchar el nuevo palacio con
pintura roja." November 27.

Página Siete (La Paz). 2019. "CEDIB: El 37.6% de la superficie de las TCO tituladas
fue sobrepuesta con áreas petroleras." June 17.

Painter, David. 1986. *Oil and the American Century: The Political Economy of U.S.
Foreign Oil Policy, 1941–1954*. Baltimore: Johns Hopkins University Press.

Palermo, Hernán, and Cynthia Rivero. 2011. "Memorias del trabajo ante los pro-
cesos de privatización en Argentina." *Nómadas* 34:151–65.

Peláez C., Rafael Ulises. 1958. *Los betunes del Padre Barba*. La Paz: Talleres Gráficos
Bolivianos.

Pereira de Lima, Cristiane. 2010. "La aportación de la UNASUR para el surgimiento
de América del Sur como actor global de relevancia en el escenario interna-
cional (2004–2008)." PhD diss., Universidad Complutense de Madrid.

Petras, James, and Jorge Lora. 2013. *Extractivismo y simulacro progresista en Bolivia y
Latinoamérica*. Puebla: Benemérita Universidad Autónoma de Puebla.

Philip, George. 1982. *Oil and Politics in Latin America*. Cambridge: Cambridge
University Press.

Pinkus, Karen. 2016. *Fuel: A Speculative Dictionary*. Minneapolis: University of
Minnesota Press.

PNUD (Proyecto de las Naciones Unidas para el Desarrollo). 1995. *Elay Santa Cruz:
Informe del desarrollo humano en la ciudad de Santa Cruz de la Sierra*. Santa
Cruz: Gobierno Municipal de Santa Cruz de la Sierra and PNUD.

PNUD (Proyecto de las Naciones Unidas para el Desarrollo). 2004. *Informe de desarrollo humano en Santa Cruz 2004*. La Paz: PNUD.

Political Database of the Americas. 2004. "Bolivia: 2004 Binding Referendum on Energy Policy." http://pdba.georgetown.edu/Elecdata/Bolivia/ref04.html.

Poole, Deborah. 2004. "An Image of 'Our Indian': Type Photographs and Racial Sentiment in Oaxaca, 1920–1940." *Hispanic American Historical Review* 84 (1): 37–82.

Postero, Nancy. 2017. *The Indigenous State: Race, Politics, and Performance in Plurinational Bolivia*. Berkeley: University of California Press.

Prada Alcoreza, Raúl. 2013. "Defensa crítica del proceso." January 16. http://www .rebelion.org/noticia.php?id=162342&titular=defensa-cr%EDtica-del-proceso-.

Prada Alcoreza, Rául. 2020. "La revolución truncada." *Bolpress*. January 7. https:// www.bolpress.com/2020/01/07/la-revolucion-truncada/.

Prudén, Hernán. 2003. "Santa Cruz entre la post-guerra del Chaco y las postrimerías de la Revolución Nacional: Cruceños y Cambas." *Historias* 6:41–63.

Puar, Jasbir. 2017. *The Right to Maim: Debility, Capacity, Disability*. Durham, NC: Duke University Press.

Quiroga Castro, Gina. 2005. "La fórmula uno de la ganadería." *Cash: Negocias y finanzas* 2 (35): 30–33.

Quiroga Santa Cruz, Marcelo. 1967. *Desarrollo con soberanía: La desnacionalización del petróleo*. Cochabamba: Editorial Universitaria.

Quiroga Santa Cruz, Marcelo. 1973. *El saqueo de Bolivia*. La Paz: Puerta del Sol.

Quiroga Santa Cruz, Marcelo. (1975) 1997. *Oleocracia o patria. Vol. 5 de Obras completas*. La Paz: Plural.

Quiroga Santa Cruz, Marcelo. (1978) 2013. "Importancia estratégica del petróleo y el gas, 1978." In *Un libro para escuchar a Marcelo Quiroga Santa Cruz*, edited by Yolanda Téllez, 111–27. La Paz: Muela del Diablo.

Raley, David. 2008. "The Origins of a Corporate Giant: Tennessee Gas and Transmission's Wartime Pipeline." *Business and Economic History On-Line* 6:1–21.

Randall, Stephen. 1976. "The Barco Concession in Colombian-American Relations, 1926–1932." *The Americas* 33 (1): 96–108.

Randall, Stephen. 1985. *United States Foreign Oil Policy, 1919–1948: For Profits and Security*. Kingston: McGill-Queen's University Press.

Restrepo, Laura. 1999. *La novia oscura*. Bogota: Editorial Norma.

Reyna, Stephen. 2007. "Waiting, the Sorcery of Modernity: Transnational Corporation, Oil, and Terrorism in Chad." *Sociologus* 57 (1): 131–39.

Richard, Nicolas, ed. 2008. *Mala guerra: Los indígenas en la Guerra del Chaco*. Asunción: Museo del Barro.

Rigirozzi, Pia, and Diana Tussie, eds. 2012. *The Rise of Post-Hegemonic Regionalism: The Case of Latin America*. London: Springer.

Riofrancos, Thea. 2018. "Ecuador after Correa: The Fate of the Petrostate." *N+1*, no. 29 (Fall). https://nplusonemag.com/issue-29/politics/ecuador-after -correa-2/.

Rivera Cusicanqui, Silvia. 2013. "Del MNR a Evo Morales: Disyunciones del estado colonial." *Upside Down World*, June 11. http://upsidedownworld.org/noticias -en-espa/noticias-en-espa-noticias-en-espa/bolivia-del-mnr-a-evo-morales -disyunciones-del-estado-colonial/.

Rogers, Douglas. 2015a. *The Depths of Russia: Oil, Power, and Culture after Socialism*. Ithaca, NY: Cornell University Press.

Rogers, Douglas. 2015b. "Oil and Anthropology." *Annual Review of Anthropology* 44:365–80.

Romero, Simon. 2008. "American Rancher Resists Land Reform Plans in Bolivia." *New York Times*, May 9.

Rosenbaum, David. 2004. "A Closer Look at Cheney and Halliburton." *New York Times*, September 28.

Rout, Leslie, Jr. 1970. *Politics of the Chaco Peace Conference, 1935–1939*. Austin: University of Texas Press.

Roy, Ananya. 2009. "The 21st-Century Metropolis: New Geographies of Theory." *Regional Studies* 43 (6): 819–30.

Royuela Comboni, Carlos. 1996. *Cien años de hidrocaruros en Bolivia (1896–1996)*. La Paz: Los Amigos del Libro.

Sánchez de Lozada, Gonzalo. (1985) 2018. "Bitter Medicine." In *The Bolivia Reader*, edited by Sinclair Thompson, Rossana Barragán, Xavier Albó, Seemin Qayum, and Mark Goodale, 507–13. Durham, NC: Duke University Press.

Sawyer, J. Herbert. 1975. "Latin America after 1920." In *Trek of the Oil Finders: A History of Exploration for Petroleum*, edited by E. W. Owen, 960–1521. Tulsa, OK: American Association of Petroleum Geologists.

Sawyer, Suzana. 2004. *Crude Chronicles: Indigenous Politics, Multinational Oil, and Neoliberalism in Ecuador*. Durham, NC: Duke University Press.

Schiller, Naomi. 2018. *Channeling the State: Community Media and Popular Politics in Venezuela*. Durham, NC: Duke University Press.

Schilling-Vacaflor, Almut. 2014. "Rethinking the Link between Consultation and Conflict: Lessons from Bolivia's Gas Sector." *Canadian Journal of Development Studies* 35 (4): 503–21.

Schultz, Jim. 2008. "That Kosovo, Goldberg, Bolivia Thing." Democracy Center blog, May 16. https://democracyctr.org/that-kosovo-goldberg-bolivia-thing/.

Seidman, J. I. 1934. *Munitions Manufacture and Arms Embargoes*. Editorial Research Reports 1. Washington, DC: CQ Press.

Seto, Karen C., et al. 2016. "Carbon Lock-In: Types, Causes, and Policy Implications." *Annual Review of Environment and Resources* 41:425–52.

Shever, Elana. 2012. *Resources for Reform: Oil and Neoliberalism in Argentina*. Palo Alto, CA: Stanford University Press.

Solíz Rada, Andrés. 2001. "Rescatemos la conciencia nacional." *Temas Sociales*, no. 22.

Soruco Solugoren, Ximena. 2011. "El Porvenir, the Future That Is No Longer Possible in the Bolivian Oriente." In Fabricant and Gustafson 2011, 68–90.

Souza Crespo, Mauricio, ed. 2011. *René Zavaleta Mercado: Ensayos 1957–1974 obra completa, Vol. 1*. La Paz: Plural.

Souza Crespo, Mauricio. 2013a. "Las figuras del tiempo en la obra de René Zavaleta Mercado." In Souza Crespo 2013b, 11–30.

Souza Crespo, Mauricio, ed. 2013b. *René Zavaleta Mercado: Ensayos 1975–1984 obra completa, Vol. 2*. La Paz: Plural.

Speers, L. C. 1935. "Issue of War Profits Is Now Taking Form." *New York Times*, March 24.

Standard Oil Company of Bolivia. 1939. *Confiscation: A History of the Oil Industry in Bolivia*. New York: Standard Oil.

State of New York. 1920. *Annual Report of the Superintendent of Banks Relative to Savings Banks, Trust Companies, Investment Companies, Safe Deposit Companies, Personal Loan Companies, and Personal Brokers*. Albany, NY: J. R. Lyon.

Stearman, Allyn Maclean. 1985. *Camba and Kolla: Migration and Development in Santa Cruz, Bolivia*. Gainesville: University of Florida Press.

Stewart, Kathleen. 2007. *Ordinary Affects*. Durham, NC: Duke University Press.

Stoekel, Alan. 2007. *Bataille's Peak: Energy, Religion, and Postsustainability*. Minneapolis: University of Minnesota Press.

Stoler, Ann L. 1989. "Making Empire Respectable: The Politics of Race and Sexual Morality in 20th-Century Colonial Cultures." *American Ethnologist* 16 (4): 634–60.

Streit, Clarence K. 1935. "League Supports First Punitive Act; Curb on Paraguay." *New York Times*, January 17.

Svampa, Maristella. 2017. *Del cambio de época al fin de ciclo: Gobiernos progresistas, extractivismo y movimientos sociales en América Latina*. Buenos Aires: Edhasa.

Tambiah, Stanley J. 1976. *World Conqueror and World Renouncer: A Study of Buddhism and Polity in Thailand against a Historical Background*. Cambridge: Cambridge University Press.

Tapia, Luís. 2002. *La producción del conocimiento local: Historia y política en la obra de René Zavaleta*. La Paz: Muela del Diablo.

Tellería Escobar, Loreta. 2016. "Wiki Revelación: Las relaciones entre las Fuerzas Armadas y la Embajada de los Estados Unidos en Bolivia (2007–2008)." In *Bolivialeaks: La injerencia política de Estados Unidos Contra el Proceso de Cambio (2006–2010)*, edited by Juan Ramón Quintana, 145–83. La Paz: Ministerio de la Presidencia.

Tinker-Salas, Miguel. 2009. *The Enduring Legacy: Oil, Culture, and Society in Venezuela*. Durham, NC: Duke University Press.

UNASUR (Unión de Naciones Suramericanas). 2008. "Informe de la comisión de UNASUR sobre los sucesos de Pando." Accessed July 3, 2019. https://www.alainet.org/es/active/27848.

United Nations. 2009. *Informe público de la Oficina del Alto Comisionado de las Naciones Unidas para los Derechos Humanos en Bolivia sobre los hechos de violencia ocurridos en Pando en septiembre de 2008*. La Paz: Oficina del Alto Comisionado de las Naciones Unidas para los Derechos Humanos.

United Nations Human Rights Council. 2009. "Report of the Special Rapporteur on the Situation of Human Rights and Fundamental Freedoms of Indigenous People, Rodolfo Stavenhagen: Mission to Bolivia (A/HRC/11/11)." February 18. http://unsr.vtaulicorpuz.org/site/images/docs/country/2009-country-a-hrc-11-11-bolivia-en.pdf.

United States Congress. 1934. *Congressional Record. Proceedings and Debates of the Second Session of the Seventy-Third Congress of the United States of America. Volume 78, Part 10*. Washington, DC: US Government Printing Office.

United States Congress. 1936. Report of the Special Committee on Investigation of the Munitions Industry. 74th Congress, 2nd session, February 24, 1936, pp. 3–13. http://mtholyoke.edu/acad/interet/nye.htm.

United States Congress Senate Committee on Finance. 1931–32. *Sale of Foreign Bonds or Securities in the United States: Hearings before the Committee on Finance United States Senate Seventy-Second Congress. First Session Pursuant to S. Res. 19. A Resolution Authorizing the Finance Committee of the Senate to Investigate the Sale, Flotation, and Allocation by Banks, Banking Institutions, Corporations or Individuals of Foreign Bonds or Securities in the United States*. 4 vols. Washington, DC: US Government Printing Office.

United States Congress Special Committee Investigating the Munitions Industry. 1934. *Munitions Industry: Hearings before the Special Committee Investigating the Munitions Industry. United States Senate, 73rd Congress, Pursuant to S. Res. 206. A Resolution to Make Certain Investigations Concerning the Manufacture and Sale of Arms and Other War Munitions. Part 10, Dec. 5 and 6, 1934 Embargoes*. Washington, DC: US Government Printing Office.

United States District Court Southern District of Florida, Miami Division. 2013. "Second Amended Consolidated Complaint for Extrajudicial Killing; Crimes Against Humanity; and Wrongful Death." Case 1:08-CV-21063-JIC. Document 156. https://harvardhumanrights.files.wordpress.com/2013/06/second-amended-complaint-english.pdf.

UNITEL (Universal de Televisión). 2008. "La verdad de los muertos en Pando." Accessed May 24, 2018. https://www.youtube.com/watch?v=VMKpEHecGJk.

USMILGRP (US Military Group). 1962. "Memorandum of Understanding Concerning the Activation, Organization and Training of the 2d Ranger Batallion—Bolivian Army." National Security Archive. http://nsarchive.gwu.edu /NSAEBB/NSAEBB5/docs/doc14.pdf.

Valdivia, Gabriela. 2008. "Governing Relations between People and Things: Citizenship, Territory, and the Political Economy of Petroleum in Ecuador." *Political Geography* 27:456–77.

Valverde Bravo, Carlos. 2012. *¡Maten a Rosza! El rompecabezas de una conspiración.* Santa Cruz: El País.

Verdery, Katherine. 1999. *The Political Lives of Dead Bodies: Reburial and Postsocialist Change.* New York: Columbia University Press.

Vilca, Nelson. 2008. "Entrevista de Nelson Vilca: Guarani esclavos en Camiri." YouTube, April 9. https://www.youtube.com/watch?gl=ES&hl=es&v =id3QoWqQdno.

Vice Ministerio de Tierras. 2008a. "Actividades realizadas para el saneamiento, reversión y expropiación de tierras en favor de comunidades guaraníes cautivas." Manuscript in author's possession.

Vice Ministerio de Tierras. 2008b. "Antecedentes históricos de la ocupación territorial del Pueblo Guaraní del Alto Parapetí." Manuscript in author's possession.

Vice Ministerio de Tierras. 2008c. "Resumen de los hechos violentos acaecidos en contra del Pueblo Guaraní y de funcionarios públicos." Manuscript in author's possession.

Vicepresidencia de Bolivia. 2009. *Informe conclusivo de la investigación de los hechos y atentados en la ciudad de Santa Cruz de la Sierra: Terrorismo separatista en Bolivia.* La Paz: Vicepresidencia de Bolivia.

Vitalis, Robert. 2006. *America's Kingdom: Mythmaking on the Saudi Oil Frontier.* Palo Alto, CA: Stanford University Press.

Wallace, Mike. 1957. "Interview with Glen McCarthy." Mike Wallace interview, Harry Ransom Center, University of Texas at Austin. https://hrc.contentdm .oclc.org/digital/collection/p15878coll90/id/17/rec/33.

Watts, Michael. 2001. "Petro-Violence: Community, Extraction, and Political Ecology of a Mythic Commodity." In *Violent Environments,* edited by Nancy Peluso and Michael Watts, 189–212. Ithaca, NY: Cornell University Press.

Watts, Michael. 2004a. "Antinomies of Community: Some Thoughts on Geography, Resources, and Empire." *Transactions of the Institute for British Geography* 29:195–216.

Watts, Michael. 2004b. "Resource Curse? Governmentality, Oil, and Power in the Niger Delta, Nigeria." *Geopolitics* 9 (1): 50–80.

Webber, Jeffrey. 2016. "Evo Morales, *Transformismo,* and the Consolidation of Agrarian Capitalism in Bolivia." *Journal of Agrarian Change* 17:330–47.

Webber, Jeffrey. 2017. "Evo Morales and the Political Economy of Passive Revolution in Bolivia, 2006–2015." *Third World Quarterly* 37 (10): 1855–876.

Weiner, Tim. 2009. "Robert McNamara, Architect of Futile War, Dies." *New York Times*, July 6.

Weintraub, Sidney, ed. 2007. *Energy Cooperation in the Western Hemisphere: Benefits and Impediments*. With Annette Hester and Veronica R. Prado. Washington, DC: CSIS.

White, Leslie. 1943. "Energy and the Evolution of Culture." *American Anthropologist* 45 (3): 335–56.

Whitehead, Laurence. 1973. "National Power and Local Power: The Case of Santa Cruz de la Sierra, Bolivia." In *Latin American Urban Research*, vol. 3, *National-Local Linkages: The Interrelationship of Urban and National Polities in Latin America*, edited by Francine Rabinovitz and Felicity Trueblood, 23–48. Beverly Hills, CA: SAGE.

Wilson, Sheena, Adam Carlson, and Imre Szeman, eds. 2017. *Petrocultures: Oil, Politics, Culture*. Montreal: McGill-Queen's University Press.

Wood, Bryce. 1961. *The Making of the Good Neighbor Policy*. New York: Columbia University Press.

World Bank. 1971. "Bolivia—Gas Pipeline Project." http://documents.worldbank.org/curated/en/443081467997579211/Bolivia-Gas-Pipeline-Project.

World Bank. 1996. "Bolivia: Preparation of the Capitalization of the Hydrocarbon Sector, Volume 1. Energy Sector Management Assistance Program (ESMAP)." http://documents.worldbank.org/curated/en/622321468743106143/Main-report.

Young, Kevin A. 2016. *Blood of the Earth: Resource Nationalism, Revolution, and Empire in Bolivia*. Austin: University of Texas Press.

YPFB (Yacimientos Petrolíferos Fiscales de Bolivia). 2017. "Información financiera: Contratos de servicios petroleros." Accessed December 20, 2018. https://www.ypfb.gob.bo/es/transparencia/contratos-petroleros.html.

Zabala, Elizabeth, and Ariel Ramírez Quiroga. 2016. *Dinámicas de la trata, proxenetismo y violencia sexual comercial de niñas, niños y adolescentes en Bolivia*. La Paz: Fundación Munasim Kullakita.

Zalik, Anna. 2004. "The Niger Delta: 'Petro Violence' and Partnership Development." *Review of African Political Economy* 101:401–24.

Zalik, Anna. 2008. "Liquefied Natural Gas and Fossil Capitalism." *Monthly Review* 60 (6): 41–53.

Zalik, Anna. 2011. "Protest as Violence in Oilfields: The Contested Representation of Profiteering in Two Extractive Sites." In *Accumulating Insecurity*, edited by Shelley Feldman, Charles Geisler, and Gayatri A. Menon, 261–84. Athens: University of Georgia Press.

Zapata Zegada, Oscar. (1964) 2015. "Pompilio Guerrero: El hombre que desafió a la Standard Oil." In *Antología del pensamiento crítico boliviano contemporáneo*, edited by Silvia Rivera Cusicanqui and Virginia Aillón Soria, 73–83. Buenos Aires: Consejo Latinoamericano de Ciencias Sociales.

Zavaleta, René. 1967a. *El desarrollo de la conciencia nacional.* In Souza Crespo 2011, 121–207.

Zavaleta, René. 1967b. "El gas, promesa económica o riesgo para la independencia." In FUL 1967, 137–86.

Zavaleta, René. 1970. "Recordación y apología de Sergio Almaraz Paz." In Souza Crespo 2011, 633–48.

Zavaleta, René. 1972. "Bolivia—Military Nationalism and the Popular Assembly." *New Left Review* 73:63–84.

Zavaleta, René. 1977. "Consideraciones generales sobre la historia boliviana." In Souza Crespo 2013b, 35–96.

Zavaleta, René. 1984. *Lo nacional-popular en Bolivia.* In Souza Crespo 2013b, 143–382.

Zook, David H. 1960. *The Conduct of the Chaco War.* New Haven, CT: Bookman.

Zulawski, Ann. 2006. *Unequal Cures: Public Health and Political Change in Bolivia, 1900–1950.* Durham, NC: Duke University Press.

abortion, 246, 252

academia, 12, 113, 152, 159

Acción Democrática Nacionalista. *See* the ADN

Achacachi, 109

activism, 17–18, 44, 60, 67, 87, 140, 251. *See also* resistance; revolution

Adair, Red, 62

the ADN (Nationalist Democratic Action), 182, 190, 260n1

advertising, 116, 142, 145

aesthetics, 130, 134–35, 138–39, 144, 185

affect, 14, 29–30, 100, 115, 125–28, 180, 190, 212, 224, 228–42

agrarian reform, 155, 158, 162

agriculture, 58, 143, 202; and agro-industry, 9, 16, 97, 118, 126–29, 136, 140–45, 156–60, 192–95, 248

Air BP, 102. *See also* BP (British Petroleum)

Alborta, Freddy, 185

alcohol, 80, 82, 104, 127, 170, 216

Allende, Salvador, 66

Almaraz, Alejandro, 16, 161–76, 189

Almaraz, Sergio: the gaseous state and, 1, 5–6, 16; nationalism of, 43, 61, 99, 161, 199, 243; on the oil-military-capital assemblage and, 28, 47–48, 51, 253; tin dependence and, 53–56

Alto Parapetí, 152–74, 200

the Amazon, 107, 160, 179, 203, 250

the American Fund for Public Service, 43

Amnesty International, 190

Amoco, 102

anarchism, 18–19, 31–32, 36–37, 47–49, 245–48, 252

anarcho-feminism, 18–19, 227, 245

Andean people: migration of, 89, 129, 137–40; ontologies of, 77, 113, 199, 226, 239; racism against, 21, 125–26, 130, 132–33, 170, 184, 256n11, 264n4; regionalism and, 142, 149; violence against, 113, 267n4. *See also* Indigenous people

Angulo, Gildo, 106–7, 109

Antelo, Jimena, 193

anti-imperialism, 2, 9–11, 16, 49, 56–59, 71, 93, 106–7, 191, 234. *See also* imperialism

the APG (Guarani People's Assembly), 159, 206

Aretxaga, Begoña, 197, 240

Argentina: Bolivian exports to, 9–10, 42, 61–62, 64; the fossil fuel assemblage and, 15, 28, 31–35, 45–49, 67–69, 80, 102–5, 191; imports from, 78–81; Indigenous people and, 6, 27; oil nationalization and, 57–58, 90–91, 101, 214, 223–24; resistance and, 73, 77, 118, 244

the arms industry, 30–32, 38, 43–47, 257n18

Armstrong, Thomas, 40–41, 55

Arze Vargas, Carlos, 243

Asamblea del Pueblo Guarani. *See* the APG

the Asamblea Popular, 65

the ASOFAMD, 188

assassinations, 33, 120, 122, 188, 194, 258n23, 260n2

assemblages, 20, 30–32, 39–40, 47, 58, 98–99, 155, 205, 223, 246

automobiles, 28, 148, 203, 220

autonomy, 5, 21, 122; Alto Parapetí and, 155–69; carnivals and, 126–29; civic coup and, 150–51; migration and, 137–40; Morales and, 215, 249–51; regionalism and, 125, 129–35, 263n19, 265n12; territoriality and, 135–37, 221–22; violence and, 182, 192–98. *See also* regionalism

the Aymara people, 104, 109, 118, 122, 189, 199, 223

the Ayoreo, 132–33

the Balkan wars, 195

banking, 17, 31, 36, 39–42, 47–48, 120, 202

Bánzer Suárez, Hugo, 52, 65–70, 91, 97–99, 103, 139, 164, 187–90, 196, 260n1

Barnes, Harry Elmer, 43

Barrientos, Juan José, 199

Barrientos, René, 59–61, 63, 88

beauty queens, 127–29, 132–35, 141–44, 148–49, 193, 264n7

Beni, 151, 182, 237, 245, 250

Benjamin, Walter, 194

the Besiro people, 132–33

biofuels, 97, 242

Black September, 122

blockades: Guarani, 134, 148, 211; land reform and, 161, 164, 166, 170, 183–84; regionalist, 122–23, 145, 217–18; resistance and, 109, 118; social movements and, 153, 248; violence and, 110, 152–53, 168

bodies: Che Guevara and, 185–88, 198; excess and, 179–81, 197–201; hegemony and, 21, 123–25; Indigenous, 27, 132, 137, 155, 166, 183; in the media, 152–53, 225; the Pando killings and,

181–85, 192–94; Quiroga Santa Cruz and, 188–89; women's, 237, 245. *See also* mass killings; necropolitics; thanatopolitics

the body politic. *See* bodies

Bohan, Mervin, 51

the Bohan Plan, 129

Bolívar, Simón, 106, 179, 191, 227

the Bolivian constitution, 16, 109, 126, 156, 180, 204, 224, 234, 247

the Bolivian government. *See* the state

the Bolivian military: the Chaco War and, 35–38, 50; Evo Morales and the, 248–51, 262n9; fossil fuel and the, 10, 30–32; the gaseous state and, 1; killings by the, 263n15; nationalism and, 51–55, 58; nationalization and, 61–68, 93, 104–13, 120–21, 149, 167, 183–94, 199–201; the US and, 19, 39–49, 59–60; the YPFB and, 69, 87–88. *See also* Rangers; the Bolivian Navy

the Bolivian Navy, 106

the Bolivian Ranger Battalion. *See* Rangers

bonds, 40, 42, 44, 46

the Bonosol, 90

Boyer, Dominic, 14

BP (British Petroleum), 102, 123

Braden, Spruille, 34

Brazil: conflict with, 31, 49, 251; drug trafficking and, 202–3; the fossil fuel assemblage and, 65–68, 103, 118–22, 181, 191–92, 194, 214, 223–24; nationalization and, 242–44; Petrobras and, 9–10, 16, 57, 102, 105, 146, 261n4; pipelines and, 69, 97–99, 187–88

Breglia, Lisa, 15

Britain, 6, 28, 30–33, 39, 43–46, 53

British Gas, 9, 102, 238

brothels, 79–83, 93, 217–21, 227–28, 238. *See also* sex-trafficking; sex work

Burgos, Elisabeth, 75

Bush, George, 121

Bush, George W., 157–58, 192, 242

Bustos, Ciro, 73, 77

Caballero, Luís, 189–90
the CAF (Andean Development Bank), 116
California, 107, 120
the Camba Nation, 140–45, 149
Camiri, 28–32, 49, 61–64, 69–96, 116–17, 146, 161–66, 187–88, 214–15, 219–21
Canada, 116
Cantinflas, 77
capital: foreign, 31–33, 51–52, 59, 89, 228, 232, 243; gas, 28, 113; global, 3, 9, 18–19, 21; oil, 14, 43; the state and, 2, 9, 20–21, 98–99; United States, 39–43, 56–57, 101, 103, 113–14, 191; war and, 45–51. *See also* finance capital; fossil capital
capitalism: fossil fuel, 2–4, 9, 13–18, 22–23, 30, 35–39, 49, 98; imperial, 2, 244; labor and, 221, 229; neoliberal, 16, 235; war and, 45, 125, 158. *See also* racial capitalism
Caranda, 60, 62
Carapari, 105
Caraparicito, 173–75
Cárdenas, Víctor Hugo, 100, 244
Cardoso, Fernando Henrique, 103
carnival, 126–35, 140–45, 245, 264n7. *See also* festivals
cars. *See* automobiles
Casa Grande del Pueblo, 226, 245
cash transfer programs, 10, 223, 228–32
Castro, Fidel, 66, 225
Castro, Jorge Cruz, 76
Catholicism, 184–85, 199, 246
CEDLA (Center for Studies of Agrarian and Labor Development), 242–43
centralism, 132, 143, 246n4
Centro de Estudios Jurídicos e Investigación Social (CEJIS), 122
Centro de Estudios para el Desarrollo Laboral y Agrario. *See* CEDLA
Cepek, Michael, 15
Céspedes, Augusto, 61, 256n10, 267n4

Chaco (company), 91, 120
the Chaco (region), 6, 9, 18–19, 29–49, 70, 77–80, 97, 104, 135, 154. *See also* the Chaco War
the Chaco War, 6, 17–19, 29–53, 70–71, 85, 93, 104–8, 120, 198, 258n23–26
the Chapare, 89, 182, 197
Chávez, Hugo, 12, 118, 121–22, 157, 165, 191–93, 242
Cheney, Dick, 209
Chevron, 10
Chicago Boys, 226
children, 61, 80–83, 109–10, 128, 149, 153, 200, 230
Chile, 6, 28, 31, 46–49, 57, 66–67, 84, 98, 103–15, 121
China, 192, 214, 224–25
the Chiquitanía, 133
the Chiquitano, 132–33. *See also* the Besiro people
Christianity, 130–31, 134, 138, 143–44, 150
the CIA, 60–61, 65–66, 259n7
CIPCA (Center for Research and Promotion of the Peasantry), 106
civic committees, 126–27, 135, 138, 140, 142
class: autonomy and, 127–33, 137, 141–45; Evo Morales and, 248–49; gas labor and, 216, 226–30; imperialism and, 50, 54–59, 65–66; nationalism and, 107, 116–17, 122, 141, 171, 214, 229; social movements and, 243–44; violence and, 171, 183, 199; war and, 31, 35, 38, 48–49; the YPFB and, 75, 78, 87, 100. *See also* workers
climate change, 13, 108, 229, 232, 270n12. *See also* the environment; global warming
Clinton, Bill, 121
Clinton, Hillary, 12
the CNPZ (Comisión Nestor Paz Zamora), 17, 190, 194, 196–98
coal, 57, 191

the COB (Bolivian Workers' Central), 67, 87, 90, 227

Cobija, 182–83, 194, 203

coca, 89, 100, 109, 138, 197, 216, 223

cocaine, 68–69, 104, 129, 138, 181, 203. *See also* drug trafficking

Cochabamba, 39, 80, 92, 176

CODEPANAL (Committee for the Defense of National Patrimony), 106–8

the Cold War, 52, 55, 59, 87, 104, 195, 199, 252

Colombia, 15, 77, 123, 166

colonialism: autonomy and, 125–26, 130–32, 138, 200, 206; fossil fuels and, 3, 13, 18, 56; race and, 139, 153, 185, 193, 227; settler, 27–28, 264n1; violence and, 36, 152–60, 171, 264n5. *See also* decolonization; settler colonialism

COMIBOL (Mining Corporation of Bolivia), 241

Comisión Interamericana de Derechos Humanos. *See* the IAHCR

Comité Pro-Santa Cruz. *See* the Pro-Santa Cruz Civic Committee

communism, 55–56, 59–61, 64–65, 199–200, 203, 256n8

communists, 199

Condorito, 83–84

the Condors, 104

consciousness, 77, 91, 108–10

Consejo Energético Suraméricano. *See* the South American Energy Council

conservativism, 52, 60, 65, 106, 113, 118, 121, 125, 132, 231

constitutional assemblies, 127. *See also* the Bolivian constitution

consumerism, 13, 58, 132, 231

consumption, 115–16, 203–8, 232, 240

Cooperativa de Telecomunicaciones Santa Cruz. *See* COTAS

cooperatives, 62–63, 91, 118, 146

Coronil, Fernando, 11, 136

corporal punishment, 185. *See also* punishment

Correa, Rafael, 191

corruption, 2, 16, 41, 45, 90–93, 106, 219, 224–25, 235, 245, 251

Cossío, Mario, 120

Costa du Rels, Adolfo, 159

Costas, Rubén, 142, 150, 220

COTAS (Santa Cruz Telephone Cooperative), 196–97

Cote, Stephen, 35

cotton, 86, 138

the Council of South American Nations, 191

the coup of November 2019, 21

coups: autonomy and, 21, 127, 136, 150–51, 157; gas lock-in and, 120–22; the MAS and, 182, 192, 194, 251–52, 255n3, 259n7, 267n2; military, 194–96, 249–50; nationalization and, 88, 188; US imperialism and, 11, 60, 65–67

the CRE (Cooperativa Rural de Electrificación), 62–63

criminality, 152, 171, 202

the Cruceño Youth Union. *See* the UJC

Cuba, 66, 112, 185

Cuevo, 152–53, 168, 170

cultural appropriation, 21, 87, 125–26, 132–35, 141–43, 237, 264n1–2

culture: autonomy and, 125–32, 135, 142–43; fossil fuels and, 13–15, 19, 30, 33, 135–38; regionalism and, 136, 142, 150; the state and, 229, 233; the United States and, 55, 58, 76; violence and, 79, 180

Cusicanqui, Silvia Rivera, 18, 189

the Dakar Rally, 237, 245

the Dallas Petroleum Club, 98, 100

dance, 127–28, 130, 142

the Davenport Code, 56, 61, 63–64, 87

death squads, 67, 256n14

Debray, Regis, 73

debt: fossil fuels and, 220, 242, 259n8; lock-in and, 99, 101–3, 116, 129, 220, 231; the oil-military-capital assemblage and, 31, 35–36, 39–43, 47; US imperialism and, 52, 54, 57, 64, 68.

See also banking; debt servitude; microlending

debt servitude, 157, 160–61, 174

decolonization, 3–5, 9, 16, 52, 155, 174–76, 182, 221, 234

Delgado Gonzales, Trifonio, 36–38, 45, 49, 256n11

the Democratic Party, 12, 121

Dennis, Lawrence, 44

Detzer, Dorothy, 44–46

development: aid, 70, 100, 120–21; distribution and, 229–32; fossil fuels and, 10, 52–53, 74, 93, 104; gas and, 106–7, 146, 176; Indigenous people and, 16, 28, 161; the MAS and, 182, 234, 242; US imperialism and, 11–12, 19, 51, 59–65, 76–77, 251

dictatorships: gas and, 52, 65, 69, 97, 103–4, 164, 181, 187–88; nationalism and, 88, 99, 196; resistance to, 17, 164, 235; the US and, 12, 33–34, 59, 61, 256n14; violence and, 181, 197

diesel, 126–27, 202, 242

Diéz, Hormando Vaca, 120

the Dignity Rent (Renta Dignidad), 230

disappearances, 67, 186–88, 221, 260n1, 267n4

domestic violence, 80–83, 220. *See also* masculinity; patriarchy; violence; women

Domínguez, Raul, 76

drinking. *See* alcohol

drug trafficking, 122, 170, 202–3, 221, 224, 238, 262n13

drug use, 165, 170, 268n4. *See also* alcohol

drug wars, 100, 267n2

DuPont, 45

Dwyer, Michael, 195

ecofeminism, 246, 252–53

Ecuador, 15, 191, 244, 261n6

education, 49, 74–75, 91–92, 115, 153, 216, 221, 236, 240

the EGTK (Túpac Katari Guerrilla Army), 189–90

the Eighth Army Division, 196

Ejército de Liberación Nacional de Bolivia. *See* the ELN

Ejército Guerrillero Túpac Katari. *See* the EGTK

El Alto, 109, 113, 121, 136

El Deber, 128, 143–44, 148, 179

electricity, 9, 14, 57, 62, 102–3, 143, 175, 203

the ELN (National Liberation Army of Bolivia), 190

embargoes, 46, 258n23

empire. *See* imperialism; the US

employment. *See* labor; workers

energopower, 14

energy: anthropologies and, 13–19; colonies, 9, 100, 107–8, 233; empire and, 11–13; integration, 12, 100, 191; policy, 107, 191, 268n7; US imperialism and, 98, 121

Enron, 69, 102

entrepreneurialism, 91, 129, 207, 221

the environment, 106, 207–8, 217, 242–44. *See also* climate change

Equipetrol (neighborhood), 58, 133–34

the Equitable Trust Co., 40–41

erasure, 21, 86–87, 113, 155, 265n9

the ESMAP (Energy Sector Management Assistance Program), 100–101, 262n6

Espinoza, Oswaldo, 189–90

Estenssoro, Víctor Paz, 89

Estremadoiro, Tanimbu, 168

ethanol, 192, 241–42

ethnicity, 136. *See also* race

evangelicalism, 246, 249, 252

excess: fighting over, 20, 223–44; fossil fuels and, 1–2, 5–6, 9, 21; gas and, 202–22, 252, 269n5; masculinity and, 19, 245; political violence and, 179–201; war and, 47, 245

EXPOCRUZ, 141–42, 145–48

expropriation, 1–2, 51, 113–23, 156, 162, 172–74, 199, 266n6 extractivism, 16–18, 21, 231–32, 255n7, 262n6, 270n12

Exxon, 9, 123

family, 71–84, 93, 112, 129, 133, 149, 157–62, 188, 199, 214–15

FARC (Revolutionary Armed Forces of Colombia), 166

farming: Andean migrants and, 104, 137–42, 183, 198, 223, 232; gas and, 202, 223, 232, 238–39; Indigenous people and, 89, 160, 170, 197, 255n6, 267n4; land conflicts and, 128, 156, 163; resistance and, 183–85; violence and, 149, 157, 179, 192–94, 198–99

fascism, 17–19, 50–58, 66, 120, 126, 141–50, 192–96, 227, 232, 252

Federación de Ganaderos de Santa Cruz. *See* the FEGASACRUZ

federalism, 118–19, 136, 158

the FEGASACRUZ (Federation of Cattlemen of Santa Cruz), 162

feminism, 16–19, 109, 227, 245–46, 248, 259n5

Ferguson, James, 228–31

Feria Exposición de Santa Cruz. *See* EXPOCRUZ

Fernández, Leopoldo, 180–85, 194, 250

Fernández de Kirchner, Cristina, 191

Fernández Terán, Roberto, 122

fertilizers, 9, 97

festivals, 127, 139, 141–42, 226, 237. *See also* carnivals

feudalism, 156–58, 182–83, 233

FEXPOCRUZ. *See* EXPOCRUZ

finance capital, 19, 30, 39–41, 98. *See also* capital; debt

FOBOMADE (Bolivian Forum on the Environment and Development), 106

folklore, 33, 127, 130, 140–42, 159, 184–85

food, 36, 78–81, 87, 121, 130, 159–60, 192, 203–5

Ford Motors, 65–66, 259n8

forestry, 140, 143. *See also* lumber

fossil capital: contradictions and, 2–6; global, 15, 20, 86; hegemony, 201, 232, 263n16; lock-in and, 21, 242–44; nationalism and, 98–102; resistance and, 18; the state and, 114–16, 150, 191–92, 223, 234–36, 242; the US and, 12–13, 38, 57, 62, 122, 192; war and, 40–42, 47–51. *See also* capital

fracking, 10, 103, 217, 242, 270n10

France, 9, 46, 102, 156, 175, 214, 234

fraternities, 127–28, 135, 140–43

the free market: gas and, 113, 120–21; poverty and, 70, 107; redistribution and, 229–31, 242; the state and, 2, 89, 108, 160, 226, 242–43; the US and, 12, 61, 98–103

the FSB (Falange Socialista Boliviana), 66, 196

Fuerzas Armadas Revolucionarias de Colombia. *See* FARC

Galeano, Eduardo, 34, 256n8

Galindo, María, 18, 227, 245

gangs, 123, 163–65, 188, 202

García Linera, Álvaro, 10, 167, 189, 202, 237, 250

García Linera, Raúl, 196

García Meza, Luís, 88, 139, 188

gas: the age of, 5–10; conflict in Alto Parapetí, 155–71; contradictions and, 2, 71, 188; dead bodies and, 179–81, 185–94, 197–201; excesses and, 205, 223–27; exploration, 102, 156, 206, 224; global warming and, 22–23; imperialism and, 19, 52, 57; Indigenous people and, 27–28, 87, 171–74; lock-in, 52, 97–124; migration and, 137–40; militarization and, 58–68; nationalization of, 1, 29, 69–96, 109–10, 118–19, 126, 156, 200, 227, 232–42; political violence and, 197; politics of, 11–17, 198, 242–44, 247–51; redistribution and, 228–32; regionalism and, 125–34, 154, 156, 188, 200; resistance and, 245–46, 252–53; the state and, 2–4,

17–21, 83, 98, 150–51, 175–76, 180, 191–92; territoriality and, 135–37; terrorism and, 194–97; transition from tin to, 53–58; violence and, 49, 86, 126, 141–50, 155, 181–85, 198; work and, 202–22

gasoline, 28, 110–11

the Gas War of 2003, 21, 99, 109–13, 121–23, 136, 151, 160, 180–82, 200, 250

Gazprom, 9

Geisel, Ernesto, 97

gender, 18–19, 83–86, 126, 132, 140–41, 150, 209, 216, 219–20, 239–52. *See also* masculinity; women

Germany, 6, 28, 36–38, 45–47, 53, 62, 142, 161, 257n18

Giannechini, Doroteo, 28

Gill, Lesley, 15, 67

Gillette, Michael, 46

global warming, 2–3, 14, 22–23, 243. *See also* climate change

Goldberg, Philip, 182

Gómez-Barris, Macarena, 218

Grandin, Greg, 11

the Gran Poder festival, 226

the Great Depression, 31, 43

Grebe, Horst, 119–20

Greenlee, David, 120–21

Green New Deal, 244

Guakaya, 222

the Guarani people: autonomy and, 135, 155–58, 163–71, 206–14, 219, 221–22; the Chaco War and, 29, 46; cultural appropriation and, 101, 132–33; enslavement of, 158–61; fossil fuels and, 6, 10–11, 18–19, 21, 27–28, 78–79, 85, 97, 217; gas lock-in and, 104–6, 118, 123; imperialism and, 56, 93; labor and, 205–14, 217–18; regionalism and, 140, 152–54; social movements and, 219–22; the state and, 166, 171–76, 206, 245; violence against, 82, 86–87, 148–55, 169, 180. *See also* Indigenous people

the Guarani People's Assembly, 140

the Guarayu, 132–33

the Guerra del Gas. *See* the Gas War of 2003

Guerrero, Pompilio, 42

guerrilla movements, 64, 189–90, 196, 199, 245

Guevara, Che: the death of, 185–88, 190, 198; the left and, 73, 87, 171, 199–200, 225, 243, 252–53; the US and, 61, 157, 197

Gulf Oil, 1, 29, 51–71, 99–103, 108, 123, 188, 190, 199, 233

guns. *See* the arms industry

Gutiérrez, Raquel, 189

Gutrie, Sonia, 169

Haarstad, Havard, 89, 92–93

Halliburton, 9, 209, 215, 268n7

health care, 36, 71, 78, 81–82, 115, 184, 230, 235

Healy, Kevin, 159

hegemony: fossil capital, 15, 57, 228, 232, 263n16; regionalism and, 138, 150, 164, 264n8, 265n8; the state and, 99, 155, 158, 161; United States, 3, 15, 21; violence and, 21, 180–82, 189

Heller, Joseph, 38

heroism, 31–49, 52, 71–87, 123–24, 171, 188, 190, 200–201, 243, 252–53

heteronormativity, 193. *See also* patriarchy

highways, 61, 203

homophobia, 85, 224. *See also* patriarchy; sexuality

the Hostal Marietta, 73

Hotel Las Américas, 194, 197

housing, 222, 230

Huber, Matt, 232

Hughes, David McDermott, 15, 22

humanitarian work, 121

human rights, 144, 157, 160–61, 171, 234

hunger strikes, 92, 127–28, 176. *See also* strikes

hydrocarbons legislation, 67, 89, 100–102, 107–8, 114, 118–21, 123, 135, 208
hydroelectric energy, 241

the IAHCR (Inter-American Court of Human Rights), 160–61
identity, 80–81, 130–36, 144, 166
the ILO (International Labor Organization), 160, 181
the IMF (International Monetary Fund), 42, 69, 89, 116, 123, 242
imperialism: the arms industry and, 39–47; the Chaco War and, 30–37, 48–52; development and, 251–52; energy and, 11–13; fascism and, 257n18; fossil capital and, 2–5; language of, 143; militarization and, 58–61; Morales and, 234–35; nationalization and, 9–10, 61–68; resistance to, 16–18, 106–7, 243–44; tin and, 53–58, 93, 106, 122 (*See also* anti-imperialism; the US)
Incahuasi, 6, 156, 158, 174–75
Indians. *See* Indigenous people
indigeneity, 4, 9, 52, 77, 85, 135
Indigenous, Peasant and Originary Peoples Fund. *See* the Indigenous Fund
Indigenous autonomy, 5, 135, 156, 164
the Indigenous Fund, 226, 230, 235
Indigenous movements, 18, 125, 138–39, 148–49, 189, 205. *See also* Indigenous organizations
Indigenous organizations, 109, 126, 140, 149, 218. *See also* Indigenous movements
Indigenous people: the Chaco War and, 45; cultural appropriation and, 128, 133, 264n7; enslavement of, 161; erasure of, 85, 265n9; Evo Morales and, 124–25, 215, 224, 249; the gas assemblage and, 2–5, 15–16, 27, 104–6, 262n6; gas labor and, 206–14; imperialism and, 121; the military and, 88; racism against, 122, 182;

regionalism and, 129–32, 142, 144–45; resistance by, 101, 118, 164; rights of, 162, 208, 233; social movements and, 218, 221–22, 244–55, 266n3, 266n10; sovereignty and, 155, 200; sterilization of, 65; territoriality and, 135; US imperialism and, 59; violence against, 86–87, 159–61, 264n5, 267n4. *See also* the Guarani people
industrialization, 113–14, 233
inequality, 18, 59, 102, 202, 231
infrastructure, 39, 51–52, 57, 61–62, 103, 117, 121, 129, 191, 203, 206
the INRA, 158, 163, 172, 183
Instituto Nacional de Reforma Agraria. *See* the INRA
intellectuals, 1, 11, 17, 31, 37, 43, 52, 61, 76, 100, 141, 161, 189, 243, 251
intelligence agencies, 67, 190, 196
the Inter-American Defense Board, 64–65
international aid, 69, 113, 116. *See also* development
the International Labor Organization. *See* the ILO
interventionism, 3, 11, 53
the Iraq War, 209
iron ore, 67
isolationists, 44, 47
the Isoso Guarani organization, 140

jobs, 115, 161, 207, 218, 229–30
Johnson, Lyndon B., 53, 59, 61
the Juana Azurduy payment, 230
the Juancito Pinto payment, 200, 230

Katari, Túpac, 189
Kaup, Brent, 16
Kemmerer, Edwin, 43–44
kerosene, 28
Khelil, Chakib, 100–101
kidnappings, 221
killings, 67, 76, 79, 157. *See also* bodies; mass killings
kinship, 79, 127

Kissinger, Henry, 65, 121
Klein, Herbert, 35, 41
Korda, Alberto, 185
the Korean War, 53, 55
Kundt, Hans, 36–37

labor: exploitation, 229; forced, 27,
    161–62, 172, 181; fossil capital and,
    14–15, 19, 21, 72; gas and, 202, 205;
    Guarani, 29, 159; war and, 47, 53; the
    YPFB and, 77–93, 153, 231
labor movements, 48
labor organizing, 93, 205
labor unions, 67, 140
land: defense committees, 162–63; grab-
    bing, 68, 129; Guarani, 27, 78, 97, 133;
    redistribution, 156, 160, 202; reform,
    125–51, 153, 155–56, 160–61, 163–64,
    166–67, 171, 176, 183; regionalism and,
    145; seizures, 149; the state and, 162;
    surveys, 153, 163–64, 172
landowners, 128, 135, 149, 153, 159, 161,
    165, 169, 172, 182
La Paz, 19, 39, 58, 66, 80, 109, 111
Larsen, Duston, 172–74
Larsen, Ronald, 164–65, 172–74
latifundia, 166
the League of Nations, 46
legalism, 112
legal regimes, 5. See also hydrocarbons
    legislation
LGBTQIA organizations, 245–6
Li, Tania Murray, 228–30, 232
liberalism, 49
libertarianism, 43, 231
Limbert, Mandana, 19
lithium, 241
LNG (liquefied natural gas), 98, 103, 107
loans. See debt
lock-in, 21, 97–124
Lonsdale, Jorge, 190
López Obrador, Andrés Manuel, 244
Lora, Jorge, 109
Lula da Silva, Luiz Inácio, 191
lumber, 33, 181. See also forestry

macroeconomics, 223, 233
Maduro, Nicolás, 12
Magowan, William, 42
Magyarosi, Arpad, 195
Malm, Andreas, 3, 40
manual labor, 28, 75, 77, 214
marches, 16, 123, 141, 143–44, 149–50,
    173, 185, 188, 193, 245–46
Mariaca Bilbao, Enrique, 16, 106, 108
Marinkovic, Branko, 196
marriage, 81, 209, 215
Marsh, Margaret Alexander, 43–44
Martinez, Enrique, 87, 92
martyrdom, 75, 91, 171, 185, 189,
    199–200. See also heroism
Marxism, 14, 31–2, 50, 189, 227
the MAS: the constitution and, 83; Evo
    Morales and, 234–42; gas lock-in and,
    123–24; gas politics and, 188, 192–94,
    198, 200, 242–53; the Guarani and,
    206; imperialism and, 15, 113–14; In-
    digenous people and, 156–61, 166–71,
    175–76, 182, 200–201, 219, 223–26,
    255n6, 266n10; land redistribution
    and, 202; the left and, 189–91; move-
    ments against, 16, 128–30; national-
    ization and, 2–3, 49, 109, 115–19, 154,
    167, 231–33; race and, 126, 137–40;
    redistribution and, 202; regionalism
    and, 141, 146, 173; social movements
    and, 165, 183–84; social policy and,
    231; terrorism and, 194–97; violence
    against, 149–51, 153, 155. See also
    Morales, Evo
masculinity, 19, 52–55, 61, 76–87, 132,
    143, 193, 198–99, 205–10, 217, 228,
    239–40. See also men; patriarchy
massacres, 184, 192, 199
mass killings, 31, 61, 110–12, 123, 171,
    179–80. See also bodies; killings;
    violence
Matkovic, Zvonko, 197
Maxus, 102, 120
Mbembe, Achille, 180
McCarthy, Glenn, 55–58

McLarty, Thomas, 121

McNamara, Robert, 65–66

media: autonomy and, 166; dead bodies in the, 179–81, 192–93; Evo Morales and, 224–25; land reform in, 174–75; regionalist, 128, 141–44, 148–50; slavery in, 160–61; United States, 65, 118–19; violence in the, 181–82

medical care, 36, 71, 78, 81

memory, 29, 49, 107, 152, 160, 188, 234–35

men, 132. See also gender; masculinity

Menchaca, Martha, 15

Mennonites, 104, 238

mercenaries, 198

Mesa, Carlos, 113–21, 123, 127, 144, 160, 162

mestizaje, 130, 132, 243

Mexico, 12, 15, 56, 103, 111, 120, 122, 219, 222, 244

Meza, Luís Garcia, 88

Miami, 112–13, 129, 192

microlending, 220

the middle class, 117, 129, 133, 142, 229

the Middle East, 14, 35

Middleton, Townsend, 180

migrants, 77, 126, 129, 133, 169, 182

migration, 89, 129, 137–40, 229

militants, 16, 189, 220

militarism, 11, 13, 19, 23, 30, 35, 47, 49–50, 52, 64, 198–200

militarization, 13, 19, 52, 58–61, 71, 109, 252

the military. See the Bolivian military

military nationalism, 107, 113, 121, 199. See also the Bolivian military; nationalism

military regimes, 139

militias, 66

minerals, 3, 39, 42, 50, 230

miners, 54, 88–90, 118, 195, 199

mining, 29, 31, 51, 53, 59, 61, 66–67, 77, 79, 84, 87, 103, 133

the MIR (Movement of the Revolutionary Left), 190

Miranda Pacheco, Carlos, 99, 102

misogyny, 81, 240

missions, 27, 71

Mitchell, Timothy, 48

the MNR (Nationalist Revolutionary Movement), 53–56, 58, 60, 65–66, 87, 89, 101–2, 160

modernity, 10, 159, 216

money, 21, 36, 39–49

Monsanto, 56–57

Montenegro, Carlos, 61

Morales, Evo: conspiracies against, 112; the election of, 123–24, 150–51; the gas assemblage and, 20–21; gas nationalization and, 118–21, 200–208; gas politics and, 74, 83, 135–36, 183, 188, 192, 198, 230, 242–44; indigeneity and, 132, 137; Indigenous people and, 153–57, 160–67, 170–71, 174, 215, 226; the MAS and, 176, 223, 228, 234; movements against, 128, 132, 182–83, 189, 224–25, 247–51; nationalism and, 108–9; nationalization and, 2–6, 9–11, 29, 49, 113–16, 215, 227; patriarchal violence and, 228, 245; racism and, 122, 125–26, 137, 158, 228; the reelection of, 204; the resignation of, 251–52; revolutionary affect of, 234–42; revolutionary politics and, 16, 64; social policy of, 231–32; terrorism and, 194–97; the US and, 12, 16. See also the MAS

the Movimiento al Socialismo. See the MAS

Movimiento de Izquierda Revolucionaria. See the MIR

the Movimiento Nacionalista Revolucionario. See the MNR

Mugabe, Robert, 157–58

Mujeres Creando, 227, 245

multinationals, 92, 100, 137, 150, 213, 218, 228. See also transnationals

music, 130, 135, 142–44, 159

Nación Camba. See the Camba Nation

Nader, Laura, 13–14

Nash, June, 18, 75, 77, 79, 84, 239
the nation, 15, 72–73, 75, 81, 85, 90–91
national consciousness, 50, 53, 56
nationalism: the Bolivian military
    and, 58; the Chaco War and, 30–32,
    35–36, 50–52; fossil fuels and, 1–5,
    20, 46–49, 93, 98–99, 106–7, 112–14,
    121–22, 136, 144; imperialism and, 42,
    55–60; Indigenous people and, 27, 85;
    Latin American oil, 217–18; of the left,
    9, 16–17, 43, 108; patriotism and, 38;
    privatization and, 100–102; regional-
    ism and, 137; the right and, 61–68; the
    YPFB and, 88
national narratives, 158
natural resources, 11, 29, 39, 55, 63,
    136–37, 158. See also gas; oil
nature, 14, 19–21, 53, 231
Nazi Germany, 47, 51
necropolitics, 180
neoliberalism, 2, 4, 14–15, 52, 68,
    87–92, 97–99, 102–15, 123, 150, 164,
    190, 218
Neruda, Pablo, 33
New Left Review, 66
the New York Times, 46, 58, 65, 165
the NFR (New Republican Force), 113
NGOs (nongovernmental organizations),
    70–71, 74, 100, 106, 108–9, 122, 155,
    157, 160–61, 182, 225, 244
Nigeria, 20, 53, 136
Nixon, Richard, 65
nongovernmental organizations. See
    NGOs
non-violence, 123, 171, x
Noriega, Roger, 121
Northtufter, Miguel, 190
Norway, 46
Nye, Gerald, 44, 47
the Nye Committee, 44–46

the OAS (Organization of American
    States), 160
Obama, Barack, 12, 125
Occidental Oil, 57

occupations, 118, 127–28, 139, 150, 170
the Oceti Sakowin, 13, 208
oil: capital and, 39–49; imperialism
    and, 33–35, 37, 48–50, 58, 61, 77, 98,
    107; Indigenous people and, 27–28;
    masculinity and, 6, 17, 34, 56, 58,
    60–61, 71–72, 74, 79, 81, 101, 214–15;
    the media and, 143; nationalization, 1;
    neoliberalism and, 15, 18; Santa Cruz
    and, 129; transition from tin to, 53–58;
    the US and, 6, 12, 30; wars, 14
oil companies, 40–41
the oil crisis of the 1970s, 67
oil exploration, 42, 85–86, 102, 224
oil infrastructure, 19, 28, 102
oil legislation, 61–62, 67
oil nationalism, 46, 50–52, 57
oil nationalization, 35, 45, 50–51, 71, 93;
    the right and, 61–68
oil prices, 48, 52, 67, 69, 121, 191, 223
oligarchs, 17, 35–37, 40, 42, 47–48, 51–52,
    76, 164
Olivera, Oscar, 118
Organization of American States. See
    the OAS
Otero, María, 12
Ovando, Alfredo, 63–64, 88, 190

Pacific LNG, 103
pacifists, 44, 46–47
Padilla, Ubaldo, 29–30, 92
Palermo, Hernán, 90
pan-Africanism, 136
Panama, 60
Pando, 118, 151, 157, 160, 181–82, 192,
    200
parades, 128, 134, 142–43, 184–86
Paraguay, 29, 32, 35, 38–39, 44–46, 48,
    67, 104, 238
paramilitarism, 15, 122–23, 163, 182, 188,
    192, 197
Parapetí. See Alto Parapetí
party systems, 3, 50, 118, 121. See also
    political parties
Patiño, Simón, 37, 46

patriarchy, 2, 13, 17, 23, 81, 84, 125, 131, 153, 159, 200, 219, 240, 252. *See also* masculinity

patrimony, 132

patriotism, 38, 67, 107

Paz Zamora, Jaime, 97, 190, 196

Paz Zamora, Néstor, 190

the Peace Corps, 65–66

Peláez, Rafael Ulises, 47–48

Pemex, 12

Peñaranda, Enrique, 51, 102

pension funds, 90

Peru, 46, 63, 108, 113, 115, 181

Petroamérica, 118

Petrobras, 9, 57, 102, 105, 120, 146, 243

petrochemicals, 67, 191

Petróleos Mexicanos, 12

petroleum, 215. *See also* oil

the Pilcomayo River, 104

the Pink Tide, 3, 244

Pinochet, Augusto, 90

the Plan Bohan, 51

Plan Condor, 67

plurinationalism, 3–4, 16, 52, 182, 227, 234

Pluspetrol, 102

PODEMOS (Social and Democratic Power), 182

Poder Democrático y Social. *See* PODEMOS

police, 16, 92, 121, 125, 148, 153, 158, 163, 167, 172–73, 183–84, 208, 225

political parties, 50, 88–90, 93, 109, 113, 118, 125, 127, 141, 206, 220. *See also* party systems

pollution, 2, 175

Pope Francis, 203

popular nationalism, 123, 125, 233

populism, 4, 16, 50, 66, 88, 161

Porvenir, 183

Postero, Nancy, 16

Potosí, 234

poverty, 2, 59, 70, 102, 113, 129, 134, 138, 202, 216, 229

power, 2, 11–15, 27, 88, 99, 111, 126, 133–35, 153, 171, 201

Prada, Raúl, 16, 18, 236

Pride marches, 245–46

prior informed consent, 20, 99–100, 208, 231

privatization, 69, 87, 89–92, 100–104, 106–9, 214–15

property, 132, 138–39

the Pro-Santa Cruz Civic Committee, 126, 140–45, 150

prostitution, 79

Protestantism, 66

protests, 109, 126–27, 148, 199. *See also* marches

public spaces, 150, 152, 166, 184–85. *See also* spatiality

punishment, 152, 171, 184–85

the Quechua people, 104, 157, 199

queerness, 85, 245

Quiroga, Tuto, 103, 182

Quiroga Santa Cruz, Marcelo, 61, 64, 67, 99, 188, 190, 243

Quispe, Felipe, 118, 244

race, 136, 171, 216. *See also* indigeneity; racism; whiteness

racial capitalism, 2, 13, 38, 49, 253. *See also* capitalism; racism

racism, 12, 17–23, 35–36, 45, 52–60, 79, 85–86, 105; anti-Indigenous, 121–22, 129–33, 137–40, 149, 152, 157, 182; autonomy and, 125–26, 161; bodies and, 185; the law and, 233; regionalism and, 150; of the right, 200; the state and, 39, 182; violence and, 193, 195. *See also* indigeneity; race; whiteness

Rada, Alfredo, 122

RADEPA, 120

radical politics, 1–2, 43, 52, 54, 63, 77, 87, 115, 118, 140, 156, 240

railroads, 44, 48, 102, 107

ranchers, 28, 33, 58, 71, 78, 122, 133, 140–42, 148–59, 162–70, 181

Rangers, 61, 186
the Rangers battalion. *See* the Second
    Ranger Battalion
rape, 82, 159, 171. *See also* sexual violence
Razón de Patria (RADEPA), 50
Read, Dillon, 44
redistribution, 229–33
regionalism, 5, 21, 62–63, 80, 125,
    133–34, 175; autonomy and, 125–26;
    civic, 140–41; migration and, 137–40;
    in Santa Cruz, 58. *See also* autonomy
religion, 49, 130, 132–33, 138
renewable energy, 13, 203
Renta Dignidad, 230
reparations, 160
Repsol, 9–10, 102, 105, 123, 242–43
Repsol YPF, 102
the Republican Party, 12, 121
resistance, 14–20, 43, 49, 52, 66, 87,
    91–93, 101, 109, 138, 149. *See also* activ-
    ism; marches
resource nationalism, 17
Restrepo, Laura, 79
revolution, 2, 38, 50, 158; the 1952 Revo-
    lution, 53, 58, 59, 156, 196
revolutionaries, 76–77, 224
revolutionary affect, 234–42
revolutionary thought, 2–3, 13–16, 20,
    36, 67, 71, 84, 87, 107, 175, 199, 227
Ribera, Maricruz, 128–29
the right, 1, 3, 17, 21–22, 44, 88, 97,
    109, 157, 175, 182; autonomy and,
    163–64; Evo Morales and, 215, 224–25,
    234–42; labor and, 221; the MAS and,
    15, 113–21, 176; media and, 166, 193;
    oil nationalization and, 59–68; racism
    of, 200; Santa Cruz, 141; social policy
    and, 232; violence and, 190–92, 196,
    198
rights. *See* Indigenous people: rights of
Río Tinto Zinc, 103
roads, 51, 115
Rocha, Manuel, 121
Rockefeller, John D., 28, 33–34, 40–41
Rockefeller, Nelson, 51

Rodríguez Veltzé, Eduardo, 144
Rogers, Douglas, 136
Rojas, Juan Carlos, 158, 160, 162, 166–67,
    169, 172, 176
Rojas, Marlene, 109–10
Roosevelt, Franklin D., 44–47
Rosza, Eduardo, 195, 197–98
the Rosza Group, 196–97
Rout, Leslie Jr., 35
Roy, Ananya, 18–19
Royal Dutch Shell, 33
rubber, 31, 33, 181
rural spaces, 139, 161, 183, 199, 216, 220.
    See also spatiality
Russia, 136, 192, 242
the Russian Revolution, 234–35

Saavedra, Bautista, 42
Salamanca, Daniel, 31
San Alberto, 6, 105
Sanandita, 188
San Andrés University, 66
San Antonio, 6
Sánchez Berzaín, Carlos, 111–12, 200
Sánchez de Lozada, Gonzalo "Goni," 69,
    89–92, 99–114, 118–19, 121, 126, 138,
    151, 200
Santa Cruz (region), 10, 19, 21, 56, 62–63,
    67–68, 80, 104, 113, 119, 121–22;
    autonomy and, 125–29; civic coup in,
    150–51; civic regionalists and, 140–41;
    elites, 162, 195; the EXPOCRUZ fair in,
    145–48; labor and, 215; migration and,
    137–40; militarization and, 58–61;
    regionalism in, 129–35, 146; the right
    in, 190; royalties to, 156; territoriality
    and, 135–37; violence and, 141–45,
    149–50, 165
the Santa Cruz Civic Committee, 58, 146
São Paulo, 97
Saudi Arabia, 44
Sawyer, Susana, 15
Schlumberger, 9
the School of the Americas, 60, 65
schools, 49, 74, 77–78, 91–92, 131, 142

secession. *See* separatism

the Second Ranger Battalion, 60, 66

secret societies, 50, 120, 143–44, 197

segregation, 133

Selich, Andrés, 67

Sempra Energy, 111, 130

Senkata, 110–11

separatism, 118, 140–41, 144

settler colonialism, 27, 29, 85–86, 132, 153, 158. *See also* colonialism

settlers' unions, 138

sex, 79–80, 82, 87, 127. *See also* sexual violence

sexism, 212. *See also* masculinity; misogyny

sex-trafficking, 217, 221, 228. *See also* brothels

sexual harassment, 215

sexuality, 18, 105, 246

sexual violence, 79, 159. *See also* rape

sex work, 79–80, 217, 221, 227–28. *See also* brothels; debt

Shearer, Derek, 157–58

Shell, 9, 57, 69, 102, 120

Shever, Elana, 15, 90, 214

the Siglo xx mine, 61

Siles Salinas, Luis Adolfo, 63

Sinopec, 9

60 Minutes, 55–56

slavery, 156–60, 181. *See also* debt servitude

soccer, 78, 80

socialism, 4, 9, 12, 16–17, 48, 50–52, 125, 162; democratic, 234; in Latin America, 191, 233

socialists, 1, 43, 61, 63–64, 67, 71, 108, 161, 188

social movements, 4, 20, 44, 51, 67, 76, 91, 109, 115–21, 141, 153, 174, 182–83, 227, 243. *See also* marches; protests; *specific organizations*

solar power, 203, 241. *See also* renewable energy

soldiers, 36–38, 45, 48–49, 51, 67, 74, 76, 78, 87, 187–88

Solis, Hilda, 12

Solíz Rada, Andrés, 16, 243

South Africa, 230

the South American Energy Council, 191

Souza Crespo, Mauricio, 17

soy, 133, 136, 140, 202

spatiality, 5, 15, 17, 19–21, 62, 83–84, 93; autonomy and, 125–29; Bolivian leaders and, 113–16; civic coup and, 150–51; civic regionalists and, 140–41; discursive lock-in and, 116–22; the EXPOCRUZ fair and, 145–48; the fourth insurrection and, 122–24; gas and, 135–37; gas lock-in and, 97–100; the Gas War and, 109–13; labor and, 218; migration and, 137–40; privatizing YPFB and, 100–104; public spectacle and, 125–29; regionalism and, 129–35; unruly subjects and, 148–50; in Villamontes, 104–9. *See also* public spaces; rural spaces; urban spaces

Spain, 28, 102, 105, 157, 206, 214

Spanish language, 130

Standard Oil, 28–36, 38, 40–44, 47–48, 55, 63, 71, 76, 86, 102, 120, 213; nationalization of, 50–51, 123

"Standard Oil" (Neruda), 33–34

Standing Rock, 208

the state, 2, 4, 27, 36, 47, 69, 74, 89, 92, 98–108, 114, 118–25, 158, 229, 240; autonomy and, 125–27; fossil capital and, 150, 191–92; the Guarani and, 211; hegemony and, 161, 164; lock-in and, 116; oil and, 11–21, 52; racism of, 39; redistribution and, 218; regionalism and, 129, 144; territoriality and, 135; violence and, 111, 123, 180, 182, 189, 194–97, 201

Stavenhagen, Rodolfo, 161

Stearman, Allyn Maclean, 133

steel, 62

stereotypes, 139–40

Stifel Nicolaus, 40

street violence, 58, 66, 110, 134, 150.
    See also violence; whippings
strikes, 61, 87, 90, 92, 118, 127. *See also*
    hunger strikes
students, 1, 31, 64, 66–67, 78, 110,
    182–85, 192
subsidies, 55, 126
subsidization, 140. *See also* subsidies
Sucre, 175, 200
sugar, 138, 160, 192
Svampa, Maristella, 23
symbolism, 144, 203

Tarija, 10–11, 105, 125, 135, 151, 182
TCOS, 155
teachers, 74–78, 91–92, 118, 152–53, 166,
    170, 183, 220
Teagle, Walter, 40
telecommunications, 102, 143, 196–97
television, 77, 141, 166, 193, 203
temporality: the Chaco War and, 27–33;
    feudalism and, 156; fossil capital and,
    5, 17, 19–20; imperialism and, 50–52;
    militarization and, 58–61; national-
    ization and, 61; of resistance, 236;
    Standard Oil and, 33–39; transition
    from tin and, 53–58; war capital and,
    39–49; the YPFB and, 69–93
Teoponte, 190
the Teoponte guerilla movement, 64
territoriality, 15, 20–21, 135–37, 154–56,
    160, 211
terrorism, 14, 194–97
Texas, 53–56, 58, 62, 136
thanatopolitics, 180, 201, 225
tierras comunitarias de orígen. *See*
    TCOS
tin, 18, 31–33, 37, 39, 50, 53–58, 61,
    77, 84
Tinker-Salas, Miguel, 58
TIPNIS (Territorio Indígena y Parque
    Nacional Isiboro Secure), 16
the Toba people, 27
Toro, David, 48
Torres, Juan José, 64–67, 88, 108, 121

torture, 67, 159, 170, 196
Total, 9, 123, 156–57, 174–75, 243
tourism, 138, 232
TRADEPA (Patriotic Democratic Transfor-
    mation), 120
transgender people, 245. *See also* patriar-
    chy; sexuality
transnationals, 64, 118, 146. *See also*
    multinationals
transportation, 136
transportation infrastructure, 102
Transredes, 91
trauma, 155, 160, 164, 171, 195
Trotskyism, 77, 109, 189, 240, 1999
the UJC, 127, 135, 140–43, 149, 163, 166,
    170, 196, 249
the UN, 157, 161, 184
UNASUR (Union of South American
    Nations), 184–85, 191–92
the UN Declaration on the Rights of the
    Indigenous Peoples, 161, 163
Unidad Tactica de Resolucion de Crisis.
    See UTARC
Unión de Naciones Suramericanas. *See*
    UNASUR
the Unión Juvenil Cruceñista. *See* the
    UJC
the Union of Sex Workers of the 12th of
    October Avenue, 228
unions, 32, 60–63, 74, 87, 90–93,
    99–100, 121, 133, 138–40, 149, 183–88,
    218, 227
the United Nations. *See* the UN
the United States. *See* the US
the United States Agency for Interna-
    tional Development (USAID), 121
the United States Geological Survey
    (USGS), 6
UNITEL (Universal de Televisión), 193
universal basic income, 228, 230–32
universities, 10, 97, 108, 199, 205
urban spaces, 79, 88, 129–51, 183, 208,
    216–18, 246, 253. *See also* spaciality
Uruguay, 67, 195

the US: energy and, 11–24, 244; Evo Morales and, 235, 243; fossil fuel interests and, 157, 191–92, 255n3; gas and, 115, 208–9; the gaseous state and, 1–10, 198, 201; global warming and, 22–23; intervention by, 121–22, 199, 257n18, 259n7, 263n16, 267n2; militarization and, 58–61; nationalization and, 61–68, 119–20; neoliberalism and, 112, 120, 233, 259n4; the oil-military-capital assemblage and, 39–49, 258n25, 259n8; politics in, 193, 198, 201, 258n23, 260n2; regionalism and, 129, 136; Standard Oil and, 28, 30, 33–34, 51–52, 259n1; the tin industry and, 53–58; the YPFB and, 76, 104, 107. *See also* imperialism

USAID, 150

the US Air Force, 121

US Green Berets, 60

the US Southern Command, 12, 121

UTARC (Tactical Unit for Crisis Resolution), 194, 198

Valverde Barbery, Carlos, 143, 196

Valverde Bravo, Carlos, 196, 224

Vallegrande, 142, 186, 188

Valle Mandepora, Ramiro, 152, 160, 168, 170–71

Velasco, Juan, 63

Venezuela, 12–14, 48, 112, 118–21, 136, 157, 191–93, 242–44, 263n16

Verdery, Katherine, 180

Vickers, 44

the Vietnam War, 52, 60, 66

Villamontes, 32, 38, 104–9

Villegas, Carlos, 106, 208

Villegas, Guido, 107

violence: autonomy and, 126, 149–51, 163–64; Carnival and, 127, 134; contradictions and, 2–3, 71, 141–45; excesses and, 5–6, 21, 205; fossil fuels and, 99–100, 112–13, 136, 253; the gaseous state and, 14, 18–20, 71; gendered forms of, 86–87, 126–27;

against Indigenous people, 27, 31, 58, 61, 122–23, 139, 155–74; political, 180, 197; the public spectacle of, 152–53; revolutionary, 190–91; the state and, 12, 118–19, 167, 192–93; against women, 16, 79–83, 93, 202–6, 220–21, 228, 240, 245–46, 252, 261n6. *See also* domestic violence; sexual violence; street violence

Wallace, Mike, 55, 259n5

Wall Street, 35–38, 43–44, 49, 57, 257n18

war, 2, 18–19, 30, 45–46, 48–49, 54; capital and, 40, 47; death and, 39; for oil, 14, 38

the Washington Consensus, 100

water, 118, 175, 238, 242

the Water War, 122

Watts, Michael, 20

the Weenhayek people, 27, 104

whippings, 152–53, 159–60, 166, 168, 184

whiteness, 55, 85–86, 129–31, 133, 193, 209, 211, 220. *See also* racism

Williams Brothers, 57–58, 62

Wilson, Web, 72, 260n2

wind power, 241

women: autonomy and, 21, 129, 132, 142–46; commodification of, 10, 237; Evo Morales and, 224, 227–28, 240–41; Indigenous, 65, 86, 149, 159, 209; labor and, 205, 210, 214–19, 228, 230; social movements and, 44, 140, 168, 183, 212, 245–46, 251–53; violence against, 2, 16, 79–83, 93, 153, 200–202, 206, 220–21, 240–41, 264n5

the Women's International League for Peace and Freedom, 44

the Women's Peace Party, 44

workers: bodies of, 225–28; the Chaco War and, 29–30; the gaseous state and, 1, 51, 105; Guarani, 206–7; land reform and, 170–74; nationalism and, 59, 64, 71–78, 87–93, 134, 200, 214–18, 227, 233–34; patriarchal violence and, 80–87, 246; resistance and, 31–32,

36, 50, 66–67, 239–40. *See also* labor; unions

the World Bank, 42, 57, 62–69, 100–102, 116, 119–20, 231, 259n8, 261n5

World War I, 31, 39, 44–45

World War II, 45–47, 51–53

Yacuiba, 218

Yapacani, 138

YouTube, 72, 179, 193

YPF (Yacimientos Petrolíferos Fiscales), 10, 48, 57, 102

YPFB (Yacimientos Petrolíferos Fiscales Bolivianos): 78, 88, 90, 92; gas lock-in and, 99–102, 106–8, 114–15, 117–19, 123–24; labor and, 215–18, 236, 269n9; oil nationalization and, 9–10, 48–51, 54–57, 62–63, 69–93; redistribution and, 226–28; the reestablishment of, 161, 208, 221

Yugoslavia, 122

Zapatistas, 219, 222

Zaratti, Francisco, 120

Zavaleta, René, 4, 17, 21, 36, 47–49, 63, 66–67, 198–99, 228–34, 243

Zimbabwe, 157–58

zinc, 65–66